DYNAMIC
HEALTH

DYNAMIC
HEALTH

Using your own
beliefs, thoughts
and memory
to create a
Healthy Body

Dr. M. Ted Morter, Jr.

BEST RESEARCH, INC

Dynamic Health: Using Your Own Beliefs,
  Thoughts and Memory to Create a Healthy Body

Dr. M. Ted Morter, Jr.

Copyright © 1995, B.E.S.T. Research Inc.

Printed in the United States
ISBN   0-944994-04-0

Morter HealthSystems
1000 West Poplar Street
Rogers, Arkansas 72756

1 800 874 1478
1 501 631 8201 (Fax)

*Dedicated to improving the health of mankind worldwide —
one person at a time*

INFORMATION FOR THE READER

The information presented in this book is a compilation of concepts and principles I have developed over the past thirty years. These concepts and principles relate to maintaining and promoting health, not to treating disease of other physical complaints. The information in this book is not intended as suggestions for self-diagnosis or self-treatment of mental, emotional, or physical symptoms or complaints. The reader is cautioned against applying the concepts in this book for therapeutic purposes in lieu of seeking professional health care. The reader is urged to consult licensed health care professionals for diagnosis and treatment of health problems mentioned in this book and for all other physical, mental, or emotional complaints. This book deals with the concepts that the body functions as a unit, that various elements of lifestyle can influence physiology, and that physiological processes respond in a predetermined manner to specific stimuli. The concepts and ideas presented are intended to offer the reader suggestions for examining facets of his or her lifestyle that can impact physiology.

No guarantee or assurance is given for obtaining specific results from the use of any of the suggestions given. The reader is reminded that regular professional health care examinations are important to early detection and treatment of all diseases. THIS BOOK DEALS WITH THE PREVENTION OF DISEASE RATHER THAN WITH THE TREATMENT OF DISEASE.

The reader is also advised that the representation of the brain that appears on the cover of this book is not a true representation of the brain's physical structure. The colors depicted in this illustration are intended only to identify general areas of the brain referred to in this book.

Dr. M. Ted Morter, Jr.

TABLE OF CONTENTS

ACKNOWLEDGEMENTS

Over the past thirty years, thousands of patients and hundreds of doctors provided clinical and mental "challenges" which spurred the development of my concepts of how the body works. Thanking each of them individually would be impossible. So, I shall offer a blanket "Thank you" to the patients from whom I continue, over the years, to gain insight into the marvelous workings and healing powers of the body. And to the doctors, especially B.E.S.T. doctors in this country and abroad, whose intellectual curiosity and support have kept me fine-tuning my concepts in the search for truth in health, I offer my sincere appreciation. Each of these major influences realizes the role he or she has played.

On the production side, a very special thanks to my wife, best friend, and resident cheer leader, Marjorie. Her patience, persistence, and computer typesetting skills transformed the draft typescript into finished "real book" pages. Concurrent thanks go to my daughters-in-law, Anna and Janna, to Petro van der Merwe, Peg Blackadar, and staff members who served as critics and proofreaders.

Also on the "behind-the-scenes" team is Pat Kelly who again, for this fifth book, transmuted the presentation of my concepts and ideas from oratorical and seminar styles to written style.

My acknowledgements wouldn't be complete without sincere thanks to the "star" of the chapters that follow — Universal Intelligence — for the opportunities to continue to learn about the perfection of the body's survival and healing responses, and to share this knowledge with doctors and patients, and others who are searching for truth.

*If you have knowledge, let others
light their candles at it.*
                                    - Thomas Fuller

Prelude

WARNING: This book may be hazardous to your
            lifestyle!

But this book may also be more beneficial to your healthstyle than any other book you have read.

This book offers some ideas about the relationship between lifestyle and healthstyle that may or may not be new to you. Either way, it presents you with an opportunity to gain a whole new outlook on how your personal health is affected by your private choices. It gives you practical tips on how to revitalize your life in ways that can lead to greater health, happiness, and success. We're talking whole health here.

This book is for you only if you are (1) open-minded, (2) dissatisfied, and (3) a risk-taker.

Why these reader qualifications?

Because within these covers I punch holes in some of our sacred-cow concepts of health — concepts such as "germs make you sick," and "we are victims of our heredity and environment," and "new, more sophisticated drugs are the answer to controlling disease." Hence, qualification #1: open-mindedness. Not everyone can handle sacred-cow punching. And not just anyone will entertain unfamiliar views about health. Views that reveal the single most important, least talked-about element of health: the vitality of the energy in and around your body. You need an open mind to look at yourself and your health from a new vantage point.

Qualification #2, dissatisfaction, is imposed because only those who are dissatisfied with something — in this case their personal health and/or our nationwide health care debacle — are willing to investigate and do something to bring about change. It's time to change tactics. It's time to stop trying to cure disease and start making disease unnecessary. Disease isn't a curse or bad luck or punishment. Health isn't a gift or good luck or reward. Disease and health are both by-products of choices in essential areas of life.

And you need to be something of a risk-taker, qualification #3, because the responsibility for your present and future health will be plopped in your lap. You — not your doctor, not the government, not your insurance company or significant other — only you are responsible for your health. That's a risky idea to entertain. It takes all the fun out of blaming your parents and grandparents for weak genes, or faulty plumbing, or frazzled nerves. It stifles our national pastime of blaming someone else — spouse, children, boss, the IRS, or "the system" — for our physical and emotional miseries.

This book is about "response-ability." Your ability to respond to life events in ways that help your body function at its best. You have the ability to choose how you are going to respond to events in your life. You don't have the ability to choose how your body will respond to those choices. Physiological responses are beyond your control. You have been propelled to your present health, happiness and success by physiological responses to lifestyle choices you made in the past. The choices you make from now on will dictate future responses and your future condition.

But I'm not passing out "guilt." Feeling guilty about past choices is not only a waste of time, it may be counterproductive. You can't change anything that's already happened. And agonizing about past faults and foibles can lay the groundwork for painful, debilitating physical problems.

In the pages to come, I explain why guilt, grief, worry, anxiety, and other negative emotions affect your internal goings-on. Gut-level physiological processes, such as sympathetic and parasympathetic responses, can be — and are — perpetuated by chronic negative emotions. And chronic negative emotions are perpetuated by habitual conscious choices, thoughts, memories, and beliefs. It's the constant presence of these stimuli that can bring on responses that result in symptoms you don't like. The responses are perfect. Stimuli of particular thoughts, memories, beliefs, and attitudes that prompt the responses may not be. The cumulation of these responses is called "health" or "disease."

Health and disease are different degrees of the same thing. Both originate from the same source — physiological responses to stimuli. With predominately appropriate stimuli you rest comfortably on the health side of the continuum. When most of the stimuli that spark physiological responses are inappropriate, you develop what we call "disease." By understanding that health and disease are effects of perfect internal responses, you'll never again look at your physical condition as the luck of the draw. And by understanding that you are an energy being, composed of, developed by, and powered by perfect energy, you will understand that there's more to you than meets the eye. You are an energy being that functions in and with the Ultimate Source of energy. This concept is a Biggie:

> *Your personal connection to the Ultimate Source is*
> *an unseen yet physical part of your body.*

A lot of "stuff" in this book — research, experience, intuition — supports the concepts presented. This "stuff" takes some time to explain. The explanations are the bulk of the early chapters. The concepts presented are rather succinct . . . you were designed to survive . . . your body is doing exactly what it should be doing for you to survive . . . the power source that runs your body isn't your heart or brain or nervous system — it's your "integrating personal field" . . . your integrating personal field is as much a part of you as your nose, eyes, blood pressure, and personality . . . your integrating personal field connects you with the Ultimate Power Source . . . the Ultimate Power Source provided the information that guided your creation and development . . . the Ultimate Power Source contains all of the information required for maximum physiological performance . . . your thoughts and conscious choices can interfere with communication between you and the Ultimate Power Source . . . and the interference factor determines your present and future health, happiness, and success.

Now that's a plateful of information.

In this book you will join me on a trip through familiar territory of your body and its functions. Much of the "scientific" information comes from the writings of physiologist Arthur C. Guyton. Although I have never met Dr. Guyton personally, a couple of his physiology texts have been some of my closest companions since my college days. They are my seat-mates on airplanes, and "recreational reading" material at home and in the office. So, as we travel, we look at the workings of physical body, and we travel further to take a romp through your integrating field of energy. We look at the body as a whole, not as a collection of parts strung together. You are alive, vital, full of energy (even if you're tired). You aren't merely a piece of animated machinery that needs to be tinkered with periodically to keep it on the straight and narrow. We look at the whole "You." Not just the bones and marrow and muscles and organs. There's a "You" inside that skin. That "You" is your personality. Your individuality. Your uniqueness. Mind. Emotions. Feelings. Memories. Beliefs. Attitudes. Mannerisms. Sense of humor. You are a unique personification of vibrant energy. It's up to you to take care of your physical body. And it's up to you to take care of your vibrant energy body.

To get the most out of, and put the best into, both physical body and energy body, it's helpful to understand what's going on in the parts that can be seen and in the parts that can't. But, most important, it's essential that you understand the relationship between the two. And that's where our scenic travels will take us — along the well-travelled paths of cells and nervous systems, conscious mind and subconscious mind, thoughts, attitudes, memories, and beliefs. In the process, we'll veer off to some less well-travelled paths to see how we can expand our health view to include electrons and electromagnetism and force fields and quantum theory.

If you choose to join me on this safari to self-directed health, we'll take in a panoramic view of the body as a whole energy unit. By the end of our journey, you will understand why I say "There's more to you than meets the eye." And (if I've done my job) you should be able to conceptualize the energy field appendage of your body. This field has been there all along, yet it remains unlisted in the glossary of human anatomy.

With the foregoing serving as a travel brochure for the land of health opportunity, you can decide for yourself if you meet the reader qualifications. Are you an open-minded, health-dissatisfied, risk-taker who is willing to venture into barely tamed lands of self-directed health? Or are you satisfied with your present condition and future prospects for health? Do you want to determine where your health is going? Or are you happy to let someone else try to "fix" anything and everything that goes wrong with you?

The concepts in this book are an outgrowth of three decades of study and clinical experience. Since 1965, I have devoted my life and my energies to helping sick people get well. My experience keeps reinforcing my conviction of the validity of the body-mind-energy connection that has skirted the fringes of healing for years. By drawing on a flood of medical and technical information blended with my personal clinical experiences, I am more and more comfortable with my intuitive conviction that the body is the ONLY healer of itself. And I am also convinced that our thoughts and beliefs are the greatest contributors to our personal health-styles.

The concepts and recommendations presented here have been effective in helping real people handle stress better, feel better, feel better about themselves, feel more alive and energetic, and enjoy life more.

The good news is that you are the keeper of your mind, body, and field — your life. You are in charge of your health, happiness, and success. No one else can give any of these to you. And no one else can take any of them away. In the pages of this book you will find the "solution" to many of your health and discomfort problems. (Actually, I believe that you can find the solution to *all* of your problems, but that sounds like hyperbole, so we'll settle for "many.") The point is that if you aren't satisfied with the way your life and/or health have been going up to now, there's something you can do about it. That something is to change the way you respond to life's wrinkles and blips. If you take the following concepts to heart, you will discover that you really aren't a "victim." You are in charge of your life, your health, your happiness, your self-esteem, and your responses to stress.

The choice is yours. If you are happy with everything in your life — health, success, happiness, and all that — you don't need to spend your time reading this book. Just keep doing what you're doing. However, if you are not satisfied — and it doesn't have to be major "dissatisfied" — with the way your life is going, the concepts in this book just might help you to "take a turn for the better." The adventure starts here.

Join me on this journey.

*Men and nations behave wisely once they have
exhausted all the other alternatives*
                                — Abba Eban

CHAPTER 1
A Journey to Health

OUR JOURNEY BEGINS

In this book, we look at a health picture bigger than symptoms and body parts. We look at the body as a whole. We look at how one part can be affected by other parts; how the whole is affected by its many individual parts and functions; how both individual parts and the whole mechanism are affected by the controlling influences of internal and external energy systems.

My purpose is to help you understand that you can live the healthiest, happiest, most pain-free life possible. I won't try to impress you with arcane "scientific jargon." Our mutual goal — yours, as reader, and mine, as tutor — is to help you get a firm grip on the tiller of your private ship of health.

We are doing "big picture" here. We don't look at infinitely small parts of the body to find the cause of physical problems. The objective isn't to tell you how to "cure" anything. The objective is to guide you on a path that will help you to live in such a way as to make pain, disease, and stress-related problems unnecessary. When you are healthy and your body is humming along harmoniously, you don't need a cure.

Health is a whole-body affair. The whole-body factor is painfully apparent during times of stress. What happens when major trauma strikes? Your whole body responds. You are mentally stressed. You are physically stressed. All too often, after the initial impact of the traumatic situation subsides, you get sick. A cold or flu. Physical and mental exhaustion. Or, in extreme cases, cancer or arthritis develop. This is not coincidence.

The idea that stress and mental or emotional turmoil lead to dis-stress and disease is far from new. Hippocrates, of 460 B.C.E. vintage, made the connection between stress and asthma. More recently, in the heyday of tuberculosis, Canadian physician Sir William Osler (1849-1919) observed, "The care of tuberculosis depends more on what the patient has in his head than what he has in his chest."[1]

What you have in your head affects what goes on in your body. Every internal physiological activity of your body is the result of stimuli or "messages" transmitted through your nervous systems. You are conscious of and directly responsible for initiating many of the messages. Every time you eat, drink, or put some substance into your body, your body responds — messages race along intricate channels to take care of the new arrival. Every thought and feeling stimulates internal signals that alert or subdue particular activities. However, no matter whether you nurse a martini or nurse a grudge, you have absolutely no conscious control over how your physiology responds!

> WELLNESS PRINCIPLE: You have no conscious control
> over physiological responses to
> any stimulus

As we wend our way through the land of health opportunity, we will focus on the concept that stress and all of its permutations can lead to physical problems that are by-products of mental turmoil — worry, anxiety, fear, and all that lot. The physiological by-product of these emotions is what I call the "Sensory Dominant Stress," or SDS. Stress messages from the sensory system dominate the way the body is functioning. Diseases, physical pain, restricted mobility, exhaustion. All of these are physiological by-products of the body responding perfectly to messages received through your five senses and from memory. There's nothing wrong with the responses; the messages are inappropriate. Sensory Dominant Stress can bring on a variety of symptoms from minor aches and pains to chronic debilitating disease.

> WELLNESS PRINCIPLE: Sensory Dominant Stress is a
> shorthand term for the body
> doing right things at wrong
> times

SDS means that your body continues to respond physiologically to stimuli (internal messages) received through your five senses. Your body can handle a stress response for a short time. And it can handle stress responses that go on for days, months, and years. But when it must continue to respond for all that time, the systems and organs involved become exhausted. Stimuli that cause the same systems and organs to respond constantly are inappropriate. The responses are fine — perfect. It's the unremitting stimuli that are inappropriate. The stimuli are behind exhaustion. Exhaustion on the inside leads to physical problems and disease. And all too often, the source of these physical problems isn't obvious. You go to a doctor (or several) to find out why you hurt or are tired all the time and, after lengthy (and costly) exams and tests, you keep getting the same response from the doctors: "Everything seems to be perfectly normal. We can't find anything wrong."

Great! Your back or neck or legs or arms or "innards" are giving you fits, keeping you awake at night, limiting your activities, and the doctors "can't find anything wrong."

Maybe they're looking in the wrong place! However, most likely, the doctors you went to don't even acknowledge the presence of "the place" that holds the key — your memories, attitudes, and beliefs.

A patient who came to me recently presented one of the most compelling examples of the "we can't find anything wrong" conundrum. Although I haven't put many "case studies" in this book, this patient serves as something of a set piece. His symptoms and his responses represent the personification of the cumulative knowledge I have gained about how the body functions and responds to its internal and external environments. As a doctor, I see similar examples of body-mind responses nearly every day. However, this man presented a graphic picture of how memory-prolonged stress can lead to incapacitating pain and general deterioration through Sensory Dominant Stress. So, to give you a real-life preview of the concepts we'll explore in the pages that follow, we'll begin with his story. In relating this real-life stress drama, I'll call the patient "Ben" which, of course, is not his real name.

THE STORY OF "BEN"

I met Ben when I was in Paris conducting seminars to help other doctors learn more about how their patients' bodies work. Ben is a "middle-aged" businessman from a small principality on the Mediterranean. The only things I knew about him before we met were that he was a former cancer patient, and he had responded well to conventional surgical intervention and radiation therapy.

For two years after recovering from the cancer surgery and radiation, Ben appeared to be in good shape. Suddenly his legs started to become weak and painful. Then he needed crutches to walk. When I encountered him, he had been on crutches for almost three years.

After I heard this brief history from Ben's friend who had arranged for our meeting, I told the friend that if Ben's cancer had returned and attacked his lower spine, there wasn't much I would be able to do in a short period of time. Or, if scar tissue had developed and affected his neurological system as a result of the radiation, there was probably very little I could do for that. On the other hand, if the original cause of whatever brought on the cancer had not been addressed, that same cause may have sparked Ben's current symptoms of weakness and pain. Only by evaluating Ben's condition could I determine which, if any, of these situations was causing his pain and weakness.

At our first meeting, Ben walked with metal crutches — the kind that brace against the forearm. He also wore ankle and foot supports in his shoes to compensate for "foot drop" — to keep his feet from dropping down at the ankle when he picked them up to walk. Without the supports, he couldn't raise his toes off the floor far enough to keep from tripping. An interesting feature that separated Ben from most of my patients was that Ben speaks no English, only French. To complicate matters, I speak no French. So all of our communication was through his friend as interpreter or by crude sign language — actually, our direct communication was more like a game of charades.

I examined Ben thoroughly. I must explain here that my "examination" of Ben did not include blood work, x-rays, CAT scans, or MRIs. Ben had been through a barrage of highly sophisticated medical evaluation tests already. He had been to notable medical physicians in Canada, and to another host of specialists in Paris. None could pinpoint a reason for his painful, debilitating symptoms. However, I wasn't looking for minute internal malfunctions with polysyllabic names to account for his disabilities. It was obvious that something wasn't working right because his body as a whole wasn't performing up to snuff. I was looking at how his body responded to specific stimuli.

My initial examination showed Ben had low-average strength in his hands, and his legs were weaker than his arms. He couldn't lift either leg enough to raise either foot off the floor completely.

As we talked through the interpreter, I learned some details of Ben's history.

Seven years earlier, Ben had been diagnosed as having testicular cancer. One testicle was removed, and four months of radiation followed his surgery. After recovering from the surgery and radiation therapy, Ben felt and appeared perfectly normal for two years. He skied, played tennis, enjoyed a comfortable, robust lifestyle, and led a very athletic life.

I asked him what symptoms he had noticed first after those two symptom-free years that made him realize he wasn't as well has he had been. He answered, "The muscles all over my legs would quiver and shake." Quivering, shaking muscles is the same type of phenomenon that follows a traumatic crisis experience.

With Ben lying on his back, I continued my examination. I found his leg muscles flabby to the touch. However, when I pressed as little as a quarter of an inch on any leg muscle he screamed in pain. When Ben hollered, his wife, who was sitting in the room with us, winced and complained to the interpreter, "This looks like mental and physical cruelty." Yet all I had done was apply a small amount of pressure to his leg muscles.

With Ben still on his back, I lifted his legs by his heels and tried to move his feet and legs apart horizontally. I could move his feet only a few inches apart. His legs were virtually rigid. This maneuver prompted Ben to comment that he had become so stiff that he could no longer flex his knees when he was lying on his back.

Ben presented an interesting contradiction of symptoms: His muscles were both weak and rigid at the same time. The muscles were so rigid that he could hardly bend his knees, yet they were so weak he could barely walk. Furthermore, he couldn't lock his knees when he stood. You might think that rigid leg muscles are strong. However, Ben couldn't stand without the support of crutches, and he couldn't get up to a standing position without help. His condition was a classic illustration of Sensory Dominant Stress. His body was responding continually to signals that should have been short-term messages from his subconscious mind. These signals may have been coming from an imbedded memory of a "crisis" in his life. Or they may have been the result of his brooding about and dwelling on by-gone real or imagined crises. No matter the source — real or imagined — the effect was the same. And I didn't want or need to know the particulars of what the crises were all about.

As I finished my evaluation of Ben's condition, I asked him if he could recall any incidents that had caused him acute stress in the six months before he needed crutches. He told me that during that time his mother had died and sister had become, and remains, very ill. "Aha!" thought I, "these are major traumas in his life that could seriously affect his health." However, when I asked him to think about each of these situations separately, his body showed no significant response to indicate that either was a primary factor at this time. Again I was surprised.

There had to be something else. So I asked, "What prompted you to go to the doctor that led to the surgery seven years ago?"

He responded, "I had pain and tenderness in my testicle."

My next question was, "Was there any trauma in your life that happened any time up to a couple of months before you went to the hospital?"

"Yes," he answered without hesitation.

"Without telling me what it is," I instructed, "think about that trauma." When he thought about it, his physical reaction was immediate. I tested his legs to see if I could separate them; I couldn't. He was frozen!

Since I couldn't move his legs apart from each other, I lifted both legs off the table. The most amazing thing happened: He didn't bend at his hips. His whole body was rigid — completely rigid. When I lifted his legs by the heels, his entire body — from feet to neck — came off of the table. He was literally as stiff as a board. I was so astonished, I repeated the move half a dozen times.

I am sure you realize that a tremendous amount of muscle strength is required to keep the entire body rigid. Here was a man who was so weak he could hardly walk, yet he had the strength to immobilize every muscle in his body from his neck down. I couldn't believe it! His thoughts about his traumatic experience — whatever it was — caused severe contraction of nearly every skeletal muscle in his body. His muscles were virtually immobilized!

This whole episode was most astonishing. I have helped people for decades who have come to me with physical complaints brought about by thoughts. I am well aware that thoughts and emotions are prime influences on muscles, organs, and complete body systems. However, never before had I seen such a dramatic display of miscued stimuli — Sensory Dominant Stress.

When I saw Ben the next day he was excited. He told me that after our first treatment session he had improved considerably. However, the improvement lasted only about twenty or thirty minutes.

Ben's report of temporary improvement told me a lot. It told me that for seven years he had been mentally defending against at least one threatening thought. After seven years of constant defense, his muscles were exhausted, and so were his adrenal glands. So I worked with him again using the non-forceful, hands-on, neurological-updating procedures I have developed and used for nearly twenty years. This time, the response to the devastating thought he had had the day before was milder. So I instructed him to think of his mother, and his muscles went weak. Then I told him to think of his sister, and his muscles went weak. Interesting!

Consciously, Ben thought that his mother's death and his sister's illness were big problems in his life. Strangely enough, his body and nervous system didn't agree. Indeed they were problems, but not as big as whatever it was he had thought about that made him stiff as a board. However, after the power of the thought of the dominant situation (the details of which remain unknown to me) had been diluted, then, and only then, did the more obvious crises connected with his mother and sister become the biggest "threat."

I continued to see Ben several times a day for the next two days. When we parted company, he was really excited. He could stand without his crutches. He could walk with the help of crutches, but without the foot braces. A big improvement over how he had been when I first saw him. Now he could walk up and down stairs one foot per step instead of laboriously planting both feet on the same step before negotiating the next.

Let's review what happened. When I first saw Ben, he was so weak he couldn't walk unaided. You will see as our whole-health story unfolds that weak muscles indicate that the body is operating in a "toned-down" mode. However, for Ben, those weak muscles were very, very tender and very, very tense. Tense muscles indicate the body is operating in a "fast-forward" mode.

> WELLNESS PRINCIPLE: For muscles, tense and weak
> don't ordinarily go together

To help Ben, we had to "update" the SDS memory-controlled physiology — signal his control centers that the SDS physiology was no longer needed. With updated signals (that we'll talk about later) his muscles could relax and rest, and his adrenal glands could rest and repair.

Since our first encounter, Ben's muscles are now relaxed and he has changed his diet dramatically. Now he can exercise. And with his muscles responding to appropriate internal messages, the more he exercises now the stronger his muscles will get. That's the opposite of his condition when he came to me. Although his doctors in Canada and Paris had told him to exercise to relieve his stiffness, the more he exercised, the worse he would have been. You'll figure out later why exercise would have been counter-productive at that point, but I'll give you a clue now. His muscles were already as tense as they could get. They had been "maxed-out tense" for so long they were exhausted. Remember, they were "flabby to the touch" on the surface but tense enough below the surface to be painful to the touch. They were tense and exhausted. Because they were exhausted, they had lost their strength. Exercise wouldn't make his muscles stronger; it would make them more tired. However, once he was back on track with relaxed muscles, they could handle exercise and benefit from it.

It was a joy for me to see the smiles on the faces of Ben and his wife at the end of our four-day association. He came to me doomed to a wheelchair within a year or so. Ironically, because Ben's body had been responding to a trauma of seven years earlier, his mobility would have declined at a rapid rate, yet his life expectancy would have been reduced only slightly. All of his problems showed up in his skeletal muscles, principally below his diaphragm. His heart was in fine shape. Although his heart is a vital muscle, it wasn't involved in the muscle weakness at all — it would go on beating for years. He would just have continued to waste away physically for no apparent reason. None of the many tests that would have been ordered for him and reviewed by the many doctors he would consult would have shown anything "wrong."

Ben's case is different only in degree from the cases of most of the people I see in my clinic and classes. The symptoms of most people aren't quite as dramatic as Ben's. They are more on the order of nagging pain, chronic fatigue, and chronic disease. Nonetheless, the basic problems are the same — trauma, stress, and lingering responses typical of Sensory Dominant Stress.

I haven't seen Ben since that series of encounters. Consequently, I can't comment on his further recovery. I know from past experience that he needed further treatment to continue his progress. The story of Ben illustrates several concepts put forth in this book: Outdated memories and emotions are behind many debilitating physical ills; subconscious physiological responses are beyond the control of the conscious mind; and, most important, change is possible — changing the stimulus changes the response.

> WELLNESS PRINCIPLE: If you don't like the response,
> change the stimulus

MECHANICAL BODY – VITAL BODY

Scientific researchers continue to learn how the human body and human nervous systems are constructed, act, and react. Sophisticated, exotic, and often confusing "scientific" labels are attached to elements, structures, systems, and tiny operating parts of your nervous systems. Labels like lingual gyrus, and arachnoid granulation, and pineal body, and interpeduncular fossa, and myelin sheaths, and neuroglial cells are used by those who are intimately familiar with anatomy. These are just some of the thousands of terms used to identify parts of the body-machine. And by using modern technology, smaller and smaller bits and pieces of your vast, intricate nervous systems — the systems we think of as the body's "control central" — are being identified and their functions documented in an unceasing (and woefully ineffective) pursuit of health. The focus is on bits and pieces gone wrong, not how these bits and pieces must respond to their environment.

Two points of view of the body and health have crossed ideological swords for centuries: the mechanistic and the vitalistic. Health care in the U.S. is dominated by the mechanistic view — isolate a part, fix it, isolate and fix another part, and isolate and fix the next part that goes wrong. Dean Black, in his unpublished book *Regulated to Death*, describes mechanism as "catabolic." He points out that "mechanists study the body's connections within itself. . . separated from the influence of its natural environment."[2] "Mechanistic science," writes Black, "grew from an entirely reasonable assumption derived from the forces of interaction — that tiny causes necessarily produce tiny effects, so we can ignore all but the most prominent ones."[3]

The vitalistic view, on the other hand, is different. It includes the "living" aspect of the body. "The living portion of the system," Black explains, "reveals itself in the rhythms the molecules pulse with as they work, for it is rhythms, not molecules, that vanish when a living body dies."[4] Black expands the concept of "vitalism" from the limited definition of the "life" or "lively" component of a living system to include the study of living wholes — "wholism." As Black puts it, "... wholism studies organisms in terms of their dynamic connections with their environment."[5] The vitalistic view boils down to, fix the whole, including its environment, and the parts will take care of themselves.

When we study health by looking at tinier and tinier biological structures of the body, we may learn whether or not certain organs or systems are functioning correctly. But if there is a problem, micro-investigations show only effects, not cause. Discovering that the pancreas isn't producing appropriate quantities of insulin may be a symptomatic pattern of "diabetes"; however, it doesn't address glitches in the system-wide communications that caused the problem. It's rather like closely scrutinizing and examining the missed-assignment tendencies of the second-string defensive tackle to figure out why the team's season has been a bummer. There may indeed be a problem there; however, the cause of the *team's* lackluster performance comes from the top down. When a team has a couple of bad seasons, the players aren't fired *en masse*; the coaches take the heat. The top-brass isn't communicating effectively with the worker-bees. So it is in the body. Communication between the top-brass directors and the "drones" is garbled. The workers are doing exactly as they are told to do; it's the instructions that are amiss.

If a unit (sports team or physical body) isn't functioning effectively, look at the big picture — the whole. For a body in trouble, find out what is being communicated internally by lifestyle, foods, rest, exercise, and most important, thoughts. These are some of the major pieces that make up your personal picture of health — and they could also have something to do with a wretched football season.

> WELLNESS PRINCIPLE: Your body is more than an ac-
> cumulation of parts zipped up in
> a common skin

Having pointed out the differences between mechanism and wholism/

vitalism, keep in mind that the road to health is paved with many "bricks." As I see it, mechanism and vitalism are two distinct types bricks in this road — crisis care and maintenance. Mechanism is the damage control needed in emergencies. Vitalism fills the need for ongoing health maintenance and improvement. The two are complementary. And since health care cost and effectiveness is a major issue as the 20th century wanes, we'll talk more about the role of mechanistic medicine as we go on.

Your best bet for health and feeling good is to make sure you send the best messages possible in order to get the best possible responses.

The concepts presented in this book are to give you some ideas about the relationship between lifestyle and healthstyle that may be completely new to you — concepts that integrate the energy fields that are a part of all matter, including you. This book presents you with an opportunity to gain a whole new outlook on how the choices you make in six essential areas of life affect your internal communication and energy supply and determine your lifestyle and health. These six areas of choice are what you eat, drink, breathe, and think, and how you rest and exercise. You will also find practical advice on how to revitalize your life in ways that lead to health, happiness, and success.

In the pages ahead, you will be introduced to explanations of how your thinking affects more than just how you feel at the moment — depressed, angry, anxious, or racked with fear. We, as a society, have long acknowledged that habitual worry can lead to an ulcer, and that constant anger can lead to high blood pressure. Now you will learn why. You will see that thoughts and health are more than kissin' cousins; they are "joined at the hip."

You will also come to see why everything your body does is absolutely perfect for the situation. You'll find it comforting to learn that your body isn't trying to do you in. Even if you don't like the results of the things it is doing, the process is perfect.

Along the way, I'll give you self-help suggestions to guide you toward identifying the CAUSE of your physical problems. And I'll even throw in the occasional "scientific" finding and opinion to reinforce the concepts. All of this will be presented in easily understood language. I believe you will find it exciting. So, let's get on with it.

WELLNESS PRINCIPLE: Health — good or bad — is a
                      do-it-yourself project

POINTS OF INTEREST

1.   Health is a whole-body affair.

2.   You have no direct control over physiological responses.

3.   The physiological by-product of negative emotions is Sensory Dominant Stress.

4.   The mechanistic approach to health views the body as a collection of separate parts that need to be controlled or fixed.

5.   The vitalistic approach to health views the body as an integrated whole.

6.   Vitalism includes the "living" element of your body.

7.   Everything your body does is perfect for current conditions.

*The solution to the health care problem
is to make disease unnecessary.*
- Dr. M.T. Morter, Jr.

CHAPTER 2
Perfect Power

THE "FLAT-EARTH" VIEW OF HEALTH

A perspective on health that may be new to you is that YOU control your life and your health. Good life, bad life; good health, bad health, it makes no difference. It's not the government's job; it's not your doctor's job — YOU are the ultimate purveyor of your personal, self-inflicted health.

How's that for an alternative philosophy of health? Rather than looking at ways to cure physical problems, we are about to delve into concepts that shed light on how to prevent them — concepts such as . . .

You were designed to survive — not to be healthy;

Your body never does anything wrong;

Your disease is your cure;

Your conscious mind runs your life while your subconscious runs your body;

Your body must respond to everything you put into it — food, drink, drugs, thoughts . . . ;

Your conscious choices in six essential areas of life lead you to disease, defeat, and misery — or to health, success, and happiness;

Your body is alkaline by design and acid by function;

Exercise can kill you;

Purely physical stress is short-term and okay; emotional stress can be long-term and not okay — it can lead to disease.

And much, much more.

Some of these concepts may seem a bit off-the-wall to you — "Your body never does anything wrong," "Your disease is your cure," "Exercise can kill you." We haven't been conditioned to look at ourselves, our bodies, and our health in these terms. However, every concept we take for granted today was new at one time. For example, not too many centuries ago, everyone *knew* the earth was flat! Five or six hundred years ago, if I had openly advocated "The earth is round," I would have been derided, ridiculed, and labeled the pre-Copernican version of "kook."

Now, at the end of the twentieth century when I say, "The earth is spherical," the biggest sin is that I am stating the obvious. However, if I say, "Your body never does anything wrong," the verdict among the closed-minded is "guilty of divergent thinking," or the greatest sin and accusation of all: "quackery." After all, everyone knows the body does "wrong" things. Hospitals are full of examples — premature babies, diseased hearts, unruly gallbladders, and an assortment of maladies labeled "Tests inconclusive."

In my opinion, the conviction that the body can do "wrong" things is a "flat spot" in our modern-day thinking. The bodies of those heart patients, gallbladder patients, or any other hospital patients aren't doing anything wrong. Everything they are doing is "right" for survival of internal conditions of the moment. The owner of the body may not be at all happy with the manifestations of these "right" things, but the manifestations are "right" all the same.

As we go along, we'll identify other flat spots. Flat spots like "Being a vegetarian is a sure road to health," or "Germs cause disease," or "I hurt because I have colitis." And when we're finished, you will understand why I say . . .

WELLNESS PRINCIPLE: Everything your body does is perfect — for survival of the moment!

THE BODY UNIFIED

The idea that everything the body does is perfect may seem as outlandish to you as the idea of manned space flight would have been to Sitting Bull. However, the concepts and health-directed principles I offer in these pages are not based on whimsy or wishful thinking. They result from over thirty years of investigating and studying how the body works as a whole unit. My ongoing pursuit is to learn more about the unifying factors that allow your hundreds of body parts and systems to function together harmoniously — not to learn why a particular organ or system breaks down. That's my pursuit; my goal is to share what I have learned with as many people as possible.

I see the body as more than just a collection of systems, organs, tissues, and fluids that independently break down or malfunction. I view the body as an integrated unit. No function of the body is independent of other functions.

If you have a cold, the problem is far more widespread than merely a runny nose. Cells throughout your body rid themselves of toxins — clean out. Your whole body is not only affected, your whole body is involved.

If you break a leg, your whole body adapts to allow the damage to be repaired. It's not just your leg that mends the bone.

If you are depressed, angry, or unhappy, your whole body responds.

If you adopt a confident, cheerful, amiable outlook, your attitude brings about a whole-body response. We see this when we get all spruced up in our "Sunday Best" or favorite "Power Suit"; attitudes and feelings of well-being get dressed up to match.

WELLNESS PRINCIPLE: Your body is greater than the
                      sum of its parts

The conventional view of health is that the body is an intricate piece of machinery that is subject to breakdowns. The focus is on systems and parts that go awry. The object is to try to fix parts that don't work right. Conventional "health care" is a "service center" for bodies with problems. Run low on insulin/oil; add the necessary ingredients to make the machine run better. An artery/hose becomes clogged; rip out the old and replace it. Parts are fixed, snatched out, or replaced all in the name of "health care."

WELLNESS PRINCIPLE: How many parts must be re-
                      moved from a sick body to
                      make it healthy?

Rather than being reactive to disease, we should be proactive for health. Instead of trying to fix symptoms, we need to address the source of the problem that caused the symptoms. What is the CAUSE that mandates low insulin levels, high blood pressure, or artery-clogging debris? What stresses has the body been compelled to adjust to over the long haul that would CAUSE such a response? What is the CAUSE? CAUSE is what we're after.

Of course, if you or someone close to you is in imminent danger of dying, or if blood is gushing from a gaping wound, your immediate concern is to survive the crisis. Retrospection and long-term planning aren't high priorities. You need crisis care.

Crisis care is the foundation of our so-called "health care" system.

However, "health" has almost nothing to do with it. Our current system is one of "crisis management" — working to correct critical breakdowns in the machinery of the body. And that's good. That's necessary. But it has nothing to do with "health." Health is MORE than the absence of symptoms!

> WELLNESS PRINCIPLE: Health is symptom-free, harmonious functioning of body and field that make up a unique "Person"

Health is more than surviving stresses. Health is a process of functioning in harmony with the creative energy that "powers" living creatures. Health care is the process of keeping the whole "You" synchronized with this energy. That's your job. Health care isn't "curing" anything. Doctors (of whatever stripe) can't cure. Drugs can't cure. Radiation can't cure. Surgery can't cure. Aspirin can't even "cure" a headache; it only masks symptoms, and as we shall see, changes stress priorities. Only the body can cure itself. So our job, as health-conscious individuals, is to make sure our bodies are able to function under the conditions best suited to allow them to cure themselves.

When your body functions harmoniously throughout, with only short-term interference we call stress, its many systems and organs can adjust to handle the occasional unusual circumstances. You are healthy.

However, (watch it, here comes a Biggie Concept) *your body wasn't designed to be healthy.* But, take heart, it wasn't designed to be sick either. Your body was designed to *survive!* It survives moment by moment. It survives by adapting to ever-changing conditions. That's the way it is supposed to work. When your body becomes "stuck" in a particular survival adaptation the way Ben's did, you — like Ben — are headed toward pain, disease, and misery.

Even more important, no matter how hard you try, no matter how many drugs you take, no matter how much is cut out or repaired, until the adaptations that caused your body to become "stuck" become "unstuck," you won't eliminate your problem. You may reduce your symptoms, but your body will be headed toward exhaustion and real trouble.

That's one of the reasons governmental health-care reforms won't solve our so-called "health care crisis." In today's world, "health care" is really "crisis care." Symptoms may be eased, but unless the cause of the problem is resolved, symptoms of some sort will crop up again. You can be assured that if you "fix" the body so that one set of symptoms can't return — like taking out the gall bladder to relieve the agony of gall bladder "attacks" — other symptoms will appear somewhere else. Doctoring and fixing go only so far. You'll keep generating symptoms until you do something about the cause that made the symptoms necessary in the first place. When the cause is eliminated or corrected, symptoms are unnecessary. When symptoms become unnecessary, the body can heal itself.

WELLNESS PRINCIPLE: Only the body has the power to
cure itself

And while we're on this health-care crisis side trip, another reason governmental health-care reforms won't work is that "health care" is an economic and political problem. "Health-care" costs are astronomical. Health care costs the government and individuals billions of dollars each year. Yet "health care" is a profitable industry. It provides livelihoods for millions of people. If we reduce health care costs, we reduce the number of jobs available in the industry, lower incomes, and play havoc with personal and national economies. What megalithic industry worth its profit-and-loss statements is going to stand still for, much less cooperate with, consumer-oriented improvements that bring large-scale reductions in the industry's income? The health-care community is as enthusiastic about reducing consumer health care costs as you would be about having a nuclear waste disposal site built in your back yard. The need is acknowledged, but "not on my turf."

You can do your part to make disease unnecessary by making choices in your life that allow your body to respond to stimuli of the moment, not to stimuli from the past. Residual stresses in your life can affect your health — and your pocket book. On our trip to self-directed health, we deal primarily with stresses brought about by the two greatest stressors — eating and thinking. Of the two, thinking is by far the greater influence on health.

WELLNESS PRINCIPLE: Solve the health-care problem
— make pain and disease un-
necessary

THE BODY EXTENDED

A well-entrenched yet seldom verbalized "flat spot" of our times runs along the lines of "A body is a body, is a body — tangible, visible, and self-contained." As we shall see, the sharp edges of this flat spot are being burnished away. Science and technology have advanced to the point where the unseen energy component of the body can be measured, if not seen.

Is your reader qualification of open-mindedness in gear? We are headed at full gallop toward a major concept of self-directed health — the energy component of you and your body. To lay the groundwork, a short primer on how this energy component fits into our picture of health might be helpful. Some of these info-bits may be familiar to you — some may not. However, the concept of ever present energy is important to understanding that there's more to health than fixing blowouts, adjusting fluid levels, and plugging leaks. The addition of the energy component helps to integrate our traditional way of looking at the body with the concept that we are energy beings designed to survive. From the instant we are conceived, the primary goal of your body is survival.

> WELLNESS PRINCIPLE: We are energy beings designed
> to survive

The visible body is tangible. We can see it and feel it. However, intangible elements are also integral components of you as a person. These intangible elements are energy. Energy is ever present in the invisible fields that surround you. These unseen yet measurable intangibles are major players in every facet of your life and health. They constitute "your personal field" that is "attached" to you as surely as your arms, legs, and eyes are "attached."

We can use the example of magnets as an illustration of fields and their connectedness. Remember the childhood joy and mystery of playing with magnets? You'd put two together one way and they clamp solidly against each other. Turn one around and try to put them together and they just won't go. They slip and slide away from each other around an unseen barrier. That unseen barrier is the type of field we're talking about. It isn't exactly the same as "your personal field" — but it's an apt illustration of the field's invisible-yet-powerful, all-encompassing nature. You can't see it, but you can feel the effects.

Your personal field is your direct link with the universe and all of the information in it. Your field, like your body, isn't isolated and it isn't static. Both body and field are dynamic. Ever active. Your field, like your body, is affected by its internal and external environments. Your field is ever-present and ever-changing. It can be vibrant; it can be subdued. We might say that your field can be "healthy" or it can be "sick." And the health of your field determines the health of your visible body. As we shall see, the biggest influence on your field-health is your thoughts and feelings. Your thoughts and feelings affect your field; your field affects your health.

> WELLNESS PRINCIPLE: As your field goes, so goes your
> health

Your field is energy. Energy fields, invisible to the naked eye yet measurable by sensitive equipment, surround the human body. We are energy beings. We shall see later that we were energy before we were physical. Energy is at the core of a vital animate being, and energy is generated by and encompasses living systems. An energy field surrounds every individual live being.

Robert O. Becker, M.D., orthopedic surgeon and author, researches energy fields that stimulate growth and development. In his book *Cross Currents: The Perils of Electropollution, The Promise of Electromedicine*, Becker writes: "... magnetic and electromagnetic fields have energy, can carry information, and are produced by electrical currents. When we talk about electrical currents flowing in living organisms, we also imply that they are producing magnetic fields that extend outside of the body and can be influenced by external magnetic fields as well."[6] Yet, the energy field that surrounds a body is not isolated. It touches and overlaps, is overlapped by, and converges with other fields.

Your energy field is connected to other energy fields, and those fields are connected to other fields, and those are connected to even more fields, and on and on and on. With all of this interweaving and overlapping and fraternizing, we can see that your energy field is directly or indirectly connected to every other energy field. We could think of these mix and match energy fields as subsets of a whole connected through uninterrupted Venn diagrams. You remember Venn circles: circles B and C partially overlap circle A and each other. So you have "pure B" and a portion that is "B + A" and a portion that is "B + C" and a portion that is "B + A + C". And that's rather straightforward when you have just A, B, and C. But extrapolate on that model and you have a gazillion fields throughout the world and galaxy and universe touching and overlapping and mingling. You have a huge pot of intergalactic energy soup.

But let's bring that concept out of the galaxy and relate it to your own energy connection. In your body, the individual energy field (Venn circle) of each minuscule bit of your body is a subset of several larger energy fields. Fields of subatomic particles interconnect with the fields of atoms and molecules. These interconnect with fields of systems which interconnect with fields of ever-larger subsets. In no time at all, each of the itsy-bitsy fields of each subatomic particle of your body is connected with all of the energy fields of the entire Universe. Energy soup. The component and collective energy bits of each human energy body are integral parts of this energy soup.

WELLNESS PRINCIPLE: Each energy bit acts on and reacts to every other energy bit

Subatomic particles within the body are always active. This activity produces energy. Some internally-produced energy can be measured externally: the electrocardiogram (ECG) on the outside of the body measures electrical variations of heart muscle activity inside the body. The kinetic energy of atoms or molecules inside the body is measured as temperature. Impulses of the brain inside the body are measured on the outside of the body by the electroencephalogram (EEG). But remember, the energy in and of your body isn't static. It's dynamic. It changes. And here's a point that keeps cropping up in various forms throughout our essay on energy. The amount of energy produced by your brain depends on your brain's activity level.

WELLNESS PRINCIPLE: Busy brain, busy energy

Guyton explains this phenomenon: "Electrical impulses called *brain waves* can be recorded from all active parts of the brain and even from the outside surface of the head. The character of these waves is determined to a great extent by the level of sleep and wakefulness at the time that the waves are recorded. When a person is awake but not thinking hard, continuous waves at a rate of approximately 10 to 12 per second can be recorded from almost all parts of the cerebral cortex."[7] The frequency of these waves picks up when the brain is working. Guyton goes on to say, "When any part of the brain becomes very active — for example, the motor regions initiating muscular activities — additional waves [have] a frequency sometimes as high as 50 cycles per second, . . ."[8] Not only does the wave frequency increase, the intensity can also increase. Brain waves are a part of the energy soup. The more alert or stimulated the brain, the greater intensity the bioelectrical energy — bioenergy. That bit of information will come in handy later. Store it in your energetic brain.

Through its electrical impulses, the brain has a direct connection with the body's personal electromagnetic field. It's one of those circles that overlaps, intersects, or combines with your greater whole-body personal field. By understanding the interconnectedness of fields, we can see that energy emitted from the brain has a profound effect on the personal field which in turn affects all fields inside and outside the body.

WELLNESS PRINCIPLE: Thinking affects your field as
                      well as your actions, attitudes,
                      and life

The concept that energy of some sort affects the body is not new. It is a concept that has sparked debate for centuries. In his paper "Electromagnetism and Life" Becker sums up the debate by writing, "This controversy, dating back to the early Greek philosophers, pitted the vitalists who believed that living things possess an 'anima' or vital spirit unaccessible to physical analysis, against the mechanists who thought that this was simply nonsense and that living entities were merely more complex than non-living things."[9]

The debate between vitalists and mechanists thrived in the 17th and 18th centuries after electricity was identified and scientists developed methods of measuring electrical currents. By the 20th century, reductionists had gained the advantage by excluding more and more physiological functions from the influence of electricity. By the beginning of World War II, the reductionist scientific community that studied the world in smaller and smaller bits had concluded that, as Becker puts it, "There were no biological effects of electrical currents below the level at which shock was produced, and living organisms made no use of electrical currents in their physiological functions."[10] The reductionist model is alive and well today — but, once again, beginning to fade.

Ever-increasing numbers of reputable scientific professionals are concluding that the body is more than the tangible bits and pieces of tissue and fluid we are accustomed to considering it to be. The body includes the energy of the parts and the energy of the whole. The energy field surrounding the body is as much a part of the human being as are the bones that give that being its form and structure. The "accepted scientific school of thought" may be shooting itself in the foot as far as the vitalistic vs. mechanistic debate goes. As the vast majority of Western civilization clings tenaciously to a Newtonian reductionist line of thought, science continues to develop instruments of greater sensitivity. With those instruments, the opportunity grows to "prove" that the living body is more than merely the mechanists' version of a more complex entity than non-living things.

WELLNESS PRINCIPLE: Energy fields are the gridiron
for the game of life

The development of the SQUID (superconducting quantum interference detector) made possible the detection of minute magnetic fields. "Today," Becker explains, "the magnetic field (called the magnetoencephalogram, or MED) produced by the brain is easily detected using the SQUID magnetometer (a device based upon the fact that a superconducting current is extremely sensitive to very small magnetic fields). The flow of electrical currents in the brain actually does produce a magnetic field that can be measured and analyzed several feet away from the head."[11] The idea that the brain generates measurable electric currents is acknowledged. As we shall see, your individual energy currents affect your individualized magnetic field. Electromagnetic fields are energy fields — force fields. And your energy field is part of your physical body.

For years I have worked with the energy fields, or "force fields," of and around the body. Now, that bioenergy is finally being investigated intensely by "scientists," I'm not quite as much of a "kook" as I used to be. Thinking about energy as part of physiology isn't as off-the-wall as it was only a few years ago. Yet even before the first glimmers of scientific acknowledgement, my clinical experience and research showed that for many patients the source of symptoms was interference in their energy field rather than interference in their physical organs and systems. And one of the most important features I have found is that this interference develops in the field before it shows up as symptoms in the body. We'll explain more about interference later.

The concept of the individual bioenergetic field as an extension of the body opens the door to viewing health and disease from a different angle. From both the mechanistic and vitalistic viewpoints, pain and disease are unquestionably real. However, by including the energy field in "anatomy," we can see that the *cause* of that pain or disease may not have originated where it hurts. In fact, I will go so far as to say that nothing happens in the body that didn't first "happen" in the field.

WELLNESS PRINCIPLE: Take care of your field and your
                                          field will take care of you

And, to take this energy-appendage concept a step farther, your energy field came into being before you did. How's your open mindedness doing?

THE POWER BEHIND DEVELOPMENT

Your original, unique, personal field was created at the moment you were created. You and your field are inseparable.

We learn early in life "where babies come from." In elementary school, most children are exposed to vivid if inaccurate tales of "where babies come from." Then in junior high or high school we are introduced to the biological mechanics of reproduction of living beings — fertilization, cell division, gestation, and the like. However, in schools other than those that are religiously oriented, nothing is said about the impetus behind the origin of a new life. The whole process is attributed to chemical reactions — which is quite true as far as it goes. We need to add that chemical reactions involve energy. Everything that is created starts as energy. Energy of some sort is needed to spark and sustain activity.

Energy is the force behind the development of the body, and energy sustains the activity of the body. Energy is your constant companion throughout life.

WELLNESS PRINCIPLE: The power that made the body
guides the body

We've alluded to the traditional junior high or high school version of sex education. But there's something your teacher didn't tell you — you were "You" before your chassis and filling came into being. Not long before, but before.

You learned in school (or on the school bus or behind the barn) that the human body develops from a single fertilized egg. You may not have been told that this fertilized egg pulsates with life. As it pulsates, this single-celled egg divides into two daughter cells. Both of the daughter cells then divide — four cells. Then that generation of daughter cells divides — eight cells. And again, and again, and again until there are trillions of cells. In the process of multiplication by division, daughter cells differentiate. They take on characteristics necessary to form the many different tissues, organs, and structures that become a complete body of predetermined shape. Some cells become blood cells. Others become bone cells. And still others become kidney cells. Cells differentiate and specialize until there are cells to make up all of the equipment prescribed for a small but complete human being. "Within one month after fertilization of the ovum," writes physiologist Guyton, "all the different organs of the fetus have already been 'blocked out,' and during the next two to three months, most of the details of the different organs are established."[12] In less than nine months, the single fertilized egg evolves into a complete person with structural, biological, and interactive communication systems precisely configured. But how?

How does the fertilized egg cell know to divide? How do daughter cells know to differentiate? How do differentiated cells that make up particular organs know the proper location for those organs? What guides the original single cell through its intricate developmental course to turn out a standard-formed, multi-trillion-celled complete human being? Or, to reduce these questions to the lowest common denominator, "How are babies really made?"

WELLNESS PRINCIPLE: Cells don't think; they "know"

Science has identified the processes of cell division and differentiation. However, process identification sheds no light on the motivation behind the process. Who, or what, directs the development process?

Assembly instructions for a new human body can't be a function of information stored in the newly-forming cerebral cortex. Conscious activity doesn't begin until after formation of the physical structure. Certainly the mother isn't the architect. The process is well underway before she's even aware that a new person is in the making. Then, is it all DNA's doing? Are cells cognitive entities?

You can see where we're going.

The "power source" we've been talking about directs the process.

Science hasn't solved the riddle of the power behind development. "Hazy"[13] is the word Guyton uses to describe their understanding. Scientists look at the mechanics of development — the "how." "We know many different control mechanisms by which differentiation *could* occur,"[14] says Guyton. Presumably, once the "mechanisms" are identified, we'll be able to fix whatever goes wrong. Right? I don't think so. Science is looking for the mechanics through which cells tailor themselves to perform particular jobs. And that's great for expanding knowledge. But it doesn't address the question of *why* cells do what they do — the *cause*. What is it that tells the cells to differentiate? That's a question that can't be answered from the mechanistic perspective. Guyton again: ". . . the overall basic controlling factors in cell differentiation are yet to be discovered; when learned, they will make a tremendous difference in our understanding of bodily development."[15]

WELLNESS PRINCIPLE: Is science looking for the carbu-
retor in a fuel injection engine?

Current physiology textbooks (such as Dr. Guyton's) deal with the mechanics of the body. They deal with chemical reactions and tangible, visible structures of the body, such as DNA. Anything else is seen as being irrelevant to physiology and counter to "science." Yet a few members of the scientific medical community have a severe case of open-mindedness. These few recognize external influences in the process of development. One such medical scientist is Richard Gerber, M.D. Gerber implies a power source behind development when he writes: "At the micro level, cells of living organisms display organizing principles which demonstrate that every piece contains the whole. Similar information storage patterns are seen in conventional holograms. At a higher organizational level, the growth of the entire organism is guided by an invisible etheric overlay or template which is also similar to a hologram in its three dimensionality."[16]

WELLNESS PRINCIPLE: You develop as a whole organism

From the time of conception, the fertilized ovum contains all of the information necessary for development to a full-sized being. In his book *The Body Electric*, Dr. Becker, premier researcher in regeneration and its relationship to electrical currents in living things, writes "... the entire genetic blueprint is carried by every cell nucleus."[17] As cells divide, development information is passed along to each daughter cell. Each cell contains the whole message — cells are holographic — each contains the "whole message." Information of cells is passed from generation to generation.

Guyton reinforces the blueprint analogy with an example of development information that comes from an unexpected source: "The nucleus from an intestinal mucosal cell of a frog, when surgically implanted into a frog ovum from which the original nucleus has been removed, will often cause the formation of a completely normal frog. This demonstrates that even the intestinal mucosal cell, which is a reasonably well-differentiated cell, still carries all the necessary genetic information for development of all structures required in the frog's body."[18] Hmmmm. Sounds surprisingly like a recurring theme of this book.

WELLNESS PRINCIPLE: "Blueprints" in each cell depict
the finished product

The Newtonian community acknowledges that fields exist. They view fields as the *result* of physical responses and activity. From my view of whole health and the energy body, fields are not the result of physical responses, they are the *cause* behind the physical. Field first, physical follows.

Much of this book is devoted to showing that your body always knows what it is doing. It knows what it is doing because it has access to all of the information it needs to do its job perfectly. This "information" is not only *available* throughout life but is the *source* of both life itself and that illusive quality we humans describe as "health."

To illustrate that cells use an intelligence that dwarfs our conscious intelligence, let's take a look at the amazing abilities of the lowly salamander. Salamanders are obviously "inferior" to us humans — a salamander can't drive a Porsche or build an 80-story skyscraper or create a soul-stirring symphony. All he or she can do is scurry around, eat, reproduce and do whatever salamanders do to survive. If, in a scuffle with another salamander from a rival gang, a salamander loses a body part — such as a leg — he or she grows a perfect replacement. And we think we're so smart!

Dr. Robert Becker, whom I mentioned earlier, has studied the regeneration abilities of salamanders. He, and other salamander researchers, have come up with some startling revelations about the unpretentious, lizard-looking creatures. It seems that salamanders, or their bodies, know exactly what to regrow where. That leg we mentioned. When a leg is lopped off, how does the salamander "know" where to grow a new one? And how does it know which kind of leg to regrow? Very likely, the salamander gives little thought to the process. But that is purely conjecture since few of us speak Salamander and we can't "get into their heads." Be that as it may, back in the nineteenth century, some embryologists tried to find out where the regeneration information comes from. Apparently they never came up with a definitive answer, but their research provided some very interesting results.

When a salamander loses a leg (and you can be assured the researchers didn't wait for a fight to break out for this to happen), a small bundle of cells forms at what we will discreetly call the "amputation site." This small bundle of cells is called a blastema. The investigators found that if they removed the blastema of a foreleg within ten days and transplanted it near the hindleg, another hindleg developed. But if they waited longer than ten days to transplant the foreleg blastema near a hindleg, the blastema grew into a foreleg.

How in the world did this happen? What told the cells to develop a hindleg before the ten day period and a foreleg afterwards? Certainly it wasn't the salamander's super brain. No self-respecting salamander would want a foreleg stuck next to a hindleg.

Was it the salamanders nervous system?

No, says Becker. Studies showed that the nerves around the blastema were not transmitting impulses. It wasn't nerve signals.

Chemical messengers — neurotransmitters?

No, says Becker. Chemical messengers can't transmit that kind of information.

With the nervous system and chemical messengers removed from contention as carriers of regenerative information, another source of information must be considered. As Becker puts it, "something similar to the morphogenic field — that could contain within itself the entire organizational plan."[19] The idea of the morphogenic field was proposed in 1939 by Paul Weiss who "conjectured that development was guided by some sort of field projected from the fertilized egg."[20] Becker suggests in his book, *Cross Currents* that fields produced by DC electrical currents could contain such information. "Even the simplest electrical field has a high degree of organizational complexity. . . . It's possible that the field serves only as a 'trigger' to instruct the cells to follow certain routines in development."[21] The field "triggers" the cells to "follow certain routines." The cells know what to do, this information is built in. It's unerring intelligent fields that "trigger" the cells to respond to their environment.

Aha! An important facet of living systems — "fields of intelligence" — that has been ignored (or pooh-poohed) in conventional analyses of life and health.

Research and investigation into the electromagnetic fields surrounding living systems show that the surrounding field is indeed the template for development to a mature entity.

At Yale University in the 1920s, neuroanatomist Harold S. Burr studied energy fields and their shapes around live plants and animals. According to an account by Gerber, Burr found that in animals "this field contained an electrical axis which aligned with the brain and spinal cord."[22] The field surrounding tiny seedlings, however, presented unexpected shapes. "According to his [Burr's] research," writes Gerber, "the electrical field around a sprout was not the shape of the original seed. Instead the surrounding electrical field resembled the adult plant. Burr's data suggested that any developing organism was destined to follow a prescribed growth template and that such a template was generated by the organism's individual electromagnetic field."[23]

Remarkable! A field around the seed indicates the shape of the full-grown plant. The field of a sprouting acorn would be in the shape of an oak tree. The field of a sprouting pumpkin seed would be in the shape of a pumpkin plant. The field of a germinating kernel of corn, the shape of a corn stalk. These findings set the stage for serious consideration of the electromagnetic field as a vital element of growth, development, and, ultimately, health.

And that's the crux of your extended body. From conception on, throughout life, we not only live within our field, we "grow into it." Your field is your template for growth. And, as I explain in the pages to come, your physical health depends on the health of your field.

> WELLNESS PRINCIPLE: Your field determines the shape
> you're in

PERFECT INTELLIGENCE

As we progress through our journey to a better understanding of how our bodies work and what "makes them tick" (an apt expression that becomes more clear later), we shall see that an unseen Intelligence is constantly at work in and around our bodies. Furthermore, this unseen intelligence is *perfect*. And it is *always perfect*. This is the Perfect Intelligence of the Ultimate Power Source that never makes a mistake. Your conscious intelligence that you use to run your life isn't perfect, but the Intelligence that runs your body is. It responds to every internal situation immediately — and *perfectly*!

Every function and response of your body is directed by this Intelligence. Breathing, digestion, insulin production, muscle movement, blood pressure, circulation — every function and response. And every function and response of your body is *perfect* for the conditions of the moment. Do you begin to get the idea that this concept of a *Perfect Intelligence* is important? You're right. It is paramount to understanding that you are in the shape you are in right now because your body has responded *perfectly* under the direction of Perfect Intelligence to everything you have done, eaten, thought, and felt in the past. You may not be in "perfect health," but the health you're in is a perfect response for survival at this moment.

To establish a working definition of the word *intelligence*, we can use a simple and practical term of Deepak Chopra, author, champion of mind/body medicine, endocrinologist, and former chief of staff of New England Memorial Hospital in Stoneham, Massachusetts. Chopra writes: "Rather than referring to the intelligence of a genius, which may seem both exalted and abstract, I define it simply as 'know-how.' There is no doubt, whatever you think about intelligence in the abstract, that the body must be credited with an immense fund of know-how."[24] The Intelligence that runs the body is "know-how." Your body knows how to do everything it needs to do for you to develop from a single fertilized egg and to survive. Your body's intelligence is complete.

WELLNESS PRINCIPLE: "Know-how" Intelligence is perfect — it contains the "whole message"

Cells constantly die off and are replaced. As Greenwood and Nunn describe the renovation process, "The cells of our stomach lining are replaced every three or four days; our livers are renewed every six weeks or so; even our bones, which seem so solid, are actually 'fluid' in the sense that they are continuously renewed, completing a cycle every three or four years."[25] Despite the complete turnover of matter, we adhere to the blueprint. We retain our personality and general appearance and are completely unaware of the renovation process.

Development doesn't end at birth. The body continues to develop throughout life. Cells are constantly renewed and replaced. That's lifetime development. It's slower and less obvious than development from toddler to roust-about street urchin, but it's development. Development that depends on what Greenwood and Nunn describe as "the flow of energy and material passing though our bodies."[26] Through this flow of energy, molecules and cells in our bodies are replaced. At the end of every seven years you are an entirely different set of atoms. We might say that in seven years, you aren't the same person you used to be. By the time you are 56, you begin working on your eighth "new you." We expect a dramatic metamorphosis in children; we tend to forget that what we euphemistically call "the aging process" is a continuation of our "development."

The perfect "know-how" information that held the blueprint for development from seed to full-blown sustainable being directs the parts-replacement of that living system throughout life. And that perfect information is contained in the thousands of overlapping fields of cells, molecules, atoms, subatomic particles, and spaces of that entity.

> WELLNESS PRINCIPLE: Fields of Perfect Intelligence
> surround all structures from
> subatomic particles to planets,
> and everything in between

Development of the fertilized egg into a complete human being is a process of Perfect Intelligence. Changes in physiological function are processes of Perfect Intelligence. Survival responses are processes of Perfect Intelligence. Perfect Intelligence not only serves as a conduit for Universal Energy but as a form or derivative of Universal Energy.

Your personal energy field is the radiant energy (literally and figuratively) of the amalgamation of the individual internal fields surrounding each minute entity of your body. As long as this energy flows through and from your body to connect with the greater fields of the external universe, you are alive. It's what we might call the "Tinker Bell Syndrome": when the "light" of internal energy goes out, you're dead. Recall the story of "Peter Pan." After Tinker Bell drinks Peter's poisoned medicine, her light begins to fade. Peter entreats all within earshot to help save Tink by clapping their hands. With the cacophony of compassionate clapping, Tink is saved. (Lives there an adult so hard-hearted as to not clap and let Tink die?) Unfortunately, for mere mortals, a bit more than hand-clapping is needed to undo misdeeds which are the results of conscious choices. But the "Tinker Bell Syndrome" holds for all of us. We are energy beings, and when our energy stops, we stop. Our purpose here is to help you understand how you can not only keep your "light" glowing, but increase its healthful intensity.

And the underlying principle for keeping your "light" — your internal energy flow — "glowing" is to provide your body with the best tools available for handling all of the stress in your life. Not just the stress of having too much to do and too little time to do it. But the much more pervasive stress that comes from the conscious actions and thoughts that only you control.

You come equipped with Perfect Field Intelligence that replaces worn-out cells and directs the inner workings of your body. You also develop decidedly imperfect conscious intelligence that recycles conscious thoughts and directs your actions. The two intelligences are decidedly different, yet inextricably interwoven.

> WELLNESS PRINCIPLE: Your field intelligence is per-
> fect; your conscious intelligence
> is not

INTELLIGENCE AND STRESS

You are conscious; you think. You think and act through your conscious-mind intelligence. Your body responds to those thoughts and actions through your Perfect Intelligence. You think; your body responds physiologically. Right now, as you read these words, your body is responding without you consciously telling it what to do. Muscles are moving your eyes to scan line after line. Your fingers may ripple the corner of the pages absentmindedly. You may be bouncing your foot. A phone rings; the status quo is disrupted; you are momentarily "startled" — however slightly; your train of thought is diverted from reading to answering the phone. None of this is high drama. Yet throughout even humdrum activities, your body responds with thousands of physiological adaptations. And you have no idea consciously that anything is going on. Yet every time something "happens" in or to your body, you have stress.

We usually think of stress as being all bad. We associate it with making us feel up-tight, uneasy, nervous, distracted, distraught, possibly sick, but generally miserable. Yet, stress is neither good nor bad. Stress is a fact of life. How you *respond to stress* is a fact of health.

Just what is stress? Stress is more than feeling frustrated, anxious, or pressed for time.

> *Stress is ANYTHING that causes your body to change the way
> it is functioning right now!*

Although we tend to think of stress as purely emotional, life is a never-ending series of three different types of stress: physical stress, emotional stress, and nutritional stress. In this book, we look at how these three types of stress act on your body, react with each other, and promote either health and vitality or symptoms and disease. More important, though, we show how choices you make in your conscious mind minute-by-minute, day-by-day produce the stimuli your Perfect Intelligence must respond to and deal with. These are the stress stimuli that determine your healthstyle. Stimuli are either appropriate or inappropriate. You survive stress in a healthful, happy, successful manner, or you succumb to the effects of perfect responses to inappropriately-timed stimuli and end up with pain, symptoms, and misery.

Your body is designed to survive all three kinds of stress. And your body is not only resilient, it's tenacious. It can survive a lot of stress. But you may not be happy with how you feel during the survival process.

> WELLNESS PRINCIPLE: Survival doesn't always feel good

The interconnections among the three types of stressors — physical, emotional, nutritional — are central to this book and to your health, so here's a general overview of each.

Physical Stress

Physical stress comes from an actual threat of injury to your body. It comes as a package deal along with physical activity and physical accidents. Bash your thumb with a hammer, heft a 40 lb bag of garden mulch, fall down the stairs, or jog through the park and your body responds with faster heart rate, heightened awareness, and other survival characteristics. When the action stops or the threat is over, the stress is gone. Physical stress is short, if not sweet.

Accidents are physical stressors. By definition, accidents aren't planned. Rare is the person who survives this life for any period of time without an accident of some sort. Most of us get our first taste of accidents while learning to walk and to navigate around obstacles the Big People call furniture or stairs. Fortunately, your body is designed to take care of most mishaps. Given the opportunity, your body will repair accident-damaged tissue and bone in a matter of days or weeks. Similarly, given the opportunity, exercise injuries heal in a short time. Although a physical accident or trauma may leave a scar of some sort on the surface or structure of your body, physical trauma should not impose long-term stress on your body. The master plan calls for your body to take care of the immediate needs of a physical stress, then return to business as usual. No problem.

> WELLNESS PRINCIPLE: Physical stress is short-term

Emotional Stress

Emotional stress, on the other hand, comes from within. It originates in your conscious mind, your feelings, memories, beliefs, and your attitudes toward events and people in your life. Emotional stress comes from your conscious responses to events around you — *events perceived with your five senses.* You can suffer emotional stress along with physical stress. Being physically attacked, beaten and robbed by a club-wielding thug is short-term physical stress that can drag with it long-term emotional stress.

Or in a considerably less violent scenario, you generate emotional stress by your response to a situation or event. For example: In six months, the company you work for will close the plant in your city. You are given the option of moving to a company branch in another city or losing your job. You don't want to do either. Your family is happily entrenched where you live now, but jobs are scarce. You are upset — emotionally stressed. The bad news is that this stress can go on for a long time — weeks or months. And as long as the emotional stress continues, your physiology, directed by your Perfect Intelligence, must adapt to handle it. One of these adaptations might be chronic high blood pressure. The good news is that you don't have to *respond* in ways that put undue stress on your body. You may not have much choice about the situation, but you do have a choice about how you respond to the situation.

> WELLNESS PRINCIPLE: Emotional stress can be long-
> term

Nutritional Stress

Nutritional stress is an ever-present companion of eating and drinking. Your body must react to everything that goes into it — a bite of toast or juicy steak, a vitamin pill or prescription drug, concentrated smog or cigarette smoke. It doesn't matter. Your body must handle it. It must change the way it was functioning before the substance entered through mouth, lungs, or injection to take care of the new situation. If you ate a banana and your body didn't switch into a let's-take-care-of-this-new-substance mode, the banana would sit there and rot, ferment. Not a pretty picture. You would be in trouble.

Your body changes the way it is functioning when you drink a glass of water, a cup of coffee, a soft drink, or an alcoholic drink. Anything! Your body MUST change its current function in order to process newly introduced food and drink. Recall our definition of stress: anything that causes your body to change the way it is functioning right now.

> WELLNESS PRINCIPLE: Your body MUST respond to
> any substance that enters it

SURROUNDED BY STRESS

You can see that everything you do stresses your body to some extent.

Stress is inflicted with every movement you make, every morsel you eat, every sip you drink, every breath you breathe, every nap you take, and every thought you think.

Running a marathon may appear to be a much greater stress to your body than sitting in front of a cozy fire reading a book. You will learn later in this book why that may be a mistaken assumption. Stress is more than being up-tight or out of breath. Stress is a whole-body condition. And your thoughts are the biggest stressors of all!

WELLNESS PRINCIPLE: All stresses are not created
equal

Stress in your life isn't a problem. If you didn't experience stress and stress reactions, you would fall flat on your face every time you tripped over a rug or your own feet. Certainly, in the fraction of a second between the time you trip and the time you marshall your anti-falling forces, you don't consciously decide to move your other foot quickly to catch yourself. You don't think consciously, "Oh, goodness me! I must prepare to cushion my fall with my hands and arms because my fancy footwork might not work."

No, indeed. Your Perfect Intelligence takes over in a flash. Adjustments for emergencies are "automatic." Adrenalin surges and you respond to the stress of losing your balance and starting to fall. Your righting reflex kicks in and you try desperately and instantaneously to regain your balance, if not your composure. And you make balance adjustments without consciously analyzing the situation or the options open to you. Good for you! Once you regain your balance automatically, you can work on your composure, which is a conscious act. And only seconds after all of the high drama, your life and your body shift back to business as usual.

Now, suppose you trip, respond, react, then hold that response reaction mode for hours, days, or decades. That's another story. For one thing, you'll look pretty silly with arms jutting out stiffly in front of you. For another, you'll get pretty tired. Adrenalin constantly flowing. Muscles rigidly tense. It won't be long before you are more than merely tired. You're exhausted! And you know from experience that when you're exhausted, you can't function at your best. But worse than that, when your organs and systems are exhausted, they can't function at their best either.

WELLNESS PRINCIPLE: Long-term stress responses are
exhausting

In essence, that's exactly what was going on in "Ben's" body. His response to a traumatic event or memory went on and on. In the process, his muscles became both weak and rigid at the same time. He was experiencing systematic sensory stress.

So you can see, stress itself isn't a problem. Your responses to stress can cause problems. How — and how long — you RESPOND to a particular stress is the key. Your responses are always perfect. How long they last determines how you feel mentally and physically. Responses also determine how healthy you are. Stress responses are key players in the game of health.

All of this may imply that physiological responses to stress are the root cause of physical problems. Not so! Responses are always perfect. They are dictated by Perfect Intelligence. You have absolutely no control over how your body will respond. But you do have a great deal of control over the stimuli that prompt the responses — mainly thoughts and actions. Responses to all of these are perfect. The timing of the stimuli that prompt the responses may not be. That's where the problem is — inappropriately timed stimuli.

> WELLNESS PRINCIPLE: If you don't like the response,
> change the stimulus

Medical science has made great strides in subduing physical symptoms and diseases generated by long-term stress responses. Modern technology brings us sophisticated techniques to detect and combat symptoms that started as trauma and turned into symptoms — techniques such as by-pass surgery, MRIs, chemotherapy, radiation, life-saving emergency remedies, and a cornucopia of pain-killers. High-tech measures have increased the life-span and improved the quality of life of millions of people.

Yet extensive and expensive measures hit us ever harder in our individual and national pocket books without getting at the *cause* of the problem. There must be a better way. Rather than devoting our resources to trying to relieve pain and cure disease, a better approach is to learn how to *make pain and disease unnecessary*. And you make disease unnecessary by providing the body with the best physical and mental stimuli that will allow it to function at its best under Perfect Intelligence. Keep in mind that your body is a whole being. Anything that affects one part — including your surrounding field — affects every other part.

POINTS OF INTEREST

1. Your body is greater than the sum of its parts.

2. Only the body can cure itself.

3. Your personal energy field is your direct link with Universal Energy.

4. Your brain is directly connected with your personal energy field.

5. You were energy before you were a body.

6. The intelligence that runs your body is perfect "know-how."

7. Stress is anything that causes your body to change the way it is functioning.

8. Stress can be physical, emotional, or nutritional.

9. Stress isn't a problem — prolonged stress responses are.

Anyone who keeps the ability to
see beauty never grows old.
                              - Franz Kafka

CHAPTER 3
The Red 'N The Green

DESIGNED TO SURVIVE

Survival! The bottom-line purpose of every function your body performs is survival.. Everything your body does is directed toward keeping you alive *right now!* "Right now" is this instant. This nanosecond — one billionth of a second. Now!

As long as you live, your body will do whatever is necessary to survive cell by cell, instant by instant. While you sleep restfully and your conscious mind is "turned down," cells are fed, surplus nutrients stored, tissue repaired, toxins and residue from food are gathered to be eliminated. Thousands upon thousands of physiological events take place constantly for the sole purpose of survival. As these instants of rest are laid end to end, your body takes care of current needs. You don't think about it; your body doesn't "think" about it. It just does what's necessary without thought. The result is that you awake ready for another day of physical and mental activity.

While you are up and around, your body carries out its usual housekeeping chores and continually adapts its functions to survive your conscious-driven efforts, thoughts and feelings. Your many parts work together, directed by your central nervous system and guided by Perfect Intelligence, for the sole purpose of survival.

Survival is the only purpose of any and every physiological function the body performs. The body was not designed to be healthy. It was not designed to be sick. The body was designed only to survive conditions of the moment.

WELLNESS PRINCIPLE: Survival is your body's #1 design feature

What are you surviving?

You could be surviving a physical attack, a "nutrition attack," or a "thought attack."

Physical attacks are not as common as "nutrition attacks" or "thought attacks." Although our society is becoming more violent and threatening with each passing year, most of us in this country don't live in danger of imminent physical destruction. For the most part, unlike those in some other parts of the world, we don't sit around consciously thinking about how to avoid being killed. We are relatively safe and secure. However, "survival" as far as your body is concerned, is a different matter. It is constantly "threatened." The "threat" comes in the form of any stimulus that requires a response. And every stimulus requires a response.

What is a "stimulus"? Taber's Cyclopedic Medical Dictionary (15th edition) defines "stimulus" as: "Any agent or factor able to influence living protoplasm directly, as one capable of causing muscular contraction or secretion in a gland, or of initiating an impulse in a nerve." That's pretty clear; a stimulus is anything that causes some element or elements of your body to do something. And, as you will see, just about everything that happens in and around you is a stimulus.

WELLNESS PRINCIPLE: You sink or swim in a sea of
stimuli

As long as you are alive, your body responds to "stimuli"; it is "threatened" in some way. As long as you're alive, your body is bombarded by stimuli from inside and out. Food, breathing, movement, and thoughts. But, not to worry. Your body was designed to handle these "threats." It just wasn't intended to handle the same threat continuously for weeks, months, or years.

But I'm getting ahead of myself.

With every minute change in internal or external conditions, some physiological processes must start, stop, speed up, or slow down in response to the new situation. Eat or drink something and your body responds. Detect through any of your five senses a change in external conditions — heat, cold, danger, mouth-watering aromas, . . . — and your body's physiology changes. Become upset by bad news or elated by good, and your body responds. Blood flow increases or decreases in strategic parts. Muscles tense or relax. Acid is generated, then eliminated. All of this, and more, for survival. Your body responds to all of these events without conscious direction on your part. Your physiological functions adapt for the sole purpose of responding to and surviving ever-changing conditions of the moment.

Your body doesn't plan ahead the way you do. You, as a forward-looking, reasoning individual, consciously plan for the future — insurance, retirement, college fund for the kids, holiday celebrations, vacations. Your body, though, lives only in the present. No long-range physiological strategy to be healthy. No calculated effort to develop disease. Just survive!

> WELLNESS PRINCIPLE: Your body wasn't designed to be healthy or sick — it was designed to survive

Survival is under the command of your Perfect Intelligence. When internal conditions change, intricate systems of your body MUST adapt their function to handle the new environment. But as smart as your Perfect Intelligence is, it does not think, reason, judge, or prepare for the future. Accommodate, survive. Accommodate, survive. If someone stops you on the street and asks, "How does the body work?" you have the answer — accommodate, survive.

Your body responds to two things: (1) messages about what's going on inside, called internal feedback controls, and, (2) messages received from the five senses through the central nervous system (CNS). Internal feedback might be described as internal status reports to your subconscious from muscles and organs. CNS messages are sensory and thought information. Merely getting up from a chair and walking across the room sends a flood of messages about changes in internal conditions. More oxygen is needed, the body's center of gravity changes, muscles and tendons coordinate activities. As a result, your heart beats slightly faster. Your delicate balancing mechanisms leap into action to keep you from falling over. Your muscles and tendons work together to allow your legs to move cooperatively. Countless coordinated, perfectly timed physiological activities take place and you don't even think about them or realize they are happening.

Physiological changes are neither directed nor monitored by your conscious mind. No matter how smart you are, you can't consciously adjust your physiology to meet survival needs continuously.

"Hold on," you think. "What about transcendental meditation, and biofeedback, and the other techniques that allow you to control your heart rate and whatnot?"

Indeed, some meditation techniques can affect a few internal systems such as heart rate and blood pressure. But what about your blood calcium level? Or your kidney function? Thousands of processes go on in your body all the time. Internal functions are so numerous, complicated, and important that they can't wait for you to "think" about them to keep them on track. Physiology is automatic — responsive. How much distraction does it take to divert your attention from the task of regulating your heart rate? Not much. As soon as you are distracted, your subconscious takes over directing the function you're concentrating on. Using your conscious mind to influence automatic functions is a waste of time and energy. Your body knows without thinking how to respond to everything you do.

Take exercise for example. You join in a friendly but lively game of basketball in your backyard. After a few minutes of running and jumping, you notice that your heart is beating faster and you are breathing faster and deeper. Happens all the time when you exercise hard. Yet you don't consciously direct your heart or breathing to speed up. Those are subconscious physiological adaptations to need. Your subconscious control systems get the message that there is a change in oxygen requirements and take the necessary steps to make sure additional oxygen goes where it is needed. Subconscious control systems don't think about what needs to be done; they are designed to respond to the need of the moment. So when you exercise strenuously, you've established a need and your subconscious responds. Your heart steps up its pace to deliver the oxygen to strategic areas. You begin to breathe faster and deeper to rush additional oxygen to hard-working muscles and to get rid of the carbon dioxide generated by running, jumping, and generally gallumping about like a teenager. If physiological changes aren't made on the spot, your muscles and other taken-for-granted parts can't work as well as you expect them to. You don't last very long in the game of basketball — or in the game of life.

Your body is a dynamic piece of equipment. Something is always going on inside. As long as you are alive, your body is never idle. Even as you vegetate in a crumpled heap with your brain in "neutral" in front of the TV, on the inside your body reverberates with organized activity. Constantly adapting. Without the bijillion adaptations your body makes every day, you would die on the spot — and they'd call it "heart attack" or "gizzard failure," or "unknown causes."

WELLNESS PRINCIPLE: If the systems of your body
don't adapt, you don't survive

Every stimulus is a "stress" to your body. Stress plays a major role in life and health. Earlier I emphasized that I use the term "stress" to refer to conditions different from those customarily thought of as "stressful." It's not just the Sturm und Drang of your worlds of work, family, or romance. Stress is ANYTHING that causes your body to change what it is doing at the moment.

As you shall find dotted throughout this book, stress in itself is not a health problem. Health problems crop up when your body must continuously respond to stimuli that are inappropriate. And any long-term stimulus is inappropriate. Long-term stimuli are generated internally by such everyday activities as worry, guilt, judgment, negative thinking, and negative attitudes.

We know that your body is designed to survive stress and that everything your body does is for the purpose of survival. Surviving a variety of stresses is a whole lot easier on you, your health, and your body than is surviving the same stress constantly.

Stress is a constant companion. When a particular stressor, such as anger, worry, or "high-stress" foods stimulates a non-stop stress response for great periods of time, something in your body is going to be worked to capacity for too long. Your body CAN adapt to a stressful stimulus for long periods; however, after a while fatigue sets in. Major tired! In time, the overtaxed organ or system will become exhausted. As Guyton puts it: "As long as normal conditions are maintained in the internal environment, the cells of the body will continue to live and function properly. Thus, each cell benefits from homeostasis, and in turn each cell contributes its share toward the maintenance of homeostasis. This reciprocal interplay provides continuous automaticity of the body until one or more functional systems lose their ability to contribute their share of function. When this happens, all the cells of the body suffer. Extreme dysfunction leads to death, while moderate dysfunction leads to sickness."[27] There it is, from the pen of a noted Newtonian-oriented physiologist: When one or more systems becomes exhausted, the whole body suffers. Unless something changes to give the organ or system a reprieve and rest, disease or death can be the outcome.

> WELLNESS PRINCIPLE: Exhaustion is the precursor to
> pain, discomfort, and disease

"NOW" PHYSIOLOGY

The intelligence that powers and guides your body is strictly present-time oriented. It doesn't know past or future. It doesn't plan ahead. Nature knows no time other than now. Nature responds to current conditions. The concept of time is man-developed.

From man's perspective, life is a continuum of events. Conditions in our personal worlds change constantly. We learn about these changes through our conscious minds. We cruise or stumble through one experience after another. Situation/Event "A" leads to Situation/Event "B" which leads to Situation/Event "C." Cause and effect. Life's events flow along a continuous, though sometimes bumpy, line. Yet motion is, in reality, a succession of present conditions strung closely together nanosecond by nanosecond. Take the observed movement of the ground during an earthquake, for example.

During an earthquake, every movement of a particular portion of the earth involves a unique interrelationship of matter. Matter intertwined in natural and manufactured configurations, such as rock, sand, tree roots, freeways, homes, and bicycles. Each separate condition of the interrelationship requires a separate response. Rocks shift, gravel is pulled along, the crust of the earth that was your front yard is yanked apart, and the bicycle dropped randomly in quieter times teeters, then disappears into the growing fissure. Each separate response becomes a new present condition which requires a unique response. Each unique response creates a new environment that becomes the present condition that brings on the next response. And the "present" pattern of "A," "B," "C" is repeated on and on. The end result, after the countless successions of "presents" have been responded to and the rumbling of the earth has ceased, may be disaster to physical beings and property. Yet the process of arriving at the end product of the disaster was perfect for the environment and conditions of each moment. Each condition of each nanosecond can be seen as a separate frame, just as each frame of a motion picture film captures a particular circumstance. Each effect was a perfect response to each cause.

In the same way, your body responds to unique conditions of each nanosecond. And each response is perfect for the conditions that prompted it. Your lifetime of nanosecond events and responses dictate your present condition. Your present condition is the effect of past responses. Pain or comfort, health or disease, happiness or despair, and all other conditions are the effects of those nanosecond by nanosecond physiological responses. In fact, everything in your life, is an effect.

> WELLNESS PRINCIPLE: Disease is an effect; health is an
> effect; life is an effect

We have seen that Perfect Intelligence is the power behind the thousands of intricate physiological and biological processes that maintain and repair your body. Your well-schooled learning and rational thinking can't adjust physiological processes. Your conscious mind can't calculate how much hydrochloric acid or which enzymes are needed to digest a meal. Digestion, growth, oxygen distribution, wound-repair and all of the other physiological processes that keep you going are "a piece of cake" for

Perfect Intelligence.

As an example, take what happens when you slice your hand instead of the pumpkin you're carving. When blood flows, you'll do something. Your conscious mind will come up with alternatives. You may just stop the bleeding and put a bandage on it. Or, if you've really done a number on your hand, you'll go to the doctor and have the wound sewn together. Afterwards, you'll adjust your activities to protect your injury. But all of that is what *you* will do. In the meantime, your body is doing what needs to be done — heal the wound. Chopra describes how your brainless cells, functioning with Perfect Intelligence, can run circles around your conscious mind when it comes to actually healing your cut. "When a blood cell rushes to a wound site and begins to form a clot, it has not traveled there at random. It actually knows where to go and what to do when it gets there, as surely as a paramedic — in fact, more surely, since it acts completely spontaneously and without guesswork. Even if we break down its knowledge into finer and finer bits, looking for the secret in some minute hormone or messenger enzyme, we will not find a protein strand labeled 'intelligence,' and yet there is no doubt that intelligence is at work."[28] Keep in mind that the blood cell doesn't think; it responds to information and reestablishes homeostatic balance — dynamic equilibrium — without thought.

Perfect Intelligence doesn't plan for the future. Neither does it evaluate the impact current responses will have on future health. It attends perfectly to situations of the moment — eating, sleeping, worrying, running. It doesn't matter. Physiological responses are always perfect for the conditions.

> WELLNESS PRINCIPLE: Survival calls for specific re-
> sponses, now!

RESPONSES PERFECT FOR SURVIVAL

Your Perfect Intelligence doesn't think, judge, or reason. It responds only to the way things are. It responds to messages of the moment generated by physical activity or mental activity. No matter what the messages, the response is always perfect. And the only purpose of any physiological response is to keep the body going for that precise nanosecond. If the messages keep coming, the response continues to address the situation.

Internal organ and system responses are primarily electrochemical reactions. Perfect Intelligence itself isn't visible, but the fruits of its labor are. Perfect Intelligence works its survival magic through commonly recognized physiological responses. We limited-intelligence Generic Men may not understand properties and "mechanics" of Perfect Intelligence itself, but that's a problem that one day may be solved. In the meantime, Perfect Intelligence isn't "magical." We may not understand what makes Perfect Intelligence work, but we know that its directives are carried out through tangible physical materials and recognized electrochemical reactions that help to keep us alive.

> WELLNESS PRINCIPLE: Perfect Intelligence is the "power-pack" behind electro-chemical processes

Although it may appear that I am belaboring the concepts of the body's survival response tactics, these principles are central to understanding how you can end up where you would rather not be on your personal health continuum. All too often, we look for the source of a physical problem by looking at the symptoms of the problem. A common example that afflicts millions may also afflict you: Periodic itchy nose and eyes compounded by a continuous flow of fluids from same that goes beyond bothersome. You have allergies. So the solution is to dry up the cascading rivulets and avoid the offending mold, or pollen, or cat dander that cause the problem. Right?

Maybe not.

Maybe the solution is to revamp your eating habits. Or change your job or where you live or your attitudes and beliefs.

Maybe your "now" responses are still contending with internal stimuli that have nothing to do with pollen or mold or cat dander but have persisted for years.

> WELLNESS PRINCIPLE: The "Now" you perceive con-sciously may not be the same "Now" your body is working with

Once more, in unison: "Every current function of your body is correct for current conditions. Every physiological response is perfect."

Perfect physiological responses may occur even when physical circumstances do not warrant them. The stimulus may be inappropriate. The responses are quite normal, natural, and necessary at appropriate times. But if the stimulus is inappropriate the response can be inappropriately-timed. High blood pressure during resting. Digestive fluids stimulated continuously although there is no food in the stomach. Skeletal muscles tense during sleep. The body's ability to respond physiologically is necessary, and the physiology itself is perfect. Blood pressure must fluctuate according to need; the stomach must be able to produce acid according to need; and muscles must adapt tonicity for smooth movement. All of these functions are responses to stimuli. However, when a perfect physiological response occurs at inappropriate times — when it is not needed to handle present conditions — the response pattern is correct but the timing of the stimulus that prompts the response is inappropriate

A physiological response is never wrong. The body can't do anything wrong any more than a new-born infant can do anything wrong. Sure enough, the things the body and the infant do can sometimes be annoying to those directly involved, but the activity itself is never wrong. The responses of both brand new baby and body are perfect for the conditions that exist. Little purpose is served by trying to alter the response. You don't stuff a sock into a newborn's mouth to stop the crying (even if you're tempted). If you want a different response, change the stimulus. Update the current stimulus of hunger, anxiety, gas pain, or cold. Feed, cuddle, burp, or wrap him/her in another blanket.

The stimulus that causes a newborn to cry (hunger, pain, fear) must be updated to one that satisfies the survival needs of the baby. The stimulus that causes your body to raise blood pressure (fear, anxiety) needs to be updated to one that maintains normal blood pressure. The stimulus (worry) that causes your digestive system to stay in high gear when no food is present needs to be updated to allow the digestive juice production to adjust to actual conditions. (And if you are an anxious new parent, all of the above may be satisfied by the first — satisfying the survival needs of a crying baby by feeding, re-diapering, or comforting.)

Your body — healthy or miserable — fairly buzzes with a continuous flow of internal messages. Often faster than the speed of sound, signals dart through highly sophisticated nerve networks. Most of the signals that prompt physiological responses are right on target as far as being appropriate for the occasion. But worry, anxiety, guilt, remorse, and other emotions that are memory-retained relics of the past are the main generators of inappropriate signals. For the most part, our bodies must contend with inappropriately-timed stimuli because we think!

Your entire internal world is carefully and delicately controlled by message impulses to and from conscious and subconscious areas of your brain and the rest of your central nervous system. Nothing happens in your body by chance. Every internal activity from altering heart rate to adjusting the acid level of your cells is an essential response to conditions in your internal environment. Instantaneous responses are made to local conditions such as low oxygen levels or high acid levels. Messages from your conscious mind on the order of "Take a deep breath," or messages from your subconscious mind, such as "Coordinate muscle contraction and relaxation for walking," ignite immediate biological and physiological responses. And the most amazing part of the whole process is that every response to a subconscious signal is precisely correct!

But how is all of this information transmitted to the appropriate responders?

Science has probed deeply into the physical structures and areas of operation of the several nervous systems that monitor and direct your body. Three dominant communication systems relay messages subconsciously. These three nerve networks act in concert to coordinate internal activities:

- The **central nervous system** of the brain and connected spinal cord;
- The **peripheral nervous system** made up of cranial nerves, spinal nerves, and part of the involuntary nervous system that is outside the brain and spinal cord; and,
- The involuntary **autonomic nervous system** that is concerned with specific functions like digestion and elimination and with regulatory functions such as body temperature, blood pressure and respiration, and is an integral part of behavioral and emotional responses and actions.[29]

We'll focus first on the conscious and subconscious areas of your nervous systems — "The Red" and "The Green."

RED 'N GREEN WORK TOGETHER

What is your name? What are the colors of the American flag? What happens if you stick your finger in a live light socket? Very good! You know the answers.

What do these questions — or answers — have to do with health? Nothing! They merely illustrate the type of information stored in your conscious mind — information you received through your five senses. They are examples of information you learned from experience, from school, or from the kids on the playground. They are examples of second-hand, learned information.

You gather facts and knowledge from your external world through your five senses. Sensory signals received through your senses of sight, hearing, taste, smell, and touch are processed in your brain — more specifically, your conscious mind. You learn through sensory stimulation. You can recall some learned information intentionally and easily; some you can't. You probably can't recall the names of all of the children in your second grade class, or the color of the shoes you wore six birthdays ago. However, given the right cues, such as reminiscing with a few old school cronies about titillating tidbits of yesteryear, you could probably dredge up the names and antics of many childhood friends and foes about whom you hadn't thought in years.

Learned information gathered throughout your life arrived through your eyes, ears, nose, mouth, and skin was processed through your conscious mind. This is the information you use to run — or ruin — your present and future. Take learned information about your job as an example: whether you are a full-time homemaker, accountant, or rock star, as long as you recall and utilize the information you learned in school or on-the-job training, your life runs smoothly. Fail to recall or utilize the requisite job-related information and skills, and your life-course could take an abrupt change in direction.

> WELLNESS PRINCIPLE: Everything you ever learned in
> your conscious mind came
> through one or more of your
> five senses

In this book, I use the term "Red" to refer to the area of your brain where conscious activities take place. Your Red is your personal learning center. It's the conduit for storing and retrieving memories. It's where activities such as walking, thinking, eating, resting, decision-making, and attitude formation are learned. And learning implies memory storage.

"The Red" identifies that part of your brain where your conscious thoughts are at work. You are aware of your world only through the workings of your Red. Your Red is your thinking, reasoning, evaluating, planning, judging cerebral cortex — the thin layer of tightly packed nerve cells that covers your brain. To give you an idea of the area of the brain we're talking about, look at the front cover of this book. The illustrated representation of the brain shows the Red colored red. Just below the Red is a larger area colored yellow. That's the memory storage area. However, since the information stored in the yellow area must come through the Red, for now we'll refer to that whole section (the cerebrum colored red and yellow) as Red. Both of these areas receive their information from the senses, and both of them are involved with learning through conscious activity. So, for now, just remember that ...

Red = Conscious

Earlier I posed a few questions that illustrate the type of information stored in your Red but have nothing to do with health — the color of the flag, and all that. Now let's try a few questions that are related to health — to how your body is functioning.

What is your blood calcium level? The pH of your duodenal drainage? The reticulocyte percentage of your red blood cells?

You don't know?

How can you take care of your health if you don't know the status of vital conditions inside?

Actually, you don't need to consciously KNOW precisely what is going on inside. Internal physiological functions are handled quite ably by your subconscious mind. As long as these thousands of functions cruise along in sync, you aren't even aware that anything is going on.

> WELLNESS PRINCIPLE: You have no conscious control
> over internal activity

Your body performs thousands and thousands of physiological feats every second of your life. Your body has a housekeeping schedule that would intimidate a queen bee. Internally, the regimen is so complex that no one has yet figured out all of the intricacies.

Here's a little exercise to illustrate this point. For the next sixty seconds, feel your pulse and count your heart beats, count how many times you blink your eyes, and while you're at it, count how many times you take a breath.

Did that get a little confusing? If you can't keep track of what's going on in only three obvious areas of your physiology, how could you ever keep track of the millions of processes that go on every second. Fortunately, (1) you don't have to, and (2) you couldn't do anything consciously about most of the processes even if you wanted to.

There's no way you can keep track of all of your internal interactions. Even if you could, the processes are so elaborate if you tried to keep up with them you wouldn't have time to do anything else, like cut the grass, or read the paper, or fill out your tax returns. And in trying to sort out the complexities of your marvelous internal system you would surely mess up vital processes. You'd fall asleep and forget to reduce the acid level of your blood. Or you'd become careless, neglect to relax a muscle when you contracted its opposite partner, and wonder why your leg locked stiff.

So, what controls your myriad life-sustaining functions? Subconscious automatic, involuntary responses to internal messages directed by your "Green."

Your "Green" refers to the subconscious faculties that run your body. The first thing we can say about your Green — your subconscious — is that it comes fully-equipped and perfect at birth. Your Green responds to survive! You don't have to "learn" anything in your Green. All of the information needed for your Green to perform its functions perfectly has been present in you from the time you were one fertilized egg. Your Green runs on "primary information." (Take another peek at the front cover to get an idea of the physical location of your Green.)

Green = Subconscious

Green primary information developed "you." Your Green started pulsations in what passed for a body before you had a heart or circulatory system. It assigned the development of body parts to the proper locations, and it directed all of the other processes that culminated in that unique being, you.

I use the term "Green" for the *director* of all subconscious physiological processes and functions you can't control — digestion, internal communication, insulin production, acid control, and the like. Your "Green" is the "boss" of involuntary internal activity.

You have absolutely no DIRECT conscious control over subconscious function. Your subconscious Green responds perfectly! When you are stressed in your Red conscious mind, your subconscious Green responds. When you are happy in your Red, your Green responds. When your Red prompts you to behave foolishly, your Green responds. All Green responses are perfect.

> WELLNESS PRINCIPLE: Green primary information is
> smart enough to survive Red
> intellect

There are two reasons I use the terms "Red" and "Green" for conscious and subconscious functions. First, our focus is on health, not jargon. The simple words "Red" and "Green" remove much of the mystique of more complicated terms like "cerebrum," "cerebral cortex," and "somatosensory cortex." The second reason is that the illustration of the brain in the printed material I use for my HealthWeek seminars shows conscious and subconscious areas of the brain in those colors. The colors themselves have no intrinsic significance; they happened to be the colors of the markers close at hand the first time I colored a picture of the areas to illustrate their differences. And over the years, I have found that the terms "Red" and "Green" prompt immediate, vivid mental pictures. Patients can easily visualize particular parts of the brain and remember the specialized functions and purposes of conscious and subconscious activities.

Your Red and your Green perform their own specific functions. They work together to allow you to do those things you want to do.

> WELLNESS PRINCIPLE: Your Red handles your lifestyle;
> your Green handles your health-
> style

YOUR CONSCIOUS "RED"

When you look at an illustration of the human brain, the dominant feature is the cerebrum — the large, furrowed, cap-like structure. This is the physical area that handles your Red conscious thinking, decision-making, evaluating, and other awareness functions. The outer layer of the cerebrum is called the cerebral cortex. "Cortex" refers to the outer layer of an organ or structure. In the case of the cerebrum, this outer layer is about 1/8th of an inch thick. Thin, but powerful. The cerebrum, along with its outer layer, is divided into two hemispheres that are connected physically by complex networks of nerve fibers. The largest of these bundles of nerves is called the corpus callosum. Networks of nerves allow information to be communicated between the left and right hemispheres. For now, we'll consider any activity of the many parts of the cerebrum to be a Red activity.

The cerebrum houses your sensory and motor areas. The sensory area *receives* signals either directly or indirectly from your five senses — sight, hearing, touch, taste, and smell. The motor area *sends* signals to various parts of the body to direct voluntary movements, such as walking or chewing or brushing your teeth or waving your arms about.

While you are awake, your cerebrum works for you continuously. It's your center of awareness for information perceived by your five senses. It's also where much of your memory information is filed. Your cerebrum is your communication center for thinking, learning, reasoning, judging, conscious deliberations, and mental wanderings. Moving, talking, decision-making, finger-tapping, eating, relaxing, choosing, all originate in your cerebrum. And the marvelous part is that you can do more than one thing at a time. During periods of intense stimulation, such as when you must act quickly and decisively, your workaholic center of consciousness — your "Red" — can take off in all directions at once.

Your conscious Red is the first port of call for information received through your five senses. By gathering sensory information, you learn through Red perception how to perform conscious activities — walk, talk, read, paint a picture, decipher quantum theory, or fix a leaky faucet. You evaluate the world around you in your conscious mind. You forge your own world view and set of values from sensory experiences and mental impressions processed through your Red. Over time, you learn about "right" and "wrong," and you learn to judge. According to your personal view of the way things are or should be you assign degrees of "good" or "bad" to events, things, places, and people, including yourself.

Your Red is the only reasoning, (presumably) rational thinking part of your body. It is where you make decisions for your life. It's where you decide what you want, or whether or not you'll go to work today, or that you have been insulted, ridiculed, or praised. The first fleeting responses of your Red are always totally self-centered. Fortunately, you learn through social enculturation that displaying this ego-centered response willy-nilly isn't always to your advantage. Your Red can evaluate whether or not each individual stimulus received through your senses is a threat to you or to your survival. Unfortunately, as we shall see, your Red isn't nearly as discerning when it comes to evaluating stimuli from itself — thoughts.

WELLNESS PRINCIPLE: Your Red is ego-centric!

When you start out in life, your conscious mind is virtually empty — devoid of learned knowledge. As you progress through life, you learn by observing and copying actions, sounds, and attitudes of the people around you. As an infant, toddler and small child, your powers of critical analysis and evaluation are underdeveloped. Lacking these skills of discernment, you accept "second-hand information" from parents, siblings, other children, and teachers as "gospel" — Santa Claus and all that. We call that being naive, unsophisticated, or just plain gullible. However, it's all very real to most children.

Second-hand information as accepted by your Red may or may not be accurate. You may misunderstand information you receive; you may be intentionally deceived; you may interpret correct information incorrectly. You may receive incorrect information such as "The earth is flat," or "Germs cause disease," or "You can't get too much protein." Erroneous information constitutes the "flat spots" talked about earlier. Despite these hazards of learning, we have a tendency to be absolutely certain that we know what we know, and that what we know is absolutely correct. That's one of the stumbling blocks to accepting a different perspective on health or anything else. **You can't learn what you think you already know.** Actually, the only thing we can say with certainty about your Red intelligence is that you can't be certain that anything stored there is totally correct.

WELLNESS PRINCIPLE: Your Red is a storehouse of
worldly knowledge that is far
from perfect

Every thought you have is a product of your Red. Every evaluation and every judgment you make is made in your Red. Every rationalization or regret takes place in your Red. Conscious attitudes of hope, love, joy, morality, value, enjoyment, and other uplifting outlooks stem from your Red. Similarly, conscious attitudes of judgment, guilt, worry, remorse, fear, anger, jealousy, frustration, and other depressing, negative stressful attitudes breed and grow — and fester — in your Red.

> WELLNESS PRINCIPLE: Your Red can be your mental
> stress-production center

A big part of your Red is devoted to storing memories of sights, sounds, feelings, and how-to's you learn along the way. Most of your memories are stored in conscious areas of your brain. Your memory might be described as a random cross-reference system. Bits and pieces of memories of a given situation are stored in various parts of your cerebrum. Rattle the cage of one memory, and associated memories respond.

But your memory component isn't limited to storing facts and figures, names and impressions. It is also where the directions for physical activities are integrated and stored. Jump on a bicycle after umpteen years and your integrated memory system kicks in. You may weave and falter for a couple of seconds. However, as soon as your integrated memory grasps the picture of what it is supposed to be doing, all (or almost all) of the old balancing and steering and pedaling coordination comes back. This is a function of your conscious mind.

Through your conscious mind, you learn how to make effective specific muscle movements. Back to the kid scene. As an infant, you weren't very good at reaching out and grasping the colorful rattle that caught your attention. When you first tried this complicated maneuver, it was hit and miss. Sometimes you hit, and sometimes you missed. Then, as you practiced and your muscles began to get the hang of it, these movements were stored in your memory. As time went on, the memories were updated and refined to allow you to target and latch onto smaller items. Confidence soared. Before long, you were a pro at rattle-grabbing. You didn't need to re-learn each time you tried your new skill. You improved upon it. Smooth, fluid movement even.

The memories that allow you to repeat a muscular movement began by you thinking about what you were doing and doing it. Initially, this is a conscious thought process of your Red cortex. Yet, as we will see later, your conscious thinking Red cortex and the memory-storing areas have their own unique jobs to do.

Learning comes through your Red cortex. Memories are formed and stored below the cortex: your "Yellow." Your Yellow, as we shall go into later, integrates the conscious functions of your Red with the subconscious functions of your Green. It's an absolutely marvelous, efficient design.

YOUR SUBCONSCIOUS "GREEN"
Your "Red" thinks. Your "Yellow," which we'll describe later, is your

main memory storage area. Your "Green," is that portion of your brain other than the thinking Red and memory-storing Yellow. Your Green is the area that directs functions over which you have no control. Your Green was developed by and runs by infallible perfect primary information. It came fully-equipped and ready for a lifetime of continuous use. You can't improve it. You can't develop it. It's perfect as is. Your Green is your direct connection to Perfect Intelligence.

Green area structures are clusters of nerve tissue housed below the cerebral area of consciousness. Below cerebral and cortical areas of consciousness. Lower brain. Sub-conscious. Subconscious areas of the brain serve as communication and control centers for countless involuntary physiological activities — breathing, acid level maintenance, muscle tone, and other physiological functions that we take for granted as long as they work right. Although we have no conscious control over *how* these subconscious functions perform their tasks, our consciously controlled lifestyle habits affect environmental conditions that determine subconscious responses.

> WELLNESS PRINCIPLE: Conscious activity controls actions; subconscious activity controls inner workings

Among the smaller structures tucked below your Red are your thalamus and hypothalamus. The thalamus receives input from the basal ganglia, brain stem, cerebellum, and all of your sensory organs except the olfactory system — your sense of smell. (Your nose has its own unique pathway.) One source describes the thalamus as "the center for appreciation of primitive uncritical sensations of pain, crude touch, and temperature."[30] So if you are into to "appreciating" pain, you can thank your thalamus.

Below the thalamus is a principle player in directing your automatic involuntary internal systems — the small, appendix-like structure called the hypothalamus. ("Hypo-" is Greek for "under".) The hypothalamus weighs about four grams, roughly 1/8th of an ounce, or about the weight of a shiny new nickel. Although this tiny structure has been described as "anatomically insignificant," as I see it, it is the focal point of your Green. It controls many vital functions of the autonomic nervous system. It directs organs and systems to speed up or slow down their activities. Hypothalamic neurosecretions (chemicals secreted by neurons) are important in controlling certain metabolic activities, such as maintaining water balance, metabolizing sugar and fat, regulating body temperature, influencing wakefulness and sleep, and regulating fluid intake and feelings of thirst.

Hypothalamic activities are subconscious — Green. Although you can't consciously direct your Green, your conscious thoughts, emotions, and choices send stimuli to which your Green must respond. So although you have no conscious control over *what* your Green does, your conscious mind provides stimuli that require your Green to do something.

Your Green doesn't think. It is completely non-judgmental. Unlike your Red, it has no conception of "right" and "wrong." It has no sense of humor; it can't take a joke. You will see as we continue our trip through our many levels of consciousness that the thoughts and choices processed through your conscious-driven Red mandate responses from your subconscious Green. Thoughts and attitudes like guilt, fear, worry, and other negative feelings force your Green to respond in particular ways. In the long run, you may or may not be happy with the cumulative effect of those responses. Nonetheless, the responses are perfect. Over time, your perfect responses can lead to health, happiness, and success — or they can lead to disease, depression, and possibly death. If your Green must respond non-stop to Red-directed negative thoughts and feelings, eventually you'll experience unpleasant symptoms. But more about that later.

> WELLNESS PRINCIPLE: There is no state of mind —
> good or bad — that is not
> reflected in the physical body

THE BODY-MIND CONNECTION

About now, you might be thinking, "Is this another one of those 'Think lovely, wonderful thoughts and the world will be peachy-keen' sermons?" Set your mind at ease. We all know that just thinking sweetness and light doesn't make the world an easier habitat. "Stuff happens!" Personal and global crises. Injuries. Catastrophes. Floods. Tornadoes. You name it; it can happen.

The focus here is not so much on *what happens* in your life as on how you and your body respond to what happens. Your responses to everyday occurrences (that we often call stress) can set you up for physical problems. We've been told this for a long time, but we're never told why or how. Well, now you know: *your conscious thoughts and attitudes dictate subconscious physiological responses over which you have no control.* And subconscious physiological responses dictate health. Fill your Red conscious mind with gloom, doom, anger, guilt, and general negativity and your physiology will respond accordingly. Keep your conscious mind alert, positive, and focused on the bright side, and you give your body the opportunity to function without undue interference.

Sincere, positive-emotion, non-judgmental, forgiving thought-habits allow your body to respond in ways that keep you pain-free, comfortable, and healthy. Now, that's worth learning more about.

> WELLNESS PRINCIPLE: Sincere, positive thoughts and attitudes allow health-prone physiological responses

Although your thoughts and attitudes directly affect your well-being, you are not just a mind entity. Nor are you just a physical mass. Neither body nor mind can function alone. As long as you are alive, both mind and body need each other. The whole-person, or holistic, concept is coming more and more to public attention. During her research at the National Institute of Mental Health in Bethesda, Maryland, PhD Candace Pert stated, "I can no longer make a strong distinction between the brain and the body."[31]

You make choices in your Red. The results of conscious choices in every area of your life either allow your Green to function in ways that promote health, or they interfere with healthful function. There's no "volume control" on your Green. You can't have "a little bit of interference." It's either on or off.

If your choices don't interfere with healthful Green function, you can expect to move through life being energetic, comfortable, healthy, happy, and successful. If the results of your choices *do* interfere with healthful function, you can be assured that you are destined for a future less pleasant than you would like.

> WELLNESS PRINCIPLE: Conscious choices either interfere with Green function or they don't

The road to health isn't paved with Red conscious learning about how to adjust different functions of your body or how to overcome stress. One of the biggest "flat spots" in today's thinking is that we can get smart enough, educated enough, and learned enough to teach the body what to do. You can't teach your body anything — it already knows more than you will ever know about keeping you alive. You can be healthy — without thought — when the choices you make in your Red allow your Green to function in ways that lead to health. Remember that your Green doesn't think, judge, or reason. That's the job of your Red. The Green is decisive — stimulus received → response performed. The only way you can assure health is to make Red choices that provide appropriate stimuli for your Green to respond to. When your Green has the appropriate raw material with which to work — stimuli from your Red — not only will you survive the moment, but the automatic physiological responses will be such that you will survive more comfortably.

Your Green responds according to plan. It doesn't learn from the past or project into the future. It responds to stimuli. Your Red provides many of the stimuli to which your Green MUST respond. All manner of stored memories of experiences, emotions, thoughts, biases and judgments are the fodder for Red-produced stimuli. Consequently, the Red is rarely decisive. Everything must be weighed and deliberated, even if the process takes only a millisecond. So your best bet for providing your Green with appropriate stimuli that will give you the most favorable responses is to get in the habit of making Red choices that are most favorable to you in the long run.

> WELLNESS PRINCIPLE: Your Green is always black or
> white; your Red is mostly gray

POINTS OF INTEREST

1.   Your body is designed to survive, not to be healthy or sick.

2.   Every physiological response is perfect.

3.   Your conscious Red runs your life.

4.   Your subconscious Green runs your body.

5.   Red information is learned.

6.   You come equipped with perfect Green information.

7.   Your thoughts and attitudes directly affect your health.

*The electric age . . . establishes a global network
that has much the character of our central nervous system.*
              - Marshall McLuhan

CHAPTER 4
All Together, Now . . .

IT'S ALL AUTOMATIC

By now you have the picture that your conscious Red runs your life while your subconscious Green runs your body. This concept is so important that it's a recurring theme throughout this book.

You become aware of something, do something, or eat something as a result of Red activity. Your body immediately adapts through Green activity to handle the new situation. You don't give any conscious thought to your internal workings. You don't consciously turn on, speed up, or slow down life sustaining internal functions. It's all automatic. For this, you should be eternally thankful. How much sleep would you get if you had to consciously orchestrate your 70 trillion cells' nutrient intake, energy production, and waste disposal? All of these crucial functions and more go on without your DIRECT conscious involvement. Your Green subconscious monitors and choreographs all internal operations while your Red conscious mind busily receives information from the world around you and decides how to handle your life.

> WELLNESS PRINCIPLE: Your Red runs your life — your
>   Green runs your body

Recall the "anatomically insignificant" hypothalamus we referred to in the last chapter. Despite its so-called "insignificance," your hypothalamus is a key player in your subconscious. This small organ exerts a major influence on processes that determine how your body responds to stimuli.

It is the center for determining whether your internal functions are on "fast-forward" or "cruise." The hypothalamus serves as "mission control" for initiating or suppressing physiological responses of the autonomic nervous system. As Guyton explains, "the hypothalamus plays a key role in setting the basic tenor of bodily function, the basic degree of excitement, and the basic level of metabolism."[32] And you have absolutely no DIRECT conscious control over autonomic (automatic) nervous system *responses*. Internal responses come from signals transmitted from lower-brain subconscious areas. Guyton again, ". . . sensory signals enter the centers of the autonomic ganglia, cord, brain stem, or hypothalamus, and these in turn transmit appropriate reflex responses back to the visceral organs to control their activities."[33] In other words, stimuli received by lower areas of the brain cause organs to respond. When you are happy, calm, content and not threatened by thoughts from the inside or stimuli from the outside, your autonomic system sets your internal homeostat on "cruise." Your whole body gets on with taking care of the business of the moment — digesting food, replenishing and regenerating cells, building health. When you are alarmed, angry or upset, your physiology responds with "Red alert" — prepare to defend against an attack. Automatically digestion slows down and blood pressure changes. You may feel tense or jittery, but you're not aware of the cascading physiological adjustments and adaptations that flood your body with activity.

Since you can't control the uncontrollable, your best bet for a happy, pain-free life is to get your Red conscious mind out of the way. How in the world would you do that?

By making sure the only threats your body must defend against are "real" threats.

Be assured that you won't have to go out of your way to drum up "real" threats to keep your defense mechanisms in practice. You encounter situations that could be "real" threats just by living in a well-populated world: sudden startling noises, the smell of smoke where no smoke should be, unexpected flashes of bright light, near-miss accidents when you're driving. Your body should and does respond to threats such as these until your conscious mind figures out that all is well. However, worry, anxiety, anger, and the like, are "false threats." They go on and on. Your Red doesn't send an "all clear" message after just a couple of minutes of worry. When your body is free of "false threats," your hypothalamus and autonomic nervous system can coordinate physiological functions in ways that let you feel good and be healthy. Later, we'll talk more about the "how's" of getting your Red out of the way. For now, we'll focus on the "why."

WELLNESS PRINCIPLE: Your defense systems don't analyze threats; they respond

Your autonomic nervous system is a highly complex subconscious system that controls a variety of vital involuntary physiological functions: arterial pressure, body temperature, sweating, to name a few. Guyton sums up the abilities of this crucial system when he writes, ". . . the nervous system, acting through the autonomic nerve fibers, can exert rapid and effective control of many if not most of the internal functions of the body. It is these extremely rapid changes that are measured by the lie detector polygraph, reflecting the innermost feelings of a person."[34] "Rapid and effective," "extremely rapid changes" the man said. Keep that in mind. Your autonomic nervous system is not only beyond your control, it is "rapid and effective."

The autonomic nervous system consists of the sympathetic nervous system, and the parasympathetic nervous system. These systems regulate the intensity of function of glands such as the salivary, gastric, and sweat, the medulla (inside) of the adrenal gland, and activities of the smooth muscle tissue of organs, and the heart.

Here might be a fine place to insert an involved scientific discourse on the magnificent, intricate, fine-tuned workings of the autonomic nervous system — paired ganglionated sympathetic trunk, motor fibers of the vagus nerve, mesenteric ganglia, and all that. But such an inspection of these physiological bits and pieces wouldn't add anything to the whole-body concepts we are dealing with in this book. Instead, we'll use general, simplified, minimally-technical, terms to describe some important health-influencing functions. If you crave additional insight into this biological system, you can find more in physiology or neuroanatomy books. However, my purpose is not to dazzle you with scientific jargon. My purpose is to help you understand the connection between fundamental lifestyle choices and health. To accomplish this purpose, we'll stick with the "simpler is better" approach to summarize the features and characteristics of the sympathetic and parasympathetic systems.

THE SYMPATHETIC NERVOUS SYSTEM

An identifying phrase for the sympathetic nervous system might be, "Rev 'Er Up, Charlie." Physical danger usually activates the sympathetic system. The sympathetic system is your first line of defense against real or *perceived* threats from the outside. The sympathetic system responds to messages and warnings of impending danger received through your five senses and *interpreted by your conscious mind.* Your sympathetic system doesn't respond to an external situation until you become aware in your conscious mind that it's a threat. View a snarling tiger securely confined in a zoo pen and neither your conscious mind nor your sympathetic system is concerned. View that same tiger loose and unfettered in your back yard and both your conscious mind and sympathetic nervous system will leap into high gear.

> WELLNESS PRINCIPLE: Messages from the five senses interpreted as "danger" ignite sympathetic responses

A consciously perceived threat jump-starts the sympathetic nervous system to engage or intensify particular involuntary physiological activities — raise blood pressure, dilate pupils, raise "gooseflesh," speed up heart rate, and more.[35] Yet the sympathetics also send some slowing down signals, particularly for digestive processes. You certainly don't need to be using precious energy to digest food when you are running for your life or trying to lift an anvil off your foot. Crisis situations that are threats to your body call for higher blood pressure, faster heart rate, and the strongest muscles you can muster.

Although the sympathetic responses increase or decrease specific physiological activities, the sympathetic system *in general . . .*
1. *affects the whole body* through responses to physical stimuli received by the five senses, and
2. *speeds up or intensifies functions.*

Sympathetic responses are the first line of defense against "threats" from the outside. The sympathetic system also responds to internally generated emotions — especially "threat" emotions. As far as your Green is concerned, danger is danger no matter where the signals come from. Your autonomic system responds. It's called the sympathetic alarm reaction, or the fight or flight reaction. "Many emotions," says Guyton, "such as excitement, anxiety, or rage often discharge the sympathetics *en mass.*"[36] Physiologist Guyton elaborates: "This frequently occurs when the hypothalamus becomes activated by fright or fear or severe pain. . . . In the state of *rage*, which is elicited mainly by stimulating the hypothalamus, signals are transmitted downward through the reticular formation and spinal cord to cause massive sympathetic discharge, and all of the sympathetic events . . . ensue immediately."[37] Getting angry excites more than your social relationships — it excites your whole body.

Even without an actual physical threat, strong negative emotions brought on by perceived or imagined danger can spark threat responses. You don't have to be standing in the path of an on-coming high-speed train to feel threatened. All it takes is a convincing hint that you are in danger — like mistaking the sound of a tree limb scratching across a window for a burglar trying to break in, or a nightmare, or a realization that the IRS is going to slap a lien on your assets for back taxes (that *is* a nightmare). And since strong negative emotions are all too often constant companions, you can keep your body in the fight-or-run mode a lot longer than you could actually sustain either activity.

> WELLNESS PRINCIPLE: How you *feel* stimulates sympa-
> thetic responses!

Most sympathetic responses prepare you for strenuous activity of defensive action. When you are frightened or in fear, your whole body is involved. Your sympathetic nervous system signals physiological changes that allow muscles throughout your body to act quickly. Your body responds without either hesitation or question. It's all automatic. And that's great. Just as it should be.

Also, when you are stressed by thought, word, or deed, your sympathetic system responds. And that's good if you need to be ready to defend yourself physically. It's not good if you are still primed for a fight when you are meditating or sunning yourself on a warm, peaceful beach. You were designed to gear up quickly for defense in an emergency. And the design includes the capacity to switch back to physiological business-as-usual after the emergency is over. Yet if you stay "geared up" for days, weeks, or years, some internal parts of will become really tired — exhausted. After exhaustion comes pain and/or disease.

However, pain or no pain, disease or no disease, you will notice that your body hasn't done anything wrong. Everything it has done is perfect. The sympathetic response is perfect. The internal hyperactivity is perfect. Your body has responded just the way it is supposed to: just the way it was designed. The only problem is that threatening "thought stimuli" prompt responses that are inappropriate for actual external physical conditions. There is no external threat to your physical safety. The threat is abstract. And abstract threats last a whole lot longer than actual threats. You were designed to handle short-term threats from rampaging tigers and the like. Long-term threats from rampaging thoughts that keep fear simmering constitute "survival abuse." Your sympathetic nervous system will respond perfectly to the stimuli, but the stimuli are ill-timed. You have a "timing problem" — Sensory Dominant Stress.

Sympathetic responses are designed to handle practical, short-term emergencies. No problem. Abstract, long-term "thought-emergencies" mimic physical threats that never end. In the "trade," this is called "sympathetic dominance." And sympathetic dominance isn't the body doing something wrong; it's the body doing right things in response to stimuli that continue inappropriately. Remember, the body never does anything wrong, and it never thinks about what it is doing.

WELLNESS PRINCIPLE: Short-term sympathetic responses to physical threats don't
cause long-term consequences

THE PARASYMPATHETIC NERVOUS SYSTEM

A summary of the function of the parasympathetic nervous system might be,"Cool it, Clyde." Your body is a magnificent system of checks and balances. For every action, there is a reaction. The slowing-down tendencies of the parasympathetic nervous system balance the speeding-up or intensifying responses of the sympathetic system.

Whereas the sympathetic system *in general* affects the whole body and *in general* speeds up functions, the parasympathetic nervous system:

1.   is *organ-specific*; it prompts increased or decreased function of particular organs to fit current need, and
2.   *in general,* has an inhibiting or slowing-down effect.

The parasympathetic system activates or suppresses the function of specific organs. It increases activity of the digestive system, slows heart beat, lowers blood pressure slightly, and, under non-threatening conditions, keeps your body from running wild under sympathetic influence. Blood pressure goes down, pupils constrict, digestion increases, your body tends to its survival functions without defensive stress.

The parasympathetic system isn't immune to being influenced by emotions any more than is the sympathetic. However, the emotions that bring on parasympathetic responses are different from those that fire-up sympathetic responses. Worry and other depressing emotions (depression, for example) activate suppressive parasympathetic responses. And how long do you worry? Usually it's more than the few minutes it takes to get over a sudden physical alarm.

"Worry" isn't the same as "fear." The body doesn't respond to worry the same way it responds to fear. Fear, as we have just seen, is supposed to be a "quick-and-dirty" response — perceive-respond, and when the crisis is over, relax. Worry is a long-term sport.

WELLNESS PRINCIPLE: Worry is a "state of body" as
well as a state of mind

Worry and other depressing emotions — emotions that slow you down, drain energy, focus inward — keep your body under unrelenting parasympathetic control. Physiologist Guyton writes, "The emotions of worry, depression, and lethargy, all of which have effects opposite to those that excite the sympathetic system, often stimulate the parasympathetics."[38] You were designed to respond to threats from the outside, survive, and get on with your life. But worry, guilt, and other "mental threat" emotions don't come from the outside — they are internal. Internally initiated physiological responses that go on and on can have a devastating effect on your overall health. Guyton tops off his list of mental contributors to physical responses by pointing out that fear can stimulate extreme reactions of both the sympathetic and parasympathetic systems. Fear can bring on the sympathetic response of elevated arterial pressure *and* the parasympathetic response of heavy-duty gastrointestinal activity that may result in uncontrolled diarrhea. That should make you think twice about living with mental turmoil. We will talk about this in more detail in a later chapter.

> WELLNESS PRINCIPLE: You can't worry yourself out of
> fear

Keep in mind that the descriptions of the sympathetic and parasympathetic systems I have given are broad generalizations. They aren't textbook answers to questions on a neuroanatomy exam. These broad descriptions are to give you a feeling for how your body automatically responds to signals it receives. Most of the signals stem from choices you make every day in six essential areas of your life.

We're moving closer to a detailed explanation of the six essentials, but we need to lay the groundwork first. In the meantime, to help you keep the terms sympathetic and parasympathetic straight, just remember: Sympathetic = Speed up; Parasympathetic = Power down.

REST, REFUEL, OR RUN

Your physiology changes constantly, moment by moment. While you may appear to be pretty much the same from day to day, stimuli from your five senses and from conscious thoughts prompt your body to respond for the purpose of survival. Everything your body does is directed toward survival of the moment — toward finding just the right balance to keep all of your many body parts chugging along for one more instant. We call this balance "homeostasis."

The term "homeostasis" refers to a process of maintaining internal dynamic equilibrium — functional balance for survival. A vast internal communications network regulates systems and organs to keep your body functioning within survival limits. Homeostasis indicates a balance of tone and functions within your body.

Throughout each 24-hour day, depending on the stimuli and stresses you encounter, your body flips through three main homeostatic patterns:

resting, digestion, and risk homeostasis. Each of these three brings about particular biological responses to serve particular purposes — to accommodate to conditions of the moment. And the ability to respond in these diverse ways is essential not only to survival but to effective internal maintenance. Problems crop up when you are locked into one homeostatic pattern. This lock-in effect is ordinarily a result of thoughts, memories and emotions.

Fortunately, the Grand Designer of these magnificent creations we call our bodies has built in checks and balances to keep our systems working harmoniously for survival. In all three phases of survival homeostasis — resting, digestion, and risk — sympathetic and parasympathetic systems work together. At any given time, one or the other may exert greater influence depending on conditions and the job to be done. Eating, for example, requires the parasympathetic to "take charge" and adjust the function of specific organs to process the food. On the other hand, responding to exercise requires the specialties of the sympathetic system. The two systems are designed to work cooperatively.

> WELLNESS PRINCIPLE: Your body keeps its balance as
> it works to survive

To illustrate the systems' balancing act, let's assign some percentages to indicate "autonomic tone." The ballpark percentages are for illustration purposes only to show how the levels of intensity of the sympathetic and parasympathetic systems adjust for each of the three phases of survival. The percentage numbers are illustrations only; they merely indicate patterns of how physiological activities adjust to handle moment-by-moment conditions. More important, these illustrations lay the groundwork for you to see how becoming "stuck" in a particular homeostatic mode can lead to dis-stress and disease.

Resting Homeostasis — *50% sympathetic and 50% parasympathetic*
— Balanced

We might term resting homeostasis as your body's "default" mode. When it's not being attacked by food or threatened physically or emotionally, it's "resting." Resting isn't exclusively a sleeping state. You might be peacefully watching a sunset, or reading an enjoyable book, or just relaxing. Resting homeostasis refers to the internal balance your body enjoys when it doesn't have to contend with intrusive substances like food, drink, polluted air, alarming situations, or excitatory thoughts. There's no long-term stress with resting homeostasis. Your sympathetic and parasympathetic systems are balanced. For the sake of example only, we can say that resting homeostasis is 50% sympathetic and 50% parasympathetic. Neither dominates physiology.

However, neither you nor your body rest all the time. So if your body isn't in resting homeostasis, it's in either digestion- or risk-homeostasis.

Digestion Homeostasis —   *25% sympathetic and 75 % parasympa-*
                             thetic — Parasympathetic Dominant

Digestion homeostasis can be thought of as being 75% parasympathetic (slow-down) and 25% sympathetic (speed-up). Remember, these are strictly pulled-out-of-the-hat percentages to illustrate the dominance of one system over the other.

Anything and everything you put into your body is a stress to your body. And, as I've said before and will say again, "Stress is anything that changes the way your body is working right now." Food, drink, drugs (including prescription and recreational, legal and illegal) stress your body. It makes no difference if you eat a banana or a hot dog, or if you drink a glass of pure water or a shot of straight whisky — your body must change the way it is functioning to accommodate the new arrival. Your body shifts into digestion homeostasis. That's good. If you didn't switch into "let's digest" when that banana came down the pike, the banana would lounge idly in your stomach and ferment. In the process it could produce enough gas in your stomach to put lethal pressure on your nearby heart.

When you eat something, your body goes immediately into digestion homeostasis. Your parasympathetic system dominates: digestive juices (including saliva) flow, blood is shunted from large muscles, heart rate slows, your pupils may even constrict. (Now that you're back in your cave with your "kill" ready to eat, you don't need to be as keen-eyed as you were during the dangerous hunt.) When you eat, your body turns its attention to handling the current stress of new arrivals in the digestive system — digestion homeostasis. And as far as your body is concerned, it doesn't make any difference if the food being handled is "good" food or "bad" food. Food in the body is a stress.

But, wouldn't you know, food isn't the only thing that triggers digestion homeostasis.

As we saw earlier, worry and depression can do the same thing. But worry and depression last longer than food in the stomach. They aren't processed or neutralized in a few short hours. Worry can masquerade as a signal to your body that "food's arrived." Digestive functions *must* handle the situation — that's their job. So you can see why worry does indeed offer an open invitation to ulcers. If digestive fluids are habitually pumped out when there's no food in the stomach for it to work on . . . holey stomach! Digestion homeostasis perpetuated by worry is a correct response happening at an inappropriate time. If this pattern keeps up, you can have a timing problem — your body doing a right thing at an inappropriate time. Timing problems that involve digestion homeostasis can lead to very unpleasant symptoms — stomach and colon problems, among others.

> WELLNESS PRINCIPLE: Stress of eating or worrying triggers digestion homeostasis

<u>Risk Homeostasis</u> — *75% sympathetic and 25% parasympathetic* — Sympathetic Dominant

Risk homeostasis is the third homeostatic mode. Like the other two, risk homeostasis can be life-saving or, if abused, health-threatening. Risk homeostasis can be illustrated as being defensively action-oriented — 75% sympathetic and 25% parasympathetic. Risk homeostasis is the virtually instantaneous sympathetically dominant physiological adaptation your body makes when you are startled or frightened, or when you become aware you are being threatened. The instant you see, hear, or smell that hungry tiger prowling and growling on the loose, your body is on guard and ready to do something dramatic. Although in our society we can probably go a lifetime without encountering a live, loose tiger, plenty of other dangers — family feuds, past-due notices, natural disasters — that prompt the same risk homeostasis dot our lives.

In addition to being a threat response, risk homeostasis is also a normal part of exercise. It's perfectly normal for your body to respond to exercise in the same way it does to a potential physical threat. That's logical. When you are threatened or alarmed, the first impulse is to move fast — create as much space between you and that tiger as possible. However, you don't have one physiology for a "tiger threat" and another physiology for a "jogging threat." Neither do you have separate "bear wrestling" and "weight-wrestling" physiologies. The same muscle and muscle-replenishment responses are required to run from a thug threatening you with a gun as to run for exercise and fun. Blood pressure goes up, circulation to the appropriate muscles increases, digestion stops. That's good.

But your body is even more attuned to physiological needs than that. Just thinking about exercise brings about an internal response. Guyton points out that merely anticipating exercise can stimulate both cardiac output and the sympathetic and parasympathetic systems.[39] How's that for turning thoughts to physical responses? But don't count on "thinking" about exercise to have the same beneficial effects as "doing" exercise. The anticipation effect is good for only a short period.

WELLNESS PRINCIPLE: "Loose tigers" and strenuous
exercise turn on risk homeostasis

Risk homeostasis should ALWAYS be a short-term response. Recognize the situation, take care of it, and that's the end of it. However, like digestion homeostasis, risk homeostasis can also be brought about by emotions — and then it isn't short-term. Unlike the depressive emotions, such as worry and lethargy, that elicit digestion homeostasis, crisis-combating risk homeostasis is prompted by expressive emotions, such as fear, anger, excitement, rage, and anxiety. The big difference between the crisis physiology of a physical threat and the crisis physiology of expansive emotions is that the emotions can linger and keep the threat-combating responses alive. Lingering risk homeostasis after an actual crisis is over can set you up for timing problems.

WELLNESS PRINCIPLE: Anger and anxiety can keep you
in risk homeostasis

Your body responds automatically to signals received through your five senses and perceived in your conscious mind. Many of the signals you receive through your five senses are strengthened by emotional reactions to those signals. If you lose your job or your house burns down, there's more to the situation than inconvenience. Strong emotions are involved. And strong emotions can "lock-in" physiological response patterns.

"Locked-in" responses are inappropriate. They keep the affected organs and systems going and going and going. This "locked-in" set of responses is the Sensory Dominant Stress, or SDS, we talked about earlier. Messages from your sensory system dominate responses of your physiology.

Messages that bring on or perpetuate an SDS are: stress-response messages; messages that originate in your conscious mind; messages that are emotionally charged and stored in memory; and messages to which your body MUST and WILL respond.

WELLNESS PRINCIPLE: SDS is stress induced, memory
retained, and body expressed

HOMEOSTASIS AND YOUR "SIXTH SENSE"
Let's look at a vignette of how you can get stuck in risk physiology.

The parking lot is dark as you leave work and walk to your car. Suddenly, you hear quick, heavy footsteps close by. A burly, menacing, weapon-wielding figure leaps out at you from between two parked cars. You freeze. Your heart is pounding, mouth dry, eyes wide. You are physically threatened. Your body immediately leaps into risk physiology.

Your initial response (unless you take the easy way out and faint) is to run, fight, or do whatever it takes to protect yourself. However, your attacker, weapon poised to do you bodily harm, presents an immediately convincing case for you to relinquish your possessions. You comply, and the attacker leaves. You survive — minus cash, credit cards, and valuables — shaken but physically unharmed. As far as your physiology is concerned, you followed the design pattern: alarm, risk homeostasis response, conclusion, cool-down, resume whatever passes for normal. No problem.

In the weeks following the attack, you re-play your mental memory tapes of the incident again and again. The initial fear turns to anger. Now you have a problem!

Day after day in your Red, you seethe with anger and rage at this person who violated your person and your life. Your emotions keep your subconscious Green responding just as it did during the actual attack. Your Green reads the anger and rage as a danger as great as the attack itself and maintains risk physiology. Muscles tense. Digestion hampered. Blood pressure up. After a while, you become exhausted and don't know why. In time, you begin to develop unpleasant symptoms.

How long will it take before you find yourself in a doctor's office looking for help for symptoms of high blood pressure, muscle pain, or digestive problems? It may take only a few weeks. Or it could be months or years. Chances are, enough time will have passed between the attack and the symptoms that neither you nor your doctor will see any connection between the two. After all, it was long ago, and you rarely mention it any more. Only your ego, pride, and wallet were hurt; you weren't physically injured. Obviously, your current problem is physical and the assault was physically non-violent. No connection. So medication is prescribed to suppress the symptoms. But the cause of the problem remains firmly intact.

You can be assured that even if the initial symptoms are cleared up by medication or any other treatment, before long the symptoms will recur or other symptoms will crop up. And it's all because your Green interprets your Red's ongoing thoughts and unreleased feelings of anger and rage as perpetual threats. Even if you rarely think about the incident, the memory of the incident and the emotions tied to the incident are parked in your Yellow storehouse of past events. Whether the stimuli come from thinking Red or memory Yellow, your Green gets the message. And it must respond. Your Green must instruct your body to defend. That's its job. Survival. The defense response is perfectly correct but the timing is inappropriate.

> WELLNESS PRINCIPLE: Inappropriately   timed   risk
> homeostasis is an invitation to
> distress

What is behind inappropriately timed homeostasis?
Stimuli.
Where did the stimuli that causes ill-timed homeostasis come from?
The attack.
No.
Your risk homeostasis at the time of the attack was good. It was better than "good"; it was great. You did what you needed to do to survive.

The stimuli that are ill-timed are those that come from your "feeling" response AFTER the attack was over. You became angry. And you stayed angry. "Angry" became "stuck" in your memory. And it is the signals from that "angry" memory that keep your body doing a right thing at a wrong time. It's a "timing problem."

We know that you and your body respond to messages received through your five senses. We also know that your body responds to thoughts in your conscious Red. You may keep your external cool when a co-worker makes a casual remark you interpret as ridicule — "Are you still working on that report, George?" — but your internal physiology jumps into "defend" or "attack" mode. Your "defend" response is not prompted as much by what was said as by how you interpreted how it was said. You remember that tone of voice from years ago. Your father used it when you were a kid, and it really made you angry. Your memory of the tone and the implied "You're a loser" is firmly fixed in your memory.

> WELLNESS PRINCIPLE: We hear with our ears; we
> interpret through our memory

Everything you perceive through your five senses makes a quick trip through your Red to your vast storehouse of memories in search of similar data that were stored in the past. You compare current input from your five senses with memories of previously experienced similar events to find the closest match. It is this match on which you base your interpretation of the present experience. Interpretation of present conditions is a function of memory. Interpreting spoken or written words is a function of memory. Recognizing faces is a function of memory. Identifying objects, sights, sounds, tastes, smells, and textures is a function of memory. And your body responds to internally generated memory messages just as it responds to sensory messages picked up from outside your body.

WELLNESS PRINCIPLE: Your memory acts as a "sixth
sense," and your physiology re-
sponds

Memories of everything you have ever done and everything that has
happened to you are processed and stored in the thinking areas of your
brain. Even if you don't bring the memories to the surface, they are there.
Assuming that your physical brain is still intact, memories of past
experiences that were stored with intense feeling can affect the way your
body is functioning right now. Experiences in themselves aren't always
positive or negative. The positive or negative quality of an experience
depends upon your perception and interpretation of the circumstances and
your feelings about the interpretation. Take the example of being dunked
in a vat of ice cold water. For most of us, this would be interpreted as a
negative experience. However, members of the Polar Bear Club seem to
find mid-winter dips in the icy waters of the North Atlantic positively
exhilarating. Their memories and interpretations are of a positive — if not
challenging — experience.

Memories are housed throughout the body but especially in the brain.
Guyton describes the cerebral cortex as "an extremely large memory
storehouse." He explains, "The cortex never functions alone but always
in association with the lower centers of the nervous system."[40] The cortex
always functions in association with lower areas of the nervous system.
Store that concept in your memory unit.

Guyton expresses current opinion that the cerebral cortex acts as the
primary storehouse of information. However, I believe from the whole-
health standpoint, that the cerebral cortex is principally a "gateway" or
"distribution center" to more versatile storage areas below the cortex. We
might say that the cerebral cortex retains the memory of events while
associated memories of feelings and physiology are housed below the
cortex. In fact, I would go so far as to say that the cerebral cortex is strictly
a "search and deploy" device for sending messages to appropriate areas of
the rest of the central nervous system. We can infer the validity of this
premise from another of Guyton's statements: "The thought processes of
the brain compare new sensory experiences with the stored memories; the
memories help to select the important new sensory information and to
channel this into appropriate storage areas for future use or into motor
areas to cause bodily responses."[41] More simply stated, the cortex receives
a sensory stimulus, memory is searched to find the closest match, and the
new information is stored along with similar information. Sort of
"neighborhood housing." Or, as we shall see later, in the energy brain,
likes attract likes. (Remember that; it may be on the test.)

On the practical side, your search-and-deploy ability gets you through the day more easily. Your cortex triggers automatic responses. When you decide to get up out of your chair to go to the refrigerator for a little something, you don't have to think about the sequence of adjustments muscles and tendons must make to get you there. Your thinking cortex organizes all of the requisite information to relieve you of the drudgery. The decision to get up is made in your Red. As soon as the thought is generated, your Red finds the information stored in lower areas that take care of "stand up" and "walk." It's all automatic. Your Red knows which retrieval system to use. Once the Red is stimulated, it stimulates appropriate, stored response information which sends signals to your Green, and away you go. It takes more than one part of your brain for you to do anything.

> WELLNESS PRINCIPLE: No part of your nervous system
> works alone

Your brain is no dummy. It practices "energy conservation." It learns as you learn. When you use the same memory over and over, each time you call it up, it greases the skids for it to come up the next time. Use facilitates future use. Or, to phrase that in proper prose, we'll let Guyton say it: " . . . each time certain types of sensory signals pass through sequences of synapses [nerve connections], these synapses become more capable of transmitting the same signals the next time, . . ."[42] Guyton calls this "facilitation." This concept will come as no surprise to anyone who has had to memorize poems, or math facts, or formulas, or the attributes of company products.

The frequency and ease with which you resurrect memories is important to why memories can have such a dramatic impact on your health.

Experiences gathered throughout your life are stored in memories. Each minute of each day, you compare current experiences with those of past seconds, yesterdays, and yesteryears, and your physiology responds accordingly. A loud bang is compared with memories of other bangs to determine if you are hearing an explosion or a plate breaking. A harsh voice is compared with memories of an abusive parent, or with memories of personally non-threatening dialogue of movie scenes. No matter how you respond outwardly to your experiences, the memories that prompt your responses are uniquely personal.

> WELLNESS PRINCIPLE: Memories are neither good nor
> bad — they are your personal
> resource encyclopedia

Memories of your life-experiences *and of your responses to these experiences* are all carefully filed away in various areas of your brain for reference. The memories act as a template to compare stimuli from current events with events that were similar in the past. Stored along with the situation identifiers are memories of responses to those stimuli — your programmed overt social response and your covert physiological response. "Please," "Thank you," "How are you?," and "Go take a flying leap" are programmed overt responses to particular situations. High blood pressure, spastic colon, and heavy breathing are covert functional physiological responses. The cumulative effect of these millions of social and functional responses describe the individual "you."

WELLNESS PRINCIPLE: "You" are the sum total of your
experiences

Each of us has compiled his or her own mental collage of life-experiences, memories, and outward responses to situations and the instructions for internal physiological responses. The more *intense* or impressive the situation that formed the memory, the more strongly imbedded are the instructions for physiological responses to that memory. These physiological responses are part of the standard survival system. Although, as pointed out, memories themselves are neither good nor bad, the physiological response instructions that accompany the memories are always perfect *for the situation at the time the memory was originally stored.* The glitch comes when the memory keeps prompting the same physiological response long after the incident is over. And the glue that sticks physiological responses to memories is *intense* feelings and emotions.

WELLNESS PRINCIPLE: Feelings "glue" physiological
responses into memory

Your physiology responds to feelings and emotions. It responds to other input also: internal signals giving "state of the organs and muscles" reports. But feelings and emotions are the most intense signals that flip through your body. "Status reports" are essential, but pretty dull, stuff. Feelings do the "exciting" stuff.

Memories and feelings are close buddies. The feelings attached to memories can upset us in the same way as the original event. When someone says, "I've put that out of my mind," they are trying not to recall the "feeling memories." Memories of events don't hurt — the feelings attached to those memories hurt. And along with the hurt of feeling memories comes physiological memories. Unpleasant experience memories can leave a lasting impression on your state of mind. Feeling memories can leave a lasting impression on your health.

Since you have no direct control over the physiological responses your body will make to any message, your best bet for health is to make sure the messages your physiology receives concern short-term current circumstances — not lingering out-dated feelings and emotions stored along with memories of past events. Feelings and memories are stored in and processed through conscious areas of your brain. Everything in your life and health begins in areas of consciousness.

And what are those areas of consciousness?

Glad you asked.

POINTS OF INTEREST

1.   The autonomic nervous system responds without thought to emotions.

2.   Emotions can perpetuate sympathetic or parasympathetic responses.

3.   Your body will find homeostatic balance.

4.   Physiological patterns of resting, digestion, and risk homeostasis address current needs.

5.   Memories can dictate risk homeostasis.

6.   Your memory is your "sixth sense."

7.   Memories come from experiences and feelings.

There is nothing in the world
to which every man has a more unassailable title
than to his own life and person.
                                    - Schopenhauer

CHAPTER 5
Of Many Minds

THE CONSCIOUSNESS CLAN

One of the pivotal concepts of this book is that your Red conscious mind runs your life while your Green subconscious mind runs your body. In the process of living and learning, you gather information in your conscious Red. This is second-hand information acquired through your sensory facilities. The information in your subconscious Green, however, is not learned. You can't add to it. It came with the package — built-in before you were born. It is primary information. Green comes from Primary Intelligence — Ultimate Power Source, Universal Intelligence, God. Whichever name you care to use is fine; they all connote perfection. Green information is always perfect.

As long as you are alive and aware, your conscious and subconscious work together for the sole purpose of survival. If you are alive but completely unaware of your surroundings, you are unconscious. Your conscious intellect is on "hold" but your subconscious intelligence continues to run your body.

The terms "conscious," "subconscious," and "unconscious" are relatively standard in the adult lexicon. Yet there are other members of the "consciousness clan" that are equally as important as the familiar big three. I term these less well-known siblings of the consciousness clan "non-conscious" and "Superconscious."

Keep in mind that we are still in the land of whole-body, whole-health. Some of the explanations and illustrations used may not fit precisely into the neat, rigid, structured pigeon-holes of mechanistic "science." Science investigates effects, not causes. My purpose is to put into perspective the correlation between how you think and how you feel both physically and emotionally. You don't need to be a certified genius to relate being constantly up-tight in your conscious mind with also being up-tight in your body. We are illustrating that everything the body does is perfectly correct. We are talking about what happens functionally. And I have found that everything I am telling you is 100% correct clinically.

We have already met "conscious" and "subconscious," but a short review might be helpful. "Unconscious" is a state rather than a process, we can quickly put that in perspective. However, the newcomers, "non-conscious" and "Superconscious" will require a more thorough introduction. So, on with our trip and a visit with the consciousness clan.

Consciousness

Your conscious mind is your Red. The conscious mind, including the learning and memory components, is a function of the cerebral cortex — that 1/8th inch nerve-rich brain covering discussed earlier. Your conscious mind is your cortical thinking machine. It's where you do your learning, evaluating, judging, calculating, and decision-making. However, keep in your learnable, conscience mind that nothing in the body happens in isolation — even thinking.

Your Red is essentially blank at birth — hardly even "pink." As time goes on, you learn. You gather and store Red information quickly. Learning takes place in the conscious mind through perceptions, interpretation, and assimilation of information received through the five senses. Information in the conscious mind is second-hand information. It is acquired. Red information doesn't come pre-packaged at birth. Learned Red information stored in the conscious mind can be accessed and retrieved — remembered and revised.

WELLNESS PRINCIPLE: You can access learned information

Much second-hand information passes for "facts" — name, address, "K" is the symbol for potassium, a red light means stop, Uncle Bill is Dad's brother. Second-hand information is learned from someone else or from observation and interpretation. Your mother may not tell you in so many words that "Uncle Bill's" first name isn't really "Uncle," and it may take you a few years to figure out why he is "Uncle Bill" to you but merely "Bill" to your parents. But eventually, being an astute child, you figure out that "Uncle" designates a particular relationship. All of this is done in your Red with a little help from memory. You receive and "interpret" information in your Red. And the primary purpose of all of this is survival. Remember that your every thought is weighed first on the survival scale. The first order of business for any stimulus, whether it comes from the outside through your five senses or from the inside through memory, is to determine its "threat intensity."

Interpretations of Red-received "raw data" are made by associating and comparing incoming information with previously stored information. Information and interpretations may or may not be correct — "flat spots" and all that. But second-hand information can be revised; or, as we say in our technological age, updated. We re-learn or replace second-hand information that we find to be incorrect. We re-learn or update "facts." A few years ago we knew about the country of Yugoslavia. Now that information is outdated. Yugoslavia no longer exists; it's Croatia, Serbia, Bosnia-Hercegovina, and assorted other independent states. We update or modify words and/or their meanings, such as "gay," and "chairperson," and "economically challenged." And we add new facts to our learned information. We learn new names to go with new faces, how to use a computer, how to program a VCR, an improved method of growing bigger and more colorful roses, and a more effective way of taking care of body and health. Our store of knowledge comes from a variety of sources including school, work, society, and family culture.

Red second-hand information that is culture-specific can be the basis for political upheaval and wars. At this writing in the mid-1990s, cultural differences concerning human rights influence political and economic policies between the United States and China. And, as we'll see in this book, second-hand information concerning diet and self-expression — often culture-specific — can impose health-threatening conditions on the body.

Since second-hand information is acquired through perception, chances are good that much of the information stored in our conscious minds is in error. Yet that's what we use to interpret new information!

Warning! Danger! Danger!

We interpret new second-hand information based on previously stored, possibly erroneous second-hand information. That's scary. We think about, analyze and interpret our current perceptions, which may or may not be the way things really are, based on equally suspect information from past interpretations. Could this be the hang-up in the fights against cancer and the common cold and our other ills?

WELLNESS PRINCIPLE: Conscious thoughts can be errors compounded by previous

errors, misinformation, or
untruths

The conscious mind is an analytical, reasoning, judging, thinking faculty that is constantly active during periods of wakefulness. During those periods of wakefulness, we move about. In addition to being control central for all of those cerebral activities (analyzing, reasoning, etc.), the conscious mind controls about 70% of your skeletal muscles. And there's more. As we shall discuss later, the conscious mind and emotions go hand in hand. But for now, we'll look at the "think-and-respond" aspect of the conscious mind.

Although the exact neural mechanism of a conscious thought is not known, apparently one "thought" is stored concurrently in several areas of the brain. As Guyton puts it, "Each thought almost certainly involves simultaneous signals in many portions of the cerebral cortex, thalamus, limbic system, and reticular formation of the brain stem."[43] Of the brain areas Guyton mentioned in that list, conscious activity takes place only in the cerebral cortex; the rest of the brain areas function below consciousness. You will see the significance of this as we go along.

We know that conscious activity (cortical) is fed by the five senses, predominantly through the thalamus. Yet the cerebral cortex, like all other body parts, does not act in isolation — you are a "whole" person and your body, including your brain, functions as an integrated unit. Guyton explains: ". . . the cerebral cortex is essential for most of our thought processes even though it also cannot function alone in this. In fact, it is the lower centers that cause *wakefulness* in the cerebral cortex, thus opening its bank of memories to the thinking machinery of the brain."[44] So, although the cortex gets all of the glory and adulation as being the font of intellectual supremacy, it's the memory storehouse that is the mental resource center. Our conscious thinking processes are responses to both perceived sensory stimuli and to memory. Csikszentmihalyi writes in his book *Flow: The Psychology of Optimal Experience*, ". . . we might think of consciousness as *intentionally ordered information*."[45]

WELLNESS PRINCIPLE: The level of your cortical intellectual ability depends on previ-
ously stored information

According to Csikszentmihalyi, contemporary wisdom acknowledges "that whatever happens in the mind is the result of electrochemical changes in the central nervous system, as laid down over millions of years by biological evolution."[46] Electrochemical — brain work is chemistry and electricity in action.

Our Red consciousness has a finite processing capacity at any given time. Too much information at one time boggles the mind. Csikszentmihalyi reports that seven bits of information is about all the information mere mortals can handle at one time. It takes about 1/18th of a second to discriminate between sets of information. However, when you do seven bits of information eighteen times a second, that means we can process about 126 bits of information a second — not too shabby.[47] Those 126 bits of information are a hodgepodge of sights, sounds, and other perceived external sensory signals, plus thoughts, memories, and emotions.

We may not know the exact mechanics of thinking, learning, and information processing, but we are familiar with the effects of tiny electrochemical reactions. They are the energy that allows us to make decisions, plans, mistakes, great strides, merry, and our mark in the world.

WELLNESS PRINCIPLE: Your consciousness is your self-director

Unconscious

The term "unconscious" refers to a condition rather than to a physical activity of the brain. "Insensible" is a term used in Taber's Medical Cyclopedic Dictionary. In "unconsciousness," for whatever reason, the reticular activating system — the waking-up system — does not function; however, the subconscious remains in good working order. In a state of unconsciousness, organs function, cells regenerate and replenish, and life goes on in a state of resting homeostasis. A person who is unconscious is alive but cannot resume cognitive awareness. One is also "unconscious" when under the influence of a general anesthetic.

The amount of actual awareness and degree of cortical activity of unconscious individuals are open to conjecture. However, surgeons and surgical nurses have noticed a correlation between what they say in the presence of an unconscious patient and the recovery time of those patients. Operating room staff are beginning to suspect that rude attempts at humor, comments such as "Ooops," and banter that ridicules or insults the anesthetized/unconscious patient can adversely affect the recovery and healing potential of that patient. "Unconscious" isn't "brain dead"; it's the inability to be aroused.

Sleep doesn't qualify as an unconscious state since we can resume full awareness either naturally or by a disturbance. A sudden sound, such as a buzzing alarm clock, a crying child, a thump in the night, or a sudden major change in lighting, is all that's necessary to rouse most of us from even a deep sleep.

Unconsciousness, on the other hand, withstands all manner of stimuli without restoring alertness. We can survive for years in an unconscious state where few, if any, Red-induced stresses interfere with resting homeostasis. As long as the bodies of comatose individuals are properly nourished and protected, their Greens carry on under nearly perfect internal environmental conditions.

> WELLNESS PRINCIPLE: "Unconsciousness" is the con-
> scious Red on "pause" while the
> Green handles physiological
> requirements undisturbed

Subconscious

When you count your blessings, remember to include thanks for your subconscious. It is the perfect "employee." Your subconscious is labor-intensive, tax-free, error-free, maintenance-free, and it never gets sick or takes a day off, much less an extended vacation. All it needs is for you to keep your intellect out of the way so it can do its job without interference.

Unlike the conscious Red that uses learned and interpreted information and can respond erratically, the subconscious Green uses "pre-packaged" Primary Intelligence and ALWAYS responds perfectly. The subconscious is impersonal, non-selective, non-thinking, and non-judgmental. It isn't analytical. It doesn't plan for the future. It responds to present need only. Its job description is simple: guide your physiological activity to maintain the best possible survival conditions at the moment. And it does all of this without thinking.

For our purposes, "subconscious" can be defined as either a specific location in the brain or a specific feature of process. Subconscious structures of the central nervous system are those located below the cerebrum — cerebellum, amygdala, thalamus, hypothalamus, and all other mid-brain and lower-brain structures including the spinal cord. The processes of subconscious are those over which you have no direct conscious control. Using this definition of "subconscious," you can see that subconscious activity goes on even in areas of the brain that harbor your conscious mind. Thousands of processes take place in your cerebral cortex and cerebrum that enable you to think thoughts, remember things you have experienced or learned, make decisions, and generally run your life. However, you have no control over the physiological processes themselves. You can change your mind, but you can't change the route of nerve impulse flow between the cortex and cerebellum or hypothalamus.

> WELLNESS PRINCIPLE: Your Green runs your physiol-
> ogy and feeds your brain

The subconscious responds to stimuli received from the conscious mind and from internal feedback mechanisms. These feedback signals carry information about internal physiological conditions such as body temperature and blood pressure, or of an urgent need for damage repair, or of the cancellation of a "severe crisis" warning. Although you have no conscious control over the activity of your Green subconscious, you do have control over your conscious thoughts. And conscious thoughts are principle instigators of both well-timed and ill-timed physiological responses.

Conscious thoughts can influence physiological responses, but most conscious thoughts don't directly stimulate physiology. That's the Green's job. Conscious thoughts influence physiology through the subconscious. As soon as you think a conscious thought, internal signals are transmitted to other areas of your brain. Once thought signals are generated by your conscious mind, you have absolutely no control over where they go or the physiology they affect. If the thoughts are packed with feeling, your Green becomes involved immediately. No matter how smart you are, your conscious has no say in how your physiology will respond to those signals. This concept is so important that it is repeated in various forms throughout this book. If you don't get anything else out of reading this book, absorb and firmly affix in your conscious mind this essential principle of health:

You have absolutely no control over the physiological responses your subconscious directs; you do have control over most of the thoughts that prompt the responses.

Subconscious physiological responses are always perfect for internal conditions of the moment. And they're perfect for the signals coming from the conscious Red. But we know that the Red can contain misinformation. It's not infallible. Red signals that prompt a response may not be appropriate for actual conditions. The response is perfect — the signals may be inappropriate at the time. Often, strong stimuli from emotions such as fear, anxiety, or anger persist although no actual physical villain threatens physical survival. But your non-thinking, non-analytical subconscious is totally literal. You think or feel "Danger!" and it responds accordingly. All your Green responds to in the outside "real" world is what your conscious Red tells it with feeling. Your Green responds to feelings, not facts.

WELLNESS PRINCIPLE: Your subconscious responds
                     perfectly to every feeling

This is the principle behind the positive thinking philosophy. Put positive thoughts into your Red that don't send inappropriate, ill-timed survival messages. If thoughts and feelings of fear, anxiety, or guilt keep you in a constant survival mode, your Green can't attend to actual conditions such as digesting food and repairing tissue. Positive thoughts don't interfere with the Green function that is addressing actual physical conditions. But there's more to thinking positively than that. As we shall see, positive and negative thinking involve the other consciousness siblings in addition to conscious and subconscious. Which brings us to the non-conscious activities of your whole self.

INTRODUCING NON-CONSCIOUS

The non-conscious mind is more of a process using latent information than a structure. If a physical location for the non-conscious could be designated, it would probably be in the mass of white matter of the cerebrum below the cortex, with "branch offices" in the muscles. The non-conscious is an integrating function rather than a specific element of the nervous system. You won't find "non-conscious" in medical, physiology or neuroanatomy books. Instead of the using the term "non-conscious," they classify the process we're about to discuss as "unconscious." However, from my perspective, "unconscious" applies to "lack of awareness"; a completely different set of circumstances.

You can see the non-conscious process at work by performing this little exercise.

Make a fist.

That's it. Just ball up your hand as though you were going to punch something.

Now. How did you do that?

You bent your fingers tightly against your palm and tightened the muscles of your hand and arm.

Again; how did you do that?

You certainly didn't go through an elaborate mental process of directing each muscle and tendon to move in a particular way. You just decided to "make a fist," and your muscle and tendon "machinery" carried out the command. The process of consciously deciding on an action followed by the nerve-muscle-tendon response that actually carries out the command is an example of non-conscious activity. Or to put it another way, you thought in your Red and your neuromusculoskeletal system responded. Your Red didn't send the "how to" directions; it merely issued the order. Your Red acts rather like the boss who says, "Don't bother me with the details, just get the job done."

Earlier I talked about the cerebrum being the focus of "Red" activity.

This is where you learn to walk and talk and do your multiplication tables. But now we are going to subdivide the tasks of your conscious mind and restrict the term "Red" to the 1/8th inch nerve-infested covering of the brain. Your Red is your thoughtful, analytical cerebral cortex. The part we are talking about now is the area below the cortex. This is where the "operating instructions" for carrying out learned activities are stored — learned muscle response activity patterns and learned intellectual activity patterns.

Your non-conscious is the area you use to carry out muscle movement patterns of well-learned activities: ride a bike, read this book, or play the clarinet. Your repertoire of non-conscious information and skills is developed through practice. Practice of motor [muscle] activity. Remember the well-worn joke, "How do you get to Carnegie Hall?", and the punch line: "Practice! Practice! Practice!" Practice hones non-conscious skills.

> WELLNESS PRINCIPLE: Non-conscious skills are developed, not inborn

Non-conscious might be seen as a subdivision of consciousness. Your non-conscious functions in conjunction with your Red. Everything in your non-conscious is learned. Information stored in non-conscious doesn't come pre-packaged at or before birth. Any learned, consciously directed motor movement is directed by non-conscious. Learning takes place through conscious repetition. The most obvious example is walking. Once you learn how to walk, you don't have to start from ground-zero to re-learn the process each time you head for the refrigerator. You repeat and reinforce previously learned motions. By repetition, you "train" your muscles to perform particular movements that you need frequently.

You "train" your muscles by storing subconscious muscle movement patterns in memory. Remember, your Red doesn't actually carry out musculoskeletal processes, that's up to your subconscious. All your Red can do is send signals of the intent. Your Green directs the physiological processes needed to accomplish your purpose.

We know that the conscious mind can't move muscles. If it could, no one would be paralyzed. If all it took was a simple, "I am going to walk," anyone, no matter what sort of internal communication problems were involved, could walk. "Walk" messages begin in the Red and are transmitted subconsciously through nerve pathways to the appropriate musculoskeletal areas.

> WELLNESS PRINCIPLE: Conscious intends; non-conscious patterns; subconscious executes

Walking involves well-ingrained patterns of muscle movements of large muscle systems. Other learned muscle responses, playing the clarinet, for example, involve more precise movement of smaller muscles. After you have survived the initial process of learning to play the clarinet, you no longer consciously focus on the delicate muscle control of mouth, lips and tongue that maintain your embouchure and ward off eardrum-peeling squeaks.

Once you have consciously learned how to walk or play the clarinet, the response patterns to repeat these skills are stored in your non-conscious. Your Red signals your subconscious when to retrieve the patterns and send them on to your Green to be carried out.

Did you notice a pattern there? From conscious through non-conscious to subconscious.

Non-conscious activity is learned initially through conscious. Once learned, the activity is carried out by responses of the subconscious. Non-conscious integrates learned Red information and primary Green information. In the light/energy spectrum, red and green are connected by yellow. Since we are dealing here with energy, we use the term "Yellow" to refer to the non-conscious. Now you can see why the brain illustration on the cover is colored red, green, and yellow.

WELLNESS PRINCIPLE: Yellow integrates Red thought
with Green responses

Yellow activity, such as walking, must be learned before it becomes "automatic." Yellow activity is "automatic"; you don't need to re-learn to write the letters of the alphabet every time you want to scribble a grocery list. It's learned material that has been learned very well. However, Yellow activity is not "auto*nom*ic." It's not "self-controlling" as are your sympathetic and parasympathetic nervous systems. You can't control autonomic activity. That's subconscious — Green. Yellow auto*matic* activity is a physical or mental reaction that happens without you consciously directing every part of the action. And Yellow activity can prompt physiological responses. It can have as strong an impact on your health as can your Red. Your Yellow is an integral — and integrating — part of your internal communication network.

The internal communication network that allows an about-to-be-toddler to get up and walk is nothing short of miraculous. Imagine smiling, roly-poly Kristopher entering the world of walking on all two's. There he is in the middle of the living room. He assumes his newly discovered though wobbly upright position, eyes focused lustfully on the floral arrangement placed "out of reach" on a table, and off he goes. Does he navigate directly from mid-floor to flowers? Not quite. With feet placed shoulder-width apart for maximum balance, and eyes fixed firmly on his prey, his chubby little legs "stump" along in a lumbering gait, in a zig-zag forward direction. "Look, Kent," chortles Kristopher's mother in great maternal excitement, "he's walking."

Well, he's walking "kind of." He may be going through the motions and taking steps. But his non-conscious hasn't yet been sufficiently "programmed" to integrate the conscious (though unarticulated) intent of "walking" with subconscious muscle control that allows "automatic" movements. His conscious intent is there, but the muscle-control pattern directed by his subconscious hasn't yet been refined enough to integrate the intent with smooth, effortless execution. The conscious and subconscious haven't quite been integrated in his non-conscious. But he's practicing, and it will be.

Back to the physiological front. Neural patterns to control particular muscles allow you to easily perform complex motor activities. These patterns are stored in what Guyton terms "sensory engrams of the motor movements."[48] The physiologist has a good bit to say about these neural patterns that we never think about but use constantly. Guyton writes, ". . . when a person learns to perform a motor function, he or she experiences in the somatic sensory areas the effects of the motor movement each time it is performed, and 'memories' of the different patterns of movement are recorded. . . . . "[49] Your somatic sensory areas are areas in your brain where feelings in particular parts of your body are sensed. Sensory has to do with feeling. You "experience" in your brain the "effects of the motor [muscle] movement." When you are a 90% free-throw shooter, a low-handicap golfer, an experienced tennis player, or an accomplished performer in a less glamorous arena that requires finely-tuned sensory-muscle cooperation, you "know" as soon as you have executed a familiar action whether or not you have done it properly. You can tell by "feel" if you've done it right.

Guyton describes part of the mechanics of "knowing" whether or not you are executing correctly. "Once a sensory engram has been established in the sensory cortex — that is, once the movement has been learned — the person then uses this sensory engram as a guide for the motor system of the brain to follow in reproducing the same pattern of movement."[50] In other words, we learn through our muscles how to do things.

Your Yellow harbors *memories* of learned information we use every day. Information that allows you to perform purposeful movements — brush teeth, hammer nail, or, to use Guyton's example, "cut out a paper doll with scissors." Patterns of movement are refined through the cooperative efforts of the sensory system and the motor system. But the movement isn't under the direct control of the motor system. It is what we can call "procedural memory," or *muscle memory.*

The conscious mind defines a desired movement: pick a soft, red, ripe tomato off the vine, for example. The motor system carries out the movement. In order to successfully accomplish this complex maneuver, two special types of sensory receptors — tiny anatomical structures in muscles and tendons (termed muscle spindles and Golgi tendon organs respectively) — signal the nervous system of the exact rate of change in muscle length and tendon tension. Muscle spindles and Golgi tendon organs are kept busy. In Guyton's more technical terms, ". . . they transmit tremendous amounts of information into the spinal cord, the cerebellum, and even the cerebral cortex, helping each of these portions of the nervous system in its function for controlling muscle contraction."[51] Without some sort of feedback mechanism to let your subconscious movement director know how fast and how far your arm is being propelled toward the tomato, you would overshoot or undershoot your target. And without feedback information to let your subconscious know how hard you are grasping the tomato once you connect, you might crush it into a handful of juicy, dripping tomato pulp or fail to get a firm hold on it. You would be in much the same situation as early-developed robots that could pick up a soft drink can but, in the process, crush the can. Their movements weren't sufficiently sensitive to regulate the amount of pressure used. Muscle memory keeps you from bloodying your own nose with a tremendous wallop when you reach up for a gentle itch-relieving scratch.

WELLNESS PRINCIPLE: Non-conscious memory patterns
protect as well as project

As we saw in the story of "Ben" at the beginning of this book, muscle memory can be perfect yet inappropriate. Instructions from "On High" (higher areas of the sensory system) can dictate that muscles stay tense in response to memories of "threat" feelings that were never "turned off" after the defining incident was over. Ben originally learned to walk with the help of his non-conscious Yellow. And when he had trouble walking, this, too, was a function of his Yellow. His original "how to walk" memories were overridden by new "how to walk" memories that were cemented in his Yellow by very strong feelings. His original "how to walk" memories were related to development; his new "how to walk" memories were related to survival.

WELLNESS PRINCIPLE: You constantly add to the memory inventory in your Yellow
storehouse

In addition to being a storehouse for memories of motor movement, your Yellow is also the repository for well-learned intellectual information. Your Yellow holds well-ingrained information that makes it possible for you to put two and two together, so to speak. To illustrate, let's get real. Think tax return preparation.

First you gather all of the relevant information together by your Red calling on your Yellow. Red searches Yellow "files" to determine what information is necessary. You know this from past years. (If you don't, take every receipt and bit of financial information you have to a tax preparer and let him/her figure it out.) After you have organized the information, Red and Yellow again work together. Red analyzes the relevance of each piece of information and decides what figures should go where on the tax forms. And in the process you read (and re-read) the instructions in your tax packet. Interpretation of the instructions is a job for the alert, discerning Red. The reading part is a function of Yellow.

Reading involves coordinated muscle movement and association. When you learned to decipher the lines and squiggles of the written or printed word, the muscle movement patterns necessary to follow the established left-to-right pattern of western writing were stored in your Yellow. If you have learned to read Hebrew, you have a Yellow "file" for eye muscle movement for reading from right to left. And readers of Chinese develop the requisite top to bottom non-conscious pattern. But most of the people who read this book are dyed-in-the-wool left-to-righters. To illustrate the point of the muscle programming, try reading a couple of lines backwards: from right to left. Aside from the word sequence not making much sense, it's rather like using the wrong hand to brush your teeth — awkward. The muscle action pattern for reading is neither intuitive nor universal. Nor is the ability to decipher meaning from written patterns.

The method of decoding symbols that represent words and sounds was stored in your Yellow, probably when you were in school. Little did you realize as a first-grader that your new-found skills would one day be put to such troublesome work as reading and filling out tax forms. However, in this dreary annual process, your Red calls up and calls on bits of information stored in your Yellow to help make sense of otherwise apparent nonsense. Reading is a Yellow function. Finding the meaning in the sequence and patterns of the words — comprehension — and being able to put that meaning to use is a Red function. And the confusion inherent in the tax forms and convoluted instructions is an IRS function. Your Green responds to your feelings about that.

So we have seen that your Yellow integrates current Red thought and learned musculoskeletal patterns. Yellow also integrates Red thought and learned intellectual information bits. Whether the topic of your Red's focus is musculoskeletal related or intellect related, signals from your Red rifle through Yellow files for associated information. When the proper information is found, it is transmitted back to the Red. Now other areas of association are relevant. More Red signals rifle through more Yellow files. Back and forth, the Red and Yellow "feed" each other. Everything you learn involves your Red and your Yellow. Without your Yellow, your Red wouldn't have any associated backup information.

> WELLNESS PRINCIPLE: Your Yellow holds learned - information your Red uses for comparisons, analyses, decisions, and judgments

When it comes to thinking, your Yellow is a two-way mediator. And there's more. Your Yellow also integrates your conscious, analytical Red with feelings.

To illustrate this concept, let's hark back to the "parking lot assault" story of the last chapter. Recall that the hypothetical "you" ended up in the doctor's office with pain and misery that couldn't be accounted for. The "cause" wasn't the attack itself; the "cause" was the antagonistic feelings you harbored long after the attack was over. Well, now you know where and why those feelings were stored. Your Yellow was doing its job.

When you stewed and seethed about the injustice of the assault, your feelings were intense. Your reminiscences about the attack weren't of the objective "ho-hum" variety. No indeed. Every time you thought about it, which was frequent, you were irate. Peeved. So what happens when you think about the same thing over and over? The same thing that happened when you learned your multiplication tables by saying them over and over. A "file" is set up in your Yellow to store the information. However, there's a difference between storing "8 x 7 = 56" and "That dirty so-and-so." Multiplication tables don't carry much emotion with them. The process of learning may, but the numbers themselves are pretty blah. The "That dirty so-and-so" thought is packed with emotion. And emotion is the "glue" of memory.

Along with the facts of the assault are stored the emotions you felt after the assault. And your autonomic nervous system responds to emotions. Emotions of fear and anger can put you in risk physiology. And sustained emotions can keep you in risk physiology. So when you store memories of the assault, you also store memories of the accompanying emotions and physiology patterns appropriate for those emotions.

> WELLNESS PRINCIPLE: Your Yellow is the keeper of memories of facts and friction

Similarly, your Yellow harbors firmly embedded, culturally-instilled learned beliefs and values. Much of the information stored in your non-conscious was acquired in childhood.

Children who grow up in an atmosphere dominated by a specific cultural attitude usually absorb the values and beliefs of that culture just as thoroughly as they absorb the elements, patterns, and intonations of speech that permeate their environment. Non-conscious values and beliefs become as thoroughly ingrained as do non-conscious patterns of motor movements and patterns of analysis. Conflict over social issues such as abortion, apartheid, "holy wars," unrestrained sexual activity, and personal responsibility may be due as much to differences in non-conscious value and belief responses as it is to differences in consciously evaluated social and political bias.

In the same vein, lessons about your self-worth are stored in your Yellow. Your self-esteem develops — or more precisely, is undermined — gradually over years. Infants don't come equipped with low self-esteem. Low-self esteem is a learned and stored "feeling habit." Like other non-conscious responses, low self-esteem is acquired through practice. Infants and small children start out life never questioning the fact that they are loveable, capable, and worthwhile. Before long, they are "taught" otherwise, by the "powerful ones" in their lives. Over and over, negative verbal and physical messages deflate their sense of self worth. "Pick up your clothes; you're a slob." "You don't know what you're talking about." "You'll never amount to anything." Each esteem-deflating incident is filed away in non-conscious. Over time, the pattern of response to esteem-bashing events becomes firmly fixed. But more about self-esteem later.

WELLNESS PRINCIPLE: Self-esteem is a non-conscious
                       feeling-memory response

What do conscious Red, subconscious Green, and non-conscious Yellow have to do with stress or health?

Everything!

Each level of consciousness plays a part in your body's responses to life-experiences past and present. Red and Yellow provide the stimuli; Green provides the responses. Your Yellow is the storehouse for previously filed information that can spark physiological responses just as surely as can current information from your Red. It's the Red and Yellow stimuli that can be inappropriate. Your Green-directed physiological responses are always perfect for each situation *at the time*.

So far we have two levels of consciousness that are subject to error, and one level that never makes a mistake. Now let me introduce you to another level of consciousness that is infinitely perfect. Another level of consciousness that is at least as, if not more, important than the conscious, subconscious, and non-conscious put together — Superconsciousness.

SUPERCONSCIOUS

Superconsciousness is the Perfect Intelligence that is the cause of all things. Superconscious — "God"; "Creative Energy"; "Perfect"; "Cosmic Force"; "Supreme Power"; or "Universal Energy." The Superconscious mind created the universe and all its constituent parts. Superconsciousness never built a part — it builds the whole! It is the power that was behind you when you were merely one cell — before you were the "You" of which you are now aware. All living things are part of Superconscious creation. And all living things — you included — were created by and are influenced by the ultimate energy of Superconsciousness.

Superconsciousness is the ultimate power source of the universe and of each individual. Its primary characteristic is that of perfection. Superconsciousness itself is perfect. Superconsciousness is holographic — the whole is present in each minute part. And Superconsciousness provides the template for the whole. We'll see this demonstrated later when we gambol through fields of energy.

WELLNESS PRINCIPLE: Superconsciousness doesn't do parts — Superconsciousness is "Wholly"

Traditionally, consideration of a Supreme Power has been the domain of philosophy and religion. Yet the emerging — or reemerging — premise that the universe and everything in it is energy in one form or another reinforces the concept of a superconscious element. If everything is energy and Superconsciousness is the Perfect Energy, then everything is connected to the Perfect Energy.

Your direct connection with Superconsciousness is your subconscious. All of that perfect information in your Green came from something. Superconsciousness is the source. (You can read "source" with a capital "S" if you prefer.) You access Superconsciousness through your subconscious Green. Just as we said that your non-conscious is a "subdivision" of your Red, your subconscious can be seen as a "subdivision" of Super consciousness. Since Superconsciousness contains all of the knowledge of the universe, we can say that its color is "white." In the energy spectrum, when all color frequencies are combined, the result is White.

WELLNESS PRINCIPLE: Perfect White creates; Green responds perfectly

Superconsciousness is perfect; yet the *effects* of Superconsciousness perfection can be tarnished by conscious thoughts and memories. Although Superconsciousness is ever present in the life of each of us, lifestyle, thoughts, and memories can interfere with communication between your lower levels of consciousness and this highest level of consciousness. Interference in communication with Superconsciousness is generated by man's conscious thoughts, memories, and actions. This interference subverts health, happiness, and success.

WELLNESS PRINCIPLE: Superconsciousness doesn't interfere with Generic Man, Generic Man interferes with communication between the two

As we continue our trip to self-directed health, we'll see more and more evidence that interference in communication with universal White is behind the ills of individual and collective Generic Man. And we'll take in a panoramic view that reveals the most amazing feature of all — the fields of vital energy. Fields of White Superconsciousness are a "physical" part of every living entity. Superconsciousness is not only the power that developed you and the power behind life itself, Superconsciousness is an integral part of you. Without the power and energy of Superconsciousness that is a part of your body, you are just a physical body. And, I might add, without that power and energy your physical body won't last long in its body-like form.

Your four levels of consciousness work together as you function in your minute-by-minute life. The primary stimulus-producers to which your consciousness responds are your five senses, your emotions, and your memories. Your Red gathers in the stimuli. Your Green, under the perfection of White, directs physiological responses to these stimuli. Your Yellow is the repository for response-pattern memories that can prompt perfect physiological responses at inappropriate times.

To summarize the attributes and limitations of the various members of the consciousness clan, we can say that:

Superconsciousness (White) is: universal; beyond your control; creative; perfect; holographic; the life-energy force that is a component of your physical body; infinite in time, space, and knowledge; all-knowing; and ever-present.

Subconsciousness (Green) is: your direct link with Superconscious White; beyond your conscious control; creative; perfect in response; infinite during your lifetime from conception to death (at least); responsive only — does not think, judge, or reason; is "time-deaf" and responds perfectly to conscious thoughts and memories in ways that promote survival at the moment.

Consciousness (Red) is: your "thinking machine"; limited awareness; perceived through any and all of your five senses; analytical; logical and rational; discriminating; judgmental; highly fallible; the source of most of life's ups and downs; essentially self-directed and self-focused.

Non-Consciousness (Yellow) is: the storage area for learned, Red, "second-hand" information; the accumulation of learned muscle responses, learned feeling-responses and associated physiology, and learned intellectual information; able to activate Green at appropriate times; and demonstrable but not explainable.

So there you have the roster of the members of your consciousness clan. We can see that it is a colorful bunch. Different facets of consciousness resonating at different frequencies. Put them all together and you have the rainbow of your mind. This is the rainbow that begins and ends in fields of vital energy that are in and around every cell of your body. These fields hold all of the information necessary for your body to function at its best throughout your life. It's time to romp through those fields for a closer look.

POINTS OF INTEREST

1. Conscious Red processes information from the five senses that may or may not be correct.

2. Non-conscious Yellow stores memories of information and feelings.

3. Subconscious Green responses run your body perfectly, without thought.

4. Superconscious White is the perfect energy behind all life.

5. Non-conscious integrates conscious thought with subconscious responses.

6. Your Yellow stores the memories and feelings about yourself that make up your self-esteem.

7. Your four levels of consciousness work together to run your body and manage your life.

8. Green and White are always right; Yellow and Red are easily misled.

You can observe a lot just by looking.
                                        - Yogi Berra

CHAPTER 6
Mind Fields

ENERGY MATTERS

We've been going on about Superconsciousness, fields, and energy being vital parts of your body, life, and health. In Chapter 2 and again in Chapter 5, I described the personal field of energy that surrounds your body. The universe is replete with energy fields. Our bodies run on energy. If we could take a panoramic view of our universe from outside its borders, we might see that everything in the universe is energy. Fields interlaced with fields that are interlaced with even more fields. Some combined fields are large enough to encompass the universe itself. Some fields are as small as an electron. All of these fields, great and small, interact; each affects every other. Overlapping circles, and all that.

Earlier I pointed out that your field is holographic (contains the whole message). Your personal field serves as the "blueprint" for your prenatal and postnatal development. The field, your connection with it, and its influence on your life and health, are recurring melodies in this book. So now it's time to dig a little deeper into the field and look at what we're talking about — matter and energy.

You know about matter and energy: the subatomic parts and features that are involved with everything in the universe — electrons, quarks, bosons, mass, acceleration, velocity and the like. Quantum stuff. But not to worry. I'm not going to wax mathematical. No big, long, alphabet soup equations to make a point. We speak "understandable" here. There's just enough of the "scientific" stuff to highlight the field concepts that are so important to your health.

For some readers, long dormant Yellow feeling-memories of past experiences in science classes may be beginning to stir. Thought responses to those Yellow feeling-memories may run along the lines of, "Yuck! Scientific stuff! I never did like science." So be it. If your interest level gauge sits around Empty when it comes to some of the finer points of energy and matter, you can just race through this part or skip right on to the next subheading. Or, if you really don't care to be bothered with the nuts and bolts of energy and matter, check out the "Points of Interest" at the end of this chapter and go from there. However, keep in mind that the nuts and bolts we're dealing with here are pretty large and easy to handle. My point is, this isn't the time to put the book down and forget it. The best is yet to come! So back to highlighting some field concepts.

The first highlight is the "quantum" part. Quantum theory is big now. It sounds so . . . , so "technical" — "physics-y." To the causal observer, it smacks of complex scientific stuff. Big bang; black holes; supernova; super colliders; quantum mechanics; quantum physics; quantum this and quantum that. But what is "quantum"? What does "quantum" mean?

Back in 1567, the word quantum came into being from the Latin *quantus* meaning "how much." Since 1942, however, "quantum" has been used outside of scientific circles as one of the "in" buzz-words to mean BIG. Quantum leap, quantum advances and all that. So, let's see what Webster's Ninth New Collegiate Dictionary has to say.

"**quan-tum**" n., pl. "quanta" — one quantum; two or more quanta. Quantity; amount; portion; part. "One of the very small increments or parcels into which many forms of energy are subdivided. One of the small subdivisions of a quantized physical magnitude (as magnetic moment)." In a word: itsy-bitsy.

And the itsy-bitsy parts we're talking about are the smallest parts discovered (so far) that make up things, such as you and trees and elk and sand and washing machines and spacecraft. Everything is made of something, and that something is energy. Energy is the itsy-bitsy parts of things. Put a bunch of energy together just right and you have "mass" — bits of mass.

Everyone knows what mass is. You learn about mass in physics class. Mass is the quantity of matter; bulk; material. But to infer that mass is big, as in bulk, may miss the mark. In his engaging book, *The God Particle: If the Universe is the Answer, What's the Question?*, Nobel Prize winner Leon Lederman quotes Greek philosopher Democritus of c. 460 B.C.E. fame: "Nothing exists except atoms and empty space; everything else is opinion." Atoms and space. That must be mass. Maybe.

Lederman questions whether mass is real or an illusion. And he answers himself: "One opinion bubbling up in the literature of the 1980s and '90s is that something pervades this empty space and provides atoms with an illusory weight. That 'something' will one day manifest itself in our instruments as a particle."[52]

Matter has been a topic of thought and discussion for centuries. Lederman relates that in the early 1700s, Roger Joseph Boscovich from Dubrovnik proposed that "matter is composed of particles that have no dimensions!"[53] And now, nearly three hundred years later, Lederman says, "we found a particle just a couple of decades ago that fits such a description. It's called a quark."[54] So here we are with more quantum stuff — a particle that has no size. Instead, it is a geometrical point — a place. And this geometrical point is part of the materials that constitute "us" — or in particular, You.

That's one of the things we focus on in this book; how quantum stuff affects You. Not just your muscles, bones, teeth, skin, kidneys and whatnot — You. With a capital "Y".

In his book *The Emperor's New Mind: Concerning Computers, Minds, and the Laws of Physics*, Roger Penrose poses some thought-provoking questions about You: "What is it that gives a particular person his individual identity? Is it, to some extent, the very atoms that compose his body? Is his identity dependent upon the particular choice of electrons, protons, and other particles that compose those atoms?"[55] The questions arise as Penrose compares Artificial Intelligence with the human mind. He points out two reasons why the physical matter that constitutes a particular person is not the person him- or herself. The first reason is that "there is a continual turnover in the material of any living person's body. This applies in particular to the cells in a person's brain, despite the fact that no new actual brain cells are produced after birth."[56] Penrose continues with the second reason: "According to quantum mechanics . . ., any two electrons must necessarily be completely identical, and the same holds for any two protons and for any two particles whatever, of any one particular kind."[57]

WELLNESS PRINCIPLE: We aren't quite the solid citizens
we appear to be

Penrose uses the examples of brick and brain to illustrate the premise that the electron is the same in any environment. Exchanging an electron in a person's brain with an electron in a brick would make no difference. Penrose writes: ". . . the state of the system would be *exactly the same* as it was before, not merely indistinguishable from it!" The distinguishing feature is the "pattern of how his constituents are arranged, not the individuality of the constituents themselves."[58]

To paraphrase one of Lincoln's pithy phrases at Gettysburg, all Generic Men are indeed created equal. The fundamental building material is identical. Electrons, protons, neutrinos, quarks and all the other quantum stuff are uniform. They are all forms of energy. We are all made up of identical forms of energy. The energy is the same; the patterns, configurations, frequencies, and vibrations are different.

Matter and energy are, as Gerber puts it, "now known to be interchangeable and interconvertible."[59] Quantum theory proclaims that photons — bits of light — have properties of both wave and particle. Photons are light particles — the material particles of sunbeams, you might say. And, Ford observes, "A material particle is nothing more than a highly concentrated and localized bundle of energy."[60] Matter is energy.

How about a little syllogism here: All particles are energy. All living entities are made up of particles. Therefore, living entities are energy. You are energy. Generic Man is a particular density configuration of energy functioning within specific energy frequencies.

WELLNESS PRINCIPLE: Tired or not, you are energy

Matter can take on many forms. The differences are in the arrangements of the identical energy materials, and the arrangement is determined by the conditions surrounding them. Bricks or brains. The specific form is determined by energy frequency of energy fields in and around the matter — the vibration rate of the molecules.

Energy frequencies determine the "state" of matter. Solid matter that makes up our visible world is at one end of the spectrum and plasma that is visible only under certain conditions is at the other end.

Plasma, according to Webster's Third International Dictionary, is "an ionized gas (as in the atmospheres of stars) containing about equal numbers of positive ions and electrons." Plasma is affected by a magnetic field and is a good conductor of electricity. Scientists estimate that 99% of the matter in the universe — our Sun, observable stars, and interstellar space — exists in a plasma state. More down-to-earth examples of plasma are lightning bolts, flames, auroras, and neon lights.[61]

A real world illustration of matter resonating at different frequencies to bring about various states is water — (H_2O).

Actually, you'd be hard-pressed to come up with another familiar form of matter to serve as an illustration. Nonetheless, we see the energy frequency differences of water as steam, liquid, and ice. In its highly electrically charged plasma state, H** resonates at its highest rate and is invisible to the naked eye. Slightly lower on the resonance scale is H_2O in its gaseous state — steam. The next in resonance frequency is H_2O in its liquid state — water. And at the bottom of the resonance frequency is H_2O in its solid state — ice. Plasma, steam, water, ice. Despite the differences in frequency and density, water is water — H_2O is H_2O: two Hydrogen atoms and one Oxygen atom.

WELLNESS PRINCIPLE: Changing energy frequency can change form and function of the energy/matter

Generic Man can be seen as "a bundle of energy" at different frequencies. One energy, different states. By using our imaginations, we can relate the various frequencies of water to various parts of Generic Man.

We can say that the personal energy field around the physical body is the invisible electrically charged plasma frequency. The energy that flows through and from the body is the steam frequency. The fluid components of the physical body — blood, lymph, bile, and the rest — is the water frequency. And the "solid" flesh and bones, that really aren't "solid," is the ice frequency. All of the components are the same energy showing up in different forms.

Now, here's one of the places where your reader qualification of open-mindedness comes in.

All of the energy that makes up the different forms emanates from the energy of the plasma state — the field. Since your personal field is a part of your body, and your field surrounds your entire body, nothing can get to your body from the outside without first going through your field. Consequently, EVERYTHING that reaches your sensory receptors — sights, sounds, tastes, . . . — is filtered through your field before it reaches your sensation receivers. Watch a gory, gratuitously violent movie or a radiant sunset, and light-spectrum energy passes through your field. Eat a well-cooked piece of steak or a ripe juicy apple, and the food along with its energy passes through your field. Touch a hot stove or caress your child, and the field around your hand "touches" before your physical hand does. Hear a scathing remark hurled in your direction by a co-worker or hear the synchronized beat of pleasing music, and the sound energy is filtered through your field.

This is another "Biggie Concept". Your field is affected by events around you before you are. Everything you perceive consciously has already passed through your field. Even sensory information that your conscious mind discards as irrelevant — sounds of traffic outside your window — invades, and is filtered through, your field.

WELLNESS PRINCIPLE: Your field knows more than you do

What does that have to do with health, happiness and success?

"Field infiltration" can affect your success and happiness, but it is a major influence on your health.

If your physical body isn't functioning at its best, the initial source of the problem is in your field — plasma. Symptoms of pain, distress, and disease show up and are felt in the interconnected lower-frequency areas of your body, but they start in the higher frequency area of your field. Field and body; matter and energy — they are inseparable.

Now you ask the logical question, "Do unpleasant symptoms mean that my field is faulty?"

No way!

Your field is perfect. It has always been perfect. And as long as you are alive it will continue to be perfect. But, if your body is exhausted in whole or in part, the vigor and vitality of your field is reduced. Field perfection remains; field "ooomph" may be reduced. Let's look at an analogy from the mechanistic view. Think of your field as a perfectly designed and crafted engine that powers you through life. A perfectly designed, perfectly crafted lawn mower engine can run perfectly. A perfectly designed and crafted Concord airplane engine can run perfectly. Both are perfect energy consuming and energy producing engines. But the two engines function at different levels of energy. The same holds true for your field. The design and craftsmanship is perfect whether the energy level is at lawn mower or Concord pitch. And the vitality of your field is interconnected with the vitality of your body. Don't expect a lawn mower field to take your body to supersonic health.

We said earlier that your personal field was created before your body developed. Your personal field is both an effect and a cause. It is an effect of the combination of your parents' fields, and it is the cause — the power source — of your development.

Your field originated at your conception as the "effect" of the combination of the fields of your mother and father. As the sperm with its field came into the field of the egg, a new field was created. The fields of egg and sperm united before the physical union was complete. More specifically, your field came into being *before* you did.

WELLNESS PRINCIPLE: Field first; physical later

As you develop throughout life, (development doesn't stop after puberty), your thoughts, emotions, and experiences affect your holographic field. Your field — the plasma part of you — affects your life. The holographic feature of the field is the source of continuity of life for the individual. The field may be damaged by internal and external events. But as long as it remains intact, life and hope remain.

As the power source of your body, your field is the "cause" of responses in your body. One of the most obvious responses of the body is illness. From colds to cancer, sick is sick. You may think you "got sick" last Thursday or in July or three years ago because that's when symptoms started showing up. However, in reality, we are "sick" before obvious symptoms reveal the problem. We "get sick" because our field is "damaged." And "damage" (interference) happens in the field before physiological responses bring about symptoms. The sequence of events (to our linear way of thinking) is: field damage (interference) → physiological response → physical symptoms.

> WELLNESS PRINCIPLE: Everything that happens in the physical body first occurred in the field

You may have wondered why I am emphasizing this energy/matter/field and quantum business. That last Wellness Principle is the crux of the whole thing. Everything that happens to you in your "solid" state happened to you first in your "plasma" state — your field. We can use the computer analogy here. Your body is the hardware; your energy field is the software, and your thoughts, perceptions, and feelings are the data base and commands. As long as you think of yourself strictly as hardware, you'll worry about trying to keep the dust and rust out of the workings. When you see yourself as an energy being that is made up of interchangeable "quantum stuff," you'll begin to understand that your body — "quantum stuff hardware" — will always respond perfectly the way it was designed. If you don't like the way your "hardware" is responding, it's because you are entering "quantum commands" (thoughts and feelings) that access only part of the information in your "quantum software" — your energy field component.

BODY OF ENERGY

We are energy beings. No doubt about it. Energy makes us, develops us, and runs us. Energy is such a biggie in our lives that, without realizing it, we gauge a person's health by the amount of energy he or she appears to have. "George doesn't look so good; he looks tired." Or, "Martha looks great; even at her age she still has all the energy in the world." Or, "Little Eric must be really sick; he isn't bouncing off the walls today." Or, "If I had half the energy of little Joe, I'd . . . ."

Comments such as these describe more than a person's "solid-state" physical condition; they describe the "plasma state" level of energy. We admire energetic people. We sympathize with or grieve for those whose level of energy is dwindling. Some of us even base our view of our self-worth by comparing our energy level with the level of others. What makes the difference in personal energy levels? The cause can't be time alone. If it were, everyone the same age would have the same amount of energy.

No. It's not just time. It's energy flow in and between body and field.

The physical body is energy of particular frequencies run by energy of particular frequencies. As long as energy flows freely between and through the your field and your physical body, your physical body has the vitality (life) to survive and repair itself. When energy flow in or between field and body is disrupted or blocked, vitality dwindles.

> WELLNESS PRINCIPLE: The energy level of your field dictates the energy level of your physical body

Your whole body has a constant measure of energy. The amount of energy allotted to you — the "volume" — is consistent. However, smooth transmission of that energy and the information (know-how) it carries isn't a given. Just because the energy is there, doesn't mean it is "circulating" freely. As we shall explore later in greater depth, disrupted or blocked energy flow within the body interferes with the information signals that direct the body. The result: pain, weakness, lack of vitality.

"Aha," you say, perceptive reader that you are. "My shoulder hurts because the energy flow to it is blocked."

Right — kind of.

The energy flow is indeed blocked. And that blockage can cause pain. But it's not that there's not enough energy running around the painful area. There's too much energy sitting in one place. It's blocked. Can't move along as it should.

> WELLNESS PRINCIPLE: Pain is an excess of energy in a localized area — energy congestion

In *The Body Electric: Electromagnetism and the Foundation of Life*, Becker writes about a "'current of injury' [that] is emitted from all wounds in animals."[62] In his book *Cross Currents*, Becker describes "current of injury" as "an electrical current found in any injured tissue."[63] This current of injury is illustrated graphically in cartoon drawings. How do artists represent the pain of a throbbing toe or head? By lines radiating from the afflicted area. They may be straight lines, star-struck lines, or wavy lines, or colorful auras. Whatever method is used, we "read" the lines as radiating pain — energy. My clinical experience shows that a "current of injury" is a current of interference and is associated with all areas of pain, not just wounds. As we all know, you don't need a gaping hole or a bone sticking out of your skin to have pain. Pain can afflict intact shoulders, knees, backs, stomachs, wrists, heads and any other part of the body.

In our pill-oriented society, we can usually subdue pain fairly easily. Flip on your TV at any time of day or night for a running commentary on the "new, improved" pain pills on the market. But subduing pain isn't the same as getting rid of the cause. The cause of pain is blocked energy flow — energy congestion.

Medical techniques and procedures that relieve pain *may* also remove energy congestion. However, for the most part, medical techniques simply mask the pain with drugs, analgesics or anesthetics, or change the priority of interference by introducing new threats (such as radiation or surgery) for the body to handle. Later, we'll talk more about interference and how it is prioritized.

> WELLNESS PRINCIPLE: Subduing pain usually doesn't uncork blocked energy

Energy and health are whole-body commodities. The deep, dark secret of the so-called health care industry is that medical applications are intended to work with individual parts. It specializes in servicing parts. Yet, as anyone who has undergone radiation therapy (bombardment with energy), chemotherapy (the politically correct term for controlled legal poisoning), or a surgical procedure (invasion of the body) knows, more than the target areas respond. The whole body is involved. Most alternative health care disciplines intentionally work with the whole body. And that whole body is energy.

For three centuries scientific thinking has focused on reducing the study of human anatomy and physiology to smaller and smaller segments or entities. However, as Davies points out, "Some problems (such as jigsaws) are only solved by putting them together — they are synthetic or 'holistic' in nature."[64] The objective of considering the body as cohesive energy in different states is to identify the source of the energy congestion behind a problem.

> WELLNESS PRINCIPLE: Energy isn't separate from the "whole" — it *is* the whole at a particular level

Holism and reductionism are not antagonistic — they are different levels of perception. The question asked determines the level of the answer. The question asked by reductionism is: "How can this 'defective' part be fixed?" The question asked by holism is: "What interference is causing parts of this unified body to function in a manner inappropriate to current conditions?" My experience has shown that the answer to the holism question is always related to energy flow — and I don't use the word "always" lightly. Energy communication inside or outside the body is *always* involved in physical "malfunction," pain, and disease.

Your body of energy functions through bioelectrochemical activity. It's a biosystem that runs by electrochemical processes. Mechanisms of internal communication include neurons, synapses, neurotransmitters, memory engrams, facilitator terminals, plus other identifiable and/or not-yet-discovered biological and physiological elements. The processes of energy communication between body and personal field have not yet been as neatly defined as have the internal processes. However, science is moving in that direction. Exploration into the quantum realm reveals features of matter that turn some concepts of Newtonian physics topsy-turvy. "Because human beings function through a physical body," writes Gerber, "the discovery by particle physicists that matter is a form of frozen energy has significant implications for science's ability to understand the subtle energetic intricacies of human physiology."[65] More and more scientists are coming to at least entertain the idea that energy in its various frequencies and amplitudes is an integral part of the condition of all life.

Many scientists have moved beyond entertaining the idea to accepting and working with this concept. Becker, Chopra, Gerber, Pert, and Hunt, referenced in this book, are but a few of this growing army. Richard Gerber, M.D., in the Preface of his book *Vibrational Medicine: New Choices for Healing Ourselves,* sets the stage for linking what he terms "our extended subtle anatomy" with our spiritual nature. According to Dr. Gerber: "That which we refer to as the spiritual domain is part of a series of higher dimensional energy systems which feed directly into the computer hardware we call the brain and body."[66] Gerber's attitude toward the spiritual domain is parallel with one of my most firmly held beliefs: We are not primarily physical beings; rather, we are primarily spiritual beings.

WELLNESS PRINCIPLE: We are spiritual beings undergo-
ing a physical experience

The mind can act quickly. The spirit can act with the speed of light. From our worldly view, the mind is the connecting point between the physical and the spiritual. The mind is energy that affects and is affected by the energy around it. This energy is generated primarily by thoughts and feelings. The mind is the connecting point between the physical and spiritual.

WELLNESS PRINCIPLE: The mind is the problem — and
the mind is the solution

FIELDS OF THOUGHT

Most of us are concerned with our physical or mental energy only when there isn't enough of either to do what we want to do. Physical energy that gives us the "oomph" to put in a day's work or weed the garden or run fifteen miles is tied closely to "mental energy." And mental energy is a function of thoughts and attitudes.

The mass-energy relationship was verified mathematically in 1905 when Albert Einstein published his special theory of relativity. This paper with its now famous footnote, $E = mc^2$, established that mass and energy are equivalent. The equation familiar to physicists and laymen alike demonstrates the relation between the mass, m, of a particle and what Ferris calls "its intrinsic energy, or energy of being, E."[67] Despite the waves this equation has made in the scientific community, most people give little thought to energy; that is, unless they suffer from an energy absence that keeps lights, production lines, lawn mowers, computers, and other power-driven equipment from working.

Although physical and mental energy are closely interwoven, they are not held firmly trussed by a Gordian knot. We can be physically tired yet mentally alert and enthusiastic. However, rare is the person who can sustain more than a moderate level of physical energy when plagued by a dearth of mental energy. But where does mental energy come from?

Mental energy comes from thoughts and attitudes. We can say that the level of mental energy is equivalent to the level of positive attitudes and positive thoughts. From this perspective, we can play with Einstein's equation and come up with our own equation: $E = at^2$. This equation describes the relationship between attitudes, a, thoughts, t, and energy, E. From our pseudo-equation, we can see that a person's energy level is their thoughts squared (t^2) times their attitudes. We can also see that the quality of thoughts has a direct bearing on physical energy. The power of thoughts is greater than just a fleeting effect on your physiology. The power of thoughts amounts to your thoughts multiplied by themselves. Thoughts affect body and mind. But that's not all. Thoughts affect your personal and corporate field energy.

Thoughts are not ordinarily included in the general compendium of energy-producers. Energy may come in many forms and from a variety of sources; but thoughts are not generally considered either form or source. Ferris describes the diversity of energy: "Like a clever actor who can assume many guises, energy appears in a variety of forms, and can shift from one role to another."[68]

WELLNESS PRINCIPLE: Thoughts are one of the many guises of energy

Thought energy affects internal bodily function, and thought energy affects the external field. Thoughts are energy. Matter is energy. Thoughts are "things."

The view of thoughts (energy) as material (mass) "things" may be difficult to accept if you are steeped in Newtonian concepts. However, researchers continue to uncover evidence that thoughts are truly things. Thoughts and emotions are more — much more — than private internal manifestations of consciousness. Thoughts are matter-producers. Neurobiologist and Nobel Laureate Dr. Roger Sperry observed: ". . . the causal potency of an idea, or an ideal, becomes just as real as that of a molecule, a cell, or a nerve impulse. Ideas cause ideas and help evolve new ideas. They interact with each other and with other mental forces in the same brain, in neighboring brains, and in distant, foreign brains. And they also interact with real consequence upon the external surroundings to produce *in toto* an explosive advance in evolution on this globe far beyond anything known before, including the emergence of the living cell."[69] That's mind-boggling! From a Nobel prize winner. Thoughts interact with each other!

It comes as no surprise that our own thoughts interact with each other. We do it all the time and call it association. You think about Aunt Martha and associate her with gardening which jerks your guilt chain with the thought that your grass needs cutting which reminds you that you need to get gasoline for your lawn mower which leads you to remember that the trusty gas can you have used for years has sprung a leak and needs to be replaced. That's logical; think of Aunt Martha to remind yourself to buy a new gas can. But Sperry tells us it's more than that. He says that thoughts interact at a distance. They affect external surroundings.

WELLNESS PRINCIPLE: Personal thoughts affect the think-
                       er's personal field; corporate
                       thoughts affect the world

Your field serves as both receiver and transmitter of energy information. Remember all of that "quantum stuff"? Quarks and leptons and electrons. They are thought of as particles that carry information. To illustrate this point, we'll concoct a little trip through fantasy land that might give you some word symbols on which to hang some mental images.

We can say that your personal plasma field is teeming with "quantum stuff." Teeny-tiny bits of point matter energy in constant motion. Your personal field receives the ubiquitous teeny-tiny point matter energy information of Universal Intelligence. Then, since your field is part of your body, that field information is available to the teeny-tiny point matter energy that is lumped together as your body. So now you have a homogenous brew of energy information coming from your field to your physical body. That brew is steeped in perfection. And as we shall see in the next chapter, the energy of your field is complete, random, and unorganized — chaotic even.

But energy communication is a two way street — the original "information highway."

Your personal field serves both as receiver and transmitter. It receives energy from your field, and it transmits energy to your field. We just saw that energy is received by your body. But your body also transmits energy: energy produced by your physical body, by your physical brain, and by your elusive mind. However, the energy information transmitted back to the field is a bit different than it was when it arrived. The body's teeny-tiny point matter energy information has been keeping some questionable company — the energy of thoughts, attitudes, prejudices, beliefs and memories. If these guys are principally negative, they're a bad lot. And you know what happens when teeny-tinies get mixed up with the wrong crowd — they're easily influenced and can pick up some unsavory characteristics. They "attack" the perfect field with negativity. But since the field is perfect and positive, it defends against the negativity by organizing itself. No more ease of movement in and out of the wilds and chaos of the field. The field is organized to restrict in and out traffic.

Your personal field is affected — for good or not-so-good — both by energy you generate and by energy of fields that intersect your field — the old Venn diagram syndrome. These intersecting fields may be parts of nature — other animate entities, flora, bodies of water, the earth itself, and so on. Or they may be fields that result from man-made contraptions — TVs, microwave ovens, power plants, high-tension wires, nuclear reactors, and the like. All of these fields affect your personal field.

WELLNESS PRINCIPLE: Even city-slickers live in fields

We live in holographic fields of energy. The whole of any system is represented in each minute part of its field. We know that matter is energy. The earth and everything on it exists in and produces measurable electromagnetic fields. Research in the realm of quantum theory reveals that chemical reactions spark barely perceptible electrical currents. Energy fields are influenced by each minute charge resulting from the interaction of atomic and subatomic particles outside and inside the body.

The process of thinking affects an individual's field which radiates and receives energy to influence interconnected fields. As LeDoux, et al, put it, "Stimuli associated with a highly charged emotional situation take on the affective qualities of that situation and can subsequently have a profound impact on mental life and behavior."[70] Or, as Chopra puts it: "In truth there is no such thing as a single messenger — each one is a strand in the body's web of intelligence. Touch one strand, and the whole web trembles."[71]

Thinking, emotions and other internal stimuli tweak strands of the intelligence web. Strand-tweaking energy is involved in conscious thinking and in subconscious responses to emotions.

> WELLNESS PRINCIPLE: Rational thinking and spontaneous
> emotions are energy in action

So what do these fields have to do with health?

Everything!

As I said before, everything that happens in the physical body has been filtered through the field.

We have established that thoughts and emotions have a profound effect on the way your body functions — your physiology. Your subconscious will activate physiological responses appropriate to your present emotions. It happens all the time. Your Green responds automatically to stimuli from your conscious mind. You blush when you're embarrassed. Your palms sweat when you're really nervous. Your heart pounds when you're frightened. These are all involuntary physiological responses. But not all responses are negative. Energy levels leap when you're jubilant. A petulant infant relaxes at the touch of his/her mother.

Physical responses to thoughts and feelings are manifest in words and actions ranging from whispered tender endearments to violent ghoulish mayhem. *Both internal and external responses affect the energy of your personal field.*

Becker puts a practical spin on this concept: "It may be a little disconcerting to know that we, and all other living things, are surrounded by a magnetic field extending out into space from our bodies, and that the fields from the brain reflect what is happening in the brain. The implications of this are enormous, . . ."[72]

Thoughts, activities, and nutrition that excite intense physiological and electromagnetic reactions can stimulate or interfere with the balanced flow of energy from the body's function-guiding energy field. My clinical research and experience indicate that of the three principle categories of energy-producers — thoughts, emotions, and physiological activity — strong emotions connected with thoughts are the most intense.

Strong emotions and feelings have the greatest effect not only on how you "feel," but on the degree of energy or interference projected into your surrounding field. Field energy is reciprocal — it affects the body and is affected by the body. Strong feelings and emotions put energy or interference into the field. The field is energized or de-energized by this input. The resulting level of energy — or interference — is reflected back to your body. Increased field energy is reflected in healthful, homeostatic equilibrium and vitality. Decreased field energy (interference) is reflected in homeostatic imbalance, pain, and symptoms or disease. Understanding the field effect of strong feelings and emotions gives new meaning of the often lightly used phrase "emotionally charged."

> WELLNESS PRINCIPLE: Emotions are physical as well as
> mental

RHYTHM AND BLUES

The energy that powers both your body and the universe is rhythmical. From plants to planets, turtles to tides, electrons to elephants, the universe and its creatures pirouette through the ages in rhythmic dances. Celestial bodies whirl in cosmic cadence. Earth spins on its axis providing an unbroken rhythm of days and nights, seasons and solstices. Flora and fauna adhere to the rhythmical cycle of life: birth/sprouting, survival, reproduction, and eventual assimilation into the earth. Generic Man, under the direction of his conscious mind and higher intellect plods, or prances headlong through rhythmic years in a cycle of infancy, adolescence, maturation, and death.

Each creature throughout the known world is sustained and refurbished by an internal cadence of renewal. Plants produce, lose, and replace cells that make up leaves, needles, fronds, or whatever, according to their own schedules. Animate creatures, including Generic Man, grow and renew themselves by producing, losing and replacing cells continuously. In Generic Man, skin is renewed monthly. Cells of the surface of the stomach lining that comes in contact with food are replaced every five minutes; the rest of the stomach takes longer — four days. Even bone that appears to be Rock of Gibraltar solid and stable sheds and replaces cells so that the skeleton is different now than it was three months ago. The body has amazing restorative powers. About six weeks is needed for most of the liver cells to be replaced. As Chopra puts it, "If you could see your body as it really is, you would never see it the same way twice. Ninety-eight percent of the atoms in your body were not there a year ago."[73] This replenishment process is particularly convenient if you happen to be short of particular types of cells — glandular cells, bone marrow cells, and subcutaneous tissue cells, among others. According to Guyton, ". . . seven-eighths of the liver can be removed surgically, and the cells of the remaining one-eighth will grow and divide until the liver mass returns almost to normal."[74]

But what is "normal"? What determines when enough is enough? Fortunately, the point at which the liver and other body parts stop growing or replacing themselves is controlled. If there were no control, your forty-year-old body would bear no resemblance to your twenty-year-old body. I believe this vital control mechanism is the field.

Fortunately for Generic Man, our replenishment parts bear a close resemblance to the original. Cellular replacement of each individual follows a personal DNA-designed pattern. As we grow and age, our outward appearance changes, but it changes relatively slowly. The cells may be new, but the patterns remain reasonably constant. That's why you and *most* of your former high school classmates recognize each other at your twenty-year class reunion.

Our cyclical patterns of change reflect a degree of order and coherence. Our bodies, our world and all that is in it march to synchronous rhythmic patterns of creation and re-creation. When those patterns are disturbed, the organism — the body or the body of community — is out of sync.

WELLNESS PRINCIPLE: When rhythm is lost, personal or
social turbulence breaks out

The universal field throbs with a ubiquitous Universal pulse that sets the rhythm not only for the cosmos but for all creatures great and small. The Universal Field pulse is magnetic, invisible, and perfect. On the individual, human level, it is the pulse that is our umbilical cord of energy connected to the Universal Intelligence that guides the development and maintenance of our bodies. As Leonard puts it in his fascinating little book, *The Silent Pulse,* "At the heart of each of us, whatever our imperfections, there exists a silent pulse of perfect rhythm, a complex of wave forms and resonances, which is absolutely individual and unique, and yet which connects us to everything in the universe."[75] The pulse referred to here is not the cardiovascular pulse that indicates heart rate. It's the pulse that begins in the newly created individual field when egg and sperm unite in the moment of conception. It is a pulse synchronized with the Universe, with the Universal Field, with Perfect Intelligence, with the Ultimate Power Source, with God — pick a name.

WELLNESS PRINCIPLE: Your body's pulses are an extension of the Universal Pulse

You acquire your particular component of the universal pulse before you acquire either a cardiovascular system or nervous system. And the pulse continues with you throughout your life. However, I have found through experience with thousands of patients, that the personal extension of the Universal pulse can get out of synch. In your personal pulse, loss of rhythm (when you're talking "scientific" it's called arrhythmia) is a symptom of interference in the connection between you and the larger field of Universal energy. Arrhythmia in the cardiovascular system (irregular or rapid heartbeat) is a symptom of interference in the physiological system. Interference in the physiological system may be caused primarily by diet and/or lifestyle. Arrhythmia in the universal pulse (asynchronous non-vascular pulses) is a symptom of interference or blockage in the creative energy field that *can* be due to inappropriate diet and lifestyle. However field interference is caused principally by negative thoughts and feelings. And negative feelings are founded on trying to improve upon perfection. Man is the only creature in the world that could botch up the Garden of Eden by trying to improve upon perfection with a "better idea."

WELLNESS PRINCIPLE: Perfection can't be enhanced by
thinking

When your personal component of the Universal pulse is synchronized with the master Universal pulse, your body is best able to handle current conditions. When your personal component of the Universal pulse is out of synch, it is out of rhythm. The beat is irregular.

Your body produces several types of pulses in addition to the cardiovascular pulse which we all know so well. Three separate pulses or "definite motions," in addition to the cardiac pulse, have been observed:

1. A pulsation which coincides with respiratory pressure changes associated with inhalation and exhalation.
2. A wave not related to either heart rate or respiration but one which constantly maintains its own cycle.
3. An undulating pulsation which has not been identified.[76]

Arterial pulses that coincide with your heart beat are easy to feel. Yet other rhythmic pulses that are neither heart-induced nor breathing-induced can be felt on the surface of the body. The pulses I'm referring to can be felt on areas of the body apart from the vicinity of major veins or arteries. They can even be felt through clothing. These pulses aren't as familiar to most people. They are the effects of resonating energy that flows throughout your body. And the beat is uniform in every body that is synchronized with the Universal Pulse. (Unfortunately, a lot of bodies aren't.)

WELLNESS PRINCIPLE: The same drummer beats for all

Most people can feel their energy pulse when they know what they are looking for. It's not an intense throbbing; it's a hint of rhythmicity. It's not rapid; it's regular. Try this pulse-detecting exercise.

Sit quietly, arms limp, palms facing upward. Relax. After about five or ten seconds you may feel a slight rhythmic sensation in your fingertips. It isn't your heart beating. It's the rhythm of your connection with the Universal pulse.

When I first encountered this pulse in a patient, I had no idea what it was. I thought it was his cardiac pulse. But there was a problem. I was feeling two arrhythmical pulses. That was really strange. But after a few minutes, the two pulses became one. They synchronized. And the fellow felt better. But I didn't. I had no explanation for what I had just observed.

Since then, I have learned that when pulses of the body are in rhythm — synchronized, the body is better able to heal itself. Pain is lessened or relieved; muscle tone, flexibility and circulation improve. Energy flows more freely through the body.

Maybe it's time for all of us to start applying energy pulse maintenance to our standard routines built around anatomy and physiology. Energy pulses are whole-body indicators. By taking the whole-body analysis approach, we can move from trying to subdue symptoms to finding the cause of the symptoms. As Gabriel Cousens, M.D., writes in the introduction of Gerber's *Vibrational Medicine*, ". . . we, as human organisms, are a series of interacting multidimensional subtle-energy systems, and . . . if these energy systems become imbalanced there may be resulting pathological symptoms which manifest on the physical/emotional/mental/spiritual planes."[77]

Energy resonates at a variety of frequencies (rhythms) and amplitudes (intensities). And do you recall the interference we've been mentioning? When the frequencies and amplitudes of the aforementioned "interacting multidimensional subtle-energy systems" are disturbed, that's "interference."

Gerber describes the effects of variations in vibratory rate on health: "Human beings may be similar to electrons in that their energetic subcomponents occupy different vibrational modes, which we might call health orbits and disease orbits. For the human being whose energetic systems are in an orbit of dis-ease, only subtle energy of the proper frequency will be accepted to shift the body into a new orbit or steady-state of health."[78] It is this "subtle energy" that can determine if your body is in a healing mode or a survival mode.

At this point your question may be, "How can I be sure the pulses of my body are in synch with the Universal Pulse?"

There are two things you can do to help keep your energy pulses in rhythm with the Universal Pulse. One is action, the other is thoughts.

First, the action part.

Your body benefits from regular physical exercise. That bit of wisdom wasn't just brought down from the mountain. And the exercise most beneficial to your body (other than exercising moderation in all things) is contralateral exercise. In essence, contralateral exercise is using opposite sides of the body in rhythm. Walking, running, and freestyle or backstroke swimming are the most obvious examples. The right leg works at the same time as the left arm. Then they switch — left leg, right arm. This working of opposites helps to keep the pulses of your body and field synchronized. I'll go into this more in the chapter on exercise.

Now the thoughts part.

Your conscious thoughts, attitudes, and choices determine the type of energy that you project into your field. The more positive, the better. For every experience you have in life, no matter how bad the experience is to you, recognize the lesson being "taught," and find some element of good in the experience. Realize that every experience — especially a negative experience that makes you "feel bad" — is a lesson for you to recognize and learn from. Identify something good in the experience. Finding the good may not make the experience any less painful; however, finding the good injects at least a modicum of positive energy into the situation. Any positive aspect of the lesson will help to neutralize some of the negative before the negative seriously interferes with your communication links with the field of Universal Intelligence.

No one who is alive, conscious, and cognizant can avoid unpleasantness in his or her life. Life's unpleasantness ranges from slight annoyance to intense feelings and a sense of extreme isolation. The trick is to not let that unpleasantness, no matter how severe, interfere with your connection to your life-support system — your field.

When you regularly incorporate these two exercises in your daily life — physical contralateral exercise, and recognizing the lesson and finding the good — you will go a long way toward keeping your energy pulse in tune with the Grand Pulse of the universe. The more in synch with the Universal Pulse you are, the better you can handle life's major and minor stresses.

WELLNESS PRINCIPLE: Rhythmic pulses chase the blues

CULTIVATING THE FIELD

Your personal field contains all of the information your body needs to function. Field information is a hodgepodge. Random. Complete.

Your body can't survive without its field. As long as your field is intact, your body can handle minor physical trauma and barely miss a beat. And with a vital, intact field, your body can survive major physical trauma that would appear to be life-ending. You may have known or read about someone who was involved in a terrible accident that appeared to be a sure killer, but the person walked away virtually unscathed. Or a child who survived a fall from a third-story window, or someone who survived being hit by lightning. People who survive severe physical trauma have healthy, intact fields.

On the other hand, there's the bumper-thumper type of accident that causes almost no damage to the car; but the driver dies. That person's field was badly damaged before the accident. It didn't take much additional trauma to "do in" the field completely.

Since our fields can be matters of life or death, perhaps we should take a look at how we can take care of them a little better.

What's the best way to improve the growth-potential of a crop field?

Cultivate and nurture it. Keep your field from getting "packed down," and expose it to only the most beneficial materials.

So it is with your personal field. You want your field to be as active as possible. And the active ingredient in this case is energy. The more active (chaotic) your field, the greater the supply of "whole" energy, the greater the selection of energy components available to your body.

WELLNESS PRINCIPLE: In your personal energy field, messy is good

Your field is White. The full spectrum of energy. White energy is complete. All frequencies and wavelengths are available. As Isaac Asimov wrote, ". . . white light introduces an uncertainty, since a whole sheaf of indices of refraction is produced by the various colors present in the light."[79] White contains the full spectrum of energy. Reduce the energy spectrum of all-encompassing White and you get colors of the rainbow. But energy is active. And since energy is active, the separations between the colors aren't clear-cut. They blend. The energy of white blends into colors from red to orange to yellow to green to blue to violet. Violet is the lowest level of color energy. We could say then that a "violet" field has considerably less information to choose from than a green field or white field.

So you can see, where energy is concerned, the only thing "pure" about white is it's completeness. We don't need limited "distilled" energy to run our bodies. We want the whole thing.

WELLNESS PRINCIPLE: Field energy should be full-spectrum, complete, white

A full-bodied field is full of complete energy. All information is available. But it's not in a neat, tidy package. You may want your life to be neat, tidy, and organized. However, if you are looking for health, happiness and success, your field needs to be disorganized. Field organization reduces information availability. Organization in the field doesn't eliminate any of the information, it reduces the availability of the information. This is an off-beat concept for our society where organizations — government, business, support groups, bridge clubs — proliferate like swamp mosquitos. Organization makes life easier. But where your field is concerned, it restricts accessibility to all of the information. Think of your field as a pot of thick vegetable soup. Lots of vegetables, no organization. Stick a ladle into the soup, the vegetables swirl with the currents and your ladle comes up with beans, carrots, okra, cabbage, turnips, and maybe even a bay leaf. Everything in the soup is available at any time.

But let's do a soup that's a little different. Suppose you built a pot of organized soup. Peas in one row, beans on another, okra, carrots, and all of the other goodies neatly arranged and segregated from each other. Now you put your ladle in the pot and come up with only some of the vegetables. The whole "spectrum" of vegetables is there, but you can get to only some of them. That's what happens when your field is organized. You don't want your peas and turnips and spices lined up like a battalion of tin soldiers in your soup.

That's all very descriptive, but it doesn't tell you anything about what you can do to keep your field from becoming organized.

Organization is the regimentation of chaos. The greatest organizers of fields are negative thoughts and feelings. They interfere with whole-energy transmission — keep you from getting to the spices in your soup. On the other hand, positive thoughts and feelings, for the most part, just "slide" into your personal field like the salt you add to your soup. Positive thoughts and feelings don't interfere with the "stirred up" condition of your field. Intense negative thoughts and feelings are like too many "starchy" ingredients in your soup. Negative thoughts gum up the works.

WELLNESS PRINCIPLE: Negative thoughts are "plaque"
that clogs your circulating energy
field

Negative thoughts are primary energy field cloggers. When you produce a continuous supply of negative thoughts, there is a constant bombardment of restrictive, organizing negative thought-energy to your field. Organization "damages" your field. When the field is damaged, the body is more vulnerable to trauma of any intensity and to all sorts of "attacks" — heart, germs, appendicitis, chronic disease, you-name-it. And it's self-inflicted.

WELLNESS PRINCIPLE: Pain and disease are symptoms of
a damaged field

No one — no matter how powerful or influential — can damage another person's field. Each individual is responsible for cultivating his or her own field. Field-therapy comes through positive thoughts, attitudes, and feelings. And you are the only one who has the power of control over your thoughts, attitudes, emotions or feelings.

The personal energy field is the key to health. The field that created and directs the body is perfect, personal, and private. No one else's thoughts can invade a personal field. No one else can cultivate your field, and no one else can "harvest" it. No one else can affect your field, make you sick, or make you healthy.

The field is receptive to positive energy. Positive energy is a great cultivator. Thankfulness, hope, and especially love are energy emotions created in the physical body. This energy is "recreated" in the field and, in turn, "recreated" in the body. Positive energy from positive attitudes can be thought of as "Type O" energy. "Love" is "Type O" energy — available to all and createable by all. It is the energy radiated by healthy, vibrant living systems that enhances the field. Positive energy is the "Green Thumb" of life — everything within its sphere of influence flourishes.

On the other hand, negative energy from attitudes such as despair, depression, guilt, self-hate, and isolation constrict both the body and the field. Thoughts that dwell on feelings of being tired go into the field and return as tired. With every thought of "I'm exhausted — tired," the field is reinforced with "exhausted" and "tired." However, controlled thoughts and feelings can reverse this trend. Silent, in-your-head declarations such as "I feel fantastic" communicate "fantastic" to the field no matter how tired you feel. When you are "tired" (which as we have seen is often mental rather than physical) the only way "fantastic" is going to get into your field is by intentionally putting it there with your thinking mind — by putting positive into the field.

WELLNESS PRINCIPLE: Positive out; Positive in

We're not talking about wishful thinking. Directing the conscious mind to generate thoughts such as "I feel fantastic" that may stretch the truth at the moment isn't merely wishful thinking. As far as your automatic Green subconscious is concerned, it's for real. The Green doesn't do reality checks on thoughts — it merely responds. It responds to signals from both your Red and your Yellow. When your Red conscious mind feeds your Yellow and Green a steady diet of positive mental repetitions, such as "I feel fantastic," topped with a liberal sprinkling of enthusiasm, your physiology-directing Green responds with physiology appropriate to "fantastic." The responses are to present-time stimuli rather than outdated stimuli. With repetition, the feeling and physiology of "fantastic" becomes just as habitual as were feelings of "tired." Better yet, with practice, you won't need to concentrate on ordering this special diet for health-promoting Green responses. The whole process takes advantage of the body's automatic response characteristic. Substituting positive thoughts for negative can be seen as "working through" an experience. You "work through" the feeling of "tired" to arrive at a feeling of "fantastic." You've cultivated your field with positive energy.

This principle for working through "tired" holds true for working through other negative feelings as well. We have seen how negative thoughts compounded by feelings such as guilt, anger, resentment, or anxiety maintained by memories of past negative experiences can affect current physiology in ways that are hazardous to your health. If an experience excites an intense emotion such as fear or anger, the whole package of the event — mental images and emotions — are stored together in Yellow memory. If the experience is extremely traumatic, the memories can influence physiology for weeks, months, or years. These memories can sustain defense physiology that eventually leads to exhaustion, symptoms, and disease.

What do memories have to do with your field?

Recall that everything that happens in your life is filtered through your field. Memories come from interpretations of sensory perceptions. The original sensations come from the outside but the memories are stored inside. And memories are indelible. Once entered, they stay. Memories that include negative feelings can damage your field. Negative memories can affect your feelings, physiology and field continuously. We call this "interference." Since health — good or ill — is a function of an individual's surrounding field, attempts to improve health or neutralize disease begin with removing interference to improve the vitality of the personal field.

POINTS OF INTEREST

1.   Matter is energy at different frequencies.

2.   Your body pulsates with energy.

3.   Thoughts are energy that affect other energy.

4.   Your thoughts affect your field.

5.   A chaotic field is a complete field.

6.   Negative thoughts and feelings can "organize" the
      energy of your field.

7.   Organized energy is incomplete.

8.   Positive thoughts and feelings allow field chaos to
      reign.

*There are children playing in the streets
who could solve some of my top problems in physics,
because they have modes of sensory perception
that I lost long ago.*
- J. Robert Oppenheimer

CHAPTER 7
Interference is Organized Chaos

LIVING IN CHAOS

Recall two of the basic premises of this book: (1) The body was designed to survive, not to be healthy or sick; and, (2) any stimulus that causes the body to alter the way it is presently functioning is a stress. Most of us consider our lives to be highly stressful — chaotic even.

Family stress, conflicting schedules, job stress, holidays, too much to do, relationship stress, and financial stress are just a few of the major areas of turbulence. Turbulence and chaos are stressful to most people. But stressful situations alone seldom lead to physical ills. It's when the stress, with or without the situation, goes on and on that we have problems. Thoughts, emotions, and memories fall into the "stress that goes on and on" category. These are the stresses that can do us in. Potent memories of personal upheavals and disorder can sustain physiological responses. And we know that there's nothing wrong with the responses — it's the duration of the stress stimuli that is inappropriate. Poor timing. Correct responses are stimulated at the wrong time. Poorly timed responses are the health hazard in our lives, not the stress and chaos.

Nonetheless, a daily diet of chaos and disorganization can be unpleasant. Most of us do everything we can to regulate and bring order to our lives. "I've got to get my life together," and "Some day I'll get organized" are recurring refrains in the search for order. Organization in our lives is often elusive. We plan our day. We plan our vacation. We plan our strategy for completing projects on time. And sometimes the plans work out. Sometimes, they don't. Either way, we tend to admire orderliness and organization in others — unless they're really good at it; we tend to resent that. We herald the super-organized in admiration, or we heckle them in envy.

Life, it seems, is much simpler, more predictable, and easier to handle when things are in a regular pattern — less confusion, less frustration, less chaos; greater stability, greater tranquility, more comfort. However, despite this quest for orderliness, nature — at the most minute levels discovered so far — appears to be anything but organized. It *appears* chaotic and unpredictable.

> WELLNESS PRINCIPLE: People strive for order; nature thrives on chaos

We've talked about "quantum stuff" — the itsy-bitsy point-like quarks and leptons that scientists have detected "scampering" around apparently helter-skelter. These seemingly unrestrained tiny points of charged energy/matter are attracted or repelled by any force that comes their way. It's these little guys that make up "bigger" structures, like neutrons, protons, and atoms. But the illusive tiny basic ingredients aren't alone in their rowdiness. A structure as large as a molecule can also be seen to move in a disorganized fashion. As Davies points out in *God and the New Physics*, ". . . even in equilibrium, the molecules of a gas do not remain inert, but are continually rushing about in a random sort of way. From time to time, purely by chance, a few molecules will find themselves in unwitting cooperation, and a tiny enclave of order will arise, fleetingly, amid an ocean of chaos."[80] Sounds like your basic job search process. You bounce around randomly (interview) until you "hit" something (are hired), find yourself in "unwitting cooperation" (you work, they pay), and a degree of order is restored in your life.

Our society has been thoroughly, though subtly, indoctrinated in attitudes of orderliness that follow orderly, logical Newtonian principles. "Every body continues in its state of rest, or of uniform motion in a right [straight] line, unless it is compelled to change that state by forces impressed upon it," wrote Newton in his *Principia Mathematica*. Newtonian logic includes such concepts as: With adequate information for the instant, the course of every atom can be predicted; when two particles of matter collide, each goes its separate way, yet the angles and velocities can be calculated; cause and effect determine every event. All events, according to Newtonian logic, are linear. "A" is followed by "B" that is followed by "C," and on and on. This is the pattern behind the oversimplified description of the earthquake sequence given in Chapter 3. Processes or patterns that move linearly and have a time and space sequence fit comfortably into our Red conscious-mind reasoning. We are conditioned to live in measurable 3-D — length, width, breadth. But when quantum theory comes along and tells us that time-and-energy and time-and-space are all the same, and that a microsecond and a million years are the same, that's not so comfortable. We use Newtonian principles to run our lives.

WELLNESS PRINCIPLE: There is no time in the Grand Plan

But "times they are a-changin'." Rigid concepts of cause and effect are called into question by advances in quantum theory. Davies again: "According to the basic principles of the quantum theory, nature is inherently unpredictable. . . . In the microworld, events occur that have no well-defined cause."[81] By interjecting the quantum factor and the theory that not every event has a cause, indeterminism rather than predictability becomes a constant. Linear time can be scrambled: "B" can come after "C" and before "A." Or they can all occur at the same time. However, we'll leave the time-space issue (which inevitably leads to a discussion of free will) to the physicists and philosophers. We'll limit our discussion of it to stating the premise that the Universal energy information of the present contains information of past and future. This energy is unpredictable, and, to Generic Man, unpredictability is chaotic.

The concept of events occurring without a well-defined — or suspected — cause runs counter to our Newtonian perceptions. But remember, we're talking about itsy-bitsy events here — subatomic size. It's this lack of well-defined cause that leaves us with an impression of chaos in the energy fields in which we live. And the concept of the chaotic nature of energy is one of many recurring themes in this book. It is behind the premise that living systems can utilize, or organize, the cumulative effect of the chaos of vast numbers of subatomic particles. Notice I said "the cumulative effect"; I'm not saying that living systems can organize the chaos of the universe.

WELLNESS PRINCIPLE: The field is chaotic; the body
is organized for survival

Living systems are bent on survival. They need only some of the information available from the complete inventory of chaotic energy. Living systems are selective. They take only the parts they need to survive. But in order to get those parts, all of the energy parts must be available — and the parts don't need to be neatly organized.

You may prefer order and stability, however, nature has an affinity for chaos. When energy systems interact, new chaotic patterns emerge. Living systems of energy can interact to bring about new living systems. The energy systems of a mother and father interact to bring about the totally new energy system of a child. Living systems bring a degree of order out of chaos. And this is a marvelous plan.

Since the focus of this book has been on the superlative organization capabilities of the body, the idea that the body thrives on field chaos may initially be startling. Keep in mind that the chaos is at the quantum level — itsy-bitsy.

The information the body gleans from the chaotic field is not of the 2+2 variety; it is a quantum wave. As Davies explains, ". . . the quantum wave is not like any other sort of wave anybody has ever encountered. It is not a wave of any substance or physical stuff, but a wave of knowledge or information. It is a wave that tells us what can be known about the atom, not a wave of the atom itself."[82] Field information, then, is about relationships — relationships of the uncountable number of subatomic particles that make the discrete particles a unit.

In the world of quantum theory, unpredictability (chaos) and the role of the observer are underlying concepts. However, chaos is in the eye of the beholder. Man (of both genders) must perceive and understand through the limitation of his/her five senses. How might Universal Intelligence view the macroscopic universe (with our little world and us in it) and the quantum world that we are just learning about? Depending on how you look at things, Universal Intelligence could be called "Supreme Being," "Creator," "Infinite Wisdom," "Perfection," "God." To avoid unwieldy phraseology, I'll refer to the Supreme Being as "God."

From God's vantage point, the view of chaos and the universe might be entirely different from our view. Now, obviously, I don't know what God's perception is, so I'll just do a little hypothesizing. Perhaps from God's view, the totality of the entire universe and the subatomic quantum world would be that of infinite simplicity — a complete pattern rather than individual pockets of randomness. From that perspective, each event, each bit of randomness that we consider chaotic — microscopic or macroscopic — is an integral part of coherency. Randomness to our limited vision and knowledge is chaotic. God may see randomness as perfect order for the whole — a celestial version of the forest and the trees syndrome. God knows that those trees *are* the forest. For us lesser beings, the chaotic arrangement of the trees gets in the way of our view of the whole picture.

> WELLNESS PRINCIPLE: Living systems work best when
> the whole spectrum of subatomic
> chaos is available

So back to earth for an everyday example of perspective, context, and chaos.

Consider a memo printed by a dot matrix printer. If you use a magnifying glass to examine the individual printed letters, you will see that the shapes appear to be made up of random dots. Individually the dots offer no information. They're just black spots on paper. However, collectively, those dots come together into letters of a particular type style. And these letters mean something to those who know the code. I believe this could be similar to God's view of the universe and all that's in it. Perhaps God "looks down" on the collective dots of energy that constitute the universe and "sees" a completely clear, coherent pattern. But, again, that is pure speculation for the sake of illustration. I certainly don't know what God "sees"; only God knows.

WELLNESS PRINCIPLE: Quantum energy is "dots"; energy
                      information is "the big picture"

We'll go off on a small side trip here to get another panoramic view of the organization-out-of-chaos principle.

In society, like-minded people get together to form a group. This group works toward a common goal — we call this group PTA, or Rotary, or XYZ Corp., or government, or a nation, or church. And as anyone who has been involved in forming a new organization knows, the initial activities of the members are hardly organized. They're pretty chaotic. The theoretical structure is there, but coherency isn't. One of the first orders of business is to set out the ground rules — organize.

Yet, even after the group or business is organized, we can see the chaos-of-the-whole phenomenon at work. You might walk into an office of XYZ Corporation where twenty or thirty people are busily at work. From your perspective, the atmosphere is chaotic. People rushing around. Phones ringing. Machines buzzing. Many seemingly unrelated activities going on in a confined area. Yet, from the perspective of the doers, the chaos you see is organization to them. They know what is going on. And they know the results they expect. Chaos and organization are in the perception of the observer.

We need organization in our individual and collective lives to keep peace and order when bunches of people are trying to live in a relatively small space like our world. The chaos and organization we're talking about is at the quantum level.

How does this super-organization fit in with health?

The body needs a degree of organization. But, as we saw in the last chapter with the vegetable soup analogy, field information doesn't need to be organized. When the field is chaotic, the body can select the type of energy, or information, it needs. It takes that info and does its own organizing at the cellular level. That's the job of DNA. Undistilled information is available in the chaotic field; the DNA of the body harvests the pertinent information and the RNA processes this information as needed.

In our physical bodies, the principal organizer is deoxyribonucleic acid, known to scientists and laymen alike as DNA. And as anyone who watches current events on TV knows, DNA has a reputation for being as individual-specific as fingerprints.

In people, DNA may be individual-specific enough to serve as evidence in court. But it's more than that. As I see it, in living systems — from plants to people — species-specific DNA serves two primary purposes: 1) as housing for genes, and 2) as a physical vehicle for communicating information. DNA communicates information of the chaotic subatomic world to the systems of the entity in which it functions. DNA, with its distinctive double-helix configuration, controls not only hereditary traits, like blue eyes or stocky stature passed to children from their foremothers and forefathers, but DNA also controls the reproduction and function of cells. In living systems, DNA-containing cells develop, differentiate, divide, function, and die. Some of these cells are replaced by new cells. According to Guyton, "Both strands of the DNA are replicated," and "two new DNA helixes are formed that are exact duplicates of each other. . . ."[83] Despite differences in cells that serve different functions in the body, the DNA is consistent. Your bone cells are different from your pancreas cells because they have different jobs to do; but all of your cells have the same DNA.

From the physical science point of view, DNA contains the "genetic code" that controls the formation of other substances in the cell. From the energy communication perspective, the primary function of DNA is to filter chaotic subatomic information from the field. In the filtering process, the essence of the chaotic subatomic information is extracted. That essence is the information that is necessary to develop and maintain the system — you — of which the DNA is a part. Using this information, DNA directs RNA (ribonucleic acid) to carry out the actual chemical functions. DNA is the master receiver that decodes chaotic energy information; RNA is the practical applicator. We can use the analogy of the military chain of command. The "Top Brass" (DNA) has access to all of the information. Select bits of pertinent information from the top filter down through the ranks of junior officers and non-commissioned officers in ever-increasing specificity for action. Finally, precise orders arrive at the private who carries out the orders. The private is the "doer," not the decision-maker. He or she doesn't have all of the information that went into making the decision. The only information the private receives is the "command" to act in a prescribed way.

WELLNESS PRINCIPLE: DNA decodes; RNA carries out

In the process of our journey, we have seen that every cell has its own field, that fields are chaotic, and that information abounds in the chaos. Information is in the chaotic energy that surrounds every individual. Chaotic energy is outside of a cell, outside a group of two, four, or 70 trillion cells. And information ("know how") is in the chaos within the molecules that make up all of those cells. There's no difference in the chaos that occurs in a field within a cell, in a field between cells, or in the combined field of cells throughout the body. In a healthy body, chaotic information is available to every DNA molecule. We all have a shot at the same information.

Until you read this book, the idea of chaos in a minute atom or molecule may have been totally foreign to you. After all, we've been exposed to the concept of atoms and molecules in school . We've seen diagrams of atoms joined together neatly and rigidly like Tinker Toys to form various elements. To bring the picture of the chaotic nature of these building blocks into sharper focus, imagine a hydrogen atom. Oh, I can hear it now. "What does a hydrogen atom look like?" Well, even though they're hard to capture and tame, take my word for it that a hydrogen atom has one proton (the nucleus) in the center with one electron revolving around it. Protons are "big" tiny bits; electrons are "tiny" tiny bits.

Now let's do a little creative thinking. Imagine that the nucleus of the hydrogen atom is as big as a baseball. The electron is the size of a golf ball. The golf ball spins around the baseball at one revolution per minute. Looking from the outside of the atom, the electron golf ball can be seen to be moving and revolving. In this view, the electron golf ball and its path are quite orderly and structured.

However, a nature-size hydrogen electron travels much faster than one revolution per minute. It travels at around 186,000 miles per second. It travels at a speed so fast that it is everywhere all the time. The electron is pure energy — an electron cloud. The electron's path and space is much more chaotic than the path and space of the hypothetical golf ball-size electron dawdling around the baseball-size nucleus at a leisurely one revolution per minute.

Now imagine that a second golf ball-size electron is right next to the huge baseball-plus-golf-ball hydrogen atom. This second electron is also revolving at one revolution per minute. Periodically, the two electron golf ball orbits cross. If the scene were magnified to large screen size the scene would still be quite orderly. However, zoom back down to normal electron size. Now there are all kinds of chaos around one electron and all kinds of chaos around the electron right next to it. A new kind of chaos has developed where the two electron clouds, or fields, overlap — even more chaos. More energy, more vitality.

This far-fetched example illustrates not only an overlapping of information but it also illustrates that the information of both fields, and all other fields they encounter, overlap instantaneously. When fields overlap or intersect, new information is available. The resulting effect is that the amount of information is greater than the sum of the two fields. And since all fields are connected either directly or indirectly in the Venn diagram mode, all fields contain all information all the time.

In our example, we went from one electron moving in a fashion we could "see," to a cloud of pure energy information that appears to our untutored eye to be chaotic. And in the chaos — the chaotic pattern — is all the information "know-how" since the beginning of creation.

WELLNESS PRINCIPLE: Energy chaos is complete "know how" information

Chaotic energy can be viewed as "creative energy," or "complete energy," or "total energy," or "collective energy." It's the information of your personal field. Your DNA receives chaotic field information, distills essential information from the chaotic completeness, and extracts the refined information and organizes it intracellularly. But for the cells of the body to do their best, the field information must be complete and completely chaotic. If the field is organized, or "sorted out," the energy frequency of the information the DNA receives is different from the frequency that would have been available from the unorganized chaotic state. The energy information available for the DNA to use lacks important ingredients. Information is available, but it lacks universality — totality.

WELLNESS PRINCIPLE: The information package from an organized field is "incomplete"

To illustrate the concept of chaotic totality on yet another, more familiar level, let's move from hypothetical electron golf-balls whizzing around a hypothetical nucleus baseball to something a little more down-to-earth — green beans. (How's that for a quantum lear?).

Green beans are a nutritious food. In taste, texture, color, and nutrition, they complement many other foods. They're good alkaline ash stuff. (We'll go into that later.) However, if you eat only green beans, your diet is incomplete. You can survive on nothing but green beans for quite a while, but, in the long-run, your body will suffer from lack of essential nutrients that are not available in an exclusively green bean diet. There is nothing "wrong" with green beans and there is nothing "wrong" with organized energy — as long as you don't rely on either as your sole "nutrient" for long periods. You need the complete spectrum of alkaline ash food energy so that your body can pick and choose what it needs at particular times. We might say you need a little alkaline ash chaotic completeness in your diet too. But that's a later chapter.

In health, the body thrives on chaos. Chaos is good. It's useful. "[T]he behavior of a chaotic system," write Ditto & Pecora in *Scientific American* (Aug. 1993, p. 78), "is a collection of many orderly behaviors, none of which dominates under ordinary circumstances. . . . If two nearly identical chaotic systems of the appropriate type are impelled, or driven, by the same signal, they will produce the same output, even though no one can say what that output might be." Keep in mind the gist of this concept: when the same stimulus drives nearly identical chaotic energy systems, you get the same result from both systems. The importance of this concept will become more evident when we get into the effects of "thought energy" on your energy fields and body.

Chaotic completeness is the raw material of development and life. When the chaos diminishes, old age begins. Researcher Valerie Hunt indicates that the younger the person, the more chaotic the field. As the field becomes more and more organized, the person begins to age. Reduced chaos, or organization, of a naturally chaotic field is one aspect of ageing. And over-organization can account for the often rapid physical deterioration of the newly retired.

When people retire, the amount of chaos in their lives is dramatically reduced. Of course, that's what most "working" people look for — a little less chaos, stress, and general mayhem. But with retirement, many people become even more set in their ways than they were before. They "know" how things should be and they have a tendency to become quite negative when the world around them is different from the way they think it should be: No one takes responsibility any more; there's no respect; no morality; things just aren't the way they used to be. As we become older in thought, we have a tendency to become "set in our ways." We have a firm "mind set." Which means that our thinking is not as flexible as it once was. Our thinking becomes more "fixed." Biased. Prejudiced. Inflexible. Rigid.

When our thinking becomes "rigid," we are not as open to new ideas and information ("know how"). And our field follows suit.

WELLNESS PRINCIPLE: A rigid "mind set" impedes thought flow; a rigid "field set" impedes energy flow

Workers face stimulating energy-enhancing situations that expose their minds to new thoughts and their fields to new quanta of chaos for the DNA to process and make coherent. Of course, "stimulating energy-enhancing situations" may not always be enjoyable. But they keep the mind active. Retirement, on the other hand, can be not only relaxing but also a retreat from positive and energizing stimulation. Too much relaxation, peace and quiet can rob us of vital chaotic energy creators. Perhaps we should uproot the retirement mindset and replace it with "reactivement."

WELLNESS PRINCIPLE: Chaos is the raw material of life

The concept that your field must be chaotic in order for your body to be healthy may seem to be stretching credulity a bit at first. First I tell you that you have an energy field that is part of you. Now I tell you that this energy field isn't even well-organized; it's all mixed up. However, neither your body nor your field is constrained by the limitations of your consciousness. Your super-charged energy field can — and needs to — handle the whole stew of chaotic energy. Your body needs all of the information available at all of the frequencies of a chaotic, complete field. Every cell of every kind of tissue needs energy of a particular frequency. Liver cells need a different energy frequency than pancreas cells or kidney cells or lung cells or any other organ cell. Consequently, if the only energy available to the body through your power-source field is "pancreas-specific," then the liver and every other organ is going to suffer.

Your system of energy information conversion works perfectly for survival until something interferes with the process. Interference in messages of your internal systems or in communication with your energy field causes "garbled" signals to run your body. "Garbled" in the field is fine; "garbled" in the body or between field and body is interference.

INTERFERENCE
We all know what interference is. It's something or someone that gets in the way. Breaks up the flow. An obstacle. In your body, interference keeps messages from getting through.

As far as reaching your personal goal of health, happiness, and success, internal interference can be a pain — literally and figuratively. In your body, interference keeps two or more systems from communicating clearly. The interference can be in internal communication between your "central intelligence" and your multiple systems, or the interference can be in communication between your energy field and the rest of your body. No matter whether the interference is in field or body, the problem lies in the energy flow. Messages throughout your body, including your field, are energy messages. No stick-on notes, no mail, no inter-organ memos. It's all energy.

We might say that in your body, interference in communication is like static. You hear static — or interference — on a radio that's not quite "tuned in" to the exact frequency of a particular station. The more out of tune the radio is with the frequency of the signal, the more garbled the messages, and the less information transmitted. If the tuning is completely off the mark, you receive complete static, another station, or nothing. Tune the radio exactly to an appropriate frequency, and the receiver mechanism of the radio resonates at the correct frequency and messages are communicated loud and clear.

The same principle holds for communicating with the body's energy field. When the many fields of the body resonate in harmony with Universal Intelligence, signals pass freely and clearly between internal systems and between body and field. When the body's resonance is "out of tune," internal messages and messages to and from the field are "garbled." If the resonance of the body and field are not in tune, "operating instructions" in the form of signals from the field to the body are interfered with. Prolonged interference means continuous garbled messages. But the body is going to respond to signals, garbled or not, for survival. The signals are inappropriate; the responses are not. If inappropriate or garbled signals continue, the same organs and systems must continue to respond. Eventually, the affected organs and systems will get tired. Enter pain, symptoms, and disease.

WELLNESS PRINCIPLE: Interference can be in body or
field

When we scan the vistas of health through a holistic lens, we can understand why uninterrupted energy transmission is vital. Previous chapters deal with the concept that energy fields are the foundation of life and health. We originate, develop, grow, and live in and through a sea of unseen energy. We know that energy flows through and from living bodies, that chemical reactions involve electrical activity, and that live brains produce electrical currents. Science has observed and documented electrical activity in and around the body. We have already discussed all of this. With these concepts in mind, you can see that since you are an energy body, the most important element of your health is the condition of your personal energy level. The vitality of your energy systems is the basic ingredient of health. And these energy systems are within your cells, your organs, your many nervous systems, your brain, and your extended field. If the energy among these various systems is "out of synch," or curbed, or *interfered* with in any way, *something* is going to happen. *Something* is not going to function up to its highest level of efficiency. The precise "something" that gets out of whack is the focal point of disease. So we label the out-of- whackness heart disease, or allergies, or Bell's palsy, or cancer, or whatever.

WELLNESS PRINCIPLE: Your field is the most basic ingredient of your health

We have said that your field develops before you do. Your field is not only an integral part of your body, it is the "core." Right — a core is usually thought of as the center. But a "core" is also "a basic, essential, or enduring part (as of an individual, a class, or an entity)," as *Webster's Ninth New Collegiate Dictionary* puts it. Your field is that basic, essential, enduring part. And since it is an integral part of your body, your field is involved in everything you do or think. Move and your field moves with you. Receive stimuli through your five senses, and those stimuli (sensations from light waves, sound waves, food, aromas, or objects you touch or that touch you) must pass through your field to get to your sensory organs. Your field is involved in every stimulus to which your body must respond which means that your field influences every response of your body. And there's more. Your field is involved in every thought you think and every memory stored for re-thinking.

We know that our conscious thought patterns grow from information we have received over the years through our five senses. Memories are stored thoughts, interpretations, and emotions concerning "external" events. And in the course of receiving information that goes into thoughts and memories, what route did the information take? Right! They came through your field. So the information behind your thoughts and memories went through your field before it landed in your brain.

So, we can say, everything that happens in or to your body has been filtered through your field. That is so important, I've said it before and I'm going to say it again.

WELLNESS PRINCIPLE: Every stimulus to or in your
body is filtered through
your field energy

By understanding this crucial principle of health, you can see why interference in any energy component of your body (which is all of your body) can affect your health, your attitudes, your happiness, your success, and anything else you care to mention.

Interference in your body is a reflection of interference in communication between your body and the field of Universal Intelligence that governs the body. Again, in Chopra's words: "Touch one strand, and the whole web trembles."[84] Interference affects the whole body. The effects of interference that we call pain may be felt in specific parts of the body, but the whole body is involved.

WELLNESS PRINCIPLE: You are energy personified

The body is energy — nothing but energy. Energy at a variety of frequencies. We've said before, the body and its personal field are the same energy at different frequencies. When the flow of this energy is obstructed, there is interference someplace in the system.

The biggest interference generators are thoughts and feelings.

We generate our own interference when the focus of any thought, action, or intention is contrary to God's positive, creative energy. We can tell when we're suffering from interference. Something doesn't feel right. It could be a physical not feeling right, or a mental not feeling right. This not feeling right is a product of interference.

Interference in the body originates with trauma, toxicity and/or thoughts. Trauma, toxicity and/or thoughts are by-products of choices you make in your conscious Red — choices that range from where you live to what you eat and how you exercise. But most interference is instigated and perpetuated by thoughts — specifically negative thoughts.

WELLNESS PRINCIPLE: Interference is a do-it-yourself
project

Negative thoughts and feelings are the greatest interference-producers of all. They keep active the most damaging stimuli to body and field. On the Newtonian/physical side, negative thoughts and feelings perpetuate survival physiology of Sensory Dominant Stress even when no physical threat is present. On the quantum/field side, negative thoughts and feelings project coherency, or organization, into the field. And you're not limited to one interference problem at a time. Since you live a complex life, you have the opportunity to interfere in a number of ways. But remember, your body's number one concern is survival. Your body will focus its attention, without thought, on the effects of interference that, at the time, are most threatening — the priority interference.

PRIORITY INTERFERENCE
Priority interference is the top-dog interference problem at any given time. Priority interference can be either in the body or in the field. The question is, which particular interference is the greatest threat to survival? Of all the threats to survival, which is of top priority?

A fanciful example illustrates the concept of priority interference. Picture poor old "Joe" limping along surveying the progress of the new addition to his building. Joe is in pain. He has an ingrown toenail on the big toe of his left foot. Although the pain of an ingrown toenail can be quite intense, the problem ordinarily is not immediately life-threatening.

Joe is constantly aware of pain. As he limps along favoring his left foot while looking up at the new roof line emerging against a backdrop of bright blue sky, with his right foot he steps on the business end of a nail that is sticking up through a board. The nail quickly goes through the sole of his shoe, his foot, and ends up with the point peeking through the top of his shoe. Instantly, the pain of the toenail evaporates as Joe realizes that he has done himself an injury. Alarm and pain signals converge in his brain. A nail in the foot accompanied by alarm and pain is interference of higher priority than an ingrown toenail.

Joe's entire body shifts to "alert" mode. His sympathetic nervous system takes charge of homeostasis. Infection-fighting white cells rush to the scene. All defense systems are primed for action. Joe and body are prepared to fight or defend against the invasion of a foreign object — an antagonist of top priority. The shift in priority is so dramatic that Joe even uses his sore left foot to steady the board on which his priority right foot is impaled. Joe's ingrown toenail just dropped farther down on his survival priority list.

The body attends first to the most life-threatening problem of the moment. However, the most life-threatening problem isn't always the most painful. And pain doesn't necessarily indicate the area of interference that is of highest priority. Undetected heart disease, for instance, is of higher priority than a painful ingrown toenail. In fact, let's add to Joe's problems. If he had a heart problem along with his ingrown toenail and puncture wound, his foot problems probably wouldn't heal as quickly as they would if he didn't have a heart problem. A faulty heart is a top priority survival problem. Consequently, most of Joe's physiological energies would be directed toward adapting to survive in a heart-crisis environment.

WELLNESS PRINCIPLE: Pain alone won't elevate an interference problem to top priority

The dichotomy between pain and priority accounts for pain that resists being cured. For example, you may be suffering from what appears to be a rather straight-forward knee pain. You figure you've been jogging too much, or too hard, or too often, or too something. Yet after several visits to your friendly chiropractor or other holistic health care specialist, your knee pain is little, if any, better. You notice, however, that your bouts of indigestion aren't as bad as they had been. Do you make a connection between the attempt to "cure" your knee pain and the improvement in your digestion? Only if you understand that your body takes care of first things first.

While you're concerned about your knee pain because it hurts, your body is concerned with disturbances in your digestive processes that are a greater threat to your survival. From your body's perspective, whatever had been causing your indigestion was more threatening to survival than the knee pain. Given the opportunity to repair itself at all, your body will repair the most survival-sensitive area first. So, after your indigestion problem is taken care of, your body's Perfect Survival Intelligence can address your knee problem — unless another interference problem that you may not be aware of rises to top priority.

WELLNESS PRINCIPLE: Survival is a matter of life or death; pain just hurts

No mere mortal can improve on your body's survival-oriented ability to identify priority interference. The Perfect Intelligence that directs your body knows all. It *knows* which organ or system should be attended to first. However, with our Red intelligence, we can inadvertently change the priority ranking of interference. Drugs, surgery, chemotherapy, spinal manipulation, acupuncture, and other remedial measures can change priority.

"Hold on," you protest. "A lot of that stuff really works."

And you're right!

All of the procedures that have withstood the test of time work. They work by changing symptom patterns. Surgery, drugs, massage therapy, and even aspirin that dulls a throbbing headache shift priorities. Your body adapts to the new circumstances because the "treatment" can be more threatening to survival than the symptom. As a result, the original symptom drops down on the priority list while one or more different symptoms replace it. With the original symptom(s) suppressed, you may feel better while your health deteriorates in another area.

WELLNESS PRINCIPLE: Changing priority isn't the same as getting at the cause

Age and life experiences can also affect priority status. A "reasonably healthy" man in his twenties is afflicted with fewer physical problems than a "reasonably healthy" man in his sixties. It's the old "he really looks good — for his age" situation. People who have physical problems at age sixty generally don't heal as quickly as they did at age twenty. At sixty, they've had more time to tax their body's survival processes. So at different ages, similar threats rank differently in priority. A physical trauma that is relatively minor at twenty may be the greatest threat to the body at sixty. An infected toe at age twenty may be the biggest interference threat when there's little else to compete for the healing energies of the body.

WELLNESS PRINCIPLE: Lots of years means lots of

opportunities to do lots of
things wrong

And conversely, as physical ills accumulate with age, a trauma that would have ranked high in priority in youth can be of lower priority in advanced years. The infected toe at age twenty when you haven't had as much time to abuse your body may be a top priority threat. But that toe can be pretty low on the priority list at age sixty if your body is also contending with hyperacidity, clogged arteries, high blood pressure, diabetes, or a bleeding ulcer. At any age, the body concentrates its energy on the most life-threatening problem — the infected toe, the heart, the pH of the blood, or whatever problem is the greatest threat to survival at the moment. But if you're older and have an assortment of serious ills, energy is dissipated to handle those that are most important. Healing takes longer the longer you live.

WELLNESS PRINCIPLE: "Young" high-priority threats can
be "old" low-priority threats

For the most part, a younger Generic Man has suffered fewer bumps, bashings, and bruises to body, ego, and self-esteem than his older counterpart. Less interference. As a result, at twenty-something the vibrancy of both body and field is higher than it is at forty-, fifty-, or sixty-something. With youth, the body has "higher octane" field vibrancy and resonance to work with. The mind hasn't been dampening the field with the interference of negativity for as long. The body's youthful resiliency has allowed the body to accommodate better to inappropriate choices in the six essentials areas of life. Consequently, injuries and interference of the moment are in priority. With age, healing comes with time and by accommodation. We accommodate at a lower level of health to the reduction of field energy brought on by interference from negativity in thought and life experiences.

Although each passing year brings with it greater numbers of stress opportunities that interfere with energy communication in the body and field, people of all ages encounter stress, trauma, and upheaval. Stress and trauma come in many forms. And symptom-causing interference can occur at different levels of internal communication. Most interference is caused by conscious processes, yet interference can occur at all levels of consciousness: (1) conscious, (2) subconscious, (3) non-conscious, and (4) information pathways to the energy field of Superconsciousness. Although interference from more than one level may be present, only one level will be in priority at a given time. And that "given time" can change second by second.

FEELINGS OF INTERFERENCE

Emotions, or feelings, are energy consumers and producers.

Mental energy — especially energy of intense negative thoughts and feelings — affects your energy field. And when you muddle your field, you muddle your body. Remember the tweaked strand that makes the whole web tremble? Although you may not be aware that a strand has been tweaked, it's your energy body that does the trembling. You tremble with bioelectrochemical responses, not with mysterious or "otherworldly" responses. Mysticism is not involved in health. We may not yet be able to precisely identify each component of the thought-energy-field relation-ship, but with continued research and investigation, all will eventually become clear in terms acceptable to even the most conservative minds.

Science has worked for a long time on understanding the intricate physical and chemical systems and reactions of physiological responses. Now, those-in-the-know are investigating how non-neural communication within the body works. Non-neural communication is communication other than that along nerve fibers. Non-neural communication occurs virtually instantaneously throughout the body. I believe that in the not-too-distant future, evidence will confirm that energy field communication is the primary non-neural communication system. When the body's internal and external fields communicate, the whole body receives the messages instantaneously.

WELLNESS PRINCIPLE: Whether you're excited, angry or
sad, your toes know

In the early 1980s, investigators found out something amazing about neuro-transmitter and neuro-peptide receptors. Neuro-transmitter and neuro-peptide receptors are part of the internal message transmission system. Messages sent along nerve fibers receive chemical "power boosts" along the way. The message signal won't make it very far along the nerve fiber without a little help from chemical power boosters, neuro-transmitters and neuro-peptides. Nerve fibers aren't unbroken "communi-cation lines." They appear to be segmented — a bit of "line" then a "break" and another bit of "line." The tiny space between the two nerve sections is called a synapse. With the help of chemical neuro-transmitters and neuro-peptides, message signals "jump" from one side of the synapse to the other. The message signal gets an electrochemical boost and speeds it on its way, under its own steam, to the next synapse. On the receiving side of the synapse are receptors (landing sites) for molecules of neuro-transmitters, such as epinephrine and dopamine, and neuro-peptides, such as ACTH and insulin.

Until not many years ago, the only known location of these receptor sites was the brain. Then receptors were discovered on white blood cells. White blood cells have free run of the body. They go where they are needed at any time. They travel throughout the body. So if receptor sites are on white blood cells, receptor sites aren't limited to the brain. The discovery that receptors are throughout the body shook the foundations of the scientifically accepted premise that messages are transmitted straight through the central nervous system only in direct lines along neurons. Instead, as Chopra puts it, "Monocytes can be thought of in effect as circulating neurons." Intelligence circulates freely "throughout the body's entire inner space."[85] That's a thought to twist your socks. Intelligence, or"know-how," that you didn't learn through your Red roams around your body willy-nilly. That's one of the ways that every cell in the body "knows" what is going on with every other cell in the body.

You can guess what that means. It's what we've been alluding to or saying directly for chapters. When survival time is stimulated by food, thoughts, accidents, insults, or memories of childhood miscues, your body is stressed; and it's stressed all over. When one cell — or one group of cells — must respond to a stress or threat, all cells must respond to that stress or threat. Since every little stress is broadcast throughout your body, imagine how many stress signals your body contends with microsecond by microsecond.

Stress is high on your body's attention priority list, and it's high on your list of concerns. Your frantic schedule can be a real stress-producer — but it is not the only one.

WELLNESS PRINCIPLE: Stress is more than being up-tight
and frustrated

Let's review our definition of stress: *Stress is any stimulus that brings about a change in current physiological activity.* By definition then, anything that stimulates a physiological response of any kind is a stress — eating, drinking, exercise, smoking, taking drugs (prescription, OTC, or illegal), and thinking. These are just a few common, everyday stressors. Of the endless smorgasbord of stress, what is the most constant and most intense? What stress producing activity goes on non-stop? It's not drinking or eating or smoking or running or missing a deadline. It's thinking. Most of your stress is brought about by thinking thoughts and memories.

But the body was designed to respond to stress for survival purposes. Stress is no big deal to the body. However, unremitting stress keeps the same survival physiology going and going and going. And what is the leading catalyst of unremitting stress? It's the hand-holding, response-generating, ever-present companion of thoughts — emotions! And what about those white blood cells that are cruising your body? Guess what they're doing. They're doing their Paul Revere bit. They're charging throughout your internal environment "shouting" the alarm "The Crises are coming! The Crises are coming!"

WELLNESS PRINCIPLE: Thoughts and memories keep cells "talking" to each other — communicating stress, stress, stress!

Emotions send non-neural messages throughout your body. They keep you up-tight. Emotions are the shadow of your soul.

This new way of looking at your body and health is coming together. This is what we have been getting at throughout this book — the long explanations about sympathetic and parasympathetic responses, and chaos in your field, and your central nervous system, and physiological responses, and your different levels of consciousness. Each points to the central theme that *your emotions and your health are tied together in a Gordian knot.*

WELLNESS PRINCIPLE: Your emotions are the key to your health!

But emotions are not solely negative. Positive emotions include (but are not limited to) joy, exhilaration, enthusiasm, excitement, delight, jubilation, and love. These and other positive emotions bring with them feelings of pleasure and well-being. They can incite laughter. They generate energy that enhances or "energizes" the body and doesn't interfere with your surrounding field. Positive feelings could be described as outgoing, expansive, light, and bright. When you're energized by positive emotions, colors appear brighter, sounds resonate more clearly, your senses are tuned with nature. Positive emotions open channels of communication between the body and the field. Strong *positive* emotions are quick pick-me-ups.

On the other hand, strong *negative* emotions, such as hate, guilt, fear, shame, anger, and loathing, bring on introverted, self-focused feelings, and defensive physiology that drains energy from both body and field. Negative feelings could be characterized as "turned inward," constrictive, heavy, depressing, and "dark." Negative feelings may briefly sharpen your senses for defense when you first detect a threat of an actual physical danger. However, if the threat is internally generated by feelings of worry, anger, frustration, helplessness, depression and other long-lasting internal "danger" signals, after a while, your senses may be dulled. And worst of all, strong, long-lasting negative feelings interfere with clear communication with the energy field. Negative feelings are your Number One interference producers.

WELLNESS PRINCIPLE: Long-term negative feelings have
a constrictive, depressive effect on
body and field energy

Where do emotional feelings come from? We generally consider that emotions always follow thought. But Neurobiologist Joseph LeDoux points out that emotions need not always be preceded by a specific thought. LeDoux investigated fear responses in laboratory rats that had had their visual cortexes removed. LeDoux presented findings in an article entitled "Indelibility of Subcortical Emotional Memories" published in the *Journal of Cognitive Neuroscience* (Summer 1989). In that article, he referred to the concept of "pre-cognitive emotion"; emotions that come before recognition or thinking. According to LeDoux, "the existence of subcortical emotional processing circuits argues that at least some aspects of emotional processing are organized in parallel to cortical functions and that affect can be processed independently of cortically-dependent higher cognitive processes, such as pattern recognition and categorization."[86] Or, to put it less academically, you don't have to consciously think about something for an emotional reaction to crop up. Non-neural communication? Could this be the origin of uneasy feelings you get about something, but you have no idea what the "something" is?

In an article about LeDoux's article written for the "Anchorage Daily News," Daniel Goleman describes pre-cognitive emotion as "a very raw form of sensory information . . . based on neural bits and pieces of sensory information, which have not yet been sorted out and integrated into a recognizable object."[87] We've all responded to perceptions of sights, sounds, and touch or movement before we had time to think about what we were responding to. The initial glimpse of a crooked stick that is mistaken for a snake, for example, or an exploding firecracker misinterpreted as a shot, or a fragment of conversation overheard and misinterpreted as threatening.

And what is our basis for misinterpreting a sensory perception?

Learned information stored in your Yellow non-conscious memory. Somewhere along your road of life you learned about snakes and gunshots. Along with the memory of factual information is the emotional memory attached to and associated with those subjects. When your senses pick up on a current snake or gunshot event, both the factual and feeling memories pop right up. You don't have to do a lot of deliberating; thoughts and feelings are glued together.

The concept of pre-cognitive emotions points to the importance of feelings. They are so important that we don't always need to consciously think about something for it to affect us. These feelings can be major motivators of physiological responses, like rapid heart rate, high blood pressure, or spastic muscles. Since survival is the body's primary goal, and since feelings can pop up without benefit of conscious thought, feelings can be seen as important survival mechanisms. That's the good news.

The not-so-good news is that feelings can keep survival responses going when they really aren't needed. And no matter how well you suppress them, suppressed feelings have a negative, organizing effect on your field. That's interference. Remember, it's your body that needs to be organized, not your field.

> WELLNESS PRINCIPLE: Body organization equals health;
> field organization equals disease

Alarm and defensiveness are important when the "snake" is first noticed or the "gun shot" heard. Yet as with anything that can be used, survival mechanisms can be abused. Long-term alarm and defensiveness are not appropriate responses to perceived threats such as misinterpretation of fragments of overheard conversation.

Continuous subtle negative feelings, such as depression, worry, guilt, self-pity, resentment, and frustration, reduce the vibrancy of your surrounding field which, in turn, interferes with the flow of health-enhancing field information.

Feelings and their accompanying thoughts can be major factors in interference in the function of the body's natural healing potential. Feelings and thoughts are energy-producers that can affect the energy field surrounding the body. Positive thoughts, like positive feelings, keep energy information pathways clear between field and body. The energy of the field is positive, so positive energy of positive thoughts and feelings fits right in -- it doesn't stifle the chaos with organization. In turn, health promoting energy information is reflected back to the body. But, as we have seen, negative thoughts serve as resistors to the smooth flow of field-body energy information — they "censor" field information. When you hear someone describe their disposition or feelings as depressed, low, weighed-down, burdened, dragging, powerless, they are describing the state of their field as much as the state of their mind.

POINTS OF INTEREST

1.   At the subatomic level, all is chaos.

2,   Living systems use chaotic energy.

3.   Chaotic energy is complete energy.

4.   You and your body are energy personified.

5.   Interference restricts the availability of complete
      energy.

6.   Interference can occur in body or field communication.

7.   Your body always attends to the greatest threat
      interference first.

8.   Negative feelings interfere with energy flow.

Sturm und drang.
Storm and stress.
— Friedrich Maximilian von Klinger (title of play)

CHAPTER 8
Feelings and Emotions

POSITIVE AND NEGATIVE FEELINGS

We have developed some strange customs in our attempt to live together in relative harmony. Customs like the virtually meaningless greeting, "How ya' doin'?" The usual answer is something along the lines of "Fine," or "Okay." Verbal exchanges such as this, for the most part, are the civilized equivalent of primordial grunts that acknowledge each other's presence as non-threatening. Neither question nor answer has anything to do with your health or how you feel. So it's a good idea to take stock every once in a while of how you *really* feel. I'm not talking about an inventory of physical aches and pains, but of a review of how you feel emotionally — your inner feelings and attitudes. How you feel emotionally determines, in large part, how you feel physically. So here's a pop-quiz.

Below are two lists. The first list is words that represent positive feelings, the second list represents negative feelings. Any of the feelings these words represent can influence your physiological function.

To get a rough idea of whether your body is functioning under predominantly positive or negative influence, assign a numerical value according the scale below to indicate the intensity and/or frequency you experience for each of the feelings listed. Total both lists.

0 = Rarely, if ever
1 = Occasionally / not intensely
2 = Often / intensely
3 = Constantly / extremely intensely

POSITIVE FEELINGS

How often or intensely do I feel . . .

_____ Creative	_____ Love	_____ Joy
_____ Peace	_____ Inspired	_____ Serene
_____ Compassion	_____ Hope	_____ Enthusiastic
_____ Sincere	_____ Contented	_____ Pleasure
_____ Tranquil	_____ Cheerful	_____ Elated
_____ Trusting	_____ Stable	_____ Secure
_____ Confident	_____ Caring	_____ Affection
_____ Excited	_____ Sentimental	_____ Spiritual
_____ Patient	_____ Exuberant	_____ Happy
_____ Calm	_____ Satisfied	_____ Accepting
_____ Fulfilled	_____ Blessed	_____ Enjoyment
_____ Warmth	_____ Expectant	_____ Delight
_____ Composed	_____ Imaginative	_____ Faithful
_____ Optimistic	_____ Sensitive	_____ Friendly
_____ Generous	_____ Productive	_____ Amused
_____ Self-assured	_____ Vigorous	_____ Jovial
_____ Attractive	_____ Energetic	_____ Pleased
	_____ Gracious	

Total Positive Feelings   _____

* * * * * * * * * * * * * *

NEGATIVE FEELINGS

How often or intensely do I feel . . .

_____ Depressed	_____ Indecisive	_____ Lonely
_____ Angry	_____ Selfish	_____ Embarrassed
_____ Regretful	_____ Guilty	_____ Inadequate
_____ Bored	_____ Self-pity	_____ Hate
_____ Apathetic	_____ Superior	_____ Despair
_____ Greedy	_____ Compulsive	_____ Spiteful
_____ Rejected	_____ Grief	_____ Self-hate
_____ Jealous	_____ Callous	_____ Worried
_____ Persecuted	_____ Irritated	_____ Frustrated
_____ Envious	_____ Unhappy	_____ Anxious
_____ Self-doubt	_____ Rage	_____ Bitter
_____ Abused	_____ Isolated	_____ Fearful
_____ Hopeless	_____ Scornful	_____ Apprehensive
_____ Lustful	_____ Insensitive	_____ Hostile
_____ Vicious	_____ Powerless	_____ Dread
_____ Unworthy	_____ Sad	_____ Shame
_____ Worthless	_____ Abandoned	_____ Useless
	_____ Out of control	

Total Negative Feelings   _____

Compare your "Totals" of the "Positive" and "Negative" groups. This will give you an idea of whether your attitudes and feelings color your inner personal world with "positive" or "negative" messages. The general "color" and "tone" of your inner attitudes and feelings determine whether or not your body is accommodating to hyperstress.

If your "Positive" total is in the neighborhood of twice that of your "Negative" total, you are exceptional. Unless you are really challenging your body with inappropriate choices in the other essential areas of life — food, drink, breathing, rest, and exercise — you are providing your body the best internal environment possible. Why are you reading this book?

If you lean to the positive side in your attitudes and feelings — your "Positive" total outweighs your "Negative" total — you are headed in the right direction, and reading this book can help you to tilt the scale even more to the positive side. To make sure you allow your body to function at its best, keep yourself "up" and work on reducing the negative numbers. The fewer negatives your body has to deal with, the less interference is projected into your field, the better your body can function, and the more you can look forward to a bright, healthful, satisfying future.

If your "Negative" total is equal to or greater than your "Positive" total, your body is working overtime to handle internally generated stress from your emotions and attitudes. Negative feelings and attitudes can be long-lasting. In time, they can be the cause of acute symptoms. These are the feelings that tell your body that you are being threatened and you had better stay ready to defend yourself. Depending upon which emotion is dominant, either your sympathetic or parasympathetic system is working overtime. If negative feelings and attitudes continue for months and years, you can expect some organs or systems of your body to become exhausted and eventually "break down." It's time for you to start working on a major attitude adjustment.

If your "Negative" total score is twice (or greater) that of your "Positive" total, your feelings and attitudes are putting a real strain on your physiology. You may be plagued by persistent feelings of anxiety, worry, or fear. All of these emotions keep your body defensive and tense although you aren't in actual physical danger — Sensory Dominant Stress. Symptoms of fatigue and exhaustion may soon be continuous, if they aren't already.

Recognizing negative feelings is the first step in getting them under control. You may be encouraged to know that you don't have to continue to live in a world of negative attitudes. You can choose how you respond to situations that affect your life. You may not like some of the events in your life, but you have more control than you may have realized over how you feel about your present and past experiences, yourself and others.

FEELING YOUR WAY THROUGH LIFE

We all know what "feelings" are. Up or down. Buoyant or blue. Delighted or depressed. Many levels of feelings and moods color our outlook and activities. Feelings and emotions are non-specific physical and mental sensations that we may not be able to describe but we know are there.

On a "good day" you feel good all over. Energy level high. Outlook bright. The world appears cleaner and move vivid. You have a spring in your step, a smile on your face, and a good word for others. We can say that positive feelings energize our complete being — physical and mental.

On the other hand, feelings of "being down" that range from having a bad day or "the blues" to more severe types of depression sap physical and mental energy. No matter how brightly the sun shines on the rest of the world, when you're "down," your world is dark and dreary. Everyday activities like eating or combing your hair become chores. Nothing is easy. Nothing is clear. Nothing is satisfying. There's not enough energy to do anything, much less do it well.

Feelings and emotions are generally seen as synonymous. Under the listing for "feelings" in the index of *The Oxford Companion to the Mind* is the reference to "emotions" and "sensations." Emotions, the *Companion to the Mind* explains, involve "a general state of visceral arousal" and "different emotional experiences arise out of the same visceral background."[88] We might say that feelings are the physical sensations attached to emotions.

Since we see ourselves predominantly as physical beings, most of us are more comfortable talking about how we feel physically — good, tired, achy — rather than about how we feel emotionally — happy, sad, grief-stricken, disconsolate. But emotions have a physiological base as well as a mental base. Emotions are products of the limbic system which Guyton describes as ". . . the entire basal system of the brain that mainly controls the person's emotional behavior and drive."[89] Some of the physical structures of the limbic system are the hippocampal formation, the hypothalamus, and the amygdala. The hippocampus plays a role in long-term memory; the hypothalamus is the guardian of our autonomic functions; and the amygdala is involved with many of the same effects as the hypothalamus plus pre-packaged movements such as chewing, swallowing, bending the body, and raising the head. The limbic system is also involved with appetite, sexual behavior, and defense behavior patterns that have evolved over the centuries. It is, according to Edelman, a "value system" that "sets adjustments to evolutionary selected physiological patterns."[90] All of these brain structures are part of your green. They are subconscious. We see, we hear, we touch, taste or smell and interpret sensations in the Red. The signals are compared with associated information in your Yellow, and our Green responds according to pre-set patterns — we become aware of a feeling.

> WELLNESS PRINCIPLE: A thought plus a physiological reaction equals a feeling

But recall the pre-cognitive emotions LeDoux identified. They are emotions that crop up before you have a chance to really analyze a situation — such as jumping back from what looks like a "snake" but is only a stick. Pre-cognitive emotions are great for instantaneous responses that keep us out of harm's way. One of the strategies of survival is a quick, unpremeditated response so we can get out of the way of trouble before we "get got." We respond — for survival's sake — to sensory stimuli that the cortex hasn't had time to process.

As professor of neural science and psychology at New York University, Dr. Joseph LeDoux studied the process of "emotional memory," particularly fear. LeDoux points out that there are two routes for emotional learning: one cortical and one subcortical. Cortical learning happens in your "Red"; subcortical emotional learning is a "Yellow" function. Once you impress an emotional memory with sufficient intensity, you don't need to practice the response, it's firmly established.

"Emotional and declarative memories are stored and retrieved in parallel," LeDoux writes, "and their activities are joined seamlessly in our conscious experience."[91] He goes on to explain that although we are not aware of the emotional memory, we are aware of the consequences of that memory in the way we behave and the way we feel. We are aware that we jump and are frightened.

Subcortical response pathways are shorter and more direct than cortical pathways. "Animals and humans," writes LeDoux, "need a quick and-dirty reaction mechanism. The thalamus activates the amygdala at about the same time as it activates the cortex. The arrangement may enable emotional responses to begin in the amygdala before we completely recognize what it is we are reacting to or what we are feeling"[92] But the "quick and dirty" process isn't supposed to be used all the time. It's like the National Guard: great to have on hand for emergencies.

Instant alarm and defensiveness are vital responses when there is a good possibility you are in danger. In an emergency, your first order of business is to respond, not analyze. That comes later. Response-before-thought in some situations is a handy-dandy, built-in survival mechanism. However, as with anything that can be used, survival mechanisms can be abused. Long-term defensive response is body abuse.

Long-term and short-term emotions and feelings come in varying degrees of intensity. The effect particular emotions or feelings have on your life and physiology is directly proportional to the strength, or intensity, of the emotions. And how is "intensity" manifest? As variations in energy flow. Emotions are internal energy fluctuations prompted by mental interpretations of sensory perceptions and thoughts. Very strong emotions, such as those experienced by victims of natural catastrophes, wars, violent crimes, irreparable loss, or other psychic shocks, stimulate strong internal energy activity and often change the life of the person involved. Minor emotional disturbances, the ho-hum variety of so-you-missed-your-favorite-TV-show-today, make few ripples on the vast flowing ocean of energy feelings. The degree of emotional intensity determines the degree of energy disturbance in body and field.

> WELLNESS PRINCIPLE: Emotions are movement of en-
> ergy through the body

Strong emotions and feelings are the cement of memory. Boring is not memorable. Excitement is. Feelings attached to a major emotionally-packed incident weld the physiological response pattern to the memory of the incident.

It's really important for that message to come through loud and clear. When something unpleasant or terrible happens to you, you remember the details in your conscious Red, and *you remember the response physiology in your non-conscious Yellow*. And your Yellow dominates Green function. Signals from your Yellow spark physiological responses in your Green. Up-tight and defensive is a physiological response. It's the way you *feel* about the tongue-lashing your boss inflicted on you that sparks a physiological response, not the "chewing-out" itself. If you are afraid that your boss' current antagonism means the end of your much-needed job, you'll have pretty intense feelings about the situation. However, if you have already made arrangements for a new and better job, the confrontation probably won't be particularly upsetting.

Negative or positive feelings, it doesn't matter — physiology changes. "Positive" feelings, such as confidence, pleasure, satisfaction, serenity, and the like, do two things. First, positive feelings resonate with the perfect energy of the power source that created and sustains you. Positive feelings don't inhibit access to the complete energy of your field or solidify its "field-set." Instead, positive feelings keep communication lines open between you and your field's great energy reservoir to "fuel" mind, body and spirit and keep you rolling along energetically. Second, positive feelings permit internal energy to flow more freely. Remember, energy flows through your body as well as around it. Smooth, uninterrupted internal energy flow allows your body to function in perfect synchronization — rhythmically, free of tempo-disrupting interference.

Positive-radiating feelings are less likely than negative feelings to interfere with healthful physiology. Positive feelings feed signals to your Green subconscious that all is right with the world and there's no need for defense. Positive feelings help to keep open vital lines of communication with your invisible, personal field. Positive feelings don't cause distress. Outgoing feelings such as joy, compassion, peace, love, creativity, and serenity usually aren't the sort that prompt physiological responses that lead to discomfort, pain, and disease. Positive feelings grow out of positive thoughts and attitudes. If you haven't formed the habit of cultivating positive thoughts and attitudes from which positive feelings grow, now is a good time to start. We'll go into the "how's" a little later.

WELLNESS PRINCIPLE: Positive feelings are warm-fuzzys;
negative feelings are a big-bang

Negative feelings are usually much more intense than positive feelings. Negative feelings throw a kink in your link with your power-generating field. And negative feelings can interfere with health-promoting smooth, well-regulated internal physiological function. Feelings such as shame, irritation, jealousy, frustration, guilt, resentment, loneliness, inadequacy, greed, despair, fear, and hate, keep your body on alert and act as resistors to creative energy. They are constrictive. Directed inward. They send signals to your Green to prepare for combat. Constant negative feelings keep you constantly defensive in attitude and physiology. Intense negative emotions and feelings introduce energy-depleting organization into your personal field. And now that you know the importance of your field, you certainly don't want that! Your field is at its greatest energy potential when total, complete, random energy reigns. As your field goes, so goes your tangible body.

WELLNESS PRINCIPLE: Your body is a reflection of your
personal field

Since your field is the template for the rest of your body, and your feelings can affect your field, your best strategy for health, happiness, and success is to make sure you feel your way through life positively.

ZAPPED BY FEELINGS

Major trauma and emotional upsets can set up a chain reaction to disease. Folklore and intuition have held this view for centuries. But for the I-want-more-proof contingent, a German doctor who had a personal experience of cancer has provided evidence that the turmoil of negative feelings can be, and often is, the root cause of severe physical problems.

In October 1981, Dr. Ryke Geerd Hamer summarized his research with the statement, "I searched for cancer in the cell and I have found it in the form of a wrong coding in the brain." Dr. Hamer presented his fly-in-the-face-of-convention findings at the Tubingen University in what was then West Germany. He reported finding evidence of a link between psychic (mental) trauma and disease. His information came from studies he had conducted involving 15,000 cases. That's a lot of cases — and behind cases are real people.

Dr. Hamer found that behind each real person's developed case of cancer was "a strong stimulus, a brutal psychic trauma, which hits the patient as a major event in his life, an acute dramatic conflict, lived in a complete psychic isolation." The primary constant Dr. Hamer found among these cases was that the cancer started with "*an extremely brutal shock*, a dramatic and acute conflict, *experienced in loneliness and sensed by the patient as the most serious he has ever known.*" (Italics are my emphasis.)

Feelings! Intense feelings! The "extremely brutal shock" isn't being hit with a few megavolts of electricity. It's a catastrophic event that rattles the underpinnings of the real person's security, stability, or sense of control. It is a cataclysmic emotional upheaval that often involves a major loss — the death of a child, spouse, parent, or other loved one; loss of a business or job; divorce; a devastating fire that destroys home and possessions. The particular forms of "brutal shocks" are legion. Just about everyone experiences a brutal shock sometime in his or her life. And when that brutal shock is experienced in an atmosphere the person considers "complete psychic isolation," the physiological effects are magnified. Now that's heavy!

Although Dr. Hamer's investigations dealt with cancer, my experience shows that more than cancer is involved. The names of other chronic degenerative diseases can be substituted for "cancer": arthritis, osteoporosis, diabetes, chronic fatigue, Epstein-Barr, Candida, the "alphabet diseases" such as ALS, MS, MD, or TB, or any long-lasting, debilitating disease. An extremely brutal shock experienced in complete psychic isolation can be the catalyst for any disease. Only the form the disease takes is variable. The particular form depends on the individual's particular lifestyle and genetic makeup.

But what is "psychic isolation"?

Psychic isolation has nothing to do with being set apart physically from other people as the sole inhabitant of an deserted island or a prisoner in solitary confinement. Psychic isolation can occur in the midst of a loving family or packed city. Psychic isolation is a state of mind and emotion. It is *perceived* rather than *physical* isolation. A state of severe loneliness in the midst of multitudes. Separateness. Exclusion. Without the support of others. The mental equivalent of deprivation in a land of plenty. Psychic isolation is possible while living and working in the midst of dozens of other people you know and/or love.

> WELLNESS PRINCIPLE: Psychic isolation is the active ingredient that turns a serious trauma into serious disease

Very likely, you have "known" intellectually or intuitively that your feelings are linked with your health. However, you may not have been aware that feelings, or emotions, are an integral part of the *cause* of serious or deadly diseases. We make a "phase transition" when we move from accepting the existence of "stress headaches" to acknowledging that "a brutal psychic trauma . . . experienced in loneliness" lays the groundwork for chronic or terminal illnesses. This is a logical step. If periodic stress brings on periodic headaches, logic tells us that long-term stress can bring on long-term symptoms. Brutal physical trauma from accidents or assaults may leave scars on your body; however, the incident is over quickly and your body can repair and rebuild tissue and bone in a few weeks or months. Psychic trauma experienced in loneliness is persistent; it leaves no visible scars, but it can "cripple" your physiology and your field.

What brings on psychic trauma?

Feelings.

Feelings connected with people!

Feelings, including psychic trauma, are "person" directed. I have never encountered a person who "made themselves sick" over a "thing." Earlier I cited the loss of home and possessions as a potential psychic trauma. It is indeed. But the trauma isn't the loss of pictures, furniture and clothing. It's the personal loss: the feeling of personal violation, the destruction of the symbols of one's life and existence that the pictures, furniture, clothing and the rest of the material objects represent. It is "My" loss. The grief is for the loss of "roots" and the continuity of life — not the things themselves.

Our feelings aren't hurt by things. Things aren't a threat. We don't have recurring nightmares about the microwave dying or deserting us. We don't feel victimized by a leaky hot water heater. When we become upset with "things," our upsetness is directed toward some inconvenience we're experiencing, but the emotion is usually short-lived. We might give a flat tire a lusty kick. In the extreme, we might really whirl out of control and shoot the TV. But such physical outbursts are expressions of frustration, not physic trauma.

WELLNESS PRINCIPLE: "Things" can't hurt your feelings;
people can

Our world is full of people. (How's that for stating the obvious.) A lifetime can be described as an accumulation of feelings and memories about people and events. We remember events that caught our attention and/or stirred our emotions, and we remember people who did likewise: the happy times of holidays and an unexpected gift or visit from a favorite relative; the unpleasant times of being humiliated by parent, teacher, or peer. These are the "yeast incidents" that cause feelings and emotions to rise.

We respond with feelings to those we know and admire or to those with whom we can relate. If a stranger accosts you on the street and rants that you are the most ignorant, unpleasant, inept, useless person in the world, you would be startled and possibly alarmed but your feelings wouldn't be hurt. Your pre-cognitive emotion would ignite your physiology into defense mode until your analytical processes recognized the apparent "snake" as a harmless, under-the-influence "stick." And when the incident was over, the only memory residual would be an amusing story. There would be no long-lasting effect on your physiology.

However, if your mother, father, spouse, significant other, or someone you know, love and/or respect tells you the same thing in graphic, high-volume terms, your external and internal responses are quite different. You may be offended momentarily as you entertain a flashing thought that there is a remote possibility of some credibility to the statement. Or you may become consumed by rage and launch into immediate violent physical action. If your self-esteem is at all shaky at the time and you are particularly vulnerable to criticism, the verbal attack does a number on your feelings. The searing comments, the emotional pain and the pattern accompanying physiological responses are sealed in your Yellow memory. Afterwards, all you need to do to cue the whole combination again is to think of something that is even remotely associated with any part of the incident and the pattern is brought together again — feelings, self-esteem, and physiological response. And the pattern was in response to emotions focused that were on a person.

Strong, negative, people-directed feelings — anger, guilt, jealousy, and the like — mixed liberally with defense physiology make for a potent symptom-sustaining cocktail. Feelings that erupt in response to people can be on-going. These are the feelings that can get you into physical and emotional trouble.

WELLNESS PRINCIPLE: People generate intense feelings about people — even themselves

SUPPRESS OR EXPRESS

"Big boys/girls don't cry." "Don't hit." "Don't shout." "Don't be angry." Our society has long advocated emotional "control." From childhood we are bombarded with instructions to sanction outward responses to emotions. In some families, showing even positive emotions such as happiness, joy or affection, is frowned on: "Don't laugh out loud" runs hand-in-hand with "Don't cry." What's a body to do with all of these robust emotions bottled up all the time? Explode?

More or less. Actually, it's more like "implode" — "collapse" inward. If the energy of emotions can't be vented to the outside, it will be released on the inside. Eventually the body "implodes" with some sort of release. It "implodes" in a headache, or back pain, or knee pain, or stomach pain, or some other kind of pain. Recall that we said that pain is an excess of energy in one place. It's congested. That congested energy can come from suppressed emotions. And all too often it "implodes" in the form of release that we call disease. Suppressing emotional responses, either positive or negative, imposes a variation of psychic trauma that cultivates a sense of isolation. How sad for society and for health.

WELLNESS PRINCIPLE: Suppressed emotions clog energy–flow "pipelines"

In our civilized society, we are trained to not express our emotions openly. So if they can't be released, they must stay inside. We keep them locked tightly within the outer skin — suppress them. We act as though we believe suppressing the outward and visible signs of emotions eliminates the emotions themselves. Not so. Even if you lock your emotions tightly in your Red and Yellow to conceal your negative feelings from the outside world, you can't conceal them from your subconscious Green. And we know that your Green is designed to respond by preparing you to defend yourself. Your Green will respond! As far as your Green is concerned, bottled-up emotions are the same as being under attack; it keeps all systems combat ready to defend against the threat. But the threat stimuli are generated continuously internally.

As a result, whether you participate voluntarily or involuntarily, your emotions will be expressed. And you probably won't even recognize the expression for what it is. As in the story of the parking lot assault, the expression may erupt so long after the incident that you don't see any connection between cause and effect.

If suppressed emotions aren't expressed in some way soon after they are sparked, they will be expressed eventually. Emotions put stress on your body. Emotions cause changes in the way your body is functioning. Your body shifts into risk homeostasis. Intense emotions cause more intense changes than minor emotions. And suppressed strong emotions, such as grief and rage, keep your physiology from moving back into maintenance homeostasis.

Now don't infer that I am advocating or condoning wanton behavioral abandon, anarchy, spousal or child abuse, or a total disregard for law and civilized societal customs in the name of "expressed emotions." I'm not! The overall theme of all my teachings, written and oral, to patients, doctors and others interested in health is the theme of personal responsibility in thoughts and actions. When I talk about "expressing emotions," I am not implying that I approve of or advocate violence or abuse in any form — verbal or physical. We can express our emotions in ways that release our pent up feelings while not harming anything or anyone — including ourselves.

How do we express our emotions without causing harm?

Adult-grade temper tantrums are out. Bosses with the power to fire employees typically direct their power toward underlings who explode in verbal violence. You don't need to endanger your long-term security by releasing emotions on the spot. And you don't need to endanger your "aura of respectability" by histrionic ranting and raving around family, friends, or the general public.

How do we express negative emotions without causing harm?

We come equipped with mechanisms to do this.

Anger and frustration don't have to be expressed immediately. You can wait until after work or another appropriate time. Just make sure you take care of your delayed expression before you go to sleep. This concept has been around for years.

Back in "the olden days," mothers often passed on to their daughters a piece of valuable advice that is apropos to this situation: "For a long, happy marriage, never go to bed mad. Resolve your differences first." This advice was directed toward the bride since she was seen as the partner who had the most to lose in a poor marriage situation. However, it is advice that is valid for everyone. Deal with anger, frustration, irritation, and other negative emotions before you go to sleep. Strong emotions require specific physiological responses. If you go to sleep while your body is responding to negative emotions, the pattern of physiological response is locked into your Yellow. Sleep embeds the response pattern as firmly in your Yellow memory as a programming command embeds a response pattern in the hard drive of your mental computer. Strike the right key or stimulus and the response will begin without thought. We might say that when you take anger, frustration, anxiety, and the like to bed with you, it's like programming a virus into your Yellow computer.

So what do you do to "deal" with the emotion?

First, recognize what's happening.

Negative emotions prime you for a fight. They spark the production of adrenalin. You need to curb the adrenalin production before you go to sleep. And you can do this by adjusting your thinking.

Before you go to sleep, find some element of good in the situation that caused the emotion. Examine the situation and find something that you learned from that situation that can benefit you. If you aren't accustomed to looking at life this way, it may take some doing at first. But, with practice, you'll learn. We'll go into greater detail about "finding the good" and "learning the lesson" in a later chapter. For now, be aware that you don't have to be ruled by negative emotions that can make you emotionally and physically miserable.

WELLNESS PRINCIPLE: Find some good in every day before you go to sleep

If you suppress the release of intense emotions for weeks or months, you're asking for trouble. If you must suppress your emotions, you and your body fare much better in life when you suppress them just long enough to be socially acceptable; then do something that allows for health-restoring release. Exercise vents emotions externally and uses residual adrenalin. A weekly game of tennis or golf, a brisk walk two or three times a week, chopping wood, digging a ditch, a vigorous aerobic workout, a session on suitable exercise equipment, or whatever form of physical exercise that turns you on, all provide therapeutic release for suppressed feelings. Physical exercise is a good way to "burn off" adrenalin that surges during emotional conflicts. Adrenalin is an irresistible stimulus. If you can't "fight back" or run during adrenalin generating confrontations, you must consciously suppress the physical response expressions that come naturally. At the time, gritting your teeth or clenching your fists is about as far as you can go. Then at an appropriate time and place you can satisfy the need for "adrenalin expression" with physical exercise.

We all know that a surge of adrenalin can make us fidgety or supercharged. And we can stay that way until the adrenalin is "worked out" of our system — released, expressed by exercise or another means. Tears, deep sighs, and laughter are some of the "other means." They are internal release valves that often erupt spontaneously. Of course, we have already established that Big Boys and Big Girls don't cry; although in my opinion, crying is OK. And sighing is good. In fact, sighing is about as uncontrollable as hiccupping (which can be a real tension-producer).

Laughter is a great adrenalin release. That's why we sometimes laugh at "inappropriate" times. Funerals. Disasters. Crises. Pratfalls. The laughter-release is used frequently in tense situations. "Comic relief" in the middle of a super-serious situation often tempers overwhelming tension. Norman Cousins used the laughter-release method in his personal crusade against his own debilitating disease. Laughter can not only save a situation, it might save your health. It can't be beat for expressing emotions.

Ferris describes laughter-release in his book, *The Mind's Sky*. He writes about the old snake/stick ploy when alarm bells ring to no purpose. According to Ferris, physical exercise and meditation are stress relievers. "But," he writes, "the quickest and easiest way to discharge stress is by emitting a convulsive bark, a paroxysm of brain and body, what one authority described as 'spastic contractions of the large and small zygomatic (facial) muscles and sudden relaxations of the diaphragm accompanied by contractions of the larynx and epiglottis' — in short, by laughing."[93]

> WELLNESS PRINCIPLE: Laughter is fat-free, tax-free, indoor-outdoor stress-relief

No matter how self-controlled you are, intense stress will be expressed. It may be expressed in temper tantrums, tears, laughter, *or disease*. This is another of the underlying messages of this book: Suppressed emotions *will* be expressed! And disease is an expression of suppression. If you're into making yourself sick, take a magnum of stress, stir in a resounding wallop of severe "psychic trauma," flavor with feelings of isolation, add the juice of suppressed emotions, and you come up with a brew of "health on the rocks." Behind every chronic degenerative disease lies suppressed emotions.

How's that for a radical statement? I'll say it again: *Behind every chronic degenerative disease lies suppressed emotions.* This statement isn't made capriciously. My clinical experience demonstrates day after day that the root cause of non-traumatically induced pain (you didn't fall off the top of a twelve-foot ladder) and chronic disease is suppressed feelings. Even in children!

> WELLNESS PRINCIPLE: Suppressed emotions grow into expressed symptoms

So the question is: Can you control your feelings? And the answer is: Yes, you can — but you probably won't. As a practical matter, you will encounter unpleasant, frustrating, ego-threatening, or lifestyle-threatening situations that pummel your Red with perceived threats — "stick-snakes" and real "snakes." And you will respond — with feeling. You were designed to respond to threats for survival; and you will. Of course, the grand design was for you to respond in order to survive external threats to your physical safety — lions and tigers and bears. But we are advanced. Sophisticated. Cosmopolitan. Urbane. We ordinarily don't have predatory lions and tigers and bears roaming around our high-rise or subdivision "caves." Most of our threats are perceived intellectually. We can't run from them or physically fight with them. But the emotional wallop these perceived intellectual threats pack is equally as response-producing as actual physical threats. So here we are, responding in just the same way our ancestors did to the lions, tigers, and bears — feelings such as fear, anger, or rage erupt immediately and automatically.

You probably can't control the initial eruption of feelings. That flash of fury or gut-wrenching sense of disaster. And that's okay. Your body was designed to handle a brief flurry of intense feelings geared to prepare you to survive. Problems develop when that brief flurry is allowed to continue. And, with practice, you can get those after-shock feelings under control so that they are not sustained.

WELLNESS PRINCIPLE: Fleeting fury is fine; constant con-
sternation can be catastrophic

Most of us settle for controlling our *responses* to feelings. We do the stiff-upper lip bit. Tough it out. Bite the proverbial bullet. Put on a happy, or wooden, face. Whatever it takes to keep from displaying our feelings to others, we do. But you can control more than your responses, you can control your feelings.

Just as you are the one who restrains yourself from thumping a rude receptionist who thwarts your access to the person you need to see to complete your business, you are the only person who can nip your own negative feelings in the bud. The first step is to recognize negative thoughts and feelings. The second step is to use your free will to take charge and change your line of thinking. The practical step when a negative thought pops into mind is to think: "Cancel that thought." However, your thought line isn't going to stop just because you cancel one thought. Another thought will leap in to take its place. It's your job to take control and make sure that the replacement thought is really positive.

Instead of responding to the surly receptionist with verbal or mental comments denigrating her parentage, recognize that (1) she has a job to do, and (2) she faces her own ill-handled pressures and stresses. Recognize that her surliness is a reflection of her problem, not yours. For you, it's a challenge. In the process, you can change your feelings from anger (which harms only you) to non-judgmental acceptance (which helps you — and might help someone else).

WELLNESS PRINCIPLE: Thoughts can guide feelings

You are the only one who determines how you are going to feel about any situation. Although most of us attribute our feelings to some outside influence, YOU hold the power of ultimate control over YOUR feelings. Feelings surge from Red conscious awareness activating associated memories stored in Yellow. Other than the pre-cognitive emergency responses we talked about earlier, you can't have a feeling about a situation or action until you become aware of it in your conscious Red and relate it to associated information in your Yellow.

If your house in the States burns down while you are relaxing on a sun-drenched beach in the Bahamas, you continue to relax as long as you don't know about it. No problem; no unseemly physiological response. Then you find out about the disaster. Now you have a torrent of thoughts and feelings. All manner of Yellow associations come to the surface. And all manner of rational Red information is reviewed — material goods lost, insurance, a place to live, . . . The disruptive financial, energy, and lifestyle repercussions of the disaster are externals you must contend with. But the feelings attached are strictly personal and internal. Only you can handle those.

Feelings that bring about the most noticeable and dramatic physical reactions are fear and raging anger — strictly Red-induced responses. With both of these emotions, your body responds in ways that are noticeable to you and, often, to others. Even if you practice rigid self-control to hide tell-tale signs of anger, your body gives subtle body-language clues that you are seething inwardly — tone of voice, pace of speech, stance, flushed or livid coloring. And it's the inward seething that sets your Green responses on "danger" and "defend."

Animals have an advantage over us "higher" species when it comes to handling fear. Their fear is aroused by physical threats to their existence and their responses are pretty straight-forward. They fight or they run. After the episode is over, an animal's "body rebounds into a state of deep relaxation and ultimately back toward homeostasis," as Pelletier tells us.[94] Father raccoon has the advantage of not working in an office or shop where stress builds up, and mother rat rarely wonders if her child will survive an evening out in a car with other teenagers. In animals, feelings of stress are handled on the spot.

However, we humans become involved in situations and predicaments that stir feelings that can't be handled by running or fighting. You may not have control over situations around you or the actions of others, however you can choose how you feel and you can choose how you will respond. You, and only you, are in control of your feelings. No one else can make you happy. No one else can make you mad. Others may provoke a situation that calls for a response of glee or anger, but you are the person who controls your feelings. As your mother may have told you, "You can get happy the same way you get mad — all by yourself."

> WELLNESS PRINCIPLE: Only you make yourself angry or happy!

FEELINGS ABOUT YOURSELF

The way you feel about yourself can color the way you feel about just about everything else. And how you feel about yourself is a reflection of your view of your "acceptability": how "acceptable" you see yourself and how "acceptable" you think others see you — your family, your neighbors, your community, and your world in general.

What determines this view?

Perspective, memories, and your non-conscious.

Memories can be quite selective. Have you ever noticed that it's a lot easier to recall past negative experiences than positive ones? Past failures and short-comings are right there on the tip of your consciousness ready to spring forth to dampen, restrict, or undermine your self-confidence and best efforts. We worry about mistakes we made in the past, are anxious that we're goofing again in the present, and are afraid that our inadequacies and general klutziness will be displayed to others in the future. What do we call this perspective pattern? Low Self-Esteem.

Nearly every patient who comes to me for help suffers from low self-esteem. Many are painfully aware that they don't think much of themselves. With others, it's not so apparent. These are low-self-esteemers in camouflage. Although they appear to have the world by the tail, they chafe under niggling feelings that they aren't quite as good as they would like to be, or as good as others seem to think they are. And one of their biggest worries is that they will be found out.

Your level of self-esteem is determined by *your view of your personal "worth" and "acceptability."* It's not how others see you. It's how you see yourself. Self-esteem has nothing to do with dollars or position or status in the community. It is internal — self-evaluation of your worth as a person. The amazing thing is that often we see ourselves entirely differently from the way others see us. We perceive ourselves from our own perspective. We begin to develop this perspective in childhood as a reflection of our interpretation of feedback we get from our significant others (like parents) and the world around us. This perspective gets locked into Yellow memory as the paradigm for self-evaluation. If your stored perception paradigms are positive, you have efficient tools with which to work; if they're negative, you have a tougher row to hoe.

WELLNESS PRINCIPLE: Self-esteem is your mental self-
portrait

Perceptions of your worth begin in infancy. They are reinforced or revised throughout life — at your mother's knee, in the classroom, on the playground, in the locker room, at social functions, in your church, temple, or mosque and anyplace else you encounter people you trust, respect, and like. And over the years you tuck all of your perceptions about yourself securely into your Yellow.

If, as a child, you enjoyed positive reinforcement from your parents, teachers, siblings, and schoolmates, as you grew, your self-esteem grew. You lived up to the favorable "picture" of yourself and your "worth" that developed in your conscious mind. You saw yourself as an asset to family and world, lovable, capable, loyal, brave, trustworthy, and true. Then the "real world" started to close in. If the feedback you received from your then-significant others was predominately negative, you developed quite a different mental picture of yourself and your abilities. You were a liability to be tolerated, guilty of major and minor crimes and misdemeanors, irresponsible, a material object to be used and abused. In short, you developed a mental picture of yourself as a worthless victim. That's a terrible experience for a child!

WELLNESS PRINCIPLE: As the paradigm is shaped, so
grows the self-esteem

As children, we depend on others to care for us physically and emotionally. We take our perceptions of the opinions of others as true. However, as adults we are *supposed to* make our own evaluations, form our own opinions and make own decisions. As adults, we evaluate our self-worth from an adult perspective — not from a knee-high view. That's what we work for all those years we spend as children — the ability to view ourselves and others on a level plane through mature eyes. As adults we recognize and appreciate strengths and accept shortcomings in ourselves and others. We set realistic goals and work toward them without expecting to be perfect, or even outstanding, in every category of life. Unlike constantly berated children, adults learn to accept their attributes and virtues even in the face of struggles and crises. Adults know that they are responsible for themselves but that they are not responsible for solving all of the problems of the world or of those around them, no matter how much others try to heap guilt on them.

Yet there's hope for those who have endured an early life of self-esteem bashing, victimization, and abuse. Even if you emerged from childhood with battered self-esteem, as a thinking adult, you can refurbish and polish your mental picture of yourself. The secret is to accept yourself as you are — the positive and the not-so-positive — without dwelling on your shortcomings. You are unique. Identify, accept, and revel in your own personal strengths. The rule of thumb for updating your self-esteem is to be on guard constantly for things you really like about yourself. The "likes" can be about your physical self or your character self. But be forewarned: physical attributes are more subject to change than character attributes — recall the atom replacement policy that is in effect throughout our lives. However, character attributes, such as generosity, compassion, loyalty, trustworthiness, honesty, tact, and all of the other socially-responsible qualities are firmly ingrained patterns in your Yellow.

WELLNESS PRINCIPLE: Update your self-esteem —
evaluate yourself as you
would evaluate a stranger

Setting unrealistic standards of behavior, attractiveness, effectiveness, productivity, or creativity can cause all sorts of inner strife. Whether you set these standards for yourself or for others doesn't matter. We constantly compare our own accomplishments, appearance, intelligence, wisdom, patience, sincerity, and any other positive characteristic you care to cite with those of others. We decide our level of acceptability by illogical comparisons. We pick out someone who excels in a given characteristic, ability, or virtue to use as our comparison piece. Not as a guide, which is helpful, but to dwell on how far we fall short. Can you realistically compete with Mother Theresa's humanitarian accomplishments, Stephen Hawking's intellectual brilliance, or Michael Jordan's athletic ability? Not likely for us common folk.

WELLNESS PRINCIPLE: You are not a watered-down
version of someone else

Comparing your least developed characteristic with "an expert's" strong point is a sure way to deflate your self-esteem. Life throws us enough challenges to overcome without building impossible barriers to positive self-esteem along the way. There's little point in setting unreachable goals for yourself when you have no control over the available raw material. If you put on ice skates for the first time when you are 25-years old, no matter how much you practice, you'll never be an Olympic figure-skating gold medalist. But you can learn to skate well enough to enjoy yourself and gain a feeling of accomplishment. You're probably out of the running for a prestigious chair at an Ivy League college unless you have accumulated the education, training and credentials needed for such an honor. However, you can continue to read, educate yourself, teach, or take classes or correspondence courses to improve your mental prowess. You can benefit from activities you enjoy on your own level, and build your self-esteem in the process.

A personal example of the futility of comparing novice abilities (apples) with those of a skilled practitioner (oranges) illustrates this concept.

My two sons invited me to join them and a friend to fill out a golf foursome. I enjoy playing golf although my opportunities to play, like my game, might best be described as sporadic. I also enjoy competing and winning; so I accepted their invitation.

The four of us arrived at the first tee and I teed off first. My drive was acceptable but hardly world class. My sons in turn performed quite acceptably. Then their friend addressed the ball. Whack! Straight down the fairway the ball flew, and flew, and flew before coming to rest in perfect position to approach the green with a comfortable chip shot. The first thought that ran through my mind was a rather disgruntled, "And I'm going to have to watch performances like this for another 17 holes." Then I realized what I was doing.

The "friend" with the textbook swing and long, straight drive is the golf coach at a nearby university. Golf is his profession. He spends hours hitting little white balls down grassy fairways. On the other hand, for me, golf is an intermittent recreational activity. I had fallen into the apples and oranges comparison trap (which is similar to the sand traps my ball landed in later). As soon as I recognized my "trapped" thinking, my next thought was, "He hits a mean drive, but how many sick people can he help get well?" Once our respective capabilities were seen through that perspective, I could enjoy the game, the company, the afternoon, and the occasional well-executed shot appropriate to my level of expertise. Oh, by the way, mine wasn't the lowest score for that game — but I reinforced a valuable lesson.

That lesson is: If you can't compete successfully with the luminaries of any given field, you have two choices: Do nothing — you certainly can't fail if you do nothing; or, do your best and enjoy yourself.

WELLNESS PRINCIPLE: Never, never, never compare your
                      weaknesses to others' strengths

A seldom acknowledged self-esteem saboteur is the habit of continually grasping at one or both of two popular but unreachable goals: (1) pleasing other people, or (2) changing other people to be or act the way you think they should. You can't do either.

Not only can trying to reach these unreachable goals deflate your self-esteem, it can be dangerous to your health. Have you ever wondered why the little lady in your community who spends most of her time happily helping others develops symptoms of a serious illness? One might think that anyone with such a positive attitude, so giving and generous a nature would be the picture of health.

My experience as a doctor shows that usually these paragons of generosity and sunny nature harbor little regard for themselves — low self-esteem. Their perceptions of life have led them to believe that their happiness depends on making others happy. They are convinced that they are not "loveable" or "acceptable" unless they do things for those they would like to have love or accept them. It's a barter system. The unspoken barter is, "I'll help you with your yard sale if you will praise me, appreciate me, and verbally applaud my efforts." Or, "I'll give you roses if you'll notice me and tell me I'm wonderful." And it often works!

However, there are self-esteem pitfalls built into unspoken acceptance bartering. The "giver" is the only one aware of the "deal" and lives in a state of anxiety until the payoff. What happens when the receiver demonstrates less enthusiasm than the giver expects? Suppose the recipient is allergic to roses and rebuffs the giver? It's a negative payoff and the giver's feelings that she is not acceptable are reinforced. Down goes the self-esteem another notch. To compensate she has to do more, give more, be more generous, more thoughtful, more . . . more . . . more.

WELLNESS PRINCIPLE: You can't please others most of the time

The second self-esteem saboteur is the I'll-help-you-be-more-like-me goal. The objective here is to change someone else's mind. Can't be done! Even when you KNOW that you know best, you can't lead anyone else's life for them, and you can't change anyone else's mind for them. Trying to do either leads to manipulation, and manipulation generally backfires in the long run. You can't force rebellious teenagers to overcome their rebellion on command. They may appear to have changed their ways, but if the change isn't of their own doing, it won't last. They'll be conforming on the outside but rebelling on the inside. And eventually, the truth will out and you will have — once again — failed.

WELLNESS PRINCIPLE: The more you try to control

others, the less influence you
have on them

It's impossible to please everyone all the time, and it's impossible to change anyone other than ourselves. Yet many of us keep trying and trying. Despite the impossibility of the situation, we mistakenly base our self-esteem on how well we see ourselves accomplishing either or both of these impossibilities. And since pleasing others continually or trying to change others to fit our standards never happens, we feel we are failures and our self-esteem suffers.

The point is, we can shoot our self-esteem in the foot by setting unrealistic goals. And, contrariwise, our self-esteem shoots up when we acknowledge each success we have in life no matter how small or large.

Your feelings, your non-conscious Yellow, and your subconscious Green don't know the difference between a small and large success. Your self-esteem goes up a notch each time you credit yourself with a positive accomplishment. Whether your success is changing a tire for the first time or cleaning out your desk drawers or designing a magnificent cathedral, it's all the same to your non-conscious and subconscious. Success does wonders for your self-esteem.

WELLNESS PRINCIPLE: Self-esteem is built one success at
a time

Unfortunately, some people's self-esteem has sunk so low that they completely lose sight of any successes in their lives. Their successes get lost in a succession of put-down's and emotional abuse. These are the patients who tell me that they no longer have "feelings." They just "don't feel anything." Their feelings have been turned off. They are neither happy nor sad, excited nor bored, pleased nor displeased. Usually, from the looks of them — their tone of voice, their actions and physical condition — they're far from happy and a long way from being healthy.

I have found that feeling-less people are those who have been "bushwhacked." They, like all of us, experienced feelings at one time. Often, very strong feelings. However, somewhere along their journey of life, they learned that when they expressed their feelings they were ridiculed. Ridicule is a lethal spear to self-esteem. They were doing what they thought was "right," but the results were disastrous. Like the first- or second-grader who tries to come to the aid of a classmate, but all the teacher sees is that the helper is "in the middle of the commotion." The "helper" thinks he is doing a right thing, but gets in trouble. He's "bushwhacked."

Bushwhacking can take the form of a severe emotional, verbal, or possibly physical "attack." To stop the hurt, "bushwhackees" turn off their emotions. Although their perception of their emotions may have been subdued, their perception of the world hasn't.

' As long as they (or anyone else) experience conscious life, sensory stimuli will be received. The body responds to these stimuli. The difference here is that the non-feeling person isn't aware of the latent emotions of fear or anger. But their body is. Threats are still threats and the body responds appropriately by assuming defensive physiology. And this can go on and on.

For the non-feeling, defensive or risk physiology was "glued in" during an incident or series of incidents that prompted feelings to be "turned off." So those who think they are unaffected by life situations and relaxed are, in reality, continually responding to one or more perilous situations of the past. And they are tired! Exhaustion has set in and they are headed down the road to chronic disease — or have already arrived at their destination.

WELLNESS PRINCIPLE: Living life without feeling isn't
living — it's existing

Non-feeling can be overcome. Low self-esteem can be raised. Negative thinking can be turned around to positive. Following the steps of forgiveness that appear in a later chapter can reduce or eliminate the threat response the body maintains for each of these. However, as you shall see, merely forgiving others and oneself for past offenses isn't enough — that is only about 40% effective. The remaining 60% of the forgiveness process is to find and acknowledge the good in the situation. Or, to put it another way, to find the lesson in each experience.

We need to recognize that life is a learning process — a giant learning experience. Everything you do and everything that happens to you is an opportunity to learn. And you can't fail. Experiences we call "failures" are, in reality, experiences of non-learning. Every experience in life is a part of a lesson. Until you learn that lesson, you will have the opportunity to repeat it. How many times do you have to marry, divorce, marry a clone of the first spouse, divorce again, and marry yet more clones a third, fourth, or fifth time before you figure out that maybe you're not learning what you need to learn. When you keep repeating the same scenario over and over — gaining and losing spouses, losing one job after another — it's time to recognize that you need to learn something that you haven't figured out yet. How many times do you have to change a flat tire because you keep running pell-mell into curbs to figure out that tires aren't indestructible and curbs aren't for running into.

You may not learn the lesson the first time or the next or the next, but you'll continue to have opportunities to learn it. When you understand this principle, you'll finally tell yourself, "I'll keep getting the lesson until I learn it or die — whichever comes first."

By viewing each experience in life as a lesson to be learned, you'll come to understand that you really can't fail at anything! You can have turbulent relationships, multiple jobs, a succession of spouses, but you can't fail. You can have pain, sickness or death by becoming upset over not learning the lesson, but you can't fail.

WELLNESS PRINCIPLE: Life is a journey of lessons; disease is being stuck in a particular lesson

Understanding this fact of life can help to motivate you to upgrade your feelings about yourself, your experiences, and the world. Remember, feelings are a driving force in how your body functions. And where do feelings — other than pre-cognitive feelings — come from? From the things that go on in your Red conscious mind — your conscious thoughts.

POINTS OF INTEREST

1. Positive and negative feelings affect physiology.

2. Feelings and their physiological responses are stored in Yellow.

3. The strength of feelings determines the degree of energy disturbance in your body and field.

4. Current Red feelings can conflict with Yellow programming.

5. Intense feelings experienced in psychic isolation are the foundation of disease.

6. Feelings about yourself set your level of self-esteem.

7. Suppressed feelings will be expressed, and the expression may be disease.

8. Feelings and emotions are "people-directed," not "thing-directed."

It is the mind that maketh good or ill,
That maketh wretch or happy, rich or poor.
- Edmund Spenser (1552/53-1599)

CHAPTER 9
Thinking About Thinking

THOUGHT POWER

Unless you are a card-carrying philosopher or make your mark in the world thinking about thinking, you probably give little thought to thoughts. Thoughts and thinking just happen. Thoughts, products of your ever-active Red, are directed toward and focused on making decisions and solving problems: decisions as trivial as what to have for lunch, and problems as vast as sorting out the current "health care" crisis. We can ride away from the reality of our physical surroundings on pleasant thoughts of a deep reverie. We can become absorbed in abstract symbols of words, numbers, and ideas during periods of intense concentration. However, for most of us most of the time, thoughts come and go while we take little notice of their origins, their tone, or how they influence our body and our health. Generally, our thoughts are reactive rather than proactive and they are associative.

Random thoughts are undirected. They are the non-stop succession of associated mental musings that bounce from one idea to another. Red thoughts "bounce" into Yellow to pick up and link associated bits of information. Random thoughts are guided and restricted by the stored information and connections that link one subject or idea with another. Thoughts trail one another randomly when the conscious Red is left to its own devices — humdrum routine, mindless activity, daydreaming, quiescence, tranquility. When sights, sounds, and other sensations can be easily ignored, an apparently independent thought pops into mind. That thought is followed by another thought. The connection between the two may or may not be obvious. But each thought, whether or not you recognize the connection, is associated in some way with past thoughts. Even incoming sensory stimuli are run through associative areas and evaluated according to those associations. Although an oversimplification, we can say that micro-energy currents flit from synapse to synapse in search of familiar companions. Each thought or energy spurt finds paths to associates.

> WELLNESS PRINCIPLE: Thoughts are generated by sen-
> sory stimuli or internal stimuli
> we call memory

Although thoughts are energy signals running around in your head, they produce energy that radiates outside your head. (This is the energy recorded by EEGs.) Your thoughts either resonate with the sea of creative energy that surrounds you, or they don't. Positive thoughts resonate with creative energy and promote personal reception of life-supporting energy from your field. Positive thoughts help keep you "in tune" with Universal Energy. Negative thoughts interfere with your reception of this vital energy. In fact, we might say that these are the definitions of positive and negative thoughts: positive thought energy travels easily through your connection with the Grand Plan Universal Energy Field; negative thought energy interferes with the flow through your connection with the Grand Plan field. Simple as all that. This is why habitual negative thinking is behind most of the physical exhaustion, pain, disease, and general distress that afflicts much of the population today. It interferes with the essential energy connection.

"But," you counter, "I know a lot of people who are pretty negative, and they have a lot of energy — they don't seem to be 'exhausted' at all."

And I wouldn't contest that statement.

For many negative thinkers, the exhaustion is relayed to an organ or system — not to an activity. And the exhaustion is in the development stage. They, the people themselves, are minor lightening-bolts of physical activity in their outside world while their inside world is running down. We might say that negative thoughts are like jolts of caffeine or nicotine or crack — they force a "high." And like just about anything else on our planet's surface that is forced to move up — swinging pendulum, tossed stone, wholloped baseball, or Wall Street stock price — it'll eventually come down.

WELLNESS PRINCIPLE: Short-term negative "highs" are
                       followed by system-threatening
                       "lows"

Thoughts are energy. Electrons are on the move as electrochemical thought impulses scamper from synapse, along fibre, to synapse. Although the voltage power of thought energy is minuscule, the influence of thought energy is great. The energy of thoughts is more powerful than most of us would care to concede. Not only do thoughts spur us to action or reaction, we now know that the energy of thoughts extends outside our personal systems. The energy of our past thoughts has taken us to where we are today, and the energy of our current thoughts sets the course for all of our remaining todays. And to make this thought-energy concept even more intriguing, the influence of thought-energy ranges far beyond our tiny personal presence. Put all of our thoughts together — yours, mine, the guy next door, city employees, shop clerks, and all the rest — and what do you have? Corporate thought energy.

The combined thoughts of mankind — corporate thoughts — direct the course of history. "Accepted scientific principles" are corporate thoughts. The many shades of cultural values and beliefs are corporate thoughts. The "hundredth monkey" premise is a function of corporate thought, to-wit: After ninety-nine monkeys have acquired a learned skill, such as using a reed as a tool to collect grubs, the "hundredth monkey" — meaning the monkeys that follow — acquire that skill without actually learning it themselves. They just "know." Redfield, in his book *The Celestine Prophecy* refers to this phenomenon as "the critical mass."[95] We reach the "critical mass" of influence when x-number of people think about the same thing.

One of the motivators that prompts researchers to publish their findings as quickly as possible is linked to the hundredth monkey syndrome of corporate thought. If Researcher #1 has demonstrated or discovered a new element, or method, or principle, chances are good that Researcher #2 in another part of the world is demonstrating or discovering the same thing. So the challenge to Researcher #1 is to publish his/her findings immediately to assure that professional credit lands in his/her lap before Researcher #2 grabs the gold ring — or Nobel Prize — first.

Generic Man is a thinker. He puts his mind to work on sorting out the mysteries, trials and catastrophes of life. Generic Man is constantly looking for a "better idea." In the health realm, this has led to disaster. From my perspective, I see the Mind of Man as the Great Transgressor in trying to control his health. Through his growing intellect, Man looks to direct his health through his own mind rather than through the mind of Creative Intelligence. Rather than allowing the non-judgmental, infallible subconscious Green to handle body maintenance undisturbed, Man comes up with "better ideas" in his highly fallible conscious Red. He imposes synthetic situations for the Green to overcome. Some of these synthetic situations are in the form of pills and procedures, but most are in the form of inappropriate thoughts.

Recall our recurring theme: The Red conscious mind is in charge of cognitive thinking, the Yellow non-conscious is in charge of storing thoughts, feelings, and response patterns, and the Green subconscious mind is in charge of adapting physiology to current needs. Although Red intelligence may be enhanced by formal education or the school of hard knocks; Green intelligence isn't. You can't improve upon perfection. From the time you were conceived, your Green has known all it needs to know in order to respond perfectly with physiology appropriate to conditions. Green and its perfect responses cannot be improved upon by Red consciousness.

> WELLNESS PRINCIPLE: The subconscious Green knows
> only perfect responses

Your Green came fully-equipped as part of the package when you were born. However, at birth, your Red hadn't yet been exposed to much stimulation. It wasn't ready for abstract logic. And your Yellow hadn't yet stored much in working memory.

Red knowledge is acquired through your senses of sight, hearing, smell, taste, and touch. The information doesn't have to be right. The impressive bits, accurate or not, are stored in your Yellow. You continually add to your store of Yellow information. However, much of the information stored in your Yellow is either erroneous or negative. And that's where problems start: problems in life and problems in health.

And what happens when we have a health problem? We attack it with the Red. However, to be effective, instead of concentrating our fallible, learned Red knowledge on how to *cure* each particular variety of ache, pain or disease, we need to concentrate on making misery-producing downers *unnecessary*. And that path takes us straight through fields of thoughts and energy. Fields that may be unfamiliar to our limited Red experience. But they are fields of thought and energy that dramatically affect our physiology.

THOUGHTS AND PHYSIOLOGY

Thoughts are behind anger. Thoughts are behind grief. They are also behind humor, joy, great and daft inventions, architecture, and music. Thoughts are creative. They can mean the difference between happiness and despondency, success and failure, health and disease. Your thoughts can guide you smoothly through life or they can put such unrelenting stress on your physiology that you can literally think yourself to disease and, possibly, death — and never realize that your thoughts, not your body, are your problem.

In previous sections we focused on identifying the jigsaw pieces that go together to make up our picture of health. Now it's time to put some pieces together so we can begin to see the big picture: and the big picture shows the intricate relationship between thoughts, physiology, and energy fields.

Keep in mind that we are looking at health from the perspective of you as an energy body. You are more than muscle, bone, cartilage and assorted fluids. At the quantum level, you are made up of tiny bits of chaotic energy that are affected by other tiny bits of energy. When we adopt this perspective, we have moved away from the mechanists' perspective that the body is merely an assortment of hoses, vacuum pumps, valves, electrical circuits, couplings, levers and pulleys that adhere only to Newtonian principles. We take a look at the body as a whole. And although we are viewing the holistic body in its completeness, we are looking at the tiniest aspects of the whole as major features of physiology and health — tiny bits of energy. Thoughts are tiny bits of energy. Yet these tiny bits make great, big waves in your ocean of life.

We, as a society, have been fighting the good fight for health according to Newtonian rules for decades now. Still, we are no closer than before to "curing cancer" or successfully combating other chronic degenerative diseases. We have ignored, or been unaware of, the concept that tiny causes can have tremendous effects. How long do we need to slog through the mud of the same old well-trodden, rut-filled Newtonian fix-the-parts path to health before we notice the more direct, lightly travelled, clearer, tiny cause/big effect, whole-entity path? It's time to take a different approach.

Viewing disease as the result of unruly physiological and biological processes is a comfortable concept; it is familiar. These processes are observable or measurable. They are usually tagged as the villain when something in the body "goes wrong." Thoughts, on the other hand, are tiny causes. The thoughts may be trivial, deep, profound, or loony, but they are still tiny. And they are nebulous. You can't put thoughts under a microscope, observe their behavior, or measure their capacity — directly. Thoughts are intangibles that don't fit into generally-accepted Newtonian views of the world. And energy, if it is taken into account at all, is considered a by-product of physiological activity. Yet hope springs eternal. The health effects of energy in and around the body is being investigated by well-credentialed, experienced scientists.

WELLNESS PRINCIPLE: Energy is the core of the body, not
a by-product

One of the well-credentialed, experienced scientists who writes about healing through the energy field is Barbara Brennan. In her book *Hands of Light,* Brennan writes: "The old Newtonian mechanics interpreted the interaction between positively and negatively charged particles like protons and electrons simply by saying that the two particles attract each other like two masses. However, Michael Faraday and James Clerk Maxwell found it more appropriate to use a field concept and say that each charge creates a 'disturbance' or 'condition' in the space around it, so that the other charge, when it is present, feels a force. Thus, the concept of a universe filled with fields that create forces that interact with each other was born."[96]

Newton says the particles exert the force; Maxwell says the force is already there and the particles disturb the force in which they move. That sounds a lot like the "parts body" - "energy body" controversy we've been talking about. Is the focus of health the physical body we are familiar with, or the energy fields we are coming to know better? When we factor energy into our view of health, we begin to recognize that everything we do — especially thinking — exerts a force that influences our personal energy fields that are connected to the Universal Power of Creative Intelligence. In turn, our energy field influences our physiology. With our conditioned Newtonian mind-set, our physiological and biological responses are considerably easier for us to understand as being the source of any physical ills. However, if you have read this far in this book, you are coming to understand that there is a lot more to "You" than merely the solid components that Newtonian scientists study. "You" are directly connected through your personal field — whether you can see it or not — with the Universal Creative Intelligence that is the power behind your development and your life.

WELLNESS PRINCIPLE: Science looks for explanations;
Creative Intelligence has the an-
swers

Previous chapters in this book have dealt with Newtonian views of the body and some broad concepts of Superconsciousness, Creative Intelligence and our ever-present energy field. These views serve as the underpinnings for integrating the familiar with the not-so-familiar. We talked about physiological functions, such as sympathetic and parasympathetic responses, muscle memory, cell division and differentiation, digestion, and homeostasis. However, these concepts are presented from the viewpoint that the body, guided by Creative Intelligence, is a self-regulating, self-healing system that responds precisely, to thoughts and feelings. That's a different perspective from "take this medicine for your cold/headache/arthritis."

As we have seen, neither the body nor the perfect Creative Intelligence is "magical." "Miraculous" maybe — but not magical. Both body and Creative Intelligence follow clearly defined, if not yet clearly understood, rules. Physiological processes of the body function according to "scientifically" accepted reactions. And these reactions are essentially electrochemical. Creative Intelligence processes, on the other hand, come clothed in a variety of costumes: as "nature," radiant colors of the Monarch butterfly; as "coincidences," seemingly unrelated synergistic events; as "intuition," knowing without knowing how you know; as "miracles," spontaneous remissions or abrupt alterations of symptoms. Despite their differences, both physiological processes and Creative Intelligence processes influence and are influenced by the energy of conscious thoughts. We run into trouble when most of our thoughts interfere with the transmission of this energy. The part of the energy realm that surrounds your own personal body , whether you can see it or not, is an integral part of your body. Without that energy, there is no "You." Your energy field is the vital element of your body. And everything you do while you are alive — energized — affects your unseen field of energy. Even thinking! And most of the thoughts that meander through our brains are recycled. We are familiar with them. Their association routes are firmly connected. Most of the thoughts we have today are the same thoughts we had yesterday. They're recycled. It's easier that way.

> WELLNESS PRINCIPLE: Recycled thoughts may not be
> pleasant, but they're easy

RECYCLED THOUGHTS

We know our thoughts originate in our brains. But no one is sure of the choreography that turns neuroelectrochemical activity into the ongoing dance of thoughts. So we'll fall back on the "mechanistic approach." We'll use the modern personal computer as a rough analogy for the workings of the human brain. We'll use everyday computer terms to illustrate illusive physiological activities. Central Processing Unit. Input/Output. Memory. Save. Search. Sort. Compare. Default. Cancel. The analogy breaks down, however, when self-awareness, common sense, and judgment are required. Nonetheless, comparing the workings of the human brain with those of a computer can help us understand why thoughts have such a decisive effect on health. The old cliché of the computer world, "garbage in, garbage out," is a succinct clue to how thoughts interfere with health, success, and happiness. Put in inaccurate or negative information, or programming, and you'll get back inaccurate or negative output.

WELLNESS PRINCIPLE: Information from the outside is recycled as thoughts

The most important link in the computer-mind analogy is that both work according to the programming stored in their respective memories. The response to particular commands is entered into either mind or computer, stored, and ready to be retrieved and used. As long as the programming is unchanged, responses to given signals are unchanged. Using the stored information, comparisons and calculations are made, patterns are established, and the machine/mind spits out "logical" responses. The responses fed back by either the computer or the mind depend upon the information entered. And for either computer or brain/conscious mind, there's no guarantee that the information entered was correct! Furthermore, we don't have a clue as to its accuracy until we witness the responses. Responses to computer programming show up on screen or printouts; responses to mental programming show up in our physical bodies, in our attitudes, and in life as degrees of health, happiness, and success.

WELLNESS PRINCIPLE: Disease is your body's "error message" display

Each of us assumes that the information programmed into our mind (or computer) is absolutely correct. We don't even question the validity of our "knowledge." We know what we know. As far as your body is concerned, whether or not the information is correct, logical, or accurate is immaterial. That's the information that will be used. Right or wrong, all of our conscious responses are based on this information. Our programmed information is our operating program. In the mind, this program is made up of data accumulated over the years. It is the personal filter through which each of us sees the world — and ourselves.

Through your programming, you "know" that you are a solid citizen, clever, energetic, and worthwhile; or you "know" that you are irresponsible, lazy, ineffective, and worthless. How do you "know" these crucial "facts" about yourself? Simple. You learned them in your Red and you stored them in your Yellow. You learned by implication, word, and deed from those you trusted. For years, parents, teachers, older siblings "told" you whether or not the things you did, said, believed, and felt were "right" or "wrong." They told you outright, or by body language, or by other responses — like a rap on some part of your anatomy. You believed these trusted others, and your computer mind stored the information. You have been programmed to believe particular assessments of yourself.

If you are very fortunate, as a child you lived in a positive, supportive environment where you were peppered with positive comments about yourself, your attributes, and your abilities. You may be one of the fortunate few who has been programmed from childhood to believe that you are worthwhile, personable, clever, dexterous, capable, valuable, lovable and an all-around neat, can-do person. These "facts" were repeated over and over to you in a loving environment in a variety of forms, and now the information is securely stored in your trusty computer between your ears. That's the information you now use to assess and successfully address day-to-day situations and challenges.

However, all is not sweetness and light in the world. Most of the people I see in my professional practice have been programmed differently. They, too, grew up in loving families and were programmed by well-intentioned parents who wanted the best for their children. As children they were taught to behave "properly" in polite society, to be cautious, responsible, and thoughtful of others. They were protected from obvious dangers, and they were schooled in "personal responsibility" and other socially acceptable behavior patterns, such as, "Don't chew with your mouth open," and "don't draw pictures in the dirt on the car." However, teaching and protecting were based more on "Thou shalt not's," and "Thou cannot's" than on "try-it's" and "sure-you-can's." Behavioral researcher Shad Helmstetter estimates that by the time children reach age eighteen they have been told "No!" more than 148,000 times — if they grew up in "reasonably positive homes."[97] That's a bunch of negative down-time. It averages out to about 22.5 "No's" a day, including weekends and holidays. However, for the most part, this negative programming was unintentional — not malicious, just effective.

If children in "reasonably positive homes" are pummeled with twenty-plus "No's" a day, children in "negative" homes may go into "culture shock" if they are told "Yes."

WELLNESS PRINCIPLE: Parents of small children "No" a
                      lot

You may have been "taught," intentionally or unintentionally, throughout childhood and adolescence that you aren't very smart, or attractive, or worthwhile, or lovable, or creative, or personable, or athletic, or capable, or whatever. If so, as you progress in life and in years, unless you *reprogram* your thinking, you continue to "know" you are afflicted with your own serious character faults and inadequacies. And whether or not you are aware of it, you continually remind yourself to live up to your own negative expectations. These bits of information are stored in your Yellow memory systems and recycled constantly for an audience of one — you.

You may or may not have specific memory entries to support examples of negative programming. Your family or teachers may or may not have declared blatantly, "You are dumb, ugly, clumsy, and worthless." Nonetheless, your personal mental computer has gathered bits and pieces of data and experiences over the years and amalgamated this information to arrive at a negative sum of your acceptability.

> WELLNESS PRINCIPLE: Your picture of yourself is a collage of stored impressions

Parents are our first teachers. They are our first role models for attitudes, actions, and values. Most parents want to prepare their children to lead happy, productive lives. However, parents also function according to their own internal programming. They may *want* to do right by their children but they aren't sure just what "right" is. Sometimes their well-meaning efforts produce effects opposite to their intention. Strict discipline may be intended to build character. However, exactly where is the demarcation between discipline and abuse? The parent's noble objective of "strict discipline" may be lost on the "strictly disciplined" child. The child may grow to resent authority of any kind, be short on compassion, and escalate the "strict discipline" to abuse of others in later life.

In contrast, parents who rarely, if ever, reigned-in their pre-school child in an effort to allow the child to develop his or her full potential may have a different problem. As the child reaches his or her teen-age or young adult years, the parents may wonder why their child lacks self-discipline and is completely self-centered. Youngsters who are given few if any guidelines during childhood may become increasingly demanding and self-indulgent.

> WELLNESS PRINCIPLE: Parenting isn't for the feint-hearted

Parents, and others we encounter in life, come in two prominent flavors: the flavor we find pleasant and want to emulate, and the flavor we find distasteful and don't want to emulate. Those whom we admire and respect we want to imitate. We want to learn everything we can from them. We want success like theirs. They are our role models. However, we also learn a great deal from those whom we find offensive or do not respect. We can learn exactly what we don't want to do or to be. Lives there a child with active Red, who never to himself has said: "I won't say that (do that) to my kids." From those we don't admire we can learn a variety of behaviors that we choose never to adopt — and that's an example of a positive lesson from a negative experience as was discussed in Chapter 7.

From childhood on, during the course of your lifetime thousands of bits of information you learn about the world and yourself are programmed into your mental computer. No matter what that information may be, and no matter its accuracy, that is the information that colors your attitudes, your success, your goals, and all of your efforts.

In the course of our conscious earthly journey, each of us acquires, through our sensory system, our own particular brew of learned information. To get an idea of the amount of information received by one person's sensory nervous system, we turn to Guyton: "It [the nervous system] receives literally millions of bits of information from the different sensory organs and then integrates all of these to determine the response to be made by the body."[98] That's millions of bits of information at a given time. Compound this over years and years of constantly receiving millions of bits of information. Pure internal stimulation chaos. But as Guyton said, "more than 99 per cent of all sensory information is discarded by the brain as irrelevant and unimportant."[99] Whew! That's a relief. If we had to consciously sort out millions of bits of information constantly there wouldn't be time left to handle major decisions, like whether to have the paper towels come off the roll from the top or bottom. From an influx of chaotic information we sort the irrelevant from the relevant and respond accordingly. And it is this sorting and storing of chaotic information that makes each of us different from anyone else.

WELLNESS PRINCIPLE: Each individual personality is a unique tapestry woven of threads spun from chaotic information

And what is the purpose of receiving and sorting this cacophony of information? Survival. We learn in order to survive. We learn important survival tactics to accommodate to our environment. For example, generally it takes only one practical lesson to learn that there's a rebound effect when you stick metal tweezers into a "live" electrical outlet, or that a wet tongue sticks fast to a frozen axe blade. But many of our lessons are considerably less obvious than that. Those examples of practicality are short-term experiences that leave long-term impressions. The lessons that have greater impact on our happiness, success, and health are those that help us learn how to live in harmony with ourselves and the rest of the world, such as acknowledging and expressing feelings without abusing or suppressing others. And in the process of learning our lessons for living in harmony with others, we are afforded the opportunity to learn to survive in harmony with Creative Intelligence. When we learn this lesson, we experience the maelstrom of life without doing major damage to our physical bodies through thoughts. If we don't learn the lesson, more opportunities for learning keep cropping up.

RECYCLED LESSONS

Every experience that excites feelings cements memories into your Yellow memory. Each of these feeling-packed experiences is an opportunity to learn a valuable lesson. Some lesson experiences are more dramatic than others, but they all are fodder for future function. Once you experience an incident and acknowledge it as a "learning experience," you choose a response on the spot. You either (1) immediately suppress, or internalize, the feelings that accompany the lesson incident, or you (2) immediately find some element of personal benefit in the incident and learn from it — see the good.

Let's look at an example of a real-life condition: employment. We'll call our leading lady "Angie." Angie's story is based on reality; "Angie" is hypothetical.

Angie is intelligent, energetic, personable, creative, attractive, and a single mother. She has been in and out of countless jobs, a couple of marriages, multiple romantic and social relationships, and hospitals. Minor catastrophe after minor catastrophe plague her. She never holds a job for more than a few months. "It's not my fault," rationalizes Angie after yet another firing. "My boss was jealous of me." Or "We had a personality conflict." Or "They didn't live up to their end of the bargain." According to Angie, her job problems are always caused by someone else. The cause is always "out there." Angie sees herself as a powerless victim of the whims and caprices of others more powerful than she.

And in the process of all of this they're-out-to-get-me attitude, Angie staunchly maintains that it's never her fault. Despite lesson opportunity after lesson opportunity, she refuses to examine her attitudes and beliefs about herself. She tells herself consciously that she hasn't done anything to deserve such abuse. Although she rants and raves and cries and gets sick over perceived injustices, she suppresses uninvited thoughts and feelings that perhaps she is responsible for her predicament.

Maybe, just maybe, the outcomes of her many relationships and jobs are in someway related to her attitudes and actions. She freely expresses feelings — invariably negative — about the motives and actions of others while she firmly refuses to examine her own motives and actions. And

periodically she lands in the hospital with an acute physical problem —
migraines, digestive distress, "nerves."

Angie hasn't yet recognized that she is being presented an array of
learning opportunities. She continues to respond in ways that have proved
unsuccessful in the past, yet, each time, she hopes for a different outcome.
She hasn't figured out that with every negative experience, the first thing
to do is to step back, take a look at the situation as a whole, and find a
positive lesson. For Angie, the positive lesson might be in understanding
that her intelligence gets in the way of her common sense. Instead of
judging employers, colleagues, former friends, and spouses according to
the way she wants them to be and to behave, she would be better off
physically, emotionally, and economically if she accepts them as fellow
wayfarers who have their own lessons to learn on this journey of life.

WELLNESS PRINCIPLE: You have a choice in every lesson:
suppress feelings or learn

If you choose to suppress feelings that accompany a lesson, not only
will your body continue to respond physiologically to the suppressed
feelings, you will repeat the lesson-opportunity through a similar
experience. There's more truth than humor to the popular quip, "Keep
trying 'till you get it right."

The key to avoiding long-lasting repercussions from negative
responses to positive lessons is to address your feelings about the
situation/people involved before you sleep. Once you go to sleep with a
heavy heart or turbulent mind, the physiological response patterns stored
along with the precipitating event is embedded on your Yellow "hard-
drive." Your body will continue to respond physiologically to those
patterns until the memory is neutralized by positive feelings. But the
feelings must be equally as intense as the feelings that accompanied the
original data-entry. Wishy-washy feelings won't do it. Whether the
feelings are positive or negative, once you "sleep on it," the "commands"
are etched into your Yellow. Switching analogies for a minute, it's rather
like taking paint off your hands. It's fairly simple to do while the paint is
still wet; but let it dry and you have to rub and scrub to get it off — and
even then you're left with stains and residue around your cuticles and
under your fingernails — some of it sticks.

Once you sleep on an intense negative incident, the only way to
neutralize it is to "learn the lesson" and to appreciate the opportunity to
learn. You learn the lesson by finding something good in the situation and
appreciating that good with feelings equally as intense as the original.
Recognize that the lesson is an opportunity for you to become more "in
tune" with Creative Intelligence — and to sincerely appreciate the

opportunity.

> WELLNESS PRINCIPLE: You can't drop Remedial Life
> 101X; you repeat it

So what can poor, persecuted hypothetical Angie do about her series of job and relationship blunders? The first thing she had better do is recognize that she hasn't yet passed one specific life-lesson "course," and that she will continue to recycle the same lesson over and over until she "gets it." Angie is the only one who can identify the lesson. However, the longer she continues to respond in the same way to situations that set her up for migraines and malcontent, the longer the same types of incidents will happen over and over. And the longer she recycles that lesson, the longer it will take her to undo the physical damage she is doing to herself. Of course, she has the choice of doing nothing and her life will continue in the same familiar, unpleasant track.

Angie has her work cut out for her. Since she has stacked up a long history of not learning her lessons, her next step is to mentally backtrack to recall the many instances where she felt abused and go through the steps of forgiveness that are described later in this book. And in the process she needs to take a look at how she really looks at herself. Despite her externally-displayed bravado, how does she feel internally about herself? What does she say to herself about herself? Does she continually remind herself that she is worthless? Or that she "deserves" all of the grief she gets? Or that she is a powerless victim?

Very likely, hypothetical Angie took to heart negative childhood programming and has never moved on to the more sophisticated personal programming of adulthood. She is stuck in "Introduction to Introspection." Her personal programming — the way she "talks to herself" internally hasn't grown with her. But she can change that, too. She learned it through her Red and stored it in her Yellow. She can re-learn it through her Red and update her Yellow.

PERSONAL PROGRAMMING

Your Red is constantly active. In addition to receiving all of the information that comes at you through your five senses, your Red also manipulates and "chews on" that information. It analyzes, compares, concludes, and generally "thinks." Thinking is internal, and thinking is Red. Your Red does the thinking, your Yellow stores, and your Green responds.

Accumulated beliefs about yourself and the way you fit into family, community, and the world are the basis for your responses to everything that goes on around you.

> WELLNESS PRINCIPLE: Your actions mirror how you feel
> about and see yourself

How you feel about and see yourself is a direct reflection of your running inner commentary. Incessant internal chatter editorializes on your every action and reaction:

"That was a pretty stupid."	"Good job!"
"I can't do anything right."	"I handled that situation really well."
"I can't do that."	"Sure I can do that — and do it well."
"Ooops, goofed again."	"Another success."
"I'm too fat/skinny/short/tall."	"I look and feel great."

Unspoken remarks such as these may reflect impressions you formed about yourself and your abilities long ago. Yet each time they are repeated in your conscious mind they are reinforced in your Yellow that harbors your learned responses — how to respond to criticism, how to ride a bicycle, how you view the world. Non-conscious information comes to you after being filtered through your five senses and Red consciousness. And we know that the Red information can be off the mark. So there you are with questionable Red information fixed in your non-conscious Yellow that has a direct connection with your perfectly-responding subconscious Green. You end up with perfect automatic physiological responses to stimuli prompted by questionable information.

> WELLNESS PRINCIPLE: Learned responses spill into the
> pot at the end of your mental rain-
> bow

Your subconscious doesn't know the difference between truth and fantasy. All it knows is feelings. Each time you pass judgment on yourself, you enter Personal Programming into your this-is-how-you've-learned-to-respond Yellow. And self-inflicted judgmental statements about yourself are packed with feelings. Nagging, down-putting comments, like "Dumbhead, you goofed again," by the motor-mouth "color commentator" inside your head incite strong feelings accompanied by strong Green responses, such as "cringe," or "throw up," or "retreat." In a word — defend! Personal Programming sets the tone for all of your responses to everyday situations.

In his book, *What To Say When You Talk To Your Self*, Shad

Helmstetter uses the term "self-talk" for this internal running commentary. "Self-talk" and "Personal Programming" are different names for the same activity. However, the term "Personal Programming" helps us recognize that the things we say to ourselves in the privacy of our minds is more than idle chit-chat. Our constant silent comments influence all of our actions and attitudes. They "program" stimuli in the Yellow which influence Red thinking and Green responses. From the selection of the food we eat for breakfast to a decision to apply for a more responsible job, Personal Programming lobbies to keep us doing those things that assure we continue to conform to our well-programmed self-image.

> WELLNESS PRINCIPLE: Personal Programming forecasts success or failure

Your personal programming isn't and shouldn't be static throughout life. The "I want's," "I won'ts," "I can'ts," and "You can't make me's" that run through the head of a six-year old probably aren't appropriate as background music for a responsible thirty-year old who's trying to make car payments and mortgage payments. As you mature, acquire a greater capacity for rational thinking and for sorting out useful and useless information, you are in a position to update thoughts, attitudes, and beliefs about yourself and your abilities. Internal mental responses to current situations should be appropriate for current conditions. In other words, if the programming you received as a child isn't appropriate for adult situations, it's time to run a "check disk" on your Personal Programming.

Since you *will* respond to non-conscious Personal Programming whether you're aware of it or not, it's to your advantage to make sure that the things you say to yourself are of big-person calibre. As an adult, you don't need to be stuck in childhood attitudes toward yourself. You can re-program and up-date obsolete mental chit-chat. The prospect of changing your internal chatter may be scary at first. The familiar is comfortable. But remember, life is a succession of lessons. One of your biggest lessons may be to realize that you are a creature that is still developing. You were created under the guidance of Perfect Universal Creative Intelligence, and you continue to develop under that guidance. You don't need to contribute static to the reception of Perfect Intelligence energy by being mired in an obsolete mental monologue. It's up to you to make sure that the on-going mental cues that influence your body and your life reflect the Perfect Intelligence that powers all life.

> WELLNESS PRINCIPLE: Lobby against underage Personal Programming

PROGRAM TO YOUR ADVANTAGE

As small fry we depend upon others to provide care, sustenance, housing, and a safe place to play. We also depend on "big people" to prepare us to succeed in the world. Without giving it conscious thought, we count on those we trust to provide us a clear window through which to view ourselves in our rapidly-approaching grown-up life. Ideally, this view will show a competent, caring, contributing, productive "big person." We trust our mentors to prepare us for things to come. And they usually do. However, as we have seen, the preparation may be well-intentioned but misdirected. The atmosphere in which we grow up may foster Personal Programming that prepares us to fail rather than to succeed.

Personal Programming can lead us in directions we don't want to go. It can make us feel bad about ourselves. And it can make us sick. But I've never met a one-sided coin. The other side of the Personal Programming coin is that your intrahead chit-chat can help you reach goals, enjoy satisfaction in everything you do, and generally live life to the fullest. And that's really what all of us are after — a full, satisfying life.

> WELLNESS PRINCIPLE: The benefits of habitual positive Personal Programming last a lifetime

Imagine how you feel when you tell yourself "I'm always so tired." Repeat that phrase to yourself — with feeling — for about fifteen seconds. While you're repeating it, develop in your mind a picture of yourself looking worn out, tired and draggy. Recapture the feeling you have when you are tired. Go ahead, I'll wait about 15 seconds.

Okay, how do you feel? Tired? Down? If you don't, you probably didn't put as much feeling into the thought as you would if you were sincere about it.

Next exercise.

Now, for about fifteen seconds, repeat to yourself — with feeling — "I am energetic and feel great!" This time picture yourself vibrant, active and excited. Recapture the feeling you have when you *are* energetic and feel great. Again, I'll wait.

Good. If you spiked your repetitions with vivid visualization and positive feelings you should feel pretty perky.

The purpose of this little exercise is to demonstrate the power of repeated standardized thoughts about yourself, your qualities, and shortcomings. Personal Programming thoughts are packed with feeling. Intense. Brief and to the point. "I'm no good." "Everyone takes advantage of me." "I'm powerless." "I WON!" "I'm good at this."

It stands to reason that when we train our inner voices to help us rather than hinder us we feel better and are more satisfied with our lives and relationships. We train our inner Personal Programming voices through repetition. Training through repetition can re-program self-defeating thoughts and turn them into self-promoting thoughts.

If Personal Programming is dragging you down, it can be changed. If you aren't happy with the way you feel physically or the way you feel about yourself and your life right now, you — and only you — can do something about it. You are in control.

> WELLNESS PRINCIPLE: Personal Programming isn't etched in stone, but it *is* firmly etched in your non-conscious Yellow

Changing Programming statements isn't quite like changing your socks. It takes a little longer and considerably more effort. As with other thoughts, programming statements aren't sorted and stored neatly in bins labeled "Classic Putdowns," and "Confidence Builders." They take up residence in your brain in several places at once. According to physiologist Guyton, "A thought probably results from the momentary 'pattern' of stimulation of many different parts of the nervous system at the same time."[100] Improving your Personal Programming would be much easier if you could open your head, pluck out an offending programming statement and replace it with one more suitable. Since we haven't reached that level of technological sophistication (thank Goodness!), we must resort to the old-fashioned way. By repeatedly bombarding Red consciousness with new self-enhancing programming information.

You change Personal Programming by *updating* the messages you've stored in your Yellow. Not erasing them. Unlike information on a computer disk, information stored in your mental computer can't be erased from your "viewing screen" at the touch of a key or two. Once information from your five senses is stored in your non-conscious Yellow, it has found a home in several places in your brain. You may not always be able to recall particular stored information, such as names, phone numbers or chemistry formulae precisely when you would like, but it is there. In the same way, Personal Programming remains intact. So the secret is to update the information already there.

> WELLNESS PRINCIPLE: Update Personal Programming language to be consistent with current conditions

Updating Personal Programming (or any other internal communication) is rather like keeping your checkbook balance current — updated. If the last balance showing in your checkbook register is six months old and you've been happily putting money in and taking money out, the six-month-old balance is misleading. The figures need to be updated. You don't have to erase the ups and downs already recorded, you merely need to factor in the "ins" and "outs" — the elements that brought you to the present point — and enter current information.

WELLNESS PRINCIPLE: Personal Programming is time-sensitive

But there's another "but." In order for the information in either checkbook or programming to reflect actual present conditions, it must be entered correctly. Personal Programming messages must reflect what you want, not what you don't want. And your programming messages must be in sync with your beliefs.

Established Personal Programming and beliefs go hand in hand. You believe the ideas promoted by your Personal Programming statements. And each time you make a Personal Programming statement to yourself, you reinforce the belief behind it. The statement "The things I do are never quite good enough" reinforces the belief "I'll never be promoted." And since you believe you'll never be promoted, you keep adhering to your Programming statement. Round and round go programming and beliefs in a reinforcing frenzy that directs the course of your life and health.

Personal Programming statements that have kept pace with your changing status in life and help you respond in ways that are satisfying and health-promoting don't need to be updated. Updating is needed only in areas of your current programming that aren't positive forces in your life. The good news is that both beliefs and Programming can be changed. The process used to update is the same as the process used to acquire them in the first place — repetition.

REPETITION, REPETITION, REPETITION

Memories are stored in your Yellow either by intense feelings or by repetition. Little emotion is involved in many of the "facts" that pass through your Red to take up residence in your Yellow. When emotion isn't intense, repetition is the key to learning. Whether it's learning how to walk, talk, shoot free-throws successfully, recite multiplication tables or the Pledge of Allegiance, repetition is the adhesive that affixes patterns for muscular and "factual" responses in your Yellow.

The same repetition principle applies to updating Personal Programming. Again, our computer analogy goes awry. With the computer, new information that is entered and stored can be quickly recalled. When incorrect information is detected, it can be put right with a few key strokes. Out with the wrong and in with the right. Not so with Personal Programming. Our tissue and blood permanent storage facility isn't an inanimate, rigid, fixed, hard drive. It is live nerves and synapses in a vital container of soft tissue that requires a sudden jolt of strong feelings or the more subtle, persistent drip, drip, drip of the same message repeated over and over to establish a permanent residence.

> WELLNESS PRINCIPLE: New information must be entered
> repeatedly — or with strong feel-
> ings — to update the original

Developing new ways of thinking takes long-term commitment. It's simple; but it's not easy. The following "Steps to Update Personal Programming" can serve as a guide to help you replace outdated thought patterns with patterns that are more appropriate to your present stage of development and life. These steps shouldn't be seen as an instant cure for habitual life-jumbling thought patterns. Rather, they can guide you in forming Personal Programming thought habits that will help you to improve your life — and health.

The main point is that you must be aware of what you are thinking. Self-awareness combined with the ability to guide our thoughts may be the only thing that separates Generic Man from the rest of the animal kingdom. To be successful in updating your Personal Programming, you must not only be aware of what you are thinking, but you must put positive feelings with each statement.

Steps to Update Personal Programming

Step 1 —   *Recognize that some of your Programming statements may
have been false from the outset, or are now outdated*

During our growing-up years we develop self-portraits of ourselves by interpreting information received through our five senses. One of the most influential sources of information during childhood is the remarks made by parents and other adults. "You're sloppy." "You'll never amount to anything." "You're irresponsible."

And cruel remarks made by other children can glue negative images of ourselves into our Yellows. "You're ugly." "You're fat." "Ha, ha, ha. Your ears stick out." "Sissy." "Dummy." Comments received and interpreted by the Red, and stored with feeling in the Yellow, have the potential to become permanently fixed Personal Programming.

However, as we grow in stature and wisdom, these programming statements acquired in childhood or adolescence need to be re-evaluated. As adults, we don't need to be directed by childhood or childish beliefs and programming.

Take a close look at some of the statements that run around in your head. Are they nearly as old as you are? If so, it's time to recognize that they may no longer be valid, and to put them to rest.

Step 2 — *Recognize Negative Programming and Thoughts*

Negative programming and self-defeating thoughts are the bricks and mortar of the wall that stands in the way of you reaching your goal of health, happiness, and success. But you can't scale or demolish a wall that you don't realize is there. The trick is to recognize negative statements and beliefs when they show up. Be aware of the impact of statements like: "If I try, I'll fail," "I can't," "I'm clumsy," "I'm powerless," "I don't deserve happiness/success/a better job." Negative internally verbalized self-fulfilling, self-directed thoughts such as these running around in your Red prompt your Yellow to point you toward fulfilling your particular less-than-ideal picture of yourself. Negative programming phrases are the highly-effective, recurring drip, drip, drip of low-intensity stimuli. How many times can you hear that you are ugly, or fat, or dumb, or incompetent before you conform to it? If someone you don't care for or respect tells you that you are ugly, or fat, or dumb, or incompetent, you recognize the malice and slough it off. However, messages that spring from inside have the ring of authority. They're not interpreted as negative; they're interpreted as facts. The internal voice is the ultimate voice of authority; it's always right — or so we believe.

WELLNESS PRINCIPLE: Beliefs about ourselves surface constantly in the form of active thoughts

As you become more aware of the presence and the power of Personal Programming, you will recognize negative self-defeating thoughts for what they are each time they pop up. Once recognized, they can be neutralized — cancelled and refurbished.

Step 3 — *Cancel Inappropriate and/or Negative Thoughts*

Once you become tuned-in to negative thoughts, you may be surprised at how often they speak to you. However, when you recognize negative thoughts for what they are, you can go on the offensive. You can cancel them. First recognize a negative thought, then "cancel" it.

How do you do this?

Back to the computer analogy for the answer.

The words you are reading were written on a desk-top computer. However, I'm going to risk exploding the fantasy that books are written by blithely pouring thoughts from brain through fingers on a keyboard onto paper/screen and *viola!*, a finished book. The words you are reading are not the first effort at putting these particular thoughts, concepts, and examples into this book, chapter, page or sentence. Words, phrases, and large sections were written, evaluated, re-written, and deleted or "cancelled." Re-reading and evaluation often revealed phraseology that wasn't quite right. But errors of omission or commission were easily corrected by essentially the same steps you can use to upgrade thinking: Recognize the incorrect parts, focus attention (the curser) on the appropriate area, hit "delete," and, Zap!, the offending words or phrases vanished. The corrected version could then be entered.

You can delete inappropriate or negative thoughts that show up on your mind's "screen." Recognize, cancel, replace. The practical application of this concept is to do just that. Recognize the negativity of the thought "I'm always broke," delete/cancel the thought with the conscious mental command "Cancel that thought," and insert the conscious replacement thought "I manage my money well."

Do these "mind games" really work?

You bet they do — if you practice them. Cancelling a negative thought and replacing it with a positive substitute — with feeling — allows your body to respond to the positive stimulus; and positive stimuli don't create static in communication with your field.

> WELLNESS PRINCIPLE: Cancelling negativity reduces
> static in life and field

Step 4 — *"Enter" Only Appropriate Positive Thoughts*

Nature doesn't do vacuums well. Nature responds to a vacuum in much the same way as a river responds when you try to make a hole in it with your fist. The hole is there for almost a nanosecond, but then the water flows in again. Cancelling a thought creates a "vacuum" that will be filled with another thought of some sort. So why not custom design that refilling thought. When you "cancel" a negative or inappropriate thought, always replace it with one that is positive.

As long as you're conscious, you'll think. So your thinking may as well be to your advantage. Keep your Personal Programming on a track that will allow you to do your best, feel your best, and be your best.

Enter only positive thoughts into your soft-tissue computer. Phrase thoughts in the most positive way possible. A half-empty glass is also half-full. Phrase thought statements positively and in the present tense. Indicate that whatever you are thinking about is a done-deal. "I am energetic." "I enjoy my job." Use present-time positivity.

If you are not experienced in positive, present-time thinking, you will need to concentrate on how you talk to yourself. At first, you'll probably find that you must really think about what you're thinking about. But it is possible, and it is effective.

Never let a negative thought go unchallenged. When one sneaks in, cancel it and replace it with positive Personal Programming that will keep you on the course you want to take.

Step 5 — *"Save" With Enthusiasm*

Your subconscious responds to feelings and to pictures. Thoughts, feelings, and pictures go together. When you replace a negative thought with one that is positive, make sure that the picture is positive and that the thought is enthusiastically positive.

Remember the "tired" and "energetic" exercises? If your picture of the "energetic" you is that of a slumped frump, the picture and thought aren't congruous. Make sure your pictures are as enthusiastically positive as the programming text.

Enthusiasm and excitement are the "save" commands for positive thoughts and feelings. Fear, anxiety, and anger are just a few of the "save" commands for negative thoughts and feelings. Your Yellow non-conscious doesn't know fact from fiction. It takes the information it's given and provides signals to the Green which directs physiological responses appropriate to the feelings and pictures associated with thoughts. So even if you don't enjoy your job, don't "tell" your Yellow. Instead, visualize yourself being up-beat and positive at your work place, and tell yourself you enjoy what you are doing. But don't just "say" it. Feel it! Be positive about it! Put positive feelings of enthusiasm and energy into the thought statement. In time you won't have to work at drumming up positive feelings — they will become a standard part of your thinking.

FINE-TUNE PERSONAL PROGRAMMING

Of the four steps to updating Personal Programming, the last step is the most important. The feelings behind the words you use for your Personal Programming are more important than the words themselves. No matter what words you use, intense feelings set the tone for your Green response. This could be a problem for you. You may not really *believe* what you are telling yourself when you begin to update your Personal Programming. At first, if you tell yourself "I am at an ideal weight," yet you "know" you need to lose thirty pounds, you will probably feel you are lying to yourself. And the negative feeling will erase the positivity of the words. But take heart. You aren't "lying," you are using your body's built-in mechanisms to accomplish your purpose. You aren't engaging in self-deception, you are applying self-direction. By synthesizing positive feelings about your weight (or whatever), you are sending messages to your Green to do the physiology that goes with your goal. The way you feel about Personal Programming statements affects both the impact and efficiency of your statements.

> WELLNESS PRINCIPLE: Your Green responds to feelings;
> your Red to words, and your Yel-
> low responds to both

Your Green is totally objective. It doesn't understand modifiers and it doesn't understand "negative" commands. Your Green is a totally black-or-white kind of guy. Even if your Red and Yellow are steeped in negatives, your subconscious Green isn't. Your Green doesn't judge. As far as it is concerned, when you tell yourself in words and feelings "I'm a klutz," this isn't a negative, judgmental statement — it's a fact. And your Green responds to feelings with physiological adaptations. Your Yellow responds without thought to the words and feelings by activating stored behavioral patterns — "Okay, we're doing 'klutz' now, just like you said."

Your Red understands "I should stop smoking" as you intend. But your Yellow memory pattern is more focused than that; it understands only the "smoking" part.

"Should" and "ought" statements are incomplete. Saying to yourself "I should eat better" leaves off the unspoken (or unthought) end of that statement, "but I really can't," or "but I'm not going to change my lifestyle to do it." The conflict between what you know you "should" do and your resistance to doing it adds a dollop of guilt to an already negative brew. The positive feelings of excitement and commitment that initiate or sustain interference-free Green activity are missing.

In Personal Programming, be positive! Be present! No "should's," or "ought's." "Should" and "ought" muddy the Personal Programming waters. It's not that your Red doesn't know what it is you "should" or "ought to" do, but "should" and "ought" are verbal vacillators. They scramble the rainbow of your mind. Your Red sends out conflicting messages — "I should, but I won't" stop smoking, or go on a diet, or get more exercise. Statements such as these generate subtle guilt. Your Yellow responds with activities appropriate to the subject. Your Green responds with physiology appropriate for guilt.

> WELLNESS PRINCIPLE: "Should" statements ease your

conscience; they don't contribute to health, happiness,
and success

In order for your Yellow to respond in ways to help you achieve positive goals, you need to clue it in to the desired results. In the stop-smoking scenario, your Red may think the goal is to avoid lung cancer. However, your physiological goal is to have clean, clear, healthy, pink lungs. And you get clean, clear, healthy, pink lungs by breathing only clean, clear air. Lung cancer is an effect of not meeting that goal, and you help your body by addressing causes, not effects. The message that points your Yellow in the right direction is: "I breathe only clean air." Remember, your Yellow harbors learned responses. It integrates thoughts with actions. Positive done-deal phraseology that right now, this minute, you have clean lungs is much more effective in accomplishing your purpose than empty guilt-producing vacillation of "I'm going to stop smoking."

In the same way, if you keep telling yourself "I hope I never get Parkinson's disease like my mother," your Yellow will respond to the part that packs the greatest emotional wallop — Parkinson's disease. Thoughts along this line are generally not casual. They are loaded with feelings. And even though you are focusing on not getting this disease, all your Yellow receives is the "Parkinson's disease" part in pictures and feelings. Then your Green responds to the strong feelings and vivid pictures associated with your mother and her symptoms. Your thoughts are converted to physiology. Strong feelings and vivid pictures are potent Green stimuli. With the convincing combination of directions, pictures, and feelings, you leave your Green no option other than to get busy and work toward producing symptoms of Parkinson's disease.

WELLNESS PRINCIPLE: Give your Yellow positive instructions for what you want and your
Green will carry them out

Well-constructed Personal Programming is not an end in itself. The purpose of Personal Programming is to send the best possible messages through your mental rainbow of Red, Yellow, and Green to allow your physiology to function in ways that lead to good health, happiness, and success. You can fine-tune your Personal Programming by paying attention to how you state your aims. Your Red Personal Programming feeds your Yellow memory patterns, and your Green responds. Your Green must respond physiologically to every stimulus. And its responses are always perfect. So make sure your Green receives the signals it needs to allow you to become your best.

WELLNESS PRINCIPLE: The Green always responds precisely to Personal Programming

At the end of this chapter is a list of some examples of "do's" and "don'ts" of Personal Programming statements. Statements that send wrong messages — error messages — emphasize undesirable attributes, attitudes, or habits — "I'm always nervous and up-tight," "I can't stand my job." Their counterpart healing messages allow your Green to point you in the direction you want to go — "I am peaceful and serene," "I do my best work and am enthusiastic about it."

Once you become acquainted with your Personal Programming, you will be able to update destructive statements so that they become constructive templates for health, happiness, and success.

Over the next three days, focus on your own Personal Programming statements. Pay attention to how you phrase your Personal Programming statements. Pay attention to how you phrase your Programming. Write down the phrases you catch yourself saying to yourself. Then edit them for content and effectiveness and re-write them so that they will work for you rather than against you. When you recognize that they are running your life you also recognize their importance.

Conscious thoughts in your Red, including Personal Programming statements, are major influences on the course of your life *and your health!* You respond to your thoughts. You act on your thoughts. *Your body responds to your thoughts!* And your thoughts are closely interwoven with your beliefs.

WELLNESS PRINCIPLE: Lurking behind your thoughts and
Personal Programming are your
beliefs

PERSONAL PROGRAMMING

ERROR MESSAGES	HEALING MESSAGES
Everything I eat turns to fat	I eat only foods that are good for my body
I never seem to finish anything	I always finish what I start
I am a victim of other people's whims and maliciousness	I am in control of my life
Everything I do is wrong	I am capable and confident
I turn everyone off	I am pleasant and personable
I can't stop smoking	I put only clean air into my lungs
I'm always sick or feel bad	I am healthy and energetic
I'm a failure	I am successful
I'm always nervous and up-tight	I am peaceful and serene
I'm too fat	I am at an ideal weight
I'm tired all the time	I am energetic and enthusiastic
I'm always rushed; I wish I had more time	I am organized and efficient
I have trouble making up my mind	I think clearly and make decisions well
My father had heart trouble so I'm sure I will, too	I eat, exercise, and rest properly; I take care of my heart and body
I can't stand my job	I do my best work and am enthusiastic about it
I'll always be a failure	I am successful because I get satisfaction from everything I do

POINTS OF INTEREST

1.   Thoughts are tiny bits of energy that interact with other energy.

2   Conscious Red thoughts find associated Yellow memories.

3.   Most of the thoughts you have today are the same as those you had yesterday.

4.   Negative thinking coupled with negative feelings are behind most physical distress.

5.   Every negative experience is an opportunity to learn a lesson.

6.   Self-esteem is learned thought patterns that begin in childhood.

7.   Your thoughts and actions are in keeping with the way you "talk to yourself" — your Personal Programming.

8.   Personal Programming that works against you can be updated.

*All I have seen teaches me to trust the Creator
for all I have not seen.*
                                    - Ralph Waldo Emerson

CHAPTER 10
Beliefs — Power Motivators

BELIEFS

Beliefs are behind just about everything we do, say, and think as individuals and as communities. And in our democratic society, the demarcation between individual beliefs and corporate beliefs may not always be clear.

We eat food that we believe to be good for us — or at least not toooo bad for us. We go to work whether we feel like it or not because we believe that responsible adults fulfil their responsibilities — or because we believe we'll be fired if we don't. We stop (or almost stop) at stop signs because we believe in driving safely — or that we might get a ticket if we don't. Even if the belief behind an activity isn't apparent, it's there. In fact, a strong belief is behind my writing this book. I believe that the concepts presented here can help people manage their health better than they have in the past, and I believe I can help many more people by writing this book than I can by just seeing patients.

WELLNESS PRINCIPLE: Beliefs are powerful motivators

Our beliefs spur us to action, or inaction — especially beliefs about ourselves, how the world works, and how we fit into the grand scheme of family, society, and the world. I'm not talking about off-the-top-of-the-head beliefs, such as "I believe the price of XYZ stock is going to go up soon," or "I believe I'll have the strawberries with sauerkraut for dessert."

No, the beliefs we're talking about here are the deep-seated, gut-level, seldom verbalized beliefs that are behind our every thought and action. These are the "The world is a perilous place and I must constantly be on my guard" type beliefs. Or, "My luck has always been bad and it'll stay that way." Or, "Health is a hereditary crap-shoot; there's nothing I can do to change that." Or, "That's the way I am and always have been and nothing is going to change." Or, one of the most devastating beliefs, "The doctor said there's no cure for what I have, so that's that; the doctor knows."

WELLNESS PRINCIPLE: Beliefs are the backdrop on our
stage of life

Individual and corporate beliefs are products of conscious Red activity. They are based on conscious mind interpretations of stimuli received through the five senses. We call these stimuli "life experiences." And life experiences begin at (or, perhaps, before) birth. Beliefs are not genetically transmitted; they develop. They begin in the conscious mind and develop as non-conscious memory patterns — once learned, they are used without conscious focus.

Newly acquired sensory-received information is dumped into our pot of existing Red information. The new information is immersed in the pre-existing stew of previously acquired Red interpretations, and the whole brew is flavored by the mental herbs and spices of resident beliefs stored in the Yellow. New information is tainted or enhanced by the flavoring of the essence of existing beliefs.

Beliefs are the underpinnings of the way you think and feel about yourself and the world. Do you believe that you are a piece of machinery that needs constant tinkering? Or do you believe that you are an integral part of a larger energy system? The way you think about yourself in your conscious Red is colored by perceptions embedded in your non-conscious Yellow. From these perceptions spring your beliefs. Carrying our color concept yet another step, we might say that your beliefs are the Orange component of the rainbow of your mind. Your Orange is the basis for how you respond to life situations. And since Orange beliefs are residents of your non-conscious Yellow they can influence both your conscious Red and your subconscious Green.

Beliefs impact your thoughts, actions, and responses. Your thinking Red directs your actions in conjunction with your Yellow. Your Yellow holds your beliefs based on reference material from past experiences. And your Green brings about the physiological responses to all of the above. Put all of these ingredients together, and you have "You" — the physical "You" who walks, talks, argues, encourages, and responds to other people, and the vital "You" who thinks, feels, digests food, enjoys, and gets up-tight. "You" are the personification of your beliefs.

WELLNESS PRINCIPLE: Beliefs are the footing on which
your castle of individuality is built

Not only are beliefs the bedrock of your self-view and world-view, they are behind most of your decisions and judgments. As we discussed in earlier chapters, your health and/or happiness and/or success are products of your thoughts and feelings. Now we see that your current thoughts and feelings are products of your current beliefs. And your current beliefs were formed by previous thoughts and feelings.

Are you beginning to get the idea that your beliefs are more than personal opinions about political and religious issues or cultural values. Beliefs lurk behind just about everything you do, say, and think. And all of these together influence the way your body responds!

A personal story illustrates the impact intangible beliefs can have on thinking, decisions, actions, and the tangible physical body.

BELIEFS COLLIDE

As a practicing chiropractor since 1965, I have long held the belief that the body is a self-regulating, self-healing, integrated unit. I firmly believe that the body heals itself on a priority basis — first-things-first, and that anything that affects one part of the body affects all parts of the body. These beliefs were put to a practical test in 1978 when I was in a serious automobile accident.

One late summer day, as I drove along a well-travelled four-lane road, I noticed off to my left a roadside pasture dotted with round hay bales. The hay bales aren't directly involved in the story, but they are a vivid picture in my memory. I was intrigued by the shape of the bales since I had grown up on a farm where hay bales were always rectangular. However, my clear recollection of the round bales does serve to illustrate a couple of points that permeate this book: 1) that dramatic events can fix seemingly insignificant details into memory, and 2) that if you are not in defense physiology at the start of a critical emergency, you'll probably not be in defense physiology after the emergency is over. But back to the story.

Since I was driving, I had only a fleeting view of the pastoral scene. Suddenly, I heard noise, and my head hit the "ceiling" of my car. Another car traveling in the opposite direction had crossed the center line and hit my car head on, driver side to driver side. The accident "started" when the other car lost a tie rod and the 18-year old driver lost control. That's when

I became involved. Wham! Two vehicles, both travelling at about 40 mph collided. Although I had been looking to my left, I didn't see the car coming — a point in my favor. My body wasn't in defense physiology at the time of impact. Although neither the other driver nor I "walked away" from the accident and we were both seriously injured, we both survived. It was a bad accident. Two piles of mangled metal and two mangled bodies. Off to the hospital we both went, but not under our own steam.

At the hospital, X-rays showed that my most obvious and most painful injury was to my hip. It was both fractured and dislocated. Contrary to the words of the song, the leg bone was not connected to the hip bone. Of course, other areas of my body were also damaged, but the damage to my hip was severely painful and serious. My head had suffered minimal injury from its encounter with the roof and, perhaps, other protuberances in the car. I had no pain in my chest, I had no trouble breathing. While I could speak with force, the effort drained precious energy. After I had answered the same questions from various hospital staff, I announced that I had finished talking. I didn't need to waste vital healing energy.

After determining the extent of my injuries, the hospital staff carted me off to the operating room to do something about my wayward hip. However, before I went, I resumed speaking enough to insist that there be no "operation." No cutting into this self-healing body to clean up the bone fragment mess and put back the misplaced femur. The orthopedist did not agree with this strategy. He believed that the small bone fragments would cause me less trouble if they were surgically put back where they belonged. Nonetheless, he followed, if not honored, my wishes; he successfully realigned the hip joint without "going in." However, since he believed the realignment to be unstable, he inserted a Steinmann's pin below my knee so I could be "hooked up" to twenty pounds of traction. Off I went to intensive care.

The next day, the orthopedist told me that it would be to my advantage to have screws put into my hip in order to hold it in place. He believed that the long-term outcome would be better if this were done.

I did not share his belief.

I followed my belief that the body — even a body that hurt as much as mine did — will heal itself unaided as long as nothing interferes with the healing processes. That meant without interference from metal screws, or traction for that matter. My belief and the belief of the medical doctor were at odds. But it was my body.

The projected course of treatment, from the medical point of view, was thirty days in traction supplemented by active and passive physical therapy. I was to stay in bed, on pain pills, and continue passive physical therapy. Then, with any luck, in about ninety days I should be able to walk with crutches to my mailbox about thirty-five feet from my house.

Eventually, according to conventional medical wisdom, I would graduate to walking with the aid of a cane. Then, some time in the nebulous future, I would hardly know I had had the accident — except for a slight limp and a smattering of pain when the weather changed. That scenario didn't fit my belief system at all!

The treatment schedule my belief system mandated was to keep my body alkaline through diet, keep my energy system balanced through frequent non-forceful, energy-directed chiropractic adjustments, and keep my overall attitude positive. I believed that by accomplishing these goals, there would be very little interference to keep my body from doing what it does best — heal itself.

During the course of my seven- or eight-day stay in the hospital, another vital premise of this book was confirmed — priority healing. The day after the accident I began to notice signs of my body's predisposition for priority healing. With my hip back in place, the damage to my chest came into priority. How did I know my chest damage was in priority? It became so painful that only very shallow breathing was possible.

During the accident and the accompanying jostling about in the car (seatbelt not withstanding), my chest had hit the steering wheel. In fact, those who saw the car after the accident said that the steering column had been bent in such a way that you could stand outside the driver's side door and grasp the steering wheel in the usual driving position. Despite the violence done to chest, steering wheel, and steering column, there was no discomfort in my chest when I arrived at the hospital. It was my hip that hurt with a capital "H." The damage to my hip was the greatest threat to my survival. However, after the orthopedist had realigned my hip, the injury to my chest took priority. It became very painful. During the early days of my recovery, the dominant pain switched back and forth between hip and chest. My body was taking care of healing both injuries depending upon which was the most important at the time. Although I wasn't really keen on the pain involved, I was delighted with the illustration of the priority healing process. The hospital medical staff was not impressed.

After a few days of intense belief conflict between doctor and patient, the orthopedist and I came to a mutual agreement. We agreed that since I wasn't doing what he and the hospital staff believed I should do, and since I steadfastly refused surgical intervention, and since I wasn't eating the food, and since I insisted on being adjusted by my fellow chiropractors, I would be better off at home than in the hospital.

So I went home by the same means I had arrived at the hospital: by ambulance. My wife had rented a hospital-type bed for me which made everyone's life a little easier. Although I had been "dismissed" from the hospital, I wasn't ready to be up and around, but I was in a position to give my body the rest and nutrition it needed. For "meals," I continued on the same diet I had devised in the hospital: fresh carrot juice and fresh peach juice. For "physical therapy," I moved as much as my body indicated I should. And for "treatment," the other doctors from my clinic continued to adjust my internal communication systems several times a day. But most important, I kept faith with my body and my beliefs.

Once I was home and able to follow the regimen that was in line with my beliefs, my recovery was quite successful. Instead of a total of months of traction, crutches, and a cane, I was up and walking with crutches ten days after the accident. On the fourteenth day I was walking with a cane. At the end of three weeks — at least a week earlier than I had been "scheduled" to come off traction — I was jogging and playing tennis. I wasn't playing very good tennis, but I didn't play "good" tennis before the accident.

As far as a lingering limp goes, there isn't one. No limp. No twinges to forecast a change in the weather. In fact, about the only time I think about my accident or my injuries is when I get to the "beliefs" section of my HealthWeek seminars. Even then, I sometimes forget it.

It is important that you understand that this personal experience story is about a conflict of beliefs. It isn't about "fighting the system." I do not suggest in any way that you or any other person in crisis rebel against, ignore, or contradict the advice and ministrations of qualified doctors, specialists, or other licensed health care providers. Beliefs won't stop a hemorrhage or a heart attack. Beliefs won't instantly bring down a fever out of control or set a bone. Medical doctors are trained to handle medical emergencies, and they are very good at their jobs. Don't come to me if blood is gushing from an open wound. That's not my job; it's the job of very capable, well-trained medical personnel. My job is to give you information that can help you change your beliefs so you can take control of your health before and after a medical crisis — not during.

The point of my accident story is that we act according to our beliefs. All of the players in this mini-drama acted according to their beliefs. The orthopedist and hospital staff acted in accord with their beliefs. They were unquestioning in their beliefs that the treatment they recommended and the recovery schedule they predicted were not only valid but tested. They are skilled, conscientious professionals who believe in what they do and they do it well. I was equally unquestioning in my belief that it was up to me to make sure that nothing was done to compound the problems my body had to handle, or to interfere with its natural healing abilities.

My belief was, and is, that it is my responsibility to provide my body with the best environment for healing. The medical belief — according to their experience — is that the effects of injuries such as those I had received would very likely be evident to some degree for the rest of my life. My holistic belief was, and is, that once the initial emergency was taken care of — which the orthopedist did very well — my body would repair itself.

Most people in our Newtonian culture can give nodding philosophical assent to the concept that the body possesses self-healing, self-regulating powers. However, for the vast majority of people, this philosophy has not yet reached the "gut-level belief" stage. Inasmuch as I have spent the greatest part of my adult life living, teaching, and treating patients according to self-healing, self-regulating, priority-intense, whole-body concepts, I am completely dedicated to these principles. *I do not suggest that you use my experience as a guide in responding to an emergency situation.* I must emphasize that my story is meant to illustrate that in human relationships we often run up against a conflict of beliefs, and that our major and minor decisions and actions are founded on our personal beliefs.

BOGUS BELIEFS

Some beliefs — corporate or personal — aren't in keeping with the way things are. Take religion, for example. Each permutation of religious belief is seen as "true" to its believers. But the divergence between these "truths" is illustrated by the great variety of religious beliefs that dot the world. Loving God. Vengeful God. Involved God. Aloof God. No God. Many gods. Little "g" god. All of these beliefs are "true" for their believers. Can such diverse views all be "right"?

Religion aside, even some commonly held secular beliefs — such as, "the government is supposed to take care of us," or "all politicians/lawyers/car salesmen are crooks" — are suspect. Beliefs, like maturity, develop from interpretations of experience. We form our beliefs throughout life. They may form quickly through interpretations of a highly intense sensory experience, or they may form slowly over time. To illustrate, suppose you grew up in a small town where everyone knew everyone else, house doors were left unlocked, and trust in others reigned. Very likely you would believe that you were safe and secure in your own home town. Then one day you come home after having been away for a couple of hours and you find your house had been burglarized. Instantaneously your belief changes. Security went out the door along with your TV, VCR, and CD player. No longer do you believe you are as safe and secure as you did when you left the house. And your new belief can keep you on edge.

You can also form a firm belief as the result of persistent exposure to the same information over and over. In school you learn and come to believe "facts": 9 times 9 equals 81; scientists have identified 108 natural or synthetic elements (or whatever the number is when this book goes to press); Earth is the third planet from our Sun. Accepting beliefs such as these is advantageous at test time.

You also develop beliefs through long-term training in cultural customs — beliefs shared and taught through example, word, and deed by family, relatives, and friends. Cultural beliefs range from "abortion is murder" or "every woman has the right to choose," to "monogamy is the only acceptable marital arrangement" or "polygamy is natural and desirable"; (notice that polyandry has never caught on as a popular belief). One of the standard beliefs that permeates our society is: "You can't get too much protein." We'll see in a later chapter why that belief is bogus.

Our personal beliefs guide our thinking. We evaluate our experiences in life according to our acquired beliefs. A person of a particular religious conviction may see the untimely accidental death of a loved one as "the will of God" or "Divine punishment." An areligious individual might view it as an unpredictable fact of life, or the predictable outcome of a particular series of events. An abused wife of one cultural upbringing might view her lot as "the way things are," while a wife in a similar situation yet different cultural environment might take steps to extricate herself from the abusive environment. Beliefs are circumstantial.

WELLNESS PRINCIPLE: There's no truthometer for beliefs

Beliefs may be bogus, but they are always true to the believer. No one continues to believe something that is illogical to that person. A belief may be illogical to others, but not to the believer. Whether or not a belief stands up to the scrutiny of science or logic makes no difference. Although beliefs originate intellectually in your Red, the "truth" factor transforms your Orange function of believing into an integral part of your health. And your beliefs may be major stumbling blocks in the way of health, happiness, and success. Take the tried and true belief "Germs cause disease" for example.

Germs do not "cause" colds. Of course, you'll have a hard time convincing the coughing, sneezing, runny-nose cold "victim" of that. "Cold germs" are always around. They are outside your body and they are inside your body. You don't have to "catch" them. When your body is functioning reasonably well, your internal environment isn't hospitable to cold germs. Those you encounter can't establish a home. But when your body is overtaxed, overacid, and leaning toward the "exhausted" side, the internal environment is a pleasant place for cold germs (and other germs) to take up residence. As you will see when we talk about foods, your body becomes overly acidic when you consistently eat too much protein.

A cold is a cleansing process. When your internal environment is too acid, germs have a field day. What does your body do? Everything it must to survive! In the process, it revs up all of its dilution and elimination processes to clean out as much junk as possible. So when you get a cold, be thankful and learn the lesson. Be thankful that your body still has enough energy to combat microscopic intruders, and learn that if you continue to abuse your body by making inappropriate healthstyle choices, your body will respond in ways you don't like. More about choices later.

Beliefs may be "true" to the believer, but they may be inaccurate, illogical, or unable to stand up to close scrutiny. Correct or not, from the believer's point of view, their own beliefs are true (they chase and chase and finally "catch" that cold.)

> WELLNESS PRINCIPLE: Right or wrong, your beliefs are "True" — for you

HEALTH-INHIBITING BELIEFS

Three particular types of beliefs are especially devastating to health, happiness, and success. I have found that patients who hold any of these beliefs (or variations thereof) are particularly vulnerable to disease and slow to recover when disease develops. I term these three crucial health-inhibiting beliefs: (1) The Victim Belief, (2) The Martyr Belief, and (3) The Low Self-Esteem Belief.

The Victim Belief — Victims are helpless: lack control and abdicate responsibility. Victims believe themselves to be powerless and at the mercy of bad luck, mean-spirited others, or uncompromising heredity. They believe they, their health, and lives are under the control of external forces. Some of the external forces may be friends, relatives, strangers, germs, heredity, the government, or circumstances in general. Indeed, all too many people are truly victims of physical and mental violence and abuse. However, many actual victims recover from their trauma without becoming career victims. Others cling to the victim attitude long after their physical injuries are healed or they are removed from the abusive situation. The victim belief nurtures a victim attitude and a belief of helplessness and hopelessness.

The hopelessness of the victim belief is self-defeating. It drains vitality and energy from body, mind, and field. Hopeless victims shed their responsibility for their actions and their lives as easily as angora cats shed hair on the carpet. In our society, we see this in the recent rash of legal defenses against charges of murder or mayhem. The defendant is characterized as a victim of past abuses, and as such, seeks to be absolved of responsibility for his or her actions. Where health is concerned, the victim belief transfers the responsibility for getting sick or getting well to someone or something else. It's the old, "I caught a cold from my husband," or "Cancer runs in my family," and the most pervasive, "Doctor, I hurt; fix it." The unspoken phrase that follows that last example is "fix it while I continue doing what I'm doing." In reality, however, only the individual — victim or not — can take charge of his or her health and life. The victim belief, and its kissin' cousins the Low Self-Esteem Belief and Martyr Belief, can be updated, but it takes a whole new mind-set.

Those who believe themselves to be victims of abuse, discrimination, "the system," or bad luck will continue in that belief until they recognize that they are responsible for their life and health. That's one of the fun things about being a *homo sapien* — we get to decide how we are going to view ourselves and the world around us. And if we don't like what we see, we can change *our beliefs*. Remember, you weren't born with your beliefs. They developed in your Red and were stored in your Yellow — they were learned. And since beliefs are learned through your Red, they can be changed by your Red. You don't have to be a victim buffeted about by the whims of others. You are the captain of your ship of life. You can take responsibility for your life. You can choose how you will respond.

WELLNESS PRINCIPLE: Victims are passive; self-masters
are active

The Martyr Belief — Ah! The Martyr — Poor Pitiful Pearl, the great and constant sufferer. While the Victim suffers, the Martyr enjoys (in both senses of the word) ill health, the abuse of others, and a general case of the miseries. It's his/her purpose in life. The Martyr believes that it is his or her lot in life to suffer — but, generally, not in silence. "It's all right; you all go on and have a good time. I'll just stay here (and be miserable). Don't worry about me." Or, "I can't hold a job — migraines, you know." Or, "I'm not very strong; I was a sickly child." The Martyr is ever ready to brag about his or her misfortunes. The Martyr believes that the crosses he or she bears are heavier than those borne by others. And if you don't give the martyr the proper amount of sympathy, you're not playing the game right.

My clinical experience shows that Martyrs who firmly believe that their pain or disease is divinely decreed and serves a higher purpose rarely respond to treatment. The strong emotions that accompany their belief and persistent negativity perpetuate the physiology that led to their disease. The intensity of their negative emotion overrides positive therapeutic effects of treatment. Martyrs will continue on their path to self-destruction as long as they hold the belief that their illness glorifies a higher authority.

WELLNESS PRINCIPLE: The Martyr feeds on adversity

Low Self-Esteem Belief — Unlike those who practice responsibility-avoidance that is part of the victim belief, those who suffer (literally) from low self-esteem believe that everything that goes wrong is their fault, somehow. As we saw earlier, through years of conditioning they have accepted that they are worthless and incompetent. They habitually evaluate themselves by comparing their weakest characteristics with the strongest characteristics of others. In an effort to compensate for their inadequacies, they devote much of their energy in trying to please others. Unless their efforts are constantly acknowledged and praised, their feelings of failure and unworthiness are reinforced. Red anxiety and fear are ever present. In time, Green physiological responses to the constant anxiety and fear exhaust overworked organs and systems, and pain, symptoms, illness, and disease surface. Low self-esteem can be devastating to health just as surely as it can be devastating to happiness and success. Low self-esteem is erosion of perceived self-worth by a drip, drip, drip pattern of beliefs. Just as no one is "all good," no one is "all bad." Low self-esteem is founded on "should's" and "ought's." It is self-directed health-inhibiting beliefs in action.

WELLNESS PRINCIPLE: Low self-esteem beats you up
while it beats you down

Beliefs that lead us down a wrong path plague rich and poor, intellectual and illiterate, sophisticate and rustic. It's more than possible that belief errors are behind many mistakes in every area of your life: personal relationships, jobs, finances, diet, exercise, and health. You can ferret out health-inhibiting beliefs and re-examine them. Although I haven't discovered a litmus test for destructive beliefs, I have found that examining past disappointments can offer some clues.

To begin your examination, consider a situation that was disappointing or didn't turn out the way you had hoped or wanted — a relationship that went sour, for example. Look at some possible beliefs (or assumptions) that may have influenced the way you thought about the other person. Did you believe that the other person was "perfect" and would put up with your less-than-perfect character? Or did you believe that you were "perfect" and could change the other person to match your stellar character? Did you believe that you were the other person's "savior" or that he or she was yours? Did you believe that the other person had only your best interests at heart? Or did you believe that everyone, including your significant other, was "using" you?

WELLNESS PRINCIPLE: Beliefs guide actions

DEVELOPED BELIEFS

Beliefs develop over time. They don't just happen.

We can learn a lot about ourselves and our taken-for-granted beliefs by asking ourselves some penetrating questions about our responses to past disappointments. We may find we have outgrown some beliefs that serve as the foundation for our actions and decisions.

Earlier we saw how childhood Personal Programming can be inappropriate for adult life. The same holds true for outgrown childhood beliefs. We don't come equipped with beliefs — they develop. We come equipped with survival mechanisms. Infinite wisdom for survival is part of the standard equipment of brand-new people. As they grow and learn, their Greens continue to work for survival even as their Reds become active. Each Red received experience is measured according to its survival hazard level. Recognizing this, you can see why crying is a perfectly "rational" activity for a baby. Cry, and food arrives — great for survival. Cry, and warmth and comfort arrive — great for survival. But with growth, things change. There's more to life than eating and being comforted. It's activity time. And some activities, such as running out into the street, bring painful consequences: pain from being hit by a car or being spanked by a parent, negative reinforcement. Pain means "not good for survival." So the developing person forms a belief that street-playing equals pain equals poor survival response.

Beliefs that are formed by negative experiences put negative energy into the field. And, as we have seen, few children escape childhood without hours of negativity. This means that a developing Yellow is subjected to and permeated with a bunch of negative energy. When beliefs are reactivated as thoughts, negative energy is also reactivated. More organizing energy goes into the chaotic field. And organizing the field decreases the availability of complete energy information.

Ideally, our beliefs mature along with us - but not always. As small children we tend to believe that the world revolves around us and our wants. As adults, we should have learned that our wants and needs aren't the fulcrum that moves the world. At age three, you may have believed that monsters lived under your bed at night. At age twenty-three, you are more sophisticated — you know that the only thing under your bed is dust bunnies. In a similar vein, at age twelve or thirteen, your beliefs about sex are (preferably) based on locker-room hearsay rather than experience, and miss the mark of accuracy. When you are twenty-two or twenty-three, your beliefs about sex should be appropriate for a mature adult ready for, or in, a mature relationship. Close examination of the beliefs that lurk behind your every action can reveal beliefs in a state of arrested development.

WELLNESS PRINCIPLE: Outgrown beliefs can pinch like
outgrown shoes

One of the most common, strongly-held beliefs that can cause problems is the belief that everyone else should think, act, respond, see things, and believe exactly the way you do. The humor in the theme of the song "Why can't a woman be more like a man?" from the musical *My Fair Lady* comes from our recognition of the absurdity of the idea, combined with the realization that we lean in that thought-direction in our own lives. The he-should-be-more-like-me belief is behind all sorts of confrontations, both personal and international. We need to remember that each of us has developed his or her own beliefs from personal experience and perceptions. Since no two lives are identical, no two belief systems are identical. Or, to put it another way, we all have our own lessons to learn.

WELLNESS PRINCIPLE: Beliefs can spark lessons; lessons
can change beliefs

The problem with living with outgrown beliefs is that they impose unnecessary stress on your body. If your mature actions don't fit your outgrown beliefs, the natural consequence is guilt that can escalate to self-contempt. Now that's negative. And you know how negative feelings can undermine your health and bring on physical pain.

The association between a very real back pain and a violated belief may not be obvious. However, on those occasions when you are in pain and your doctor tells you, "I can't find anything wrong," it's time to think about the congruency of your beliefs and actions. Examine the things that are going on in your life and examine your beliefs about the situation and yourself. You may find some big dichotomies.

BELIEFS AND LIFESTYLE

In a contest between beliefs and actions, beliefs always win in the end. If beliefs and lifestyle are not in synch, beliefs will dominate. Beliefs will dominate because you will "shoot" yourself in your metaphorical foot. You will have an adverse reaction — either functional or physical — to your "belief-abusing" actions. Your body will respond non-consciously and/or subconsciously in ways that force you to fall back in line with your belief patterns. Did you ever try to sell a product or service you didn't "believe" in? You can't do it effectively — your beliefs always show through. Or, how about a friend or relative who is "his/her own worst enemy"? They constantly act in ways that undermine their alleged goal.

The problem is that their "goal" isn't in line with their beliefs, so their non-conscious sends them off in directions that keep them from reaching their destination.

On the physical side of "foot-shooting," the story of a young woman who sought my advice on a physical problem is a beautiful case in point. To set the scene, she was a professional woman in her late twenties, and engaged to be married. Her complaint was that the sex act had recently become very painful for her. "Did you grow up in a religious family, and are you living with your fiance?" I asked without prying into the particulars of her physical complaint. Startled, she replied, "How did you know?"

I explained to her that if she had been taught as a child that sex outside of marriage is wrong, and if she still held this belief, her Green subconscious and Yellow non-conscious were responding to that belief. Her Green responses that guide her physiology were reflecting her Yellow-stored emotionally-charged beliefs. I suggested three options for solving her problem. Any of the three would bring her lifestyle and beliefs into harmony. The options were: 1) She could marry the young man; 2) move out; or 3) change her beliefs.

> WELLNESS PRINCIPLE: Your body lets you know when
> you are violating your beliefs

Beliefs are spawned in your Red, programmed by emotion into your Yellow, and responded to by your Green. Establish a belief pattern in your Yellow and it will be followed until the program is changed or updated. Do something that is contrary to your beliefs and you get the same response as you do when you try to change any other firmly fixed pattern. Take trying to change your golf swing, for example. At first, no matter how hard you try to modify your movements, your old programming hangs on. Yellow-responding muscles seem to have a mind of their own. They keep doing what they've done for years. The same type of internal resistance crops up when you act in ways that are counter to your beliefs. Beliefs set a pattern for what we might call "activity homeostasis" — "steady state" activities. Once an activity pattern is programmed, — that is, a belief is recorded — if you deviate from the belief pattern you interfere with Yellow function. Your Yellow send signals to your Green to adjust your physiology to defend. Recall that beliefs are survival oriented. If your actions threaten your survival/beliefs, your Green will respond with defense physiology. The physical discomfort of the young woman in our illustration was a defense response. Her actions were "adult Red"; her beliefs were "child Yellow."

WELLNESS PRINCIPLE: The Tooth Fairy vanishes before
your wisdom teeth arrive

However, all is not doom and gloom. A belief pattern may be
inappropriate for current conditions, but beliefs can be changed.

Most beliefs are formed by the drip method from a succession of
similar "survival" experiences. A succession of jobs that are neither
satisfying nor long-term. One job for three months, another for six, and a
third for two or so. Drip, drip, drip. After a while, you begin to believe
that you are a congenital failure. But instead of having a built-in failure
gene, perhaps you are sabotaging yourself by shooting for the wrong type
of job. A prospective job looks good when you start out (which is another
way of saying paychecks are disbursed regularly), but after a short time
you find that you are at odds with the people around you. Chances are you
either overshot or undershot your beliefs. "Matt" is a good example of the
thirty-something classic undershooter. The survival belief instilled in him
is that a "job" means lots of hard work for little pay. In reality, Matt is an
energetic people-oriented person with an engaging personality, a
multitude of talents, and well-developed technical and practical skills. But
he has been doing a lot of foot-shooting.

Matt grew up in a rather turbulent single-parent working-class
household. His mother worked two or three jobs at a time to support Matt
and his two siblings. When he was old enough Matt worked after-school
jobs to pay most of his own expenses and to ease the family financial
strain. He was instilled with the belief that one must work, work, work at
minimum wage jobs just to almost stay even financially. After high
school, Matt went into the military. Good pay, interesting work, a safe,
secure environment. He earned college degree credits in a technical field.
He enjoyed his experience and his life. He progressed well, became an
instructor of recruits in a technical area, and flourished. In general, he
succeeded. On his road to success, he reinforced the "work hard" belief
his mother had instilled in him, but his personal experience led to a new,
more solidly-fixed belief — he was not only capable of leadership, he was
good at it, and he enjoyed it. The recruits under his supervision benefitted
from his instruction and his counsel.

After four years in the military, Matt was honorably discharged and
worked his way through college. Again, he did well. More successes. He
graduated with a business degree and a completely refurbished sense of
self-esteem. He set out to make his mark in the world. Problem: slow
economic times; college graduates not able to reap employment benefits
they had been led to believe a college degree would bring. Few "real"
jobs. It's back to the minimum wage, hourly, scrape-enough-together-to-
pay-the-bills-and-college-loan type jobs. But recall that Matt's beliefs had

been upgraded by his series of successes. His belief now was that he was no longer the "hourly worker." And his job performance reflected this belief. He worked to help improve the businesses he worked for and attempted to do more than just "do his job." Tilt! That wasn't what he had been hired to do. His employers didn't see his efforts as contributing to their growth and advancement; they saw them as cockiness, meddling, uppitiness. The upshot was lots of jobs but no recommendations.

Matt's difficulty stems from him taking jobs — for economic reasons — that didn't fit his personal-experience beliefs about himself. They fit his pre-success beliefs, not his current beliefs. So Matt is pretty much in the same situation as the young woman with the sex problem. His lifestyle didn't fit his beliefs. But he, too, has options: 1) Continue to do what he has been doing which is a conflict of beliefs, 2) change his beliefs back to the "work hard at lots of jobs for little pay and be satisfied," or 3) devote his energies to finding a job more in keeping with his talents, energies, abilities, goals, and beliefs about himself.

These two stories, the young woman with the sex problem and "Matt," illustrate how a conflict between beliefs and lifestyle can spill over into everyday life situations. The solution isn't the same for everyone. Matt would benefit from changing his lifestyle/workstyle to fit his education, talents, skills, and beliefs. The young woman, on the other hand, could solve her problem by changing — updating — her childhood beliefs to fit her adult lifestyle.

WELLNESS PRINCIPLE: If your beliefs don't fit, change them

Beliefs can be changed in the same way they were formed — by conscious thoughts accompanied by feeling (the same way you change your golf swing). Your non-conscious Yellow recognizes whether or not you are conforming to your beliefs. If you believe that you will fail at anything and everything, and you succeed by mistake, your Yellow notices. If your Yellow non-conscious receives feedback information of deviation from your prescribed "failure" belief response pattern, it gets a little "excited." You're not following your prescribed formula. Your Yellow will make sure you accommodate your programmed belief by directing actions and reactions that lead to familiar failure. Ahhhhhh! Deep sigh of relief. Survival threat eliminated; defense not necessary. Things are back to normal.

WELLNESS PRINCIPLE: Your comfort level is set by your beliefs

Your Green doesn't think, judge, or reason, However, it does respond to information coming from Red and stored in Yellow non-conscious memory. When lifestyle and beliefs are at odds, non-conscious memory patterns — survival beliefs — dominate and subconscious responses follow. Beliefs provide the stimulus for responses. The body responds with non-conscious actions accompanied by feelings. It's these feeling that prompt physiology for survival. Whether you consciously work at it or not, eventually your lifestyle will accommodate to your beliefs, or you'll end up with mental or physical pain or disease.

POINTS OF INTEREST

1.   Beliefs motivate actions.

2.   Beliefs form in your Red, develop in your Yellow, and are responded to by your Green.

3.   Since beliefs form in the Red, their substance can be inaccurate.

4.   Right or wrong, beliefs are true for the believer.

5.   Self-esteem is a belief pattern.

6.   If beliefs and actions are incongruent, beliefs eventually win out.

7.   Some beliefs can be health hazards.

8.   Outgrown beliefs can be updated.

Man is ultimately self-determining.
                                    - Viktor E. Frankl

CHAPTER 11
Life is Just a Bowl of Choices

CHOICES IN SIX DELICIOUS FLAVORS

As thinking, feeling creatures we have the opportunity to enjoy choices in every essential area of life. We can choose to recognize the positive side of each life experience and situation and to be considerate of others, or we can choose to dwell on the negative and to think only of ourselves. We can choose to eat foods that our bodies can handle easily; or we can choose to live on junk food.

Each of us makes choices in six essential areas of life. The cumulative effect of these choices is either long-term health, success, happiness, and general physical and mental well-being, or the cumulative effect is exhaustion, pain, disease, and all-encompassing physical and mental misery. The "six essentials," as I see them, are: 1) what you eat, 2) what you drink, 3) how you exercise, 4) how you rest, 5) what you breathe, and 6) what you think.

"Six?" you wonder. "Precisely six? Not two or five or eight? How did you come up with six?"

I'm glad you asked because, as you might have guessed, I'm going to elaborate.

In my pursuit of "finding the cause" and "health made simple" for patients and doctors alike, I began to notice a pattern among the patients I treated. In every case, the people who came to me for help had a "cause" problem in one of two areas: toxicity or timing. Their bodies were either overly acidic (toxicity), or they were doing right things at inappropriate times (timing). Since I knew that the body never does anything "wrong," the "cause" of the acidosis or inappropriate timing had to be correct responses to "incorrect" stimuli. Something — or several somethings — was forcing the body to respond in ways that produced undesirable results. That is, the results were undesirable from the patients' points of view. From the body's point of view the results were perfect: it survived. And since the body doesn't do long-range planning, the symptoms were perfect for the stimuli that caused the responses. Where did these stimuli come from?

After much pondering and arguing with myself, I concluded that all stimuli come from either inside the body or from outside the body. And activities in six essential areas in the lives of alert, thinking individuals prompt most of the stimuli.

I concluded that if the choices made in these six essential areas prompt short-term stimuli, the choices are "correct." Short-term changes in its internal environment don't put undue wear and tear on organs and systems. With "correct" choices, the body takes care of short-term survival threats then returns to business as usual.

If "incorrect" choices in most of the six essential areas are made consistently short-term stimuli that pose no problem become long-term stimuli. The body survives, but the survival processes require particular organs or systems to go full-tilt continuously. Eventually, the result is exhaustion, pain, and disease.

> WELLNESS PRINCIPLE: Good health is simple — not nec-
> essarily easy

Most of us occasionally become so overwhelmed by external circumstances that we lose sight of the fact that we have control over how we respond to those circumstances. We tend to blame our health, financial, relationship, or career problems on our background, genes, family, associates, government, providence, or luck. Not so! In reality, those of us who survive the dependency and hazards of childhood to emerge as independent, reasonably well-functioning adults direct our life circumstances by conscious choices we make day after day. And our health, happiness, and success of today is the result of choices we made in the past.

> WELLNESS PRINCIPLE: What and where you are today is a
> product of your choices in all of
> your yesterdays

Every waking moment of your life, you make choices. On a life impact scale, choices range in magnitude from life-changing careers moves to non-events of choosing to take off your sweater when you are too warm.

You make these choices in your conscious Red. You, and only you, have control over the choices you make from the many options constantly available to you. But, and this is a capital "B" but, *you have no direct control over your body's physiological responses to the results of your choices*. It works like this.

Every choice you make in your Red is filtered through your Yellow and prompts a response by your Green — turn on, turn off, speed up, slow down — all of the things we've talked about. Once you make a choice and act on it — quit your job, take off the sweater, have steak and ale for dinner, run three miles, take a nap, smoke a cigarette, lose your temper — new stimuli are introduced into your internal environment. Something has changed — feelings, temperature, activity level, whatever. And your Green *must* respond to the new condition. *You have absolutely no control over the subconscious responses.* Your Green (which is smarter than your Red will ever be) dictates the physiology necessary to accommodate to the new conditions. So it's in your best interest to make choices that allow your Green to call for "least stress" responses. And "least stress" comes from short-term stimuli.

Since we haven't talked directly about stress much lately, recall that a stress is anything that changes the way your body is functioning. Your body is constantly stressed — and that's fine. It was designed to handle stress in order to survive. Your job, as sole keeper of your body and health, is to cause as little *inappropriate* stress to your body as possible. And you do that by making "correct," or "appropriate" choices in your six essential areas of life.

WELLNESS PRINCIPLE: You can change your life-course for the better by making better choices

Your body must respond with particular physiology whenever you are engaged in any of the six essentials. And if you are able to read these words, you are conscious enough to be making choices that affect at least one of the six all of the time — you're breathing, or for some strange reason, holding your breath; you're relaxing or squirming; you're thinking (positively or negatively) about what you're reading, and you may be snacking and drinking a beer, or cup of coffee, or tea, or whatever. All by choice. And your conscious choices are impacting your physiology. When you make the same choices over and over — if you do nothing in your life other than sit there and read, wriggle, snack, and drink — your physiology responds the same way over and over. It doesn't get "stuck" because each stimulus is "new." But the organs and systems that are kept at work without rest will eventually get tired; exhausted. Fortunately, you aren't going to spend your entire life sitting in one spot reading.

Of the six essentials, thinking and breathing are constants — on a minute-by-minute basis you give little conscious attention to either. As long as they don't cause you problems, breathing and thinking are pretty much ignored. Nonetheless, you can consciously control both. The other four essentials — exercising, resting, eating and drinking — range from important to imperative, but they're not continuous; they're carried out "on command." You consciously choose when, where, how and what. When you make the "correct" choices regularly in each of the six categories, you create the best working environment for your body and the least interference in your field.

> WELLNESS PRINCIPLE: "Correct" choices promote less-stress survival

In the long run, "incorrect" choices in any of the six essential areas put more stress on your body than it can handle gracefully. Again, the rule of thumb that defines "incorrect" choices: Any choice is "incorrect" if it: 1) raises the acid level of your body to extremes — that's "toxicity", and/or 2) keeps your body doing a "right" physiological response at an inappropriate time — that's "timing."

Timing and toxicity are the two by-products of incorrect choices that are the *cause* of most of the illness, pain, and disease in our country today. And it's a toss-up whether "toxicity" or "timing" is more prevalent in our society — both are at epidemic levels. Toxic acidosis is primarily a function of incorrect eating and drinking choices. And since some acid is eliminated from your body when you exhale, breathing is also involved with toxicity. Timing is a function primarily of inappropriate conscious Red thoughts, and Yellow-stored memories, beliefs, attitudes, and feelings. Eating, drinking, and breathing are toxic-specific; the exercise, rest, and thinking are toxic-timing blends.

Toxicity, or acidosis, is too much acid. Toxicity ruins the neighborhood of your cells — acid moves in. Toxic acidosis means that your internal environment that was designed to be slightly alkaline is too acid. Acid isn't a foreign invader in your body. Your body produces acid as it functions. Cells produce acid as they function. Thinking produces acid. My clinical experience indicates that thinking, especially negative thinking, is a mass-producer of acid. However, you come equipped with systems especially designed to neutralize and eliminate acid that comes from internal functions or food. Acid in itself isn't a problem; too much of the wrong kind of acid is a major health-inhibitor. And the "wrong kind" of acid comes from incorrect food choices.

When body fluids become too acidic from acid-producing foods, your whole body must direct its energies and resources toward keeping the acid level under control. Survival, you know. To keep the acid level tolerable and cells alive, vital neutralizing minerals (particularly sodium and calcium) are taken from other areas and systems to keep the internal environment slightly alkaline.

WELLNESS PRINCIPLE: The body is alkaline by design and acid by function

But I'm getting ahead of myself. "Food choices" is another chapter. Right now we're talking about what makes a choice "correct" or "incorrect."

The second criterion that tilts a choice into the "incorrect" category is that it sparks perfectly correct physiological responses at inappropriate times. These are choices that compel your body to stay in a particular physiology, particularly defense or risk physiology, when no external threat is around. Defense responses are absolutely essential patterns of internal behavior — when they are prompted by external stimuli of perceptions of a physical danger. But most of us don't face physical danger on a non-stop basis. Most of the things we perceive as threats are in the form of symbols and interpretations of those symbols. Words. Ideas. Thoughts. Symbols packed with such an emotional charge that our Green switches us into risk physiology. However, if a risk we're responding to isn't physical — such as a lion crashing toward us through the brush — we can create a timing problem.

In keeping with my premise that health should be simple, here's a quick summary of how choices in each of the six essentials fit into the "timing" and "toxicity" categories when incorrect choices are the norm.

Eating: A major-league acid-level raiser — Toxicity
Drinking: Also an acid-level raiser — Toxicity
Exercise: An acid-producer with timing-problem potential — Toxicity and Timing
Rest: Acid-producing if you are "up tight," not completely relaxed, and "work" in your sleep — Toxicity brought on by Timing
Breathing: A prime regulator of physiological acid — Toxicity
Thinking: Acid-producer and major timing-problem culprit — Toxicity and Timing

WELLNESS PRINCIPLE: Choices have short-term or long-term effects on your body

As you have probably figured out, this book deals primarily with the relationship between thoughts and timing. My book *Your Health, Your Choice*[101] deals primarily with the relationship between diet and toxicity. Most "diet" books tell you what to do to improve your health through eating. *Your Health, Your Choice* tells you *why* you should make vegetables and fruits the centerpiece of your diet. And the answer to that revolves around how your body must handle the acid factor. We'll summarize that for you in Chapter 14. Meanwhile, back to your choices.

In this chapter we scan the horizon of how your choices in the drinking, breathing, and resting categories contribute to your healthstyle. And although we have had chapter after chapter about the effect of thoughts, we'll take a short refresher tour. Then, since "what you eat" and "how you exercise" take a little more explaining, exercise and food will follow in their own chapters. So, take a deep breath and charge on.

THE IN'S AND OUT'S OF BREATHING

Of the six essentials, breathing has a distinguishing characteristic. It is the only one of the six that you can't put off for more than a few minutes without major repercussions. Breathing isn't a learned skill. You aren't plagued by trying to fit "breathing time" into an already overcrowded schedule. You don't need to go out and gather air or wait for it to go on sale. For the most part, your Green takes care of your breathing while you tend to more pressing matters. Yet, despite its automatic nature, you can consciously control your breathing: you can pant, huff and puff, take in deep gulps, hyperventilate, hypoventilate, or stop for a while. But, under normal circumstances, if you stop for more than ten or fifteen seconds, you must concentrate on what you're doing. It doesn't take much breath-holding before you "explode" as your survival-intense Green searches for air. It's at that point — the I've-got-to-breathe "explosion" — that your conscious and subconscious work together in total synchronization. More about that later. But keep it in mind; it's another potential test question.

WELLNESS PRINCIPLE: Controlled breathing melds conscious with subconscious

Since your body is designed to do everything it can to survive the moment, and since you must breathe to survive, you *will* breathe; or, you will pass out — become unconscious. When you are unconscious, your conscious mind is out of the way and your subconscious takes exclusive control of vital internal functions and restores the breathing process. Your Green wins again — another moment of survival.

But let's get down to basics. Why do we breathe? We know we must, but why?

The primary purpose of breathing is to get oxygen to the cells. Cells need oxygen in order to function. Cells work on the micro level in much the same way we do on the macro level. They take in oxygen to use in their functioning, and as they function, they produce carbon dioxide (CO_2). But CO_2 is a waste product. And if the cell is full of CO_2, there isn't enough room for new oxygen. So the CO_2 must be eliminated. Red blood cells carry oxygen from your lungs to other parts of your body. And they take the CO_2 waste back to the lungs to be eliminated. The purpose of breathing, then, is not only to bring oxygen into your body but also to get rid of waste carbon dioxide. Your blood cells can carry the greatest amount of oxygen when your internal environment is slightly alkaline. So it is important that the CO_2 be disposed of as quickly as possible.

WELLNESS PRINCIPLE: Breathing out is just as important
as breathing in

So now that we have determined that you *will* breathe, and that breathing is an essential housekeeping activity, what are the choices involved in the process? Quality of air!

Clean, fresh air is at a premium in our technological, energy-hungry world. The air we breathe is saturated with particles of man-made chemicals that get into our bodies. Fuels, noxious emissions, pesticides, chemical fertilizers, and other impurities infest our breathing material in cities, rural areas, factories, processing plants, businesses, and homes. Chemical-laden air is not healthy air to breathe. However, your body comes equipped with marvelous cleansing and detoxifying systems that have served Generic Man well for thousands of years. But these systems of your body must work overtime when you are constantly immersed in a murky, chemical-intense atmosphere year after year. Coping with man's technological effluent continuously puts undue stress on our bodies. However, our bodies can handle nature's by-products without any problem.

WELLNESS PRINCIPLE: Man-made airborne products can
stress your body

Nature's aromas shouldn't be toxic to your body. Scents that waft from trees, flowers, and other types of foliage titillate our senses to bring enjoyment to life. They are part of the grand scheme of nature. You can lift your spirits and "feed your soul" with a walk in the piney woods with its natural smells and clean, fresh air.

"Hold on," you may think. "If nature's aromas and odors are so good for us, why do my family and I sneeze, cough, have watering eyes, and general misery when we're in the great outdoors?" The answer to that is very simple: incorrect choices in all, or too many, of the other five essentials leave you vulnerable. There are limits to how many choice-crises the body can handle gracefully. If your body has to jump through hoops just trying to neutralize the effects of acid-producing foods, lack of exercise, stress-causing drinks, contaminated air, insufficient or ineffective rest, and turbulent thoughts, the end result is "allergies" to pollen or other natural particles that are normally non-threatening.

WELLNESS PRINCIPLE: Allergies are a toxicity problem

No discourse on breathing would be complete without a few words on smoking. And in the fewest words, "Don't!"

Unless you have been living in an isolated, underground, communication-free vault for the past thirty years, you are well aware of the dangers of smoking. Government agencies and health associations have waged extensive, expensive public-awareness campaigns to drive home the message that smoking can kill you — or, at the very least, cause you and/or your family great physical and economic pain and suffering. Among the perils of smoking cited in the anti-smoking campaign are the increased potential for lung cancer, interference with blood circulation and the absorption/retention of some vitamins and minerals, and a host of other health negatives. Although I've never smoked (other than the usual couple of teen-age trials that made me sick), if I had, I would have quit on the spot in college when I saw the black, gunk-filled "smoker's lungs" of a cadaver in anatomy dissection lab. The smokers' lungs were as black as coal — a comparison that may be lost on the under 50s. The lungs of the non-smoker cadavers, although just as dead, were pink and "clean." If we wore our lungs on the outside, no one would smoke.

WELLNESS PRINCIPLE: Smoking is Big Time Bad!

Smoking dumps potentially lethal toxins into the body. The toxins from smoking a cigarette go directly to the blood stream without being processed through physiological protective mechanisms. Unlike food that is neutralized by stomach acid or detoxified by the liver, no denaturing process tempers the direct hit of pollutants of cigarette smoke. Noxious ingredients that make up the largest portion of a lusty drag on a smoldering cigarette invade the lungs then pass directly into the blood stream. Smoking puts a direct toxic hit on your body.

WELLNESS PRINCIPLE: Smoking wages chemical warfare

on your body

So what choices do you have in the breathing category? The most obvious is the smoke-or-not-smoke choice. Choices of the type of environmental air you breathe are not so clear-cut. However, you do have choices. You have some say in where you live and where you work. These two life factors aren't always easy to change. In fact, as a practical matter, moving to a different location or changing jobs may be more than merely difficult — either may be virtually impossible. Personal circumstances are usually the deciding factor in both of these situations. Picking up family and possessions and traipsing off to another part of the country or finding a new job are major steps in anyone's life. However, if you live or work in surroundings that are heavily polluted by industrial or agricultural activity, your body could suffer needlessly. Your decisions are a matter of priorities.

You may have more options in your choice of where and how you live and work than you realize. The decision to accept a job in a chemically-intense environment, such as a printing company or the spray-painting department of an auto body shop, is a conscious choice; the decision to smoke or not smoke cigarettes is a conscious choice; the decision to live in an area of heavy air pollution is a conscious choice.

Respiratory toxicity from smoking or environmental pollution imposes severe stress on the body. That stress can exacerbate weakening or exhaustion of vulnerable organs and systems that are trying to cope with other stresses. The additional stress of being immersed in environmental toxic waste can tip the scales to the development of disease. You can make conscious choices regarding the quality of air your body must contend with. If you suffer with severe respiratory allergies or respiratory disease, quality of life can be synonymous with quality of air. Radical choices and changes may be required.

But, again, hope springs eternal. You can make the best of an unchangeable situation by making sure your choices in the other five essential areas of your life are conducive to the highest possible level of health. When you are truly healthy, your body is slightly alkaline, your energy field is healthfully chaotic, and you are in the best overall condition possible to overcome negative situations.

WELLNESS PRINCIPLE: Health is simple, not necessarily easy

THE REST OF YOUR CHOICE

Rest is part of the cycle of life. Your body needs time to repair itself and recoup energy. During your rest cycle, your energies are "turned inward" to allow cells to regenerate and your body to gather debris for elimination. Proper rest is vital to health.

So what is "proper" rest?

Proper rest is a state of complete relaxation — a state many of my patients haven't experienced in a long time. They think they rest, but they don't. "Doc," they tell me, "I sleep ten or eleven hours a night and I wake up just as tired as I was when I went to bed."

How can this be?

Simple.

Thoughts and attitudes get in the way of healthful, restorative rest. These patients are as tense when they sleep as they are when they're awake. That's sleeping — not resting.

WELLNESS PRINCIPLE: Rest is your maintenance mode

Your body can't rebuild and repair when you crawl into bed at night exhausted, then lie there and re-live all of the frustrations, hurts, injustices, indignities, and general negativities of the day and the past. How can your body slip out of its defense mode when you constantly feed it "threatening" thoughts? When disturbing anxiety-provoking thoughts run rampant through your conscious mind as you finally fall asleep, you program patterns into your Yellow that dictate defense physiology. And you aren't even aware of it!

Earlier we talked about the "save" mechanism of sleep. Here's where it comes in. Falling asleep while you're in defense physiology "saves" that physiology on your mental "hard drive." You don't even need to think directly about the original thought to bring it up again. All it takes to call up the whole defense physiology pattern again is to meander into a nearby thought neighborhood. Get close to the original thought with an associated thought in your mental musings and you hit the "restore" command for the original thought physiology — defend. That's a misuse of survival design. You're designed to survive Red-perceived physical threats. Responding to Yellow memory threats is physiology abuse.

The first clue that something is interfering with your rest and rehabilitation is that you wake up just as tired as you were when you went to bed. Then you spend the rest of the day becoming more tired. In an effort to get more rest, you try going to bed a little earlier. The big accomplishment there is that you lie awake longer fretting and stewing about everything that went wrong that day. And you have the added frustration of not being able to go to sleep when you want to.

WELLNESS PRINCIPLE: Sleep isn't always restful

To solve the restless sleep problem, make conscious choices. When you go to bed, exercise your freedom of choice over your thoughts and refuse to allow negativity to creep into your consciousness. Always finish your day with positive thoughts. To help you keep negativity at bay at bedtime, don't watch the late night news on TV. That's nothing but negativity. If you must rehash the day's events, find favorable or positive aspects to think about. And if you can't find anything positive about today's activities, think about something you enjoy — something that is fun or exciting, or that you are going to do in the future. You can imagine that experience to be as terrific as you want because you haven't formed unpleasant memories about it to muddy the waters. Focus on a vacation you plan, or the fishing trip scheduled for next month, or the party you have been invited to attend, or a project you are eager to complete.

If you are going to weld a physiological response pattern into your central control system when you go to sleep, it may as well be the best response pattern you can generate.

WELLNESS PRINCIPLE: Create designer thoughts to sleep
on

Sleep is akin to eating and drinking inasmuch as "you gotta' have it." Sleep affects physiology of both the nervous system and body structures. Of the two, the nervous system is the most vulnerable. According to Guyton, sleep has a greater effect on the nervous system than it does on organs and other structures. He uses the example of those with "a transected spinal cord in the neck. . . ." That's "scientific talk" meaning a cut or severed spinal cord. Without spinal nerve communication from the neck down, ". . . lack of sleep and wakefulness causes neither significant harm to the bodily organs nor even any deranged function. On the other hand," Guyton continues, "lack of sleep certainly does affect the functions of the central nervous system."[102] He likens sleep to "rezeroing" a computer after extensive use to restore the "base line" of its operation. Guyton postulates that "the principal value of sleep is to restore the natural balance among the neuronal centers."[103] Right on, Dr. Guyton.

Lack of adequate rest and sleep can do more than make you grouchy and petulant. Long-term sleep deprivation can have profound effects. A sleep deprivation study showed that the 17-year old student who voluntarily went a marathon 264-hours (11 days) without sleep exhibited "brief hallucinations and easily controlled episodes of bizarre behavior" after five to ten days. On the whole, the young student experienced "irritability, blurred vision, slurring of speech, memory lapses, and confusion concerning his identity."[104] Fortunately, no long-term after effects were evident. This bit of trivia underscores the physiological need for refreshing sleep. Rest is a physiological requirement just as eating and drinking are physiological requirements. Abuse your rest requirements at your own risk.

You can increase your rest potential if you make sure you go to bed early enough to allow yourself time for enough sleep before you must get up to start the next day. Just how much sleep is "enough"? That's a personal thing. Some of us require eight or nine hours each night. Others are ready to bounce out of bed and greet the world with only five or six hours of pillow time. One way to find out how much sleep you need is to NOT set an alarm to wake you. When you allow yourself to wake naturally your body reaches its own level of sleep-need. Waking to an alarm short changes your sleep needs. If you need an alarm to wake you in order to get to work on time, go to bed earlier. Determine the amount of sleep you require and make sure you arrange your daily schedule to meet that important need. You were designed to go to sleep naturally for regular periods of relaxing, restful sleep and to awaken feeling refreshed. You weren't designed to need a pill to go to sleep, an alarm clock to wake up, and another pill to face the day.

WELLNESS PRINCIPLE: Your body is designed for cycles
of rest and activity

During restful sleep, your body repairs and maintains itself. Internal "housekeeping," such as healing processes and preparing debris for elimination, takes place during restful sleep. Insufficient or ineffective rest interferes with these processes, and interference leads to exhaustion and paves the way for pain, symptoms, and disease.

Restorative rest is followed by waking naturally and feeling energetic. Even if you are most productive in the evening and consider yourself a "night person" you can wake rested — though probably not eager — when your body has had adequate time to recoup from the previous day.

If the volume of sleep-aid TV commercials is an indicator of the level of consumer use of these products, an unseemly number of people must depend on over-the-counter medication to help them sleep. Popping sedatives to get to sleep, then gulping stimulants to stay awake imposes artificial rest/activity cycles on the body. Those who program their sleep patterns by artificial means are rarely truly rested or truly alert. They are drugged during sleep, jolted into semi-wakefulness by an alarm clock, and dragged into activity by will-power and stimulants. Health restoring rest is aborted. They spend much of their day feeling sluggish as their internal systems respond to man-made devices that force their bodies to switch from an otherwise natural cycle of rest and recuperation to an active state.

If you usually wake up tired and draggy, try this rest-inducing exercise for a week.

When you go to bed at night, concentrate on thinking positive thoughts. Focus on a positive aspect of each experience of the day, and on what you learned from each experience. Even if an experience appeared to be negative, find something positive about it. If you look, you can find *something* positive in each of your activities and encounters. Concentrate on feeling that positive. When you concentrate on positive thoughts and feelings, your conscious Red feeds "No-Threat" signals to your subconscious Green and your body responds with relaxation. Very likely you will be surprised at how much better you feel not only when you get up in the morning but also throughout the day.

Regular restful sleep is a boon to performance of body, mind, and daily tasks. And rest from those daily tasks is a boon to mind and attitude. Although time off from work may not be a Constitutional right, periodic relief from the pressures of our work-centered culture can improve your attitude and boost your mental energy. "All work and no play makes Jack a dull boy" is an established adage because it is true.

Pleasurable, restful, rejuvenating vacations revitalize body, mind, and spirit. The length of a "vacation" doesn't determine its value; value is determined by "changing gears" — changing your focus of interest to something you enjoy. Just as performing the same physical movements over and over brings on muscular fatigue, performing the same mental activity of work, work, work brings on mental fatigue.

A well-rounded life of rest and work provides positive stimulation to body and mind.

FLUID CHOICES

You can survive for weeks without food, but for only a matter of days without water. Cells function in a fluid environment. Without adequate fluids, cells can't function.

The 42 quarts of water contained in the body of an average 155 lb. male make up 57 percent of his total body weight. Blood is approximately 78% water and 22% solids. About 26.4 quarts of fluid are inside the cells; the remainder is outside the cells — extracellular fluid. Although fluid replacement is essential to life, each time fluid (or any other substance) is put into the body, the body is stressed — it must change the way it is functioning to process the new substance. Even water must be processed. It stands to reason, then, that in the pursuit of stress-reduction, you are better off when you choose drinks that your body can handle with the least internal upheaval.

It will come as no surprise to you that drinking some common, everyday drinks, such as coffee, tea, cola, and alcoholic beverages, puts greater stress on the body than does drinking pure water. The body must not only process the various substances contained in the drinks, it must also contend with their stimulating effect. Drinking stimulating beverages *occasionally* probably won't ruin your health. Problems can arise when stimulants are an integral part of your regular diet. Unremitting stimulation, whether from worry and anxiety or from coffee and alcohol, is unremitting stress.

We can choose from a wide assortment of drinks. Each has its own special effects. Coffee, tea, and soft drinks are acid producers. Simulated fruit drinks, either powdered or prepared and packaged to appeal to children, pack more sugar than a body needs at one gulping. Alcoholic beverages both stimulate and depress the body, to say nothing of keeping you from functioning at your best. And milk is a negatively-beneficial high-protein food in liquid form.

What's that? An unkind cut about milk,"nature's most perfect food"?

Mother's milk is ideal for babies. Cow's milk (especially in large quantities) is not appropriate for older children or adults. In my book *Your Health, Your Choice*, the chapter entitled "Osteoporosis by the Quart" points out the long-term hazard potential of milk as a regular part of adults' daily diets. For now, I'll just say that the more milk you drink as an adult, the greater your chances for developing osteoporosis.

The very best liquids for the body come from a diet heavy in vegetables and fruit. Fruits and vegetables are convenient little packages of beneficial nutrients, minerals, fiber, and water all rolled into one. And the water is fresh, pure water. The plant has already filtered out the impurities. Water in plants is not only pure, it's tasty. The water captures the distinctive flavor of the plant itself.

The more food you eat from the vegetable kingdom, the less liquid you need to drink separately. Your body is about 80% water. So the food you eat should contain a lot of liquid — and meat, fish, or chicken don't. Vegetables and fruits do.

WELLNESS PRINCIPLE: Thirst during or just after meals means you are making wrong food choices

As a practical matter, we all get thirsty. The fluids lost through elimination, perspiration, and breathing must be replenished. We need to drink fluids. The most healthful beverages you can drink to satisfy this thirst are juices extracted from fresh fruits and vegetables, and/or pure water. Unfortunately, we have out-smarted ourselves with technology to the point that there isn't any "pure" water left on the face of the earth. It's all contaminated in some way. Even the snow on the highest mountain tops is tainted. And, for most of us, the water that comes out of our home faucets is either laden with chemicals from water treatment plants or with inorganic minerals from a well. The body doesn't need either chemical purifiers or inorganic minerals.

So when you yearn for a glass of water, reverse osmosis water is the most healthful choice. Reverse osmosis is a space-age water filtering process. Water treated through this process is virtually free of contaminants and extraneous materials. Several brands of reverse osmosis filtering devices are available. Check with your local health food store or the 800 number shown.

Distilled water is the next best alternative. Yet by itself, distilled water is "dead." To revitalize distilled water, squeeze about a teaspoonful of FRESH lemon juice into it. This brings "dead" water back to life and adds flavor.

Of course, few of us are willing to drink nothing but water. For a health-enhancing, thirst-quenching, pleasant-tasting, body-alkalizing beverage, the drink of choice is fresh fruit juice or fresh vegetable juice. The ideal juice is prepared in your own home with a juicer. Vitamins and all-important neutralizing minerals stream from FRESH fruits and vegetables juiced to a health-enhancing ready-to-drink nectar.

Freshly juiced vegetables and fruit are ideal for people who are too sick to process whole foods. Carrot juice made from fresh, sweet carrots is more than merely a refreshing taste treat; carrot juice is one of the best sources of vital vitamins and usable neutralizing minerals.

The vegetables or fruits used for juicing must be fresh, and the juice produced must be sweet. The quality of the produce being juiced determines the sweetness of the juice. When I began juicing vegetables, my wife would sometimes accuse me of having added sugar to make the juice sweeter. I hadn't and I don't. You don't need to artificially sweeten the juice of fresh carrots and other vegetables that have been grown in rich soil — it's naturally sweet. However, some carrots are of such poor quality that their juice is bitter. If the juice isn't sweet, pour it onto your garden where it can be recycled productively.

WELLNESS PRINCIPLE: If fruit or vegetable juice isn't sweet, it's not complete — don't drink it

The juice of fresh vegetables or fruits can be so appealing that you may have a tendency to go overboard on the quantity you drink. As with just about everything else in life, you can get too much of this good thing. Juice is "concentrated" food that contains generous amounts of water and nutrients but little filling fibre. When vegetables or fruits have been reduced to juice form, you can *drink* a lot more carrots, apples, celery or other produce than you could ever *eat* at one sitting. Too much juice may bring on symptoms of a cold — runny nose, cough — as the concentrated nutrients stimulate your body to cleanse itself of toxic materials. Cleansing is good. Rapid cleansing, you won't like.

Too much juice can also have an "expansive" effect. Not that your waist line expands, but you become "spacy" — you have difficulty focusing your attention. Your concentration takes a holiday and you don't know why — and if you're "spacy" enough, you won't really care why.

Children who drink large quantities of fruit juice can appear super-charged and out of control. Too much juice poured into a small body can turn a normal, active child into a fireball of frenzy. An expansive child is stress for all concerned — child, parents, teachers, former friends, neighbors, and anyone else unlucky enough to be in the path of the turbulent tot.

So your conscious choice of the amount of juice you drink is just as important as your conscious choice to drink it. You can't eat enough carrots, apples or oranges in a day to equal several glasses of their juice. The rule of thumb for determining how much juice you — or your child — should drink in a day is . . .

> WELLNESS PRINCIPLE: Drink only as much fruit juice as
> you would get from eating your
> fill of the whole fruit

Beverages are not consumed by chance. Conscious thought goes into choosing the type and quantity of liquids you drink. Any beverage that adds to the acidity of your body or artificially stimulates your body (and that includes most man-made or processed drinks) puts undue physiological stress on your body. "Incorrect" drinking choices compounded by other "incorrect" choices can contribute to chronic symptoms.

THOUGHT ATTACK

Mix Red conscious activity into a soup of Yellow non-conscious memories and a series of thoughts appear. Thinking. The intricate, unexplainable processes of thinking are behind all of the monumental achievements of mankind: building of the pyramids, invention of the wheel, harnessing of energy, creation of great symphonies, works of art, literature, and architecture, development of great religions and social principles. These are just some of the steps on the march of progress, including the "giant step for Mankind." Thinking is also behind the kaleidoscope of brutal horrors of Man's inhumanity to Man. And thinking is behind most pain and misery.

Your thoughts can stimulate and prolong intense physiological activity. That's one of the key points of how the body-mind connection affects your long-term health. As we have seen, thoughts generate energy. Proven scientific devices have recorded the energy generated by the brain. The body is surrounded by energy. This, too, has been established scientifically, which leads us to the second key point — *the connection between thoughts and health is the mind-field connection.*

Without going through the whole field concept again, to stir your Yellow a bit, we'll just say that the energy fields that surround your body are chaotic, all inclusive energy. A chaotic field is complete. It contains all of the energy information available. Your personal energy field that surrounds your body is an integral part of your physical body. But the attraction qualities of your energy body are different from those of your physical body.

In the physical world — the world we learn about in school, and the world we can perceive with our senses — opposites attract. Positive forces attract negative. In the metaphysical world that we are just beginning to understand, however, likes attract. Positive attracts positive. Negative attracts negative. Hence, the oft-heard complaint, "I seem to attract bad luck," is more than idle grousing. The folks who say this may think they are kidding, but what they say is true. Negative thinkers attract negative energy and negative experiences. Consequently, negative thoughts put a double whammy on your body. Negative thoughts interfere with balanced homeostasis by keeping the body in a constant state of upheaval and defense, and they interfere with the chaotic nature of the body's field by constantly reducing the amount of positive field energy that's available.

WELLNESS PRINCIPLE: Thoughts affect mind, body, and
field

We have also seen that most thoughts are initially quick evaluations of how events, words, ideas, proposals and possibilities affect the thinker personally. Since we are survival oriented, our first thought in response to new information received through our five senses is something along the lines of "Will it `hurt' me?" or "How does this affect me?" or "Is this a threat?"   As a result, our first response to any external situation is defensive. The response may not last long but we lean toward the "defend" side much more frequently and easily than we lean toward the "relax" side.

But we aren't constantly thinking about external situations. For the most part, thinking is more of a recycling process than a creative one. Most thoughts are repetitions or extrapolations — reruns, and reruns with color commentary — of previous thoughts. Very little effort is required first thing in the morning to hit mental "replay" and review past events, problems, injustices, slights, and hurts that have come from the "outside."

Thoughts and thought patterns become habitual. Daily, hourly, or minute-by-minute we recycle disturbing thoughts: "Ooooh, I don't know how much longer I can stand this crummy job." "How am I going to get all the bills paid this month?" "I'll never forgive Uncle George for the way he treated me." Thoughts such as these can surface frequently, apparently for no particular reason. They are parenthetical or offhand or out-of-context thoughts. They interrupt your flow of thought about whatever you're doing at the time. A recurring offhand thought (ROT) can be particularly health threatening. The subject of a recurring offhand thought is generally a condensed replay of a highly emotionally charged event or perception from the past. And it is nearly always negative. When ROTs are combined with inappropriate choices in the other five essential areas, the physiological results can be particularly damaging to health.

The upshot of all of this is that we have plenty of opportunity for negativity to dominate our thinking. And when negativity dominates and scores the most points, health loses. Organs and systems become exhausted, energy goes out the window, and communication with the field is riddled with static. It's a rout.

How's that for a heap of negativity? Sounds like we are all doomed to negative-dominance. If I really believed that, I wouldn't be writing this book or trying to help sick people get well. I'd go off in a corner someplace and watch the dust collect. The point isn't that we live in a negative world and there's nothing we can do about it. The point is that we live in a world that provides each and every one of us opportunities to grow. We grow by learning that every challenge, crisis, and disappointment, is an opportunity to learn a lesson about living, and that perfect Universal Intelligence that is behind the whole thing.

The greatest accomplishment you can make in life is to learn to control your thoughts. You control your thoughts by excluding thoughts that are not beneficial to you and allowing only positive thoughts to take hold in your mind. And you can do this by making choices. Choose to think positively. At the outset, you can choose how you think by following the steps of recognizing negative thoughts, cancelling those thoughts, and replacing them with positive thoughts. After you get the hang of it, positive thoughts can become a habit.

WELLNESS PRINCIPLE: Correct thought choices increase your control over your health, happiness, and success

INDECISION AND JUDGMENT

Two thought-habit patterns that may appear initially to be positive are, in reality, negatives in disguise. These two masquerading thought habits are *indecision and judgment.* Indecision can masquerade as open-mindedness positive. Judgment can masquerade as helpful, benevolent, knowledgeable advice. However, both are forms of fear or anxiety that send mixed messages to your Green.

Ooops! Mixed messages to Green? How is your "on" and "off" Green going to respond to mixed messages?

Perfectly! But probably in ways that can cause you problems.

Indecisiveness is "should's" and "want's" and "ought'a's" contradicted by "can't's" and "must's" seasoned with expectation and anxiety. Habitual indecisive thoughts grow into an indecisive attitude. Indecisive thoughts are negative thoughts masquerading as positive: "I should lose weight — but I can't curb my appetite," or "I want to go back to school — but I have to keep my job to support myself." Indecisiveness is characterized by the pattern "should ⇒ but." Indecisiveness sends mixed messages. It rapidly flips survival responses on and off — keeps your physiology in turmoil with little time to rest. Yet indecisiveness can be countered by developing the habit of decision-making. The decision itself is immaterial. The act of making the decision is crucial. If a decision is the right one, so much the better. However, most decisions can be changed. If the original decision isn't quite on target or doesn't produce the desired results, make a different one. The goal is to be decisive.

WELLNESS PRINCIPLE: Decisive doesn't mean rigid

Decisions that are in your best interest and do not intentionally harm anyone else are generally the best decisions as far as life-path, peace of mind, and health are concerned. Decisions that follow this course usually have no adverse effects on others. However, as a rule of thumb, when you make decisions based on trying to please others or on making them happy, you'll find that neither party is satisfied. The other person won't be satisfied and you, the decision-maker, won't be satisfied. Besides that, if your good intentions are thwarted, you'll end up feeling frustrated. And frustration is a negative feeling that weaves interference into your field. We talked about this pattern earlier in the "Martyr Belief."

Decisiveness is the opposite of indecision. Decisiveness breeds commitment. Commitment gives the body clear-cut instructions. No on-again, off-again.

WELLNESS PRINCIPLE: Indecision keeps you and your
body on a tightrope

Indecisiveness is a habit that comes from looking at the world through a murky window. When your view isn't clear, you figure you don't have all of the information you need to make a clear-cut decision. And you're right. The only problem in trying to correct this problem is that you can never have all of the information available. You work with the equipment (information) you do have. No need to analyze every situation to death. Gather as much information as you can, then take what you have and run with it. Make a decision. Become committed. If you are chronically indecisive, learn to overcome your indecisiveness by starting small. For example, you're going to lunch with a friend. The first question is always, "Where shall we eat?" Ninety-nine times out of a hundred (not the results of a scientific study), the answer is "I don't care; where do you want to eat?" "Well, I don't care, either," comes the reply. And so it goes. Indecision coupled with trying to make the "other person" happy. A great way to go if you are an accomplished mind-reader. Since most of us aren't, practice your new decisiveness skills and make a decision!

Practice making small decisions — "I feel like Chinese/Italian/ whatever for lunch today." Become committed to working toward your decisions as long as they point you in the right direction and don't hurt anyone else. If you're companion is allergic to Chinese or whatever food, unless he/she is a complete wimp, you'll hear about it. Then you can make another decision that is beneficial to you, amenable to your companion, and easy on your Green.

WELLNESS PRINCIPLE: Take small decision steps first

The negative attitude twin of indecision is judgment. Not the judgment you use when you decide between remodeling your house or moving. That's evaluation that we'll talk about later. Judgment says, in effect, "Dummy, you should do things my way." Judgment of others is a mental exercise in asserting that you are smarter, more astute, and better equipped to handle someone else's situation than they are. And you may be — but it's their lesson. Keep your mental nose out of it.

Judgment is equally as detrimental to your health as is indecision. The difference between judgment and indecision is that the "should's" and "ought's" are directed toward others rather than toward yourself. Judgment is a function of your conscious Red. You receive current information through any of your five senses and compare the new with stored memory information of life-experiences. Webster's Ninth New Collegiate Dictionary defines judgement as "the process of forming an opinion or evaluation by discerning and comparing." However, health-deterring judgment is more than an evaluation and comparison. Judgment imposes your personal standards and beliefs on others. Most — but not all — judgment is negative. Judgment, like indecisiveness, is made up of "should's" and "shouldn'ts," "ought's" and "oughtn'ts" — "John should keep his grass cut"; "Mary shouldn't spend so much time on the phone"; "The company ought to provide better benefits." From politics to parenting, from appearances to actions, judgment by an onlooker or outsider is futile and frustrating. Judgments, such as, "The government should intervene in/keep their nose out of the situation in Somewhereland," or, "That mother should discipline/stop abusing her child," excite and frustrate the judge, yet they have absolutely no effect on the judged. Judgment does not change those being judged; it merely fosters anxiety and field interference in the self-appointed judge.

WELLNESS PRINCIPLE: Judgment is an attempt to control
                      the uncontrollable

Despite the dictionary description of judgment as a process of evaluation, from a health standpoint, judgment and evaluation are not synonymous. The process of evaluation poses no threat to the body. Evaluating the pros and cons of a situation in an effort to make an informed decision is based on determining which of two ar more courses of action has the greatest potential for the most beneficial outcome. An element of control over the outcome distinguishes evaluation from judgment. Evaluations look for the best resolution to achieve a future condition; judgment deals with conditions of the present or past. For example, investment possibilities can be evaluated to determine those that have the greatest potential for the greatest yield in the future. That's evaluation. Judgment is made after you have bought the stock and see whether or not your evaluation and decision were wise.

WELLNESS PRINCIPLE: Judgment is current concern over
                      the wisdom or value of past ac-
                      tions or present situations

True evaluation is cortical, non-emotional and analytical. Evaluation presumes a degree of control over the outcome. Judgment is cortical, emotional and opinionated. Judgment is devoid of outcome control. But more important than the semantic differences between evaluation and judgment is the difference in physiological responses. True evaluation is made through your Red using information gathered by the five senses. Evaluation is a rational function of your Red, tinged with beliefs and, perhaps, a whisper of emotional personal preference. Judgment is emotional. Emotions can (and usually do) stimulate and sustain inappropriate defense physiology. That's what makes judgment hazardous to your health. The judgment itself isn't the problem, it's the effects on your body (and relationships) that is the problem.

KEEPING THE RIGHT BALANCE

Your body's #1 goal is to survive. Your body was designed to survive moment-by-moment. It does this by meeting threats to its existence head on. When threatened internally or externally, your body immediately changes what it is doing (stress) to handle the new situation and to hang on right now. The most persistent threats your body must survive — threats you may not even recognize consciously — come from choices you make in your Red. Choices that have become habits you no longer consciously think about — like flopping in front of the TV instead of exercising, short-changing your sleep needs, or engaging in unrelenting cynicism about everyone and everything.

Your body can handle most short-term physical stress — other than violent trauma — with no lasting effects. You may be startled from the middle of a deep sleep to full, immobilized alert if you think you hear an "intruder" fumbling with your bedside window. Yet once you realize that your conscious mind had misinterpreted your sensory perception and the "burglar" was really that overgrown shrub you had been meaning to trim, your heart beat returns to normal, saliva again flows in your mouth, muscles begin to relax, and you become flexible again. Your body has done its job. It prepared you for defense against a threat to your survival. In this instance, your body's survival tactic wasn't fight or flight, it was paralyzing "fright". Your Green responded in a way that reduced your ability to move and call the predator's attention to you. "Scared stiff" is a descriptive term for survival physiology. After the "crisis" was over, you and your body regained non-threat composure.

Such is not the case with Red and Yellow threats that are churned up constantly by incorrect thought choices. Incorrect choices made day after day, year after year, are intense non-stop stress that can lead to timing problems. Survival physiology to Red and Yellow threats doesn't turn off. "Ben" illustrated that. Incorrect thinking leads to extended stress that leads to timing problems, and timing problems lead to exhaustion. And as we have said before, on-going exhaustion leads to symptoms, disease, and possibly death. Physiological stress that results from correct choices, such as high blood pressure from exercising, is your body's cup of tea. Respond, relax, and it's over.

WELLNESS PRINCIPLE: Short-term stress is a health non-
event

When you make correct choices of the six essentials, you ALLOW your body to do what it does naturally. You aren't throwing obstacles in its way. When you make choices of the six essentials that interfere with the way your body works best, you set up patterns that can lead to chronic pain and disease. When you make the same interfering choice over and over and over so that you no longer give much conscious thought to making the choice, you have formed a "habit." You have become "stuck" in the choice, and your body becomes "stuck" in a response.

Suppose your body is "stuck" in an anxiety response. When you are anxious, you are constantly on guard against a potential disaster. An actual disaster, hasn't occurred but you're convinced in your conscious mind that it might, or will, or could. When you are anxious, your body is on Red alert — defending against conscious-mind threats. And when you are anxious all the time, your body is on Red alert all the time.

Every habit is a pattern of activity that has — or had — a positive payback. Every thought pattern or activity pattern that is habitual was a pleasure-producer at some time. From alcoholism and smoking to anxiety and self-pity, even if the payback has lost its glow, at sometime the outcome of the activity was positive, or pleasurable.

WELLNESS PRINCIPLE: No one has a habit he/she never
enjoyed

Your body can't maintain continuous defense indefinitely. Eventually, some part of it will "wear out." Maximum defense is like the sprinter - all out for a short period. You can't expect your "sprinter defense system" to run a marathon. You were designed for your alert systems to turn on when danger is present and turn off when the danger is over. However, when the danger signals never end, the parts or systems that are continuously geared up become exhausted. But they keep going anyway. The stage is set for disease.

WELLNESS PRINCIPLE: Habits are conscious choices set
on automatic pilot

The best way to keep distress and disease at bay is to make sure the choices you make in the six essentials areas of life are the choices that allow your body to function without becoming exhausted. Sure, it may become "tired" periodically. But "tired" and "exhausted" are different. You can recover from "tired" in fairly short order by overcoming the situation that brought on fatigue. Rest, recreation, positive actions and attitudes all restore appropriate internal function.

Conscious choices made habitually in the six essential areas of life mandate physiological responses. The mind-body relationship concept enters the realm of practical reality when you realize that thoughts become actions, and both thoughts and actions bring about physiological responses. Like it or not, conscious choices made in the six essential areas of life impact physiology constantly.

Of course, how you live your life is your business. Eat and drink what you want, exercise and rest as much or as little as you want, smoke cigarettes or live in highly polluted areas, and take a negative view of everything and everyone. All of these options are yours — it's a free country and you exercise free will. The thing to remember though is that the choices you make determine how your body must respond. You can't "will" your body to respond the way you would like. Your body can only try to survive your choices — and that's the domain of your Green. Make incorrect choices consistently and your body does what it must. Make correct choices consistently and your body still does what it must. The big difference is that with incorrect choices it must do pain, distress and disease, and with correct choices, your body must do health.

The trick is to keep a healthful balance in the choices you make. When you make *mostly* correct choices in the each of the six essential areas, there's room for a bit of slippage on occasion. Pig-out on acid ash-producing foods at holiday time. Take some time off from your regular exercise program. Burn the midnight oil, or visit your old school chum in Pollution City. When you habitually make choices that allow your body to be in the best shape possible, your body can handle the occasional "incorrect choice" fling without suffering long-term ill effects. But when you make *mostly* incorrect choices, your body is fighting an uphill battle all the way and there's little margin for error. It's already working toward just plain pooped. So when you pig-out at a festive gathering or cut your rest to the bare bone you set yourself up for one final fatal dump of stress.

Your best bet for health is balance. Balance in the run-and-rest processes of your organs and systems, and balance in the acid-alkaline internal environment of your body. Balance your choices in the six essential areas of life and you give your body the best internal environment possible for it to do what it does best — function perfectly for survival.

> WELLNESS PRINCIPLE: You alone make choices that can keep your internal climate temperate

POINTS OF INTEREST

1. Your life today is a product of yesterday's choices in six essential areas.

2. Inappropriate choices made consistently in any of the six essential areas lead to toxicity and/or timing problems.

3. Breathing supplies oxygen to the cells and eliminates carbon dioxide from the body.

4. Choices in where you live and where you work can be inappropriate if the air you must breath is "toxic."

5. Adequate relaxing rest is essential for body maintenance and repair.

6. If you are thirsty after a meal, you are eating the wrong types of foods.

7. Since "pure" water is no longer available, reverse osmosis water is the most healthful.

8. When you make mostly "right" choices in the six essentials, you can easily afford an occasional "slip."

Better to hunt in fields, for health unbought,
Than fee the doctor for a nauseous draught.
The wise, for cure, on exercise depend;
God never made his work, for man to mend.
                        - John Dryden (1631-1700)

CHAPTER 12
Health Before Fitness

HEALTHY ENOUGH TO EXERCISE?
　　The exercise area of the six essentials may appear to be out of synch with the other five. Exercise isn't imperative to life as are eating, drinking, breathing, and resting. Exercise isn't in the same survival league as the other essentials. But we're talking about more than just surviving. We're talking about "surviving healthy." And proper exercise advances the cause of "surviving healthy."
　　If we're mobile at all, we get exercise. We bend and stretch to pick up crumbs or clothes off the floor. We do moderate knee bends each time we sit down and get up again. We lift children and/or bags of groceries. We garden, shovel snow, climb stairs and move around frequently. And that's good — as far as it goes. Your body works better when it is "in shape." And your conscious choices in the exercise area play an important part in the "shape" you're in. But as we shall see, "in shape" does not necessarily equate with "healthy."
　　You may or may not be healthy enough to start an exercise program. And even if you are already on an exercise program, you may not be healthy enough to continue. It all depends on your health lifestyle. Even "good" exercise can pose a problem if you aren't healthy. Take this little "test" to see if you arc a candidate for beginning, or continuing, a regular exercise program. Respond "yes" or "no" to each of the following.

1. When I lift weights or work out for 5 minutes, I become short of breath. ❑ Yes ❑ No

2. I feel sick or light-headed after I exercise hard. ❑ Yes ❑ No

3. After I walk one block, I'm out of breath, have difficulty talking, or have a headache. ❑ Yes ❑ No

4. I breathe faster than normal when I walk up two flights of stairs. ❑ Yes ❑ No

5. After work, I have to go home and rest until bedtime. ❑ Yes ❑ No

6. I wake up several times during the night. ❑ Yes ❑ No

7. When I play tennis or golf three times a week, my muscles or back hurt. ❑ Yes ❑ No

8. When I exercise, my heart pounds. ❑ Yes ❑ No

9. I can feel my heart beat when I go to bed. ❑ Yes ❑ No

10. I feel exhausted, or my legs or hands cramp when I do normal work or exercise. ❑ Yes ❑ No

If you responded "yes" to any of these questions, you may have a health problem that would make strenuous exercise potentially dangerous for you. Before you launch into a fitness frenzy, check with your doctor to make sure you are healthy enough to handle the added stress of exercise.

EXERCISE, ANYONE?

You need exercise. No matter what your age or physical condition, you need to move those parts that will move. Properly executed exercise benefits both young and "well-seasoned" bodies, as well as those in between. At any age, men and women who exercise regularly enjoy increased mobility and muscle tone, improved cardiovascular function, and improved balance. Yet regardless of age, exercise doesn't guarantee health.

Many Americans are virtually obsessed with trying to be healthy and fit. Jogging, aerobics, racquetball, walking, swimming, weight-lifting, you name it, Americans are panting to be sleek, in-shape and fit. One indicator of our passion for perspiration is the number of TV ads touting various types of exercise equipment and keep-in-shape videos. Your biggest choice there is the type of body you want to emulate: super-muscular, slim-hipped male, or long-legged, firm-fleshed female — both models, of course, fat-free. Although few of us will ever look anything like the perfect-body role models that are featured on TV and in magazines, thousands of people stretch, bend, high-step, and bounce rhythmically and regularly in an attempt to reach the impossible dream. And in the process they may or may not be getting *health-enhancing* exercise. There's more to healthful exercise than huffing and puffing.

> WELLNESS PRINCIPLE: You don't GET healthy by exer-
> cising, but you need exercise to
> STAY healthy

Any exercise affects muscles and joints. Lifting feed sacks or sweeping floors. Hammering nails or writing a report. Cutting grass or washing windows. However, for exercise to be beneficial to your health, relieve stress, and improve strength and muscle coordination, four major systems must be affected. To be truly beneficial whole-body exercise, movements must:

1. Improve joint articulation, muscle tone and resiliency ("grease the knees" and loosen up muscles),
2. Enhance cardiovascular efficiency (tune-up your heart and tone-up your blood vessels),
3. Contribute to physio-neurological integration (improve body-mind balance), and,
4. Improve timing signals to opposing muscles (remove "internal static").

Your body is a unified structure in which everything affects everything else. To reap the greatest health rewards of exercise, you need to work your whole body as a unit. This means you should be sure to involve those areas of the body that aren't involved in your work-day activities. Involve those muscles that you don't realize are there until the day after you shovel snow or romp through a game of tag football at a company picnic. Concentrate on whole-body exercise. You are more than independent sets of lower body and upper body muscles, biceps, triceps, "delts," "pects," "traps," and other weight-room designated muscle favorites. In this book, we deal with whole-body exercise — the kind that improves overall health — as opposed to muscle-specific body-building exercise.

Although we usually equate a slim, well-muscled physique with fitness and health, rippling, bulging muscles don't necessarily mean that your body is functioning under the best internal conditions. The purpose of body-building exercises is quite different from the purpose of health-building exercises. Exercises to develop a Mr. Universe type physique are geared to increase muscle mass of particular muscle groups. If that is your goal, fine. Go for it. Just don't confuse body-building with health-building.

Before you launch a campaign of body-building or any exercise program, check with your doctor to be sure you are healthy enough to withstand the rigors of the intensified physical activity. Your doctor will check to make sure your heart and cardiovascular system can tolerate the increased work load that is part and parcel of strenuous exercise. But there's more. You need to know whether or not the acid level of your body is within acceptable limits — that is, on the alkaline side of neutral. Exercise produces physiologic acid. That's fine. If your internal environment is in the neutral to slightly alkaline range, the additional physiologic acid is no problem. As we shall see, physiologic acid is eliminated when you breathe. However, the sudden bursts of acid that accompany strenuous exercise can put an already overly acidic body at risk. So a controlled acid-alkaline (pH) test is essential to determine the acid level of your body before you start a rigorous exercise program. This test should be performed and evaluated by a qualified physician to make sure your body is not overly acidic. If your internal environment registers on the acid side of neutral, your priority concern should be to reduce the acidity before you try to build muscle or fitness. An overly acid body is not a healthy body no matter how strong it is. Your top priority is to have a healthy body. You can improve your health and control your acidity level by diet. We'll go into the best way to do this in the next chapter.

WELLNESS PRINCIPLE: Build health before you try to
build muscles

Exercise takes time and planning. And it's worth the effort. The benefits of following a sound, regular, whole-body exercise program far outweigh the minor inconvenience of adjusting your schedule to fit regular exercise into your busy lifestyle. One of the first benefits of regular exercise is that you feel better. More pep and energy. Sharper concentration. A feeling of well-being. These are among the overt benefits — benefits you and your friends can observe. Less observable long-term benefits are found in the way your body works and responds to stress. You can move with greater ease and grace (men can read "fluidity" for "grace"). Your heart muscle gains strength with exercise as do other muscles. Your muscle responses are fine-tuned, and you avoid or lose some of the characteristic plodding gait that can creep up on us when we're "getting on in years" — you regain a spring in your step.

The objective of an exercise program is to reap the greatest benefit possible. The most beneficial exercise improves whole body physiology. "Proper" exercise tones up your neurological systems as well as musculo-skeletal system. It enhances internal communication as it refurbishes your muscles. Let's take a closer look at some important physiological benefits.

Improve Muscle Tone and Elasticity —   *"Grease the Knees" and Loosen Up Muscles*

Muscles were designed to be elastic, and joints were designed to bend. However, both of these features can be impaired or diminished by lack of exercise. Muscles can lose their elasticity and resiliency, and joints can "stiffen up" if they are not used. And it doesn't matter if immobility is caused by lifestyle or need. Eight-hour days at a sedentary job followed by six hours in front of the TV can effect muscles and joints in much the same way as immobilizing them in a cast — weakness and ineffective function. The biggest difference is that when an arm or leg comes out of a cast, one of the first things a patient is taught is how to exercise in order to restore flexibility and strength. However, the weakening effect that comes with lack of exercise is so gradual that the changes are hardly noticed until they have reached the dramatic stage.

WELLNESS PRINCIPLE: Muscles and joints were meant to be used

Enhance Cardiovascular Efficiency —   *Tune-Up Heart and Tone-Up Blood Vessels*

The second qualifier for healthful, stress-reducing exercise is that the activity improves heart function and blood circulation. The cardiovascular benefits of regular exercise are well publicized. Generally speaking, regular exercise strengthens the heart, lowers resting heart rate, and reduces blood pressure.

Your heart is the most important muscle in your body. If your heart can't adequately pump oxygen-carrying blood and nutrients to your brain and other cells, it doesn't make much difference how strong your other muscles are. A sound exercise program dramatically increases your heart's capacity for carrying out its life-sustaining function.

Your body is finely attuned to the need to adapt to physical exercise. According to Guyton, "Simply thinking about exercise has the psychic effect of exciting the autonomic nervous centers, which increases the heart rate, increases the strength of heart contraction, and constricts the blood vessels throughout the body to increase the mean systemic filling pressure.

Together, these effects can increase the cardiac output instantaneously as much as 50 per cent even before the exercise begins."[105] But don't put away your athletic gear yet. Although you prime your body by thinking about exercise, you need to move on to the actual "doing" to reap beneficial results. Thinking about exercise is the first step; it's the steps that come after the thinking that count.

Athletes who exercise regularly build up their heart muscles to pump more oxygen-carrying blood per beat. While most of us fall short of being true "athletes," exercise less intense than Olympic training can strengthen the heart to provide more oxygen to cells throughout the body. More oxygen means more energy. Muscle tone improves AND you respond healthfully to stress more easily. Cells function with ten times greater efficiently when they have adequate oxygen.

WELLNESS PRINCIPLE: The comment "No sweat" is slang
— not a directive

Vigorous exercise not only delivers more oxygen to your cells, it also counteracts negative reactions of stress. When you are emotionally stressed you subconsciously defend against an "invisible" threat. Your body primes itself physiologically to survive an impending attack. Your adrenalin level raises. Increased adrenalin production is a principle component of defense preparation.

While we are up-tight and defensive, adrenalin flows. And many of us spend large portions of our lives fending off on-going "threats" — not to our lives but to our egos or feelings. So if we are constantly stressed, adrenalin is ever present. Unfortunately, in our "civilized" society, we usually can't fight or run to use up the adrenalin on the spot. Exercise can help to relieve the adrenalin-stress that accumulates when you consciously restrain your built-in "fight or flight" response. A program of regular exercise that systematically releases adrenalin tension is much more socially acceptable and healthful than destructive stress-prompted "explosions" — like punching your boss's lights out.

WELLNESS PRINCIPLE: Exercise is a socially acceptable
way to "blow off steam"

Balance Body and Mind — *Remove Internal Static*
"Correct" exercise is more than pumping muscles and working off adrenalin. "Correct" exercise helps keep your hidden neurological systems in synch. The best synchronizing exercise is contralateral exercise — opposite side exercise, such as walking. We might call it the "swinging X." Walking is a "swinging X." Right arm and left leg. Left arm and right

leg. When one leg extends, the opposite arm extends. Contralateral exercise that synchronizes opposite side movement synchronizes, "re-times," or balances neurological systems by updating internal messages to reflect present need.

How does contralateral exercise balance your internal communication systems? The right side of your brain controls the left side of your body, and *vice versa*. So when you coordinate right leg movement with left arm movement, you are coordinating left brain and right brain activity. You're coordinating, or "re-timing," energy signals in your central nervous system. Recall that memory patterns for walking and other learned movements are stored in your Yellow. It's your Yellow that compares what you are actually doing with what you have done in the past. If the two aren't the same, the Yellow "tells" the Green to "fix it." But now you're doing new "step aerobic" exercises. You have to think about what to move when. Step up and forward with left foot, raise right arm, step up and forward with right foot, raise left arm, step back and down with left foot, bring right arm down, and on and on. You have to think about what you are doing until the new pattern is fixed in your Yellow. When you consciously emphasize the contralateral movement, you create new patterns in your Yellow to which your Green responds. While all of this is going on, you are also sending signals through your memory pattern Yellow to your subconscious Green that, although vigorous physical activity is called for, there's no crisis. Your central nervous system is "re-timed" and exercised along with your muscles, tendons, and sweat glands. The "re-timing" benefits of contralateral exercise are similar to those of periodic chiropractic well-patient adjustments.

Contralateral movement isn't strictly a Red activity. It plays a big part in physical development. Most babies begin their purposeful navigation with contralateral movements — crawling on all fours. Crawling does more than get a pre-toddler from the middle of the floor to great grand mother's irreplaceable crystal vase. Contralateral crawling develops neuromuscular coordination in babies. The crawling motion integrates sensory and motor signals.

Parents might brag about precocious "Little Billy" who bypasses the crawling stage and moves right into early-onset walking. But "Little Billy" misses an important developmental process. Nature included crawling in the development schedule to integrate the function of nerves and muscles. And the cross-crawl pattern of movement helps sustain neuromuscular coordination in adults. It's a pattern often used to help rehabilitate adults, or children, who have suffered brain damage — a therapy technique called patterning. The patient is guided through active or passive cross-crawl patterns by the therapist. The purpose is to establish neural pathways that will allow undamaged areas of the brain to develop the ability to perform functions that had previously been handled by the injured areas of the brain. When you realize the importance of contralateral exercise, you can see why little tykes should be encouraged to crawl before they walk.

> WELLNESS PRINCIPLE: Contralateral exercise re-times muscle groups

As noted earlier, the most common example of contralateral movement is walking. But walking is more than just forward movement. Merely moving one foot a few inches ahead of the other isn't "walking." And shuffling along with head drooping, shoulders hunched, and hands stuffed into pockets isn't contralateral walking. It lacks the health-enhancing movement of one arm forward as the opposite leg extends.

Some of the exercises that provide good contralateral action are: purposeful, head-up, shoulders-back, arm-swinging walking; riding a stationary bike* that has articulated handlebars; cross-country skiing on snow or machine; and free-style or backstroke swimming. But there are a couple of cautions about some of these "good" exercises.

Caution #1: Exercise bikes with stationary handlebars allow only leg movement. These are great for cardiovascular exercise, but they lack the contralateral benefits of bikes that allow opposite arm and leg movement. When you push down with your right leg, you should be able to either push or pull with your left arm. The objective is to have opposite limbs "working" at the same time.

And Caution #2: Freestyle swimming loses some of its contralateral benefit if you turn your head to the same side each time you take a breath. If you turn your head alternately to right and left while swimming, you improve the contralateral effect. But if you can't do that, after you have finished your swim, walk "freestyle" for a while — head up, arms and legs moving contralaterally. This will help to reintegrate the neurological systems.

Some active exercises that may appear to be contralateral, aren't. These include (but are not limited to) tennis, racquetball, rowing, and weight-lifting. Although legs and arms are involved, alternating opposite-side involvement is missing.

Please do not infer from the previous paragraph that I am implying that tennis, racquetball, skiing or any other vigorous exercise is bad. Heavens to Betsy, no! As you'll recall from the story of my automobile

---

*   WARNING: Keep small children away from stationary exercise bikes. The moving parts of exercise cycles can sever small fingers.

accident, I enjoy tennis. Tennis is a lot of fun. So are show-jumping, golf, curling, baseball, diving, luging, and just about any other sport you can mention. And most of them are great cardiovascular exercise. But we're talking more than heart and lungs. We're into whole-body exercise — cardiovascular, neurological, and muscular. And contralateral is the best for that.

Your neurological systems reap greater benefits from contralateral exercise than they do from same-side (homolateral or ipsilateral) exercises such as racquet sports. And with opposite-side exercise you are less prone to developing a stiff neck, backache, or muscle problems.

Weight lifting and rowing are good overall body exercises if your neurological systems are balanced when you begin. Weight lifting, rowing, and other exercises for which you use your upper and lower body, strengthen muscles and the cardiovascular system; however, they don't balance the neurological system. If your neurological systems are well integrated and balanced when you begin these all-body exercises, your whole body benefits — muscles, cardiovascular system, the works. However, if your neurological systems aren't well integrated and balanced when you do these exercises, the imbalance will be increased. So make sure you walk for ten minutes before you exercise. That way you'll get the integrating effects of contralateral exercise along with your tennis, horseback riding, rowing, or weight-lifting. Then top your session off with another ten minutes of head-up walking. The best of all worlds.

WELLNESS PRINCIPLE: Integrate all areas of your body —
                      top-bottom, front-back, left-right
                      — in your exercise

If you have a physical condition, such as severe arthritis, that prevents you from engaging in vigorous movement, you can still benefit from more subtle exercise. Slow or passive exercise that fits your personal situation is a suitable alternative to pound-and-puff exertion. When the choice is between slow exercise and no exercise, "slow" wins hands-down. And if self-directed exercise isn't possible, passive exercise — arms and legs flexed and exercised with the help of someone else — can relieve the stress of defense physiology.

The bottom line is to regularly move what you can. Even if you can't do the whole-body thing, use the parts you can. You may be surprised to find that as time goes on, you can do more.

Fine-Tune Muscle Movements
In discussing the first three characteristic benefits of whole-body exercise we focused on "the big picture"; agility of large muscle groups,

the cardiovascular system, and body-mind integration. The fourth element that qualifies an exercise as a beneficial whole-body exercise deals with improving internal communication. This is the communication that affects the timing of neurological signals so that your muscles do what you want them to do; and do it smoothly. It is the neurological facility that keeps track of the length of muscles and how fast they are contracting or relaxing. They are the signals that keep you from bashing yourself in the face when you reach up to scratch your nose, or squashing the ripe tomato, of a few chapters back, in a vise-like grip.

Whether you are running, lifting a child, or drumming your fingers, the muscles involved work together. As you run, for example, one set of muscles in your leg contracts as opposing muscles relax. Without this coordinated contraction and relaxation, your muscles would play a game of tug-of-war and nothing would move. Fortunately, you were designed by a Perfect Intelligence that knew about physics long before any of us did.

> WELLNESS PRINCIPLE: You were engineered by a "Master
> Physicist"

The intent to run is the result of a Red process. The actual mechanics of running are essentially a Yellow prompted Green process. You decide in your conscious mind to start running. You also decide in your conscious mind to run around a puddle of water or leap over a hole in the pavement. The actual process of running and leaping is directed by subconscious activity. When you make the decision to run or leap a puddle, your muscles respond with the muscle version of "Look alive, we're going to do something special." How does your subconscious know what the tone of a particular muscle is at the time you make the decision to leap?   Internal communication through feedback systems. Your conscious Red initiates intent of the activity. Your non-conscious Yellow gets into the act by providing the learned pattern, and the Green comes through with the physiology required to accomplish what the Red has directed. Your Green is a beehive of communication activity. Signals come and go constantly. Your Green receives status reports from all over your body, including muscles and tendons. It also sends instructions out to the muscle and tendon "troops" that do the work. The Green is the "field headquarters" that receives "status reports" from muscles and tendons and sends back signals to adjust in particular ways. So consciously inspired movement of any sort results from integration of *sensory signals from* muscles and tendons *to* the central nervous system, and *motor signals sent from* the CNS to muscles and tendons.

For our purposes, we will give a simplified version of the process of neuromuscular communication. Again, this isn't a medical treatise; the purpose is to give you the flavor of how your body works. And a vital component of its working is effective neuronal (nerve) communication between your muscles and your Green. Nerve impulses transmitted along the large fibers stimulate skeletal muscle fibers to contract. Along with these messages, signals are sent along smaller fibers to parts of the muscles themselves — to parts called muscle spindles and Golgi tendon organs. Physiologist Guyton describes these mechanisms as ". . . two special types of sensory receptors: (1) muscle spindles, which are distributed throughout the belly of the muscle and which send information to the nervous system about either the muscle length or rate of change of its length, and (2) Golgi tendon organs which transmit information about tension or rate of change of tension."[106] Your sensory system knows what your muscles are doing.

But what does this have to do with exercise?

We can see that every skeletal muscle is controlled by two basic nerve networks: one comes from the Red, the other from the Green. The large fibers from the Red control what you are going to do — pick up a pencil, or run, or move a forkful of food from plate to mouth. The small fibers controlled by your Green allow opposing muscles to work together — in synchronization. One contracts while its opposing partner relaxes.

Slow, deliberate movements improve this vital synchronized process. Exercise that accentuates precise control of muscles helps to retime non-conscious responses. Exercise such as yoga, ballet, and Eastern forms of movement that emphasize the discipline of controlled motion and use the T'ai Chi concept of active and passive integration help to fine-tune muscle responses and enhance fluidity of movement. These exercises emphasize stretching, balanced breathing, and relaxing mind and body into various poses.

Slow, controlled exercise retimes and retunes the body. It doesn't build muscle as does weight-lifting. Big muscles don't necessarily mean efficient muscles. Slow, controlled exercise doesn't put an excessive load on the cardiovascular system the way aerobics or jogging can. However, slow, deliberate motion is good training for fast, deliberate motion.

Exercise that promotes precise synchronization of the neuromuscular system provides an added bonus to any exercise program. And it is appropriate for all age groups.

> WELLNESS PRINCIPLE: Fine-tune your body with slow,
> deliberate movements

EXERCISE FACTS AND FICTION

In our fitness-crazed, exercise-intensive society, we have built up a great storehouse of exercise lore. Many of our ideas about exercise come from locker room chatter, fitness enthusiasts, and the popular press. Much of the information is based on solid evidence. However, some popular concepts and mottos about exercise border on folly. Not only are they not correct, some can be downright dangerous. Here are some common "exercise myths."

Exercise Myth #1   *If you're fit, you're healthy*

Despite the pervasiveness of this myth, being fit does not assure health. No matter how fit you are, as we have seen, if your internal acid level is perilously high from a long-term high-protein diet, every time you exercise you risk your life. Now that may sound overly dramatic, but I can't stress it too much. I firmly believe that strenuous exercise of an overly acid body can be fatal.

Acid is a constant commodity in your body. Aside from the acid you get from acid ash-producing foods (that we'll talk about in the next chapter), acid is generated by cellular function. During strenuous physical exercise, physiological functions speed up and cells produce more acid than during tranquil periods. Strenuous exercise releases great quantities of carbon dioxide (CO_2) into the blood. When carbon dioxide combines with water, the result is carbonic acid — a weak, organic acid. This organic acid is eliminated through the lungs. That's why you huff and puff when you exercise hard — or, if you're in terrible shape, when you exercise even slightly. "Carbon dioxide is one of the major end-products of the oxidative reactions in cells," writes Guyton. "If all of the carbon dioxide formed in the cells should continue to accumulate in the tissue fluids, the mass action of the carbon dioxide itself would soon halt all the energy-giving reactions of the cells."[107] Carbon dioxide is an acid-producer, and too much of it is a cell-stopper. Although carbonic acid is easily eliminated through the lungs, it is still acid. And when even a weak acid is dumped into your system along with other acid, the result can be devastating.

WELLNESS PRINCIPLE: Even a weak acid added to too
much acid is acid overload

Breathing is ordinarily considered to be directed primarily toward bringing oxygen into the lungs; and of course that is correct — but incomplete. The substances exhaled are as important as the substances inhaled. The body not only takes in additional oxygen, it cleans out increased amounts of carbonic acid. That's what is was designed to do. The lungs can dispose of weak, organic acid with no problem. And excess acid from exercise wouldn't be a problem if carbonic acid were the only acid cells produce as they function. But it isn't. Skeletal muscles — the muscles that make it possible for you to do all of that bending, bouncing, and ball-whacking — produce lactic acid. If this acid isn't carried off in rather short order, it builds up in the muscle and the muscle becomes painfully tired. And no matter when the lactic acid is "carried off," the lactic acid adds to the acid overload.

Are you beginning to see the difference between being "fit" and being "healthy"? You are "fit" when your musculoskeletal system is in good shape. Strong, well-coordinated muscles. Strong, well-aligned skeletal system. Lots of muscle tissue "hung" attractively on a well proportioned frame. That has nothing at all to do with "health."

WELLNESS PRINCIPLE: "Fit" and "healthy" are
                      not synonymous

"Fitness" indicates lean, strong, stamina, agile, athletic — in a word, fit. "Health" is more nebulous. Although we often think of "health" in the same terms just used to describe fitness, more generally we think of "health" as an absence of symptoms. But for our purposes, "health" means a slightly alkaline internal environment in which systems and organs must respond only to appropriately-timed stimuli.

WELLNESS PRINCIPLE: Health is the absence of toxicity
                      and inappropriately timed stress

Keep in mind that being fit is no guarantee of health and a long life without pain. In fact, being fit may ultimately have the opposite effect. Fitness doesn't guarantee good health anymore than good health guarantees fitness.

Exercise Myth #2   *No pain, no gain*
No doubt about it — pain is an attention-getter. Pain is "body language" yelling, "Hey! You up there in the Red — the one making the stupid choices. You're botching up the works down here."

All right, that's a little fanciful since there's no thinking or yelling at all; but you get the picture. Pain is a message from your body's "worker drones" that something is out of synch, out of time, or in trouble.

WELLNESS PRINCIPLE: Slight pain means something is
                      amiss; major pain means some-
                      thing is a mess

Among the many talents of your Green is its ability to communicate with your Red. We have seen that your Green communicates directly through feedback mechanisms with muscles and tendons, sending and receiving impulses in response to what your Red wants them to do without getting carried away — hit that tennis ball into the opposite backcourt, not into the next county. This is your Green's direct "telephone line." Pain, on the other hand might be seen as a fax message. It takes a little longer to send and receive, but when the message gets to its destination, you have something of substance you can feel.

Pain is your body's early warning signal. You can interpret pain as an alert that your subconscious has had to respond too long to the results of your inappropriate choices — too little rest, too much protein, excessive strain on muscles, or other stress-producing choices.

Overexertion is an inappropriate choice that often brings on muscle pain. When you overwork a muscle, it tears ever so slightly. However, the body repairs itself when an injury occurs. An injury is a high-priority item. The body's damage control team gets right to work. Scar tissue forms to repair the muscle, and the muscle gets bigger. If this process continues, the muscle becomes larger because of the scar tissue; but it loses strength. You build muscle mass — not health — through pain.

> WELLNESS PRINCIPLE: Pain is initiated in your subcon-
> scious and you become aware that
> something is wrong

Never put the body through pain to try to stay healthy. When pain begins, exercise should end. Or even better, exercise should end *before* pain begins. Beneficial exercise should improve communication and cooperation among Red, Yellow, and Green. It isn't a contest between conscious and subconscious. We're looking at health-enhancing exercise, not training for World Cup competition. Competitive exercise — better known as "sports" — is a whole different ball game. You don't have to push yourself to your physical and emotional limits to get the most out of health-enhancing your exercise program. In fact, in his book *Perfect Health; The Complete Mind/Body Guide*, Deepak Chopra offers the realistic yet unconventional observation that exercise should leave you ready for work, not be work itself. He recommends that you exercise to 50 percent capacity. "If you can bicycle six miles, go for three; if you can swim twenty laps, make it ten. These lower limits are not detrimental to fitness; in fact they make exercise more efficient, because you are not giving your body so much repair work to do afterward, and your cardio-vascular system will have an easier time returning to normal after your workout."[108] How's that for a liberating concept? You really don't have to approach an exercise program with "grim determination." Positive enthusiasm is a much more pleasant and advantageous attitude.

Exercise Myth #3   *"I get enough exercise at work/around the house."*
A comforting thought, but inaccurate. Although the exercise you get at your job moves muscles and joints — whether that job is in the home, in a factory, in the great outdoors, or in an office — you don't reap all the healthful benefits you can get with regular, enjoyable, recreational exercise.

Repetitive physical movements are the stock in trade of a job or regular schedule. Data entry at a keyboard, hammering nails, stocking shelves, vacuuming floors, and countless other on-the-job tasks call for the same muscle movements over and over. Repetitive movement is a principle contributor to an assortment of painful physical maladies such as muscle strain, backache, headache, and one of today's more prevalent work-related diseases — carpal tunnel syndrome.

On-the-job physical activity can have another shortcoming that knocks it out of the "healthful exercise" category: undue mental stress.

On the job, you are mentally alert — you think, analyze, make decisions, and, in general, pay close attention to what you are doing. That's good. That's what your thinking processes are for. And that's probably what you're paid for. However, if your mind buzzes with restrictions, requirements, and obligations necessary for you to fulfill your job responsibilities, you are moving into the negative realm. Negative responses to time schedules, production requirements, zero-defects goals, deadlines, dealing with the cantankerous public, contending with a badgering supervisor or surly subordinates keep your body continuously on guard.

WELLNESS PRINCIPLE: Job stress can be a mind-body
hazard

Or perhaps the activities of your job call for minimal mental effort. Tasks are dull, routine, tedious, repetitive, or just plain mindless. If so, you are in as much danger of mental stress as those in high-pressure jobs. While you are physically occupied completing your assigned duties, you are mentally unchallenged — a perfect setting to dwell on worries, frustrations, and perceived slights.

In both of these situations — stressful high-pressure or stressful frustrating tedium — any beneficial effects of job-related exercise is overshadowed by the drain of emotional distress.

WELLNESS PRINCIPLE: Emotional stress of job stress is a
breeding ground for disease

Despite the level of physical activity involved, just about any job involves emotional pressures. Look to yourself to reduce the effects of the pressures. A well-balanced exercise program outside of work can be a great stress-reducer. And to complement your physical exercise program, add a generous portion of mental exercise in the form of controlling your thoughts on the job. You are the only one who can control your thoughts. To relieve emotional stress, each day set yourself a goal of keeping your mind filled with positive thoughts as much as possible. Look for the good in each circumstance minute by minute. It takes discipline, but it's good stress-reducing mental exercise.

Exercise Myth #4   *You can't get too much exercise*

This myth follows the principle that if a little is good, a lot is better. Sort of the exercise version of the famous quote "You can never be too skinny or too rich." (To add to your store of irrelevant trivia, three people have been credited with originating this quote: Babe Paley, the Duchess of Windsor, and Gloria Vanderbilt.) As with all extremes, too much *is* too much. Studies have shown that, depending on your goal, over exercising — too much, too fast, too hard — may not bring the best results. Running, for instance.

In an article entitled "The Cold Truth About Hard Workouts," in the Mar/Apr 1991 issue of *In Health*, writer Peter Jaret told of interesting and unexpected results of strenuous training found by David Nieman. Nieman, a distance runner and director for health promotion at Appalachian State University in Boone, North Carolina, had observed that he and other runners often came down with a cold or the flu after competition. He investigated. Nieman found that all-out exercise seems to *reduce* the amount of "some protective antibodies." But less strenuous exercise improved "the body's defenses."

Moderation is the key to health-enhancing exercise. Reasonable amounts of exercise strengthen. Excessive amounts of exercise can exhaust. And not only muscles get tired. Organs and systems that work overtime become exhausted. This opens the door to allow in those unwelcome militant guests, Private Pain and General Misery.

Remember, exercise shouldn't be work that leaves you gasping, panting, and scowling. Exercise should be enjoyable and refreshing.

WELLNESS PRINCIPLE: Enjoy the exercise you do, or change it

EXERCISE WITH AN ATTITUDE
Exercising should make you feel good both mentally and physically.

How you feel about the exercise you do — your attitude — enhances or diminishes the overall benefits you gain from your efforts. In addition, your attitude affects your performance as well as your benefits. Ask just any athletic coach worth his or her championships about attitude. You will find a strong advocate of a positive mental attitude. Players must be winners in their heads before they can be winners on the fields of competition or life. Regular exercise, like competitive sports, takes self discipline; and this discipline is strengthened by a good attitude. Notice the facial expressions of champion athletes in competition. Although they are concentrating intensely, they usually appear to enjoy what they are doing (unless they are getting stomped).

I am constantly amazed at the pained expression I see on the faces of some dedicated runners who glide or lumber along our nation's roadsides. Perhaps the expression comes from fear of being the target of an inattentive or malicious driver. I suspect it has more to do with the runner's grim determination to prove something to himself or herself.

Many recreational runners pursue their hobby (or addiction) because, as they say, they feel better after running. You shouldn't have to run, or work out, or "do" anything else to feel good. If you exercise because you feel good and you want to, that's great. Go for it! If you exercise because you "should," you are catering to guilt rather than improving your health.

> WELLNESS PRINCIPLE: Exercise because you want to, not
> because you should

The most effective exercise program is one that you enjoy. Your mind, as well as your body, works when you exercise. Negative thoughts about your regimen or circumstances in your life put your body in a defensive mode which tightens muscles that should be supple. A negative attitude while exercising can diminish the stress-reducing effect, bring on a painful injury, or abort the whole program.

> WELLNESS PRINCIPLE: Smile on the inside while you
> sweat on the outside

Positive attitudes and thoughts boost the stress-relieving benefits of exercise. In his book *Mind as Healer, Mind as Slayer*, Kenneth Pelletier describes a controlled study by Psychologist Richard Driscoll (1975). Groups of high-anxiety students witnessed a sequence of stressful scenes. Pelletier writes of the researcher's findings: ". . . the group that succeeded in most effectively reducing their anxiety was a group that used the physical exertion of running in place plus positive imagery of themselves being calm and tranquil. . . . the critical factor in his study was not increasing or decreasing stress during the anxiety scenes, but insuring that positive feelings followed immediately afterward."[109]

Enjoy your exercise to increase stress-relieving benefits.

REMEDIAL EXERCISE 101X

Exercise, like literature, comes in degrees of complexity and sophistication. *Cat in the Hat*-level "athletes" soon become discouraged if they launch into *War and Peace*-level exercise. So, begin where you are, not where you would like to be.

The first exercise you should do, whether or not you are a seasoned fitness buff, is a subtle self-check exercise: the shoulder stress-check. You can do this right now. Notice whether or not your shoulders are "up." If your neck has disappeared into your shoulders you are tense! Relax. Let your shoulders ooze down to their normal relaxed position. As you do this little exercise, you will feel the tension drain from your body.

Remember, when your body is tense, you are ready for a fight; your body is in defense. If you are tense even though you aren't in the midst of a confrontation, your Red sensory system is being dominated by your sixth-sense memory Yellow. Inappropriate "danger" messages are being sent to your Green. So your Green responds with perfect, but ill-timed, physiology. Your Green can't evaluate the accuracy of the situation; it just responds. As far as your Green is concerned, warding off an attack is the number one priority for survival. Be thankful for that. But you can't sustain your best work, play, or exercise when you are trying to survive.

WELLNESS PRINCIPLE: Tense means defense

To make your shoulder-lowering exercise even more effective, you may as well get out of survival mode while you're at it. You can "tell" your Green that all is well. To do this, forcefully lower your shoulders, relax, take a deep breath and hold it as long as you can. This pattern of consciously controlling both muscle tension and breathing integrates conscious and subconscious responses to present conditions. When you hold your breath, the priority threat to your body is lack of oxygen. Since you are controlling the breathing situation through your Red, and since you can hold your breath for only a limited time, you are in no actual danger. In due time you will breathe. But your Green doesn't know that. It isn't in the forecasting business. It merely responds to "not enough oxygen" of the moment and runs a quick "status check" on all available sources of oxygen. So you breathe. What has happened is that your conscious Red and subconscious Green have worked together toward the same end — to keep you alive. You have integrated their functions. One of the best things about this drill is that you can do this several times a day. You will feel better, be less tense, and no one around you will even realize that you are "exercising."

This subtle integrating procedure is also a good pre-exercise exercise. Make it part of your pre-warm up exercise. Along with the stretching we'll talk about in a page or so, this pre-exercise exercise helps reduce tension in your muscles. It takes them out of the "run for your life" mode and allows them to work better in the "run for the fun of it" mode. You'll enjoy the effects more and/or less. You'll enjoy "more" flexibility and agility because your muscles will be more supple, and you'll enjoy "less" muscle stiffness and pain afterward.

> WELLNESS PRINCIPLE: Stress tenses muscles; exercise
> tones them

The need for stress and tension relief isn't limited to peak activity times. A variation on the shoulder stress-check can help you to get to sleep faster and rest better after you get there. The pattern for this remedial stress-relief exercise is similar to the shoulder stress-check, but you do it when you are ready to sleep. It's simple, and relaxing.

Lie down, take a deep breath, hold it, and consciously relax the muscles of different areas of your body. Start with your toes and work up — relax feet, legs, buttocks, back, torso, arms, neck, face, even your scalp. Depending upon how tense you are to begin with, you may need to take several breaths along the way. Breathe when you must, then take another deep breath and hold it. You may not make it all the way up your body before you fall asleep. Even if you don't get from toes to scalp, you have given your body the best conditions possible for a good rest and a period of effective maintenance and repair. Pleasant dreams.

WARM-UPS AND COOL-DOWNS

All exercise sessions — like Gaul — are divided into three parts: the warm-up, the work-out, and the cool-down. Leaping full-tilt into a strenuous workout without preparing your heart and other muscles is an invitation to strains, sprains, and pains. Give yourself and your body the same consideration race horse trainers give their four-legged athletes.

> WELLNESS PRINCIPLE: Warm up before you work out

The first part of each exercise session should be a warm-up period to get your heart up to speed, limber up joints. and gently stretch muscles. Let's repeat that — *gently* stretch muscles. Gentle stretching and slow exercise not only increase your heart rate gradually, they reduce the risk of muscle injury. Stretching is very important. Slowly and gently stretch the muscles. That's s-t-r-r-r-r-e-t-c-h; not yank or wrench. None of this bending to touch your toes and bouncing down the last three inches. "Bouncing" and yanking muscles isn't stretching. Stretching is a steady controlled tension. Bouncing does violence to muscles that prompts them to respond defensively — tighten up. That's not what you're after.

Tight muscles can be damaged by sudden violent pulling. Although a muscle beneath the skin of your arm or leg may feel like a solid mass to your fingers, in reality it is made up of many tiny fibers. Delicate fibers run the full length of some muscles or diagonally between tendons of others. Blood vessels and nerve fibers are associated with muscles. Messages flit between muscles and the central nervous system with information about the state of the muscle, velocity of movement, and length of the muscle. This is part of the body's intricate feedback mechanisms we've talked about. They keep the Green apprised of conditions within the body. The whole system is quite remarkable. But what does it have to do with warm-up stretching?

By implication, muscles are strong. However, like a rope made up of many fibers grouped together, individual strands can be damaged. A warm-up period of stretching and moderate exercise before the strenuous work-out phase reduces the risk of muscle damage and next-day stiffness. Warm up before you exercise, and continue your warm-up until your heart rate reaches about 120 beats per minute. Then, have a good time working out.

The cool-down phase after you have finished your workout is equally as important as the warm-up phase. Again, take your cue from race horses and Olympic athletes. If they can cool down, you can too — and should. Your cool-down period allows your muscles and your brain to agree that the vigorous activity is over, and it allows your heart rate to return gradually to its normal pace. Also during cool-down, you breathe out more of the exercise-produced acid.

And speaking of acid, one more caution concerning the timing of eating and your exercise sessions. Give your body a break, let it handle one major stress at a time. Eating and exercising are not a good combination. Both eating and exercising are stresses to your body. No big deal. You were designed to handle stresses. However, the body handles the stress of eating differently from the way it handles the stress of exercise. Recall that exercise calls for physiological responses similar to those of a physical threat. Your body goes into risk homeostasis. Sympathetic processes dominate. Blood pressure goes up, blood is flow to major muscles is increased, and digestion slows or stops! However, when you eat, your body switches into digestive homeostasis. The job of blood then is to see that nutrients are distributed to cells and that muscles aren't primed for action. It's parasympathetic dominance time. So, what's a body to do if you eat a meal or hefty snack then career down your favorite jogging path. I'll tell you what it'll do. It will take care of the "threats" as they come into priority. It's the old priority survival game.

Your physiology flips back and forth. Defend. Digest. Defend. Digest. There's food in your stomach, but the digestive process is sporadic. Food sits there longer than usual. Not a good environment for an extended stay. Your stomach is supposed to be a way-station, not a warehouse. And in the process, blood goes to major muscles to take care of them, then it focuses on the digestive process. Defend. Digest. Defend. Digest. The problem with the backing and forthing is that your muscles can cramp when digestion is in priority, and the food in your stomach just sits there when threat is in priority.

When you realize that your body is trying to survive the things you do to it, you can understand why you should wait at least an hour and a half after eating before you do any strenuous aerobic exercise.

> WELLNESS PRINCIPLE: It's not polite, or wise, to eat
> and run

You may notice that you aren't hungry when you have finished exercising. Your body is still recovering from its hard work. A short period of transition time between exercising and eating allows it to regroup before you send it off into digestive physiology. A little rest never hurt any body.

THE EXERCISE OF CHOICE

The exercise of choice requires minimal preparation and equipment, nothing to plug in, no membership fees, no reservations, scant training, is suitable for solitary, pairs, or group participation, and it's free. All you need to get started is a conscious choice, appropriate shoes and seasonal clothing. What is this gem of an exercise deal? Walking.

Walking in fresh outdoor air is the aerobic exercise of choice for people of all ages. You reap all of the benefits of healthful exercise during a brisk walk. Properly done, walking improves muscle tone and elasticity, tones up your cardiovascular system, is contralateral, and helps to fine-tune muscle movement.

> WELLNESS PRINCIPLE: Walking-for-exercise gives you all
> the perks with none of the hassle

One of the great things about walking is that you learned the rudiments of the "sport" as a little kid. For most people, though, some of the finer points of healthful walking are lost somewhere between "little kid" and "big kid." For "little kids," form comes naturally. We tend to lose this as we become more "sophisticated." We lose the freedom of movement we had. As we become more tense and rigid in our thinking, we become more tense and rigid in our walking. So when you make a conscious choice to walk for body and mind, also make a choice to loosen up. Walk as though your joints were strung together, not welded together.

How much and how far should you walk?

Ideally, if you are in reasonably good condition you should be able to step off a mile in about 15 minutes — but not the first time you step out the door. If you are a novice at walking-for-exercise, you probably won't be able to click off the ideal distance in the ideal time.

Begin your program slowly. Remember the importance of warming up, cooling down, and resting. After you have warmed up and limbered up, walk as fast as is comfortable for you to get your heart rate up to 120 beats a minute. (Wear a watch; it won't throw you off balance.) Your overall physical condition will let you know if you can sustain this pace for 10 or 15 minutes. Your body gives you plenty of clues as to how it's handling the stress. If you find you are gasping for breath, or if you can feel your heart pounding, slow down or stop. After you have regained your breath and your heart beat returns to normal, continue at a more moderate speed. As long as you can talk and smile as you walk, continue.

Your goal should be to walk at 120 paces per minute with your heart rate at 120 beats per minute for 15 minutes. This speed puts you in the aerobic exercise realm. However, if you are new to the game, set short-term goals that are realistic for your particular circumstances. As you and your body become more accustomed to the new stimulation, raise your sights and shoot for increasingly longer walks in the same amount of time.

WELLNESS PRINCIPLE: The purpose of exercise is to help
your body become more healthy
— not to punish it

Now, back to the contralateral action we discussed earlier. Walking was cited as one of the best contralateral exercises you can do. Take comfortably long, purposeful strides, and let your arms swing freely at your sides, your hands empty. Right leg-left arm left leg-right arm rhythm is the basis of contralateral movement. On cool days you may be tempted to walk with your hands in your pockets. Resist this temptation. If the weather is cool, wear gloves so your arms can be active participants. Arm movements coordinated contralaterally with leg movements synchronize your neurological systems — take the "static" out of your internal communications. But don't get carried away with the swinging-arms bit. On your "backswing," your hands shouldn't go back much farther than your hips, and they shouldn't cross over in front. An overly long forward swing lengthens your stride, slows your speed, and tires you more quickly.

Don't carry weights while you walk. Carrying weights in your hands or wearing them on your wrists and/or ankles may seem to be just the thing to add a little resistance and oomph to your walking workout. The theory is fine. But the practice isn't. Your body is balanced for its own weight distribution. Do you honestly think that you would ever gain an additional half-pound or pound of natural weight just in each wrist and ankle? Paints a pretty ludicrous picture, doesn't it? Adding "synthetic" weight disturbs the body's balance and puts unnecessary strain on joints. The pounds added by carrying or wearing weights don't burn off enough additional calories to compensate for the unnecessary strain on elbow, knee, and shoulder joints.

> WELLNESS PRINCIPLE: Your body balances its
> own weight distribution

Although one of the benefits of walking outdoors is that you can enjoy the scenery, there's more to a total exercise program than meandering through flora. Both fast walking and slower walking have therapeutic benefits. Walking at a quick pace benefits your cardiovascular and neurological systems. Walking at a slightly more leisurely pace is neurologically beneficial and, as we shall see in the next section, can bolster a weight-loss campaign. Therapeutic *aerobic* walking isn't a stroll in the park. Walk with purpose. Head up. Smile. And leave your worries and audio headset at home. Allow your body and mind to cavort freely. Some of your best thoughts can come along when you're walking. Walking without undue sensory interference is a great time for imagination and creativity to soar. We might call it "creative walking."

In our electronic instant-information age, we are accustomed to being shielded from our own thoughts by outside noises. At home, in the car, in the workplace, in stores we are constantly bombarded with manufactured sound — TV, radio, public address systems, Muzak, cassette players. Listening to a radio or cassette player while exercising dumps concentrated "verbal static" into your mind. Even if you are listening to a motivational tape, your mind constantly assesses the ideas coming through the earphones. Your body is influenced by these intrusions. You judge the merits of the information. Judgment at any time can lead to stress. Judgment while exercising waters-down benefits you would otherwise enjoy.

"What about music?" you ask.

Music comes in a variety of qualities, types, and rhythms. The problem with listening to music while you walk is that the rhythm of the music and the rhythm of your body may not be in sync. The body rhythm we're talking about here is not the outward rhythm of your stride but the internal rhythm of your personal energy field. Your field is always with you. While walking, let your body resonate to the tempo of your field without imposing unnecessary outside influences.

Walking (or running) is a whole-body experience — physical and mental. Direct your thinking as you direct your course. This is not the time to accentuate the negative. Instead, concentrate on good, positive thoughts. No matter how bleak a situation in your life may be, you can always find something good. One "good" is that despite the situation you're still alive and able to walk. Putting positive thoughts into your conscious mind allows your subconscious to respond with risk-free, stress-free physiology. In the process, the contralateral physical movements re-time your internal communication systems to respond in the most stress-reducing manner possible.

> WELLNESS PRINCIPLE: Reinforce positive attitudes with
>   positive thoughts while walking

WEIGHT-CONTROL

We all know that exercise helps to burn some of the calories we take in along with our pasta, cheeseburgers, truffles, bouillabaisse, and other sources of sustenance. A "calorie" is an energy-producing value. And logic tells us that in order to keep our weight under control we need to use at least as many calories, as much energy, as we consume — or, conversely, consume only as many calories as we intend to use. Exercise can help to keep this balance.

An added perk of regular, vigorous exercise is a process that has been termed "exercise afterburn." Exercise afterburn is the residual calorie-burning effect you get after working out. According to a "Body Notes" sidebar in *Health* magazine, researchers at the University of Missouri found that "Your body is revved up for nearly half a day after a workout." How's that for interest on your exercise investment? As the unidentified writer puts it, "Seven subjects put through a hard workout sweated off an average of 600 calories in an hour. But over the next nine hours they burned 120 calories more than on a non-workout day."[110] A real boon to the weight conscious!

And there's more good news. Another study, this by cardiologist James M. Rippe, M.D., found that faster isn't necessarily better for burning calories. For 24 days, three groups of walkers walked three miles a day at different speeds: a comfortable 20 minutes per mile for one group, a brisk 15 minutes per mile for the second group, and a smart clip of 12 minutes per mile for the third. In his article "Walk This Way," John Poppy described how the different speeds affected the members of the different groups: "All three improved. The two faster groups gained the most in endurance and overall fitness, but the strollers — to the researchers' surprise — burned off the highest proportion of calories from fat and outscored the others on reduction in blood pressure and several cholesterol tests."[111] So even if you aren't up to "brisk" or "smart clip" walking, the benefits of a more sedate pace are well worth the effort.

If you are up to "brisk" or "smart clip," or even running, the ideal routine is to walk at a comfortable pace — somewhere between "stroll" and "purposeful" — for ten minutes. Then up your pace to get your heartbeat up to 120 beats per minute for ten minutes. The first ten minutes of slow walking will "burn off fat," and the second ten minutes will benefit your cardiovascular system. The best of all worlds — lose weight and gain health in one pleasant exercise.

Exercise certainly plays a role in weight control. However, exercise alone isn't the answer to either slimming down or beefing up. Correct choices in all of the six essential areas of life — eating, drinking, resting, breathing, exercising, and thinking — will help you to reach or maintain your most healthful weight and, in the process, help you to eliminate inappropriate physiological stress.

> WELLNESS PRINCIPLE: Exercise is part of weight control,
> not the bulk of it

We have reviewed the cardiovascular and muscle tone benefits of exercise. And there's more. Although it may appear to be oxymoronic, exercise can make you less tired. One of the best ways to overcome fatigue is to exercise. Within limits, the more energy used, the more there is available. And while exercise is acid-producing, it also facilitates acid-elimination.

Choosing to exercise or not exercise is a conscious decision. Choosing to exercise regularly as a part of your schedule is a conscious commitment — what we might call an ongoing conscious decision. However, choosing to enhance health through exercise is a relatively easy mental choice — sustaining that commitment is another matter. Unfortunately, failing to carry through with the commitment can often stimulate feelings of guilt that are more hazardous to your health than lack of exercise.

Remember, you don't have to exercise to the point of exhaustion. A moderate routine of exercise can be more beneficial to overall health than

Olympic style training. If you are already firmly embedded in a regular exercise program, keep it up. However, don't expect exercise to cure all of your ills. Although it is important to all-around health, exercise is not the single most important factor in health anymore than it is the single most important factor in attaining ideal weight.

Your overall health is determined by the choices you make consistently in all of the six essential areas. The road to health is paved with choices that pump the least amount of interference into your body and your field, and that help your internal environment to stay slightly alkaline. One of the biggest factors in the condition of your internal environment is the food you eat. "Inappropriate" food selection choices piled on top of other "inappropriate" choices will eventually tip your health scales from tolerably mediocre to intolerably terrible. Improving your conscious choices to the correct side can tip your health scales to your own highest level of wonderful.

WELLNESS PRINCIPLE: Living the good life comes from
making good choices   ·

POINTS OF INTEREST

1. Make sure you are healthy enough to exercise strenuously.

2. Exercise won't make you healthy but it will help you to stay healthy.

3. Whole-body exercise improves: muscle tone, heart and blood vessel efficiency, mind-body balance, and internal timing.

4. Contralateral movement — especially walking — is the most effective whole-body exercise.

5. Regularly scheduled, brisk, outdoor walking is ideal exercise for people of all ages.

6. Begin and end exercise sessions slowly; exercise vigorously between warm-up and cool-down.

7. Slow walking burns the highest proportion of fat calories; brisk walking improves endurance.

8. Exercise is an important part of weight control; not the only part.

*The destiny of countries depends on
the way they feed themselves.*
- Anthelme Brillat-Savarin

CHAPTER 13
Food Choices and the Acid Factor

EVERYBODY'S DOING IT

We all eat. Generally, we eat several times a day — meals, snacks, nibbles. In our society of abundance, food is ever present. Food does more than sustain life — it greases the wheels of social harmony . From morning business breakfasts to evening friends-in bar-b-ques, from birthdays to bar mitzvahs, when two or more are gathered together food is featured. Indeed, there's more to eating than meeting nutritional needs. Eating can be comforter, companion, and emotional crutch. We eat to ...

- satisfy hunger
- provide fuel which cells convert into energy
- fight boredom
- celebrate
- assuage the "blues"
- reward ourselves
- spite someone else
- be sociable

For the most part, our food choices are based on habits, culture, what we like, what we are accustomed to eating, and what we expect the food to do, or not do, for us or to us. In the U.S. of the mid '90s, only a certified hermit has missed all of the hoopla about the health hazards associated with eating copious quantities of fatty foods. The current popular trend in diet is toward eating more fruits and vegetables. The rationale for this trend is that vegetables and fruits provide needed vitamins and minerals without undesirable fat tagging along. Those in the know have also observed that folks whose diets are fruit- and vegetable-centered seem to have fewer incidents of cardiovascular disease and other physical maladies than those whose diets are meat-centered or high in fat.

As we shall see, the real reason veggie buffs fare better in the health department than meat mavens goes far beyond the plugged-artery rationale. Lower fat and cholesterol intake is indeed helpful. But that's not the bottom-line reason vegetable-intense diets are better for you than meat-intense diets. Dietary fat and cholesterol in moderation pose little threat to health. Your body needs both, is designed to handle both, and produces both. Your body produces its own cholesterol and, to the chagrin of many, converts excess energy-source glucose into fat.[112] The health threat lies not so much in the fat and cholesterol that's in the food we eat but in the fat and cholesterol carriers — high-protein foods such as meat.

"Great snapping turtles, Agnes!" you protest. "First he says our thoughts, memories, and beliefs can make us sick. Now he's telling us that protein's bad. Is nothing sacred?"

Before you get your socks in a knot, hear me out.

Mothers, doctors, collective "Aunt Harriets," and coaches have conditioned us to "Get plenty of protein; it builds muscles — you can't get too much protein!" That's one of our modern-day "flat spots." I'll not careen off on a tangent of who is promoting this belief to the mothers, Aunt Harriets and coaches, or why. Instead, we'll take a quick tour of part of the internal processing plant that handles the protein-laden cholesterol/fat carrying meat. I'll not argue the "protein builds muscle" point here. But when you realize how your body must respond to the by-products of protein you'll see why excess dietary protein is the health-inhibiting culprit rather than the cholesterol and fat. Keep in mind that I am referring to *excess* protein — excess according to your body's needs, not according to the USRDA.

The amount of protein recommended for adults 19 to 51+ years old ranges from 46 grams to 63 grams per day. The wide range in the recommended amounts reflects the lower protein needs of older females and the higher needs of younger males. In the government's current effort to make nutrition requirements more user-friendly, the 46 to 53 grams of protein translate to 12 to 15 percent of daily calories. I believe that no matter how you phrase it, that's too much protein. Half that amount would be more appropriate from your body's point of view.

Recall the two internal conditions that are behind disease: excess acid and inappropriate timing. Most of this book concentrates on inappropriate timing with short forays into toxicity. Now we're into the "meat" of the toxicity story. Your body becomes toxic when it is too acid. Too much dietary protein is the foundation of acidotic toxicity. Your body MUST keep its internal environment slightly alkaline.

Again, a reminder. We're talking about quantities of protein , not protein itself. Your body needs protein. Your body also needs water, but not a gallon at a time.

The problem with high-protein food is that it leaves an acid residue — acid ash. These leavings must be eliminated. Unlike the acid produced from exercise, the acid from acid ash-producing foods, such as meat, can't be eliminated through the lungs. It must be neutralized, processed through the kidneys, and eliminated. The process of neutralizing uses essential alkaline minerals from your store of neutralizing minerals. These are the minerals used to keep the acid level of your blood under control — your alkaline reserve. That's according to the Grand Plan. However, as anyone who has dipped into a saving account knows, even a reserve has a limit. When you take out all that's been put in without replacing the withdrawals, the reserve is gone. High protein foods are long on protein and short on alkalizing minerals. If you eat mostly high-protein foods, you use more neutralizing minerals than you replace. If this pattern continues for long periods, eventually your alkaline reserve will dwindle. If more minerals aren't replaced, ultimately your reserve will be depleted. Very important! Another potential test question.

WELLNESS PRINCIPLE: Eating mostly high-protein foods
can empty your alkaline reserve

Your body is alkaline by design and acid by function. Yet the overall acid level of your internal environment must stay slightly alkaline. As explained in the exercise chapter, cells produce weak acid as they function. This weak acid can be eliminated through the lungs, and the process helps to maintain healthful internal homeostasis. It keeps the overall acid level of fluids within the body within tolerable limits. Another method of keeping your internal acid level within tolerable limits is to neutralize the strong acid that is left from eating high protein foods. Sodium and calcium are the major neutralizing minerals. But when either sodium or calcium is used to neutralize strong acid left by high-protein foods, it is eliminated from the body along with the acid.

The good news is that these minerals can be replaced. Vegetables and fruits replenish the supply of minerals your body needs to process moderate amounts of dietary acid. And when you eat mostly vegetables and fruits, you get enough neutralizing minerals in your diet to replenish your alkaline reserve. A well-stocked alkaline reserve means a favorable climate inside the body — a favorable internal environment.

WELLNESS PRINCIPLE: Vegetables and fruits help keep

your acid level under control

We, as individuals, work better, when we aren't under persistent major stress. We are more likely to be generally healthy when our personal world offers comfortable temperatures, adequate food, ample oxygen, and generally pleasant surroundings. Similarly, our life-sustaining cells work better and are under less stress when their world allows "easy living." Your internal temperature, oxygen supply, and psychological stress level all affect the health and well-being of your cells. And since your cells live in a fluid environment, the condition of this environment is very important to health, longevity, and work load of your cells. Your cells work best in a slightly alkaline environment. And your diet is a major factor in keeping your internal environment a pleasant slightly alkaline place for your cells to live.

ECOLOGICAL ALKALINITY

One of the most important environmental characteristics of extracellular fluid is its pH level. The term "pH" is a convenient expression, or shorthand, for describing the hydrogen ion concentration in a fluid. In science circles, "pH" stands for potential of Hydrogen. In "just plain folks" terms, we can think of pH as telling us how acid or alkaline a fluid is. On a more familiar note, we might think of it as the difference between vinegar (acid) and bicarbonate of soda (alkaline). The acid value scale runs from pH 0, which is completely acid, to pH 14, which is completely alkaline. The neutral point at which a fluid is neither acid nor alkaline, is pH 7.0. You might visualize this scale as a see-saw (or teeter-totter, depending upon the part of the country you're from). At pH 7.0, the see-saw is balanced — a straight line; neither acid nor alkaline outweighs the other. As the numbers go down — 6.9, 6.8, 6.7, . . . 6.0, 5.0, . . . 4.5, 4.4, . . . 0.0 — the see-saw tips toward the acid side. As the numbers get higher — 7.1, 7.2, . . .8.0, 8.1, ...8.9, 9.0, . . . 14.0 — the see-saw tips toward the alkaline side.

WELLNESS PRINCIPLE: Low pH numbers indicate acid;
high pH numbers indicate alkaline

Unlike the see-saw, however, small tips in the balance of pH in either direction mean relatively large swings in acidity or alkalinity. Each unit on the pH scale represents a logarithm — each whole number represents a value ten times greater or lesser than its adjacent whole number. For example, pH 5 is ten times more acid than pH 6, and pH 9 is ten times more alkaline than pH 8. So when we talk about small changes in pH numbers — like pH 6.2 to pH 6.8 — we are talking big changes in the internal environment. Blood, for example, must, repeat, MUST, be kept within the range of pH 7.35 to pH 7.45 in order to sustain life for more than a few hours. Now, wouldn't you think that the Master Planner would have allowed a greater range than a mere tenth of a pH unit for our all-important blood? The difference between 7.35 and 7.45 doesn't seem to be very big but in pH land, it's huge. In fact, when it comes to blood, a difference of any more than a tenth in a specific pH range is the difference between life and death. Your blood must be slightly alkaline. And, as we have noted, most of the fluids of your body SHOULD be slightly alkaline — they should tip the scale to just above pH 7.0 neutral.

WELLNESS PRINCIPLE: pH indicates your potential for Health

All fluids of the body are — or can be — alkaline. The fluids in which our cells live are, for the most part, *slightly* alkaline. Even in the stomach where much of the arduous task of breaking down food fibers and other tough materials takes place, fluids are occasionally alkaline. Guyton points out that, during the "interdigestive period" when little or no digestion is going on anywhere, only very small amounts of highly acid gastric juice are produced. During digestive down-time, the stomach secretes essentially only mucus that contains little pepsin and almost no acid. "In fact," writes Guyton, "on occasion, the fluid is actually slightly alkaline, containing moderate quantities of sodium bicarbonate."[113] However, for the most part, the job of digestion calls for stomach fluids to be considerably more acidic than other physiologic fluids. And since we are concerned here with demonstrating that the body has an overall propensity and preference for alkalinity, to avoid confusion and needless repetition, when I refer to "internal fluids" I'm talking about all fluids of the body EXCEPT the fluids in the stomach (even though they are occasionally alkaline).

One of the most prevalent fluids in your body is the fluid Guyton describes as the "mass of fluid that constantly bathes the outside of the cells"[114] — extracellular fluid. Each of us (standard size adults) has between 9.5 to 23+ quarts of extracellular fluid, the average being about 16 quarts.[115] This is the liquid from which cells gather their working materials, and it is the liquid into which cells dump the end products of their labor. Your extracellular fluid is a crucial element of your physiological infrastructure — a veritable highway of commerce by which "goods" of raw materials, finished products, and wastes are constantly transported to their appointed destinations.

WELLNESS PRINCIPLE: Cells live and work in a
sea of fluid

Your body is made up of roughly 70-75-trillion cells — give or take a few billion. Some sources say 70 trillion, others 75 trillion - who's to quibble? Written numerically with all of its zeros, the number seventy-five trillion — 75,000,000,000,000 — brings to mind the national debt. That's a lot of zeros and cells (or dollars). Of these 75-trillion cells, about 25-trillion are red blood cells. The rest are muscle, bone, nerve, and tissue cells that, in concert, make up all of the parts and systems of your body. Each cell is a specialist; each has a designated task. Although cells may differ in appearance and duties, they all share some common characteristics. All cells, other than red blood cells, convert nutrients into energy, and all cells, as Guyton describes, "deliver the end-products of their chemical reactions into the surrounding fluids."[116] Cells accomplish all of this in a sea of extracellular fluid. And the pH of extracellular fluid is about 7.4 - slightly alkaline, just like blood.

Despite the natural propensity of blood and extracellular fluid for slight alkalinity, you can see from the table that follows that there are wide variations in the pH of body fluids. The pH ranges from extremely acid (pH 1.00) to relatively alkaline (pH 8.30). But notice that the fluids showing the lowest pH are those involved with processing or eliminating food and drink. The pH of the duodenum, urine, and feces can be very acid, very alkaline, or anyplace in between. Yet the others, such as blood, pancreatic fluid, and spinal fluid, are on the alkaline side of neutral. That tells us something. Actually it tells us a lot. One of the bits of information it imparts is that organs work best in an alkaline environment. The body doesn't need acid anyplace except in the stomach (gastric). As you look at these numbers, keep in mind that the lower the number (pH value) the more acidic the substance. (Low numbers, like vinegar; high numbers, like bicarbonate of soda.)

pH NORMALS OF BODY FLUIDS[117]

Blood	7.35 - 7.45	Spinal Fluid	7.30 - 7.50
Saliva	7.30 - 7.50	Liver Bile	7.10 - 8.50
Pancreas	8.00 - 8.30	Gall Bladder Bile	5.50 - 7.70
Gastric	1.00 - 3.50	Duodenum	4.20 - 8.20
Urine	4.80 - 8.40	Feces	4.60 - 8.40

The wide range of internal pH indicates that these wide fluctuations CAN occur. It does not necessarily indicate that they SHOULD occur. We shall see that the ability of the body to produce highly acidic internal fluids is a survival device — not a maintenance device. And since the body can't do anything it wasn't designed to do, highly acidic internal fluids aren't "wrong." They are necessary under certain circumstances but they are inappropriate as long-term conditions.

Extracellular fluids are (or should be) slightly alkaline (about pH 7.4. Why would some of the fluids, such as urine and gall bladder bile, be considered "normal" on both the alkaline side and acid side? That is one of the major questions that prompted my investigations into the relationship between food choices and health. Answers began to become clear when I related the body's purpose with its function. The purpose of the body is to survive. One of the functions of the body is to keep the internal environment slightly alkaline. To accomplish its purpose, the body must get rid of highly acidic substances. Recognizing the relationship between purpose and function set the course for understanding puzzling questions concerning the wide-ranging pH "normals." When I realized that the body must maintain slight alkalinity, to survive, I realized that the wide range of "pH normals" for urine and gall bladder bile had something to do with survival. The body doesn't do anything just for grins and giggles. The wide range of pH normals is associated with the overall availability of acid-neutralizing sodium.

> WELLNESS PRINCIPLE: The body is alkaline by design
> and acid by function

The body works best when it is slightly alkaline. But cellular activity produces acid. Strange. Why would the body produce acid when survival depends on a slightly alkaline internal environment? Why would the body do something that appears to be not in its best interest?

It doesn't.

Green responses are always correct. And internal ecology is the specialty of your Green.

We know that cells produce acid as they function. According to Guyton, "Carbon dioxide is continually being formed in the body by the different intracellular metabolic processes, the carbon in the foods being oxidized by oxygen to form carbon dioxide."[118] He also says that an "increase in carbon dioxide concentration in the body fluids decreases the pH toward the acidic side, whereas a decrease in carbon dioxide raises the pH toward the alkaline side."[119] Let's run that by once more: Carbon dioxide is formed in the cells, and it is formed from carbon in food. And the more carbon dioxide in the body, the more acidic the body is (lower pH). When the carbon dioxide level goes down, the body is less acidic (higher pH). So the amount of carbon dioxide in the body determines the pH level. But the body wasn't designed haphazardly. As long as the body is not *overly* acid, the acid produced by the cells poses no threat to survival. Cellular acid is carbon dioxide. Carbon dioxide can be combined with water to form carbonic acid. And carbonic acid can be eliminated through the lungs. We can get rid of CO_2 when we breathe.

WELLNESS PRINCIPLE: Clever body; clever design

We noted earlier that high-protein foods, such as meats, leave an acid ash residue. A bit of clarification about "ash" — acid and otherwise.

Food that goes into the mouth must be processed. All food that enters the body is a stress to the body. The body must do something with it. All consumed food is divided into three parts.

(1)   Parts that *CAN NOT* be digested and used, such as fibrous cellulose. These form natural bulk and are sent on their way through the digestive tract and eliminated.

(2)   Parts that cells can use as fuel and building material, such as proteins, vitamins, and minerals. These are extracted, dispersed, and put to work.

(3)   The residue that is left after the usable materials have been extracted — the remnants from the parts that were "burned" as fuel.

This residue is termed "ash." (It's rather like the ash left in your fireplace after a log has burned.)

The ash from most foods registers either alkaline or acid on the pH scale. (A few foods, like sugar and honey are essentially neutral, but let's not muddy the waters any more than they are). The body must do something with the ash and any accompanying acid — like get rid of it. The ash itself is eliminated and poses no problem; it goes out with the rest of the "trash." The acid feature of the ash may pose a problem. Strong acid of acid ash-producing foods must be neutralized. More to come about that.

Not all foods leave an acid ash. Most vegetables and fruits leave an alkaline ash. Why "most vegetables and fruits"? Are there any absolutes in this world? While the majority of fruits and vegetables are alkaline ash-producers, few plant-life products, such as grains, lentils, blueberries, and other select "plant foods," leave an acid ash. Others, such as cranberries and plums, leave an alkaline ash, but they have an acidifying effect on the body. Despite these aberrations, *as a general rule*, vegetables and fruits are alkaline ash-producers. The pH of the ash left from *most* fruits and vegetables is alkaline. The ash registers on the alkaline-side of neutral —above pH 7.0. The acid it contains is weak and can be eliminated through the lungs. No problem.

Acids from fruits and vegetables can be processed in the cells of the body and the acid eliminated through the lungs — exhaled. That's a "plus" for vegetables and fruits. No big strain in keeping this acidity under control. Another "plus" for fruits and vegetables is that the body can use the alkaline minerals that are part of the package of good taste, pleasing appearance, and useful nutrients to help to bolster the alkaline reserve.

But the ash from meats, fish, poultry, and grains is a different story. The ash from these goods has an acid pH. It adds to the overall acid level of the body. This acid is relatively strong and can't be eliminated through the lungs. It must be neutralized, or toned down, before it can be eliminated from the body through the colon, or processed through the kidneys. Therein hangs the problem — maybe.

Remember our recurring themes: the body can't do anything wrong, and the body will do anything and everything in its power to survive. One of its survival mechanisms is its ability to maintain the most favorable internal environment possible — slightly alkaline.

A slightly alkaline internal environment is essential to life and health. You, as sole proprietor of your body and life, can give your body the kind of food that will cause the least amount of internal ecological stress.

Most consumable plant life offers the vitamins, minerals, dietary alkaline ash, and protein that help our bodies function with a minimum amount of dietary stress. Food choices that are heavy on the fruits and vegetables and light on meat, poultry, and fish that allow your body to maintain the most favorable internal environment. You've heard for years that you should eat fruits and vegetables. Now you know "why" you should.

> WELLNESS PRINCIPLE: Fruits and vegetables help keep
> your internal environment slightly
> alkaline

The body is a fanatical environmentalist. It tends to its ecological problems no matter what the cost. No environmental budget. No restrictions. No regard for pain or disease. The body WILL maintain the best possible internal conditions as long as it is alive. And alkaline ash-producing fruits and vegetables help keep the climate of the internal environments "balmy."

> WELLNESS PRINCIPLE: Our bodies are "vegiecentric" at
> heart

EXCESS PROTEIN = EXCESS ACID

Eating fruits and vegetables helps your body maintain slight alkalinity. But our society and economy appear to run on high-protein flesh foods — meat, poultry, and fish. We have been schooled to believe that we need protein and lots of it — the more the better. Not so! Certainly we NEED protein. But we don't need as much as we have been led to believe. Protein is necessary. There's nothing wrong with protein. However, excess protein can be fatal. But the process is so slow and the effect is so far removed from the cause, the connection is never made. "Death by protein" isn't a common phrase in our society.

Americans are a people of excesses who generally function on the premise that if a little is good, a lot is wonderful. But that's risky business when it's applied to eating acid ash-producing foods such as meat, poultry, fish, and grains.

Yes, grains. Grains, such as wheat and oats, leave acid ash that must be processed. But we'll leave grains for a few pages and see what the pH and cell and internal environment we talked about have to do with protein and health. We have seen that the body easily handles weak acids produced by the cells by "blowing it off" through the lungs. Acid from acid ash-producing foods can't be "blown off." Acid ash toxic waste removal is considerably more involved. However, we've laid the groundwork for understanding the protein paradox. Now it's time to see how Green-directed physiology responds if the body must contend consistently with great gobs of powerful protein.

WELLNESS PRINCIPLE: Protein is good; *excess protein* causes problems

Recall that blood pH should be between 7.35 and 7.45. If the blood pH strays too far outside of this narrow range, coma and/or death can result. "When the pH of the blood falls below 7.0," writes Guyton, "the nervous system becomes so depressed that the person first becomes disoriented and, later, comatose. Therefore, patients dying of diabetic acidosis, uremic acidosis, and other types of acidosis usually die in a state of coma."[120] The level of blood pH is important. Since the foods you eat have a direct effect on your internal pH, including the pH of the blood, an appropriate blood pH level is more than a physiological convenience. It's essential.

No matter whether dietary protein comes from meat, fish, poultry, or grains, it leaves remnants of a strong acid such as sulfuric acid. This acid must be eliminated through the urinary tract or bowels. It can't be eliminated through the lungs the way weak acid from exercise and cellular function can. However, before strong acid can be processed through the kidneys and eliminated, it must be turned into a weak acid — it must be neutralized, or buffered, to protect delicate tissues.

Neutralization takes place through the workings of intricate buffer systems. Three major systems work together to keep your internal environment under control. These systems are the bicarbonate buffer system, the phosphate buffer system, and the protein buffer system. Each of the three has a specific job; each uses different substances to do its work; and each is effective in specific ranges of pH.

With the first bite of succulent steak or juicy hamburger that slips past your tongue, your bicarbonate buffer system goes to work cleaning up your internal environment. This is the system that affects the environment outside the cells — the extracellular fluid. The bicarbonate buffer system goes to work to adjust acid-alkaline balance within seconds of a change in the environment. "The bicarbonate buffer system is the first equilibrium-maintaining system to respond to a change in the acid/alkaline balance. This system operates extracellularly and is important in regulating blood and interstitial fluid pH. When protein (either animal or vegetable) digestion produces an acid, such as sulfuric, that has a pH of less than 6.1, the bicarbonate buffer can react in seconds."[121]

The other two buffer systems — the phosphate and protein buffer systems — fine-tune pH inside and outside the cells. The phosphate and protein systems can raise the pH higher (toward alkalinity) than can the bicarbonate system.

The phosphate buffering system works outside and inside — but mostly inside — the cells. The phosphate system is crucial in keeping pH under control, yet it is far less powerful in extracellular fluid than the bicarbonate system.

The protein buffer system works inside the cells. The three systems together — bicarbonate, phosphate, and protein — make a powerful pH stabilizing team. However, in this brief synopsis of the perils of protein, we will focus on the bicarbonate system. Although the phosphate and protein buffer systems are major players in pH control, understanding how the lead-off hitter, the bicarbonate system, works can help you to see how excess protein can set you up for exhausted internal systems. Remember, any system — like any person — can become overwhelmed if it is worked continuously. And since we spend a lot of time eating, we have a lot of opportunities to work our buffer systems overtime.

The bicarbonate buffer system reacts in seconds to neutralize the acidity as soon as the pH level of extracellular fluid drops (becomes more acid) below "acceptable." One of the system's principle buffering agents is organic sodium. Although the bicarbonate buffer system can react quickly, if it must react constantly to a protein-intense diet, in time, the organic sodium will be used up. And the only way to replenish the supply is with foods that contain accessible organic sodium.

What do you need to eat to replenish organic sodium?

You guessed it — vegetables and fruits. Vegetables and fruits take from the soil, process it through their "plant factory," and when we eat the vegetable or fruit , we get sodium that is perfect for your physiological needs.

WELLNESS PRINCIPLE: Sodium in plants is the salt of the earth

Unfortunately for our salt-conditioned taste buds, our vital sodium supplies *cannot* be supplemented or replenished by sodium chloride (NaCl) — table salt. The sodium and chloride of table salt are connected by a strong bond that keeps the two partners closely associated even when dissolved in water. The sodium in table salt is not readily separated from its "significant other" chloride

Although the salt we sprinkle on our steak and eggs comes from the ground, it is not in a form that is usable by the body. The sodium we get from carrots, broccoli, tomatoes, and other plant-food has been processed through the plant. Good stuff for the body. Not so with table salt. Table salt is not only ineffective as a buffering agent, it is a burden to the body. It is an unusable product, but it mimics an essential product. The body doesn't view table salt as a dangerous invader so the body doesn't "throw it out" immediately as a poisonous threat. As far as the body is concerned, table salt "looks" like one of the work crew, so it's not evicted. But the salt isn't productive. Some leaves through the skin — salty perspiration. But most is stored and "isolated."

The body's first line of defense against useless intruders is dilution. This is why you get "puffy" when you eat a lot of salty food. It's Green-inspired, protective, retained fluids. So how do a lot of people rid themselves of retained fluids? They take a "water pill." That forces the protective dilution out, but it leaves the salt. Your Green is double-crossed by your Red. Your Green knows how to handle unusable sodium, but your Red comes along and sabotages its efforts.

If your diet is long on meats and short on veggies, in time you will come up short in the good usable sodium department. Does that mean that when your sodium supply runs low your blood pH will drop? No indeed. Remember, your body is designed to survive. It won't let a little thing like sodium deprivation do it in. Your body, under the direction of your perfect Green, is a teeming mass of backup systems.

If sodium is in short supply, your body will use the next best buffering agent — calcium. And where do you store most of your calcium? You've got it — in your bones. You have virtually an unlimited supply of calcium just sitting there waiting to be used. Of course, when calcium is comman-deered from your bones day-after-day, year-after-year, your bones don't fare very well — but your blood pH is in good shape.

WELLNESS PRINCIPLE: Better brittle bones than acid blood

One of the end results of long-term protein abuse is osteoporosis. We saw in the pH table that there is a wide range of pH"normal" for gall bladder bile - 5.5 to 7.7. That wide-range is a function of the overall availability of organic sodium. And the availability of organic sodium is linked to the pH of gall bladder bile and the development of osteoporosis. I go into that whole scenario at great length in *Your Health, Your Choice*.

"So," you might ask, "how do I know if I have enough usable sodium in my body?" And the answer is, you probably don't know. But one clue that indicates you are extremely short on alkaline reserve is urine that smells of ammonia. When you reach the ammonia-odor stage your alkaline reserve is *really* in bad shape. The odor of ammonia in urine can indicate that your neutralizing organic sodium supply is seriously depleted.

Ammonia in the urine is a backup system. Ammonia is used to combat high-intensity acid. You may recall from your high school chemistry that ammonia turns litmus paper blue which indicates its alkaline (or base) properties. Physiological ammonia has a pH of 9.25. For the body, that's a strong base. Remember what happens when you accidentally take a small whiff of "cleaning" ammonia; you catch your breath, cough, and try to get away from it. Ammonia is a STRONG alkali. It's poison. Caustic. It can "burn." Ammonia has a very high pH value. When the buffer systems are overwhelmed by very low pH value acid, physiological (not cleaning) ammonia is great for neutralizing excess acid in the body. And that's precisely what happens. The ammonia makes the acid less potent. But that's physiological ammonia that is produced by your cells. It isn't the same as household ammonia. You can't "take" ammonia to keep your body from being too acid!

> **AMMONIA IS POISON! DON'T drink ammonia or put ammonia into your body any other way to try to neutralize the acid in your body — it will kill you! You will die! Painfully!**

Back to our internal affairs drama. Have I made my point? Or was that too subtle?

If too much protein is continually dumped into the body, the buffer systems will work as best they can. In the process, sodium, that is the mainstay for the function of the alkaline reserve, is lost. When the supply of sodium and other neutralizing minerals reaches a low ebb, ammonia comes to the rescue as a backup. The odor of ammonia in the urine is a signal that the body has had too much dietary protein for too long. It's past time for a change to foods that replenish the alkaline reserve.

> WELLNESS PRINCIPLE: Ammonia in the urine is a backup
>   system, even in babies

The crux of all of this buffer system and backup system review is that acid ash from high-protein foods must be, and will be, neutralized in order to maintain the pH of the blood within a narrow range of levels. Survive! Your body will do whatever it takes to survive. Survival of the moment is paramount. Your Green doesn't plan ahead. It's business is survival now! Your Green doesn't know time. Since your body survives nanosecond by nanosecond, it doesn't make any difference if bones will become brittle, your gall bladder will act up, or you will develop a chronic, debilitating disease like diabetes, arthritis, multiple sclerosis, "Lou Gehrig's" disease, or cancer. Your body will handle the physiology of any of those developments when they come along. You won't feel very good in the process, but you'll survive as many nanoseconds as possible.

Remember, diseases are labels devised by people. Your body doesn't do diseases. It doesn't do health. It just survives conditions as they are.

If you eat eggs and bacon for breakfast, a hamburger and soft drink for lunch, and steak or chicken for dinner, your body must contend with a barrage of acid ash-producing protein. Over time, your blood pH level drops precariously low. Your body will contain the pH as long as possible. But if your blood serum pH constantly hovers around the pH 7.35 extreme, just a little more acid from any source — exercise, emotional upsets, one too many steaks or hamburgers — you can tip the scales to disaster. The disaster can be immediate, such as a heart attack, or it can be chronic, such as osteoporosis. That's why you need to make sure you get ENOUGH vegetables and fruits. One of my reasons for writing this book is to help you understand *why* you should eat more vegetables and fruits to be as healthy as you can — not just to tell you that you should.

A diet designed consistently around vegetables and fruits offers two major health-promoting benefits: (1) acid from most vegetables and fruits is eliminated through the lungs thereby conserving vital neutralizing minerals of the alkaline reserve, and (2) the body's supply of alkalizing minerals is replenished. If you think of your alkaline reserve as "money in the bank," focusing on alkaline ash-producing foods is rather like good economics. Spend dollars wisely and at the same time replenish the funds in your account. You'll come out ahead financially if you are frugal with your dollars and replace more than you spend. You'll come out ahead healthfully if you are frugal about "spending" your alkaline reserve and "deposit" more than you use.

WELLNESS PRINCIPLE: Fruits and vegetables conserve
and replace neutralizing minerals

A more complete explanation of the perils of protein and how the body maintains survival alkalinity is found in my book *Your Health, Your Choice*. For now, just keep in mind that every time you eat too much hamburger or chicken, you may be getting more than you bargained for — the pain and suffering of disease or brittle bones.

WELLNESS PRINCIPLE: Eating more fruits and vegetables
raises your "potential for Health"

Now you can see more clearly how diet and exercise are related and how exercise can kill you. It's not the exercise, it's the internal environment. Strong acid that accumulates from a diet of predominantly high-protein foods, must be eliminated through the kidneys. This takes time. And in the interim, your internal pH drops. Even weak acid can send it plummeting. The lungs eliminate weak acid very effectively. But this buffering action is not immediate; it takes a matter of minutes. And it's not the whole answer. As Guyton explains: "Unfortunately, respiratory control cannot return the hydrogen ion concentration all the way to the normal value of 7.4 when some abnormality outside the respiratory system has altered the pH from the normal."[122] And that "abnormality outside the respiratory system" is acid ash-producing food.

Your body can survive only within a rather narrow range of blood serum pH — between pH 7.35 and 7.45. Additional, easily-disposed-of "exercise acid" spilled into a system already overly acid from a diet of high protein foods can be a major problem. The rapid influx of even a weak acid may shove the blood serum acid level over the "danger" threshold into the "fatal" zone. Have you ever wondered why strapping, apparently healthy young athletes collapse during or just after exercising? The body works in the present; it can't wait for conditions to get better.

However, just eating *more* fruits and vegetables won't solve all the problems. If you continue to consume excess protein regularly, there comes a point where just *more* vegetables won't cut it. For an average adult, 47 grams of protein per day is more than adequate. I believe that even 47 grams is too much. However, since most Americans consume considerably more protein than 47 grams (it's more like 147 grams), this figure is a good place to begin. Above 47 grams of protein, research has shown that you are more likely to lose more calcium than you consume in a day. Studies involving "young adult males" (translation: college students) have shown that "urinary calcium of the men was markedly affected by level of protein intake, with every subject excreting much higher amounts when given the high protein diet than when given the low."[123] The study also showed that when the calcium intake of the men was 95 grams and 142 grams, they lost more calcium than they took in. And at those higher levels, according to the Anand and Linkswiler, even when fruit and vegetable intake was increased by 50%, the calcium balance didn't improve.

This is a major concept. *When you eat too much protein, you lose calcium!*

And the reason you lose calcium is that your body is using the calcium to neutralize the strong acid left by the protein. Calcium is used to neutralize strong acid when there's not enough sodium to do the job. I can't emphasize this enough. When you eat great quantities of protein, it doesn't matter how many vegetables and fruits you eat — your body will still lose calcium!

If you eat excessive amounts of protein you can't eat enough fruits and vegetables to overcome the mineral leaching effects of a high volume of protein. The only thing you can do is to reduce your protein intake as you increase your fruit and vegetable intake.

A quick rule of thumb is to make sure that your diet is made up of about 75 to 80% fruits and vegetables. If you do that, the other 20 to 25% are yours to do with as you will.

> WELLNESS PRINCIPLE: When you choose correct foods most of the time, it probably won't kill you to eat fun foods once in a while

VEGGIES ONLY?

If eating MOSTLY fruits and vegetables is good, then eating ONLY fruits and vegetables must be better. Right?

Not necessarily.

Your objective for health is to provide your body with fuel and tools — fuel it needs to keep itself and you going, and tools it needs to handle the variety of food traffic that enters your digestive "on ramp." Fuel includes a variety of ingredients, such as: vitamins, minerals, fats, amino acids (the building blocks of proteins) and glucose producers, tools, such as enzymes, for putting that fuel to use and other substances with names too hard to spell. To be healthy and to make correct food choices, you don't need to be a Nobel Prize-winning chemist who can figure out how much of this mineral or that enzyme is in everything you eat. All you need to do is to give your body foods that offer enough of the requisite raw materials. Your body take cares of the rest. Vegetables and fruits offer your internal V-8 engine more appropriate fuel components than do meats. And in the process, they leave a non-threatening alkaline ash and a supply of neutralizing minerals.

However, a total conversion from meat-eater to veggie-fanatic isn't necessary. As long as you are relatively healthy, the *occasional* steak, hamburger, or ham sandwich probably won't seriously impact your long-term health. There's no need to become obsessed with food. Eating is only one facet of life. There are five other health-essential areas of choice. You don't need to dump the added stress of fear-of-food thoughts into your body. Once you have decided you are going to eat something, keep judgment out of it. If you choose to eat a 12-ounce steak (more power to you), eat and enjoy. The time to deliberate about the pros and cons of eating it is before you start putting it into your mouth. When the process is underway, just enjoy. Your body will be more stressed by worrying about the effects of the protein on your body than it will by the protein itself. Besides, if you are prone to worrying about how much protein you are getting, you are probably conscientious about balancing the acid-ash producers with alkaline-ash producers.

> WELLNESS PRINCIPLE: Choices precede action; once chosen, enjoy

Strict vegetarianism can alter your mental attitude — your friends may point this out to you. We know that the body is a whole being. Everything, including food, that affects one part affects the entirety.

As a general rule of thumb, meats and their kindred acid ash-producing foods can have a restricting/constricting effect on the body and thoughts. Up-tight. Rigid. "Turned inward." Acid ash-producing foods are "contractive." Consumables that range from highly contractive to moderately contractive include salt, red meat, fowl, eggs, fish, chicken, cheese, and butter (real butter, that is). Foods that are slightly contractive are beans, seeds, nuts, and grains. Contractive foods are energy-gulpers. The body "turns inward" — focuses its attention and energies on processing and getting rid of less-than-desirable elements.

On the other side of the coin, fruit and veg alkaline ash-producing foods can have a diffusing effect on the body. Laid-back. Loose. "Spacy," even. They are "expansive" foods. "Expansive" foods have a relaxing effect on the body. Fruits and vegetables fall into the slightly expansive camp.

> WELLNESS PRINCIPLE: Expansive and contractive foods affect blood vessels, cells, and

(Saints, preserve us) thinking

Highly expansive to moderately expansive consumables include drugs, alcohol, sugar, coffee, tea, and fruit juice.

Fruit juice?

Yes, fruit juice.

If you drink nothing but apple juice, pineapple juice, orange juice, grape juice and just about any other fruit juice you can think of, you can end up with a fruit juice high. You can get too much of an apparently innocuous, healthful drink and wonder why you can't concentrate or focus on those things that need to be done. Notice I said, "just about any other fruit juice." Cranberry juice doesn't fall into this category because cranberries are acid ash-producers — not alkaline ash-producers.

> WELLNESS PRINCIPLE: When you o.d. on fruit juice you won't have a hangover, you'll try to hang on

Equally as important as the expansive repercussions of a strict vegetarian diet is the hidden acid ash potential. When most vegetarians learn of the pH factor in meat-inclusive diets, they mentally pat themselves on the back. "I must be in great pH shape since I don't eat meat," they rationalize. Sounds logical, but it's not necessarily so. Just because a food is grown in the ground doesn't mean it is devoid of an acidifying effect.

Grains are acid ash-producers. Vegetarians who are heavy into breads, pasta, beans, nuts, and seeds can be putting excess amounts of acid ash-producing foods into their systems without realizing it. Grains, beans, nuts, and seeds contain a lot of protein. Vegetarians who center their diets around wheat, rice, corn, oats, barley, and other grains, are very likely consuming too much protein. You can get too much protein from these staples of vegetarian diets just as you can get too much protein from meat-intense diets. The difference is that vegetarians also include a lot of alkaline ash-producing foods, such as carrots, cauliflower, melons, and the green leafy stuff, that provide neutralizing elements and enzymes along with the high protein pasta and its cousins.

> WELLNESS PRINCIPLE: Too much protein is too much protein no matter the form it comes in

One more hitch can crop up for strict vegetarians. If they avoid meat on ethical and moral grounds, this issue can be a source of interfering judgment. Those who not only don't eat meat themselves but who object to others eating meat can create timing problems that go along with judgment. Remember that judging is trying to impose your standards on others. This may work in law courts, but for the rest of us judgment is counterproductive. The judge becomes frustrated and irritated. An "issue vegetarian" can put static into his or her field by judging the eating habits of others; and the "others" who are meat-eaters are quite happy.

However, this book is about more than just food choices. Suffice to say, for most people, I do not recommend an exclusively vegetarian diet. You can learn more about this from *Your Health, Your Choice*.

THE WEIGHT GAME

Correct food choices and correct exercise choices go hand in hand in keeping you in good shape — literally and figuratively. It's the whole-body thing again. For vast numbers of Americans, food choices, like exercise choices, are made with weight control in mind. The fewer calories and the less fat the better. Yet food is more than merely a weight regulator. Food choices contribute to overall health — either good or not-so-good health. And in our "thin is in" society, we hear and read constantly that "too much you" can be hazardous to your health. Excess poundage is equated with greater potential for heart problems, diabetes, joint pain, and you-name-it. However, food choices are more important for acid control than for weight control.

Bodies that are alkaline from high veggie intake — not from ammonia production — are more disease resistant than are acid bodies. And alkaline bodies are more fat resistant. Fat is retained more readily in an acid environment. Folks who resist the idea of modifying their food choices as a health-enhancing measure may be more receptive to the idea of modifying their food choices if it will enhance their shape. Motivation is the key to changing eating habits. When you understand the consequences of eating habits that revolve around acid-producing hamburgers, fries and soft drinks it's easier to take the first step.

WELLNESS PRINCIPLE: Fat flourishes in an acid environment

We have seen that the fat in meats isn't the only culprit in chronic and acute health problems, such as heart disease. We now know that the real culprit is the fat *carrier* — the meat itself.

Ounce for ounce, lean meat can raise more havoc with your acid level than fatty meats. Fat leaves a neutral ash that doesn't lower your pH. Protein is in the muscle tissue of meat. In lean meat, you get more protein per ounce. In fatty meat, you get less protein than you would in the same amount of lean meat. Now, I'm not saying that eating fatty meats is fine — or even okay. I'm saying that you should not only be aware of the hazards of fat, you should be aware of the hazards of the meat itself.

The same principle applies to skimmed milk. If you are over twelve- to eighteen-months old and insist upon drinking milk, you could at least do your body a favor and make it whole milk rather than low-fat or skimmed milk. At least in whole milk some of the volume is fat. It's the same principle as lean meat vs. fatty meat. Fat is easier than protein on your pH. The fat generates acid also, but it's similar to the acid of exercise in that it can be eliminated through the lungs. It's acid that doesn't need to be neutralized before it is sent on its way. So fat is less destructive to your alkaline reserve than protein. When your body's pH is within comfortable limits, it is less likely to retain fat.

Since your body is survival oriented, it attends to its most pressing needs first — and accumulated fat removal isn't a high priority. When your body is acid and concentrating on keeping itself slightly alkaline, it can handle the fat very easily — just store it. When your body is pH-comfortable, it can handle excess dietary fat. But, of course, if you focus on fruits and vegetables, you don't take in overwhelming amounts of fat in the first place. Nor do you take in overwhelming amounts of cholesterol. Fruits and vegetables aren't cholesterol carriers. You get cholesterol in meats and meat products. So if you are looking to lose weight — or keep from gaining excess weight — begin by giving your body foods that will keep it on the slightly alkaline side.

WELLNESS PRINCIPLE: Excess weight begins with
excess protein

As far as weight control is concerned, keep in mind that it is not just a matter of selecting the correct foods. Exercise is an integral part of controlling your weight. And heredity — your genes — determines the general shape you're in. If you are short and stocky and come from short, stocky stock, no matter how well you eat or how much you exercise, you'll retain your genetically inspired configuration. Generic Men may all have been created in the same way, but they come in a variety of packagings. Remember, God didn't decree that everyone should be long and lean — Hollywood and Madison Avenue have perpetrated that hoax. So select foods and exercise that enhance your health. In the process, your shape will take care of itself.

TAKE TIME FOR CHANGE
A few words of caution.

Quick radical changes in eating habits can unleash turmoil in your life and your digestive system. All too often, those who get "nutrition religion" go overboard and leap fork-first into a radically new diet plan. The rationale goes something like, "If fruits and vegetables are what my body needs, I'll do it right and eat nothing but fresh fruit and raw vegetables."

Wrong choice! Although that sort of diet change may sound logical, it's tough on your body — and tough on your feeling of well-being.

Your body is accustomed to handling the foods you are accustomed to eating. If you suddenly begin to deluge your internal systems with nothing but raw fruits and vegetables in an all-out attempt to improve your alkalinity, you will experience immediate results; but you won't like them. You will probably have diarrhea, flatulence, stiffness in muscles and joints, burning on urination, and an overall feeling of "terminal terrible." Unless you are truly committed and something of a masochist, you will decide within a few days that the whole eat-better concept is a bunch of bunk and will revert to your old comfortable ways.

Changing your diet-style is an incremental process. If you have been heavy-into-meats, don't go cold-turkey into heavy-into-vegetables. Begin gradually. Add an additional serving or two of cooked vegetables to your daily fare. Then, in four or five days when your body has had time to adjust, add a few more cooked vegetables. You might even throw in some raw carrots. Then, after a few more days, try a piece of raw fruit. Give your body a chance to adjust to handling foods different from those it is accustomed to handling. Unless you are so sick that you are about to check out any minute, you should make dietary changes gradually.

WELLNESS PRINCIPLE: Quick drastic dietary changes can upset your internal systems and your routine

And another word of caution. Even if you reach the point of ideal eating so that your body is a constantly unwaveringly alkaline delight at all times — (and few people ever achieve this lofty goal) — you may be disappointed that you have not reached Nirvana. Here you are, making all of those "correct" eating choices and still neither your life nor health is perfect.

Eating proper foods is not the be-all, end-all, absolute guarantee of perfect health, wealth, happiness, success, thick hair, and a flawless physique. Proper food choices are but one of our six essential areas of life. Indeed, it is one of the biggies, but still, it's only one piece of the "Big Picture." For example: You eat perfectly — almost exclusively alkaline ash-producing foods. You make sure that everything that goes into your mouth is pure, organically grown, nutrient-filled, and devoid of man-made chemical preservatives, enhancers, growth hormones, or stabilizers to contaminate your being. But you live in a smog-intense environment, rarely exercise, hate your job, and resent that jerk who's at the work station next to you. In a situation such as this, the negatives in your other essential areas of life can overshadow even the best of diets.

WELLNESS PRINCIPLE: There's more to health than
eating right

To get the most from your new outlook on food, you need to make sure that the rest of your life is in the best shape possible. And the rest of your life is a product of the many conscious choices you make minute by minute. You are more than a piece of biological machinery. The biological part is the visible part. The real "You" includes not only your body but also your mind and its connection to your personal field. For real health, all of these must be in harmony. And when they are in harmony, the whole package is in harmony with the power source of life.

The mind-body connection is very real. A body supplied with a perfect diet can't withstand a constant onslaught of negative thoughts and emotions.

WELLNESS PRINCIPLE: Negative thoughts and emotions
can negate positive eating

Keep in mind that while diet can be a prime suspect in negative health, it isn't the only suspect. Your private thoughts — your private Red thoughts — are your most powerful health regulator. Your thoughts and emotions have a dramatic effect on the way your body functions. And your thoughts and emotions have a dramatic effect on the amount of perfect information that is available to you through your field. The greatest producer of discord in your potentially harmonious field is your mind and thoughts.

You have control over all of the six essential areas of life, including your thoughts. Your thoughts are behind your choices, and your choices affect your physiology.

WELLNESS PRINCIPLE: Your thoughts are your mind-body
connection

POINTS OF INTEREST

1.   Your body needs protein; it does not need excess
       protein.

2.   Excess dietary protein is a greater health hazard than
       dietary fat.

3.   The body works best when the internal environment is
       slightly alkaline.

4.   Meat, poultry, fish, and grains leave an acid ash; most
       fruits and vegetables leave an alkaline ash.

5.   The acid from dietary protein must be neutralized
       before it is eliminated through the kidneys.

6.   Organic sodium is the principal neutralizer of acid
       from foods.

7.   Fresh fruits and vegetables are the principle source of
       neutralizing minerals.

8.   Rapid, sudden diet changes can cause short-term
       unpleasant symptoms.

Even God cannot change the past.
                              - Aristotle

CHAPTER 14
Don't Forget to Forgive

ANATOMY OF FORGIVENESS

Now that we've seen how inappropriate choices in your six essential areas can muddy your river of life, it's time to examine a process I have referred to many times in the preceding pages — forgiveness. Forgiveness is the best way to "neutralize" the "toxicity" of past negative responses that is stored in Yellow memory.

When I introduce the concept of forgiveness and health to my Health-Week patients, usually someone says something along the lines of, "Forgiveness is a cornerstone of my religion. I don't hold a grudge; I forgive 'those who trespass against' me." (To avoid the unwieldy he/she problem, we'll say the patient is a he.) Yet, in the course of examination of the self-proclaimed forgivers, I find clinical responses that indicate the forgiving hasn't always been successful. How do I know this? I observe subtle physiological reactions when I instruct him to think about a specific situation or person he had already "forgiven." If he had really forgiven the other person, I would have found no physiological response when he thought of the person he had "forgiven". The "forgiving" was a conscious Red activity, but the reaction of his body indicated that the forgiving was only Red deep. The negative memory hadn't been "neutralized."

WELLNESS PRINCIPLE: Forgiveness is more than a
                                          Red process

And here's a concept that will spin your kneecaps: effective "neutralizing" forgiveness ultimately centers on self! However, this self-centeredness isn't egocentric as we usually think of it. Here's why.

Every negative situation you have ever experienced involves at least one person — you. It may also include others, but you are the focal point. We see this "my view" demonstrated on TV when a reporter asks a witness to a news event to tell what happened. Most of the time, the observer will begin with something like, "Well, I was walking the dog and . . . ," or "Well, I saw this guy . . . ." The account is given from the observer's perspective. We are the center of our own universe. We perceive life through our senses, we filter the perceptions through our memories of previous perceptions, and we respond with the feelings stored along with those perceptions.

> WELLNESS PRINCIPLE: The outside world is pictured
>   through the very narrow lens of
>   our senses

Most of us like to think that we're not all that self-centered. But we are. Our own view is the only first-hand view we ever have. We start out in life aware only of ourselves. We spend our first several months flat on our backs, literally looking up at the world. "Things" come into and fade from our field of awareness. The experts tell us that from our infant point of view things "are" only when we perceive them. Objects "are" when we are aware of them and "aren't" when we are not aware of them. From our completely dependent flat-on-the-back perspective, only those "things" that impact our young sensory system exist. And that's logical. When we're born, our Red hasn't learned much, and our Yellow is virtually empty. How can we compare and analyze new situations with similar past situations when there are few past situation "files" stored in our young Yellow.

So we learn about the "things" in our life day by day. Some of these "things" move. Some are warm and soft and big and move and make noises. They are associated with comfort and a feeling of well-being. Other "things" are cold or hard or squishy or brightly colored and interesting to our senses of touch and sight. As the days pass, we become increasingly aware of all sorts of "things" that mill around our small universe. And we are the center of that universe. The information we acquire about our universe is processed through our developing Red and begins the life-long process of stocking our Yellow.

The very first patterns that become fixed in our Yellow are those stored along with Red-detected sensations of comfort or discomfort. We develop Yellow patterns associated with experiences. We interpret these experiences either as "This is warm, comforting, satisfying, and makes-me-feel-good," or as "I don't like the way this makes me feel." Well, maybe we don't use those exact words, but the feelings are there.

As infants, we are not degree oriented; life is comfortable or not comfortable. We don't have shades of a little comfortable or a little uncomfortable. But we do have the ability to stock memories of our Yellow with Red interpreted perceptions along with Green generated physical feelings.

At the flat-on-the-back stage, we can't assess these sensations by using Red-formed language. The whole process is strictly feelings — Red processes, Yellow stores, Green responds. No well-phrased thoughts such as, "Mercy, I wish Mom would bring me something to eat." Instead, we let out an uninhibited yowl in response to a feeling of discomfort that we later learn means "I'm hungry." Tiny Gabriel doesn't holler because he knows he is "hungry." And he probably doesn't even know he is "holler-ing." All he knows is that he is not satisfied — not comfortable. Physical feeling-physical response.

The very first sensations that form the Yellow backdrop for all experiences are centered around "me" and whether or not a sensation "makes *me* feel good." As we progress through the various stages of physical and mental development, our horizons broaden. Our perception universe expands. It moves from recognizing the small immediate circle of our own craving for food, warmth, and comfort to recognizing a larger circle of "things" that we now know to be "people" in our lives. Familiar people are good. Strange people may not be good.

We attach feeling to sensations. With experience, we branch out to include more things and people. We are shoved into contact with other small people and big people — neighborhoods and schools. Some of them make us feel good; some don't. We continue to become aware of ever larger universes of even larger groups of things and people. Sooner or later (and with any luck, sooner) we begin to realize that others are their own "me's." The big people call this "maturing." But, mature or not, the original patterns that are reinforced minute-by-minute are those that center around our own specific, center-of-the-universe "me." And it's all for the purpose of survival. Everything we do is tinged with a concern for our own survival.

WELLNESS PRINCIPLE: Even the most considerate people are programmed to be "Me" oriented

Our basic drive in life is toward survival. To accomplish this, each experience is instantly evaluated for its threat value. And we fill our Yellows with strategies for combating an assortment of threats. Threats are negative experiences that project negative charges into the Yellow. Little children form behavior strategies to combat threat feelings that come with losing a toy. As adults we adapt our survival strategies to handle feelings of more serious threat to our person, security, or ego. And in the process, we put negative "charges" into our Yellows.

What does all of this have to do with forgiving?

Effective, health-enhancing forgiving "neutralizes" patterns stored in the "this doesn't make me feel good" files. Forgiving doesn't "erase" files, it updates them. It brings them in line with current conditions. "Filed" in your Yellow storage units are memories of people, places, facts, things, and feelings. The information in these files is your interpretation of the stimuli — threat or non-threat — plus feelings. Some of the information remains current, some doesn't. The information about bike riding never becomes out of date. The information about how your former partner "done you wrong" remains constant. But the feelings that go along with the information are time-sensitive. They can become outdated. Current or not, every time you think about your former partner, the Yellow patterns of the feelings stored in your "partner files" are activated. Feelings that keep you stirred up and defensive when you can no longer do anything about the situation are out-of-date. But out-of-date or not, your body responds to them. And these are the feelings that forgiveness neutralizes.

WELLNESS PRINCIPLE: Yesterday's memories color
today's health

We have acknowledged that our bodies respond perfectly to every stimulus. This is a recurring theme. But think about it for a moment. It's a monumental concept! Your physiological *responses* have never been inappropriate or wrong. They have never been ill-timed. The stimuli that prompt physiological responses may be ill-timed, but the responses themselves are always correct. Physiological responses are never wrong! No matter what has gone on in your body, the process has always been perfect *for the stimulus that caused it!* And stimuli of yesterday are, or should be, in the past. Yesterday's experiences are over — finished, done. You can't do anything to change what you had for breakfast this morning much less anything that happened yesterday or last year or ten years ago. You may be able to repair damage wrought in the past, but you can't snap your fingers and make past events disappear. Yet despite this fact of life, regret over the past runs rampant. And the patterns for feelings and physiological responses to these regrets are stored in your Yellow.

> WELLNESS PRINCIPLE: Facts, feelings, and physiology
> are "filed" in Yellow

The good news is that you don't have to continue to live in your emotional past. This doesn't mean that you are going to magically forget past events that cause you ongoing emotional pain. You can't forget anything. Your Yellow is a most efficient archival system. You may relegate disturbing thoughts and memories to the hinterland of your Yellow, but the memories are still there ready to pop up when an appropriate cue is given.

Negative thoughts and memories can be likened to the hand-painted Eiffel Tower "collector's plate" that Aunt Maud sent you years ago. You stored it away and forgot about it, but it's still there. You may think about it when someone mentions Aunt Maud, or when you learn that she is coming to visit. Or you may find it when you are looking for something else in the area where it is stored. That's how unpleasant memories you thought you had dealt with resurface. They have been right where you stored them all along. They aren't in your Red "active" files, they are in your Yellow storage files. You aren't conscious of them in your Red, but they are in your Yellow. And Yellow memories can keep your body in defense. And as we noted earlier, memories filed away in Yellow are like a sixth sense that can activate physiological responses. So when your body is responding with physiology that isn't entirely appropriate for current conditions, it is responding to sensory information from your Yellow — signals from the past. And physiological responses to past sensory stimuli are inappropriate. They are Sensory Dominant Stress.

> WELLNESS PRINCIPLE: Even when you don't remember,
> you can't forget

Since you can't forget unpleasantries of the past, how do you handle them?

You can do something better than "forget." You can neutralize the impact past experiences have on your physiology and life. You can forgive the person or persons who caused you harm in any way. But forgiveness is more than a perfunctory cerebral Red "I forgive John for getting that job that I wanted."

To be effective, forgiveness must include *positive emotion*. Don't just say it, mean it. To be totally effective, the positive emotion must be as potent as the original negative emotion. And conjuring up positive emotions when you are the injured party can be difficult. After all, if negative emotions weren't involved, there wouldn't be anything to forgive. But you don't have to try for an instant love-conversion for the emotion to be effective. Remember the two methods of storing information in your Yellow: short-term intensity or long-term repetition. Forgiveness can come in instant intensity, or it can come as a steady drip, drip, drip. You don't necessarily need a downpour of positive; a gentle sprinkle will do for starters. Then when you get your feet wet with a little positive in the situation, you can gradually wade in deeper and deeper. And you will find that once the seal of negative has been broken, positive will seep in more easily.

WELLNESS PRINCIPLE: A little positive attracts more positive

We can't "forget" the memories stored in Yellow, but we can change the "charge" of the feelings that are stored with the memories. Adding any amount of positive reduces the potency of the original negative. That's the objective: to transform negative "not comforting to Me" feelings in your Yellow to positive "comforting to Me" feelings. Your Yellow responds with patterns of feelings that evolved from your initial "comforting to Me" or "not comforting to Me" assessments. Negative experiences are "not comforting." They conjure up feelings that came with "not comforting" experiences of all your yesterdays. The focal point of your Yellow began and continues to be on yourself. Forgiving anyone for anything revolves around you.

WELLNESS PRINCIPLE: Forgiveness is "Me" centered

Most uncomfortable feelings involve other people. You may not be able to attach a proper name to these other people, but at least one other person may be involved. The other people may be a large bureaucratic agency that has inflicted economic or judicial trauma on you or on one of your significant others. Or you may feel slighted or hurt by a group of people or by an individual. No matter how large the cast of characters, you can generally find one person who is the focal point of your rancor. Forgiveness needs to be specific, focused. Forgiving the entire IRS or the whole membership of your church won't cut it. You need to be able to envision a person. Your visualization may not be accurate if you've never met the "I. M. Supreme" person who signed the letter from the IRS that sent you into orbit. But the more vividly you can visualize, the more associative areas of your Yellow will be stimulated and neutralized by the forgiveness process.

The purpose of forgiving is to help your body to respond only to currently appropriate stimuli. It's not to absolve the person who is being forgiven. Your body is survival centered, your consciousness is "Me" centered, and forgiveness is "Me" centered.

MOLEHILLS FROM MOUNTAINS

Each of us faces our own obstacles in life. Obstacles often bring hurt feelings or feelings of injustice, or enduring bitterness. To give ourselves and bodies the best chance of fulfilling their potentials, we must leave hurt and bitterness and other negative feelings behind. By following a specific formula of forgiveness, you can neutralize negative residue of the past — for your sake, not the sake of the person who offended you.

"Forgive" does not mean "approve." You don't have to condone or sanction actions that hurt or offend you. However, if you want the best internal operating environment for your body, when you are hurt or upset, you must forgive the person involved, even if that person is yourself.

WELLNESS PRINCIPLE: Forgive the person, not the deed

Forgiveness on your part does not lessen the seriousness or tragic nature of a situation. Forgiveness doesn't change the situation. It changes your physiological responses to the memory of the situation. You forgive for your sake! When you forgive another person, your forgiveness doesn't affect him or her any more than your hate or animosity does. You can hate someone else for years without altering his or her success and happiness. In fact, while you are making yourself sick with hate, the other person is going merrily along in life, completely undisturbed. *You don't forgive for the sake of the offender; it's for your sake.*

Forgiveness is more than a mental exercise — it is a deep down inner feeling. When you really forgive, you experience a sense of mental peace you may have missed for years. That in itself can make your life more pleasant. But there's more.

Forgiving those who have hurt you in some way — or forgiving yourself — has long-term health benefits that may save you years of pain and suffering. Practicing true forgiveness on a regular basis relieves stress to your body and allows it to function at its best. When your body functions as effortlessly as possible, you reap benefits of feeling better and having increased energy, a brighter outlook on life, and a better shot at satisfaction in life.

Forgiveness is a feeling. True health-enhancing forgiveness starts with a rational thought and is followed by a sincere positive feeling. You can go through the forgiveness process any time you can concentrate on what you're doing. A particularly effective time for neutralizing the toxic residue of negative feelings can be just before you go to sleep at the end of your day. This is when your body is still reverberating from the day's events. Remember, sleeping stores information on your "hard drive." So if you are going to store information on your "hard drive," the information might as well be the best it can be. By going through the process of forgiveness at night (or whenever your longest period of sleep is), you "save" positive feelings that are non-threatening. Your body doesn't have to defend against forgiveness. When you go through the forgiveness process just before going to sleep, you "tune" your body to the most beneficial frequency for relaxation and repair.

The forgiveness process is simple:

When you go to bed each night, recap the day's events. Ferret out instances where someone did or said anything that you responded to with distress. Or perhaps you did or said something to someone else that provided that person opportunity to respond with distress. You may be on either the giving or receiving end of the opportunity for distress. The situations you're looking for may be as serious as a physical attack or as innocuous as a mumbled snide remark. No need to assign a value of gross-injustice to the incidents; just recognize that each incident may have been the catalyst for you or someone else to be upset.

For each incident, follow this three-step forgiveness process in your mind:

- Forgive the other person
- Forgive yourself
- Give the other person permission to forgive you

Sound difficult? At first, it may be. Let's look more closely at these steps.

1. *Forgive the other person for any harm he or she may have done to you that day.*

This means REALLY FORGIVE. Not just lip-service. None of this "I forgive Jane — the wench!" To help you forgive "Jane" or anyone else, picture that person in a vulnerable state. Realize that Jane is also a real person who is threatened, has feelings, and is working on a particular agenda. You aren't approving of the "wrong" done to you; you are acknowledging that everything anyone does is prompted by something in that person's life. Forgive him or her for interfering with your life.

2. *Forgive yourself for any harm you may have done to yourself or to anyone else.*

   Again, you need to reach the sincere, strong-feeling stage in forgiving yourself. An off-hand "I forgive myself" won't do anything other than keep you awake for another second. We're talking industrial strength forgiveness here. Some people find this the most difficult part of the exercise. They can forgive someone else more readily than they can forgive themselves. We often have much higher expectations and standards for ourselves than we do for others. If you really have a problem with this step, try a little imagining. Assign to someone you admire and respect the role you played in the event that you are trying to forgive yourself for. You will probably be better able to forgive your surrogate more easily than you can forgive yourself . Then you can put yourself back into the picture. Give yourself the same consideration you give others.

3. *Give the other person permission to forgive you for any harm you may have caused him/her.*

   "What?" you ask incredulously, "he's the jerk who cost me my job! Why should I give him permission to forgive me? Fat chance!"

   A couple of points are involved in this step. The first is that only rarely is a situation completely one-sided. Generally, we contribute some small element — perhaps unwittingly — to bring about stressful events. The contributing factor may be as small as merely being at the wrong place at the wrong time.

   The second point is the "Me" concept. Each of us sees personal negative occurrences from our own perspective. We bring our own personal attitudes, prejudices and values to every event in our lives. And our perspective is probably entirely different from that of the other person. From the other person's point of view, his or her actions or words may be completely rational, logical, and true. A brief session of family reminiscence illustrates how people with similar histories and backgrounds differ in their perspectives of common experiences. Just bring up with a sister, brother, cousin, or childhood friend a story about a mutual experience of long ago and see how the "facts" differ.

   The third point about giving the other person permission to forgive you is that it helps to reduce a mountain of distress to molehill size. It ties up loose ends of any incident that has caused you stress and emotional upset. If you neglect or refuse to complete this step of the exercise, you will find that the forgiveness process is neither completely satisfying nor effective.

> WELLNESS PRINCIPLE: Forgiveness means to give up
> the chance to get even

You will probably find one of these steps much more difficult than the others. You might not have much trouble forgiving the other person or giving them permission to forgive you, but you just can't bring yourself to forgive yourself. Or, if you were the wronged party, you vehemently rebel at the thought of giving the other person permission to forgive you. The step you find most difficult is the step you need to work on. That step addresses the message stored in your Yellow that is causing the most interference in your body. You may lie awake for hours trying to get on top of that one giant step. However, after you have made it the first time, the next time will be easier. And it is absolutely essential that you successfully march through the three stages of forgiveness. Why? Because, 1) you are doing this exercise for yourself, not for the other person, and 2) you need to lay the forgiveness groundwork to get to the final health-restoring step — finding the good in the stressful situation that benefits you.

FINDING AND FEELING THE GOOD

The three-step forgiveness process takes you almost half-way to your goal of neutralizing specific negativity in your Yellow. Forgiving is about 40% of the process. The other 60% is accomplished by finding some element of good *for you* in the negative experience. Whether the volume of that good equates to only a tiny molecule of good or to an entire galaxy of good doesn't matter. You MUST find some aspect that is positive for you.

Finding a benefit for yourself upgrades the energy of the memories stored in Yellow. The original negatively-charged Yellow memories are stored information that came through the Red. It's part of that 1% of information received through your five senses that your Red acknowledges and processes. Information that goes into your Red is there on a short-term basis. When it is stored in the Yellow it's there for the long-term. As long as you dwell on how your former partner took advantage of you, you continue to reinforce in your Yellow the negative energy associated with that incident. So to recharge the Yellow with positive, start with the Red. You "find the good" with your thinking Red. You store the positive of this good in your Yellow with positive feelings. And these positive feelings are stored right on top of the previously stored negative feelings. Negative overlaid with positive equals neutral.

The critical point of finding the good is to attach positive feelings with your Red thoughts. Recall that we are "Me" oriented. You must feel some positive emotion of benefit to "Me" in every situation. This isn't self-centeredness; this is self-preservation.

WELLNESS PRINCIPLE: Find the good first; then
feel the good

You may determine in your conscious mind that there is absolutely NOTHING positive that you can find about the situation. It was bad, bad, bad, all the way through. And you may be right. However, the initial "good for you" that is inherent in every stressful situation is that you survived. You can start with that and build from there. For example, suppose "Uncle George" molested you repeatedly when you were a child. You were frightened and ashamed. You never told anyone about it because "Uncle George," being the sweet loveable person that he was, threatened you with your life — and you believed him. Terror; shame; disgust; physical hurt. All of these emotions and more swam in your mind for years. And although you are now an adult and "Uncle George" has gone to his reward, the memories still swirl in your Yellow and resurface frequently. Is there any "good" to be found in this situation?

The first is, you survived. The second "good" is that you have carried on with your life despite the childhood abuse. And in the process you are more conscious of the feelings of others. (If you had used these childhood traumas as an excuse for a destructive nature and to hurt others, you wouldn't be reading this book.) The feelings of accomplishment and self-satisfaction that can come by sincerely acknowledging some "good" from an experience begin the process of "neutralizing" the negativity that accompanied the experience. The secret to success is the feeling. Really feel good about yourself in relation to the "bad" experience. The purpose of finding the good in any experience is to learn from that experience.

WELLNESS PRINCIPLE: Every experience benefits you

Some element of good can be found in any stressful situation. Finding the good in an extreme situation was illustrated by a patient who had a persistent eye problem. As a child, had seen her father shoot and kill her mother. That's extreme trauma. It took a lot of looking, but she finally saw some good for herself in that trauma. And when she did, both her outlook and her eyes improved.

We should be able to find at least an atom of good in each of our stressful experiences. When you have attached the step of Finding and Feeling the Good to your process of forgiveness, you allow your body to get on track to heal and prosper. In addition to rationally recognizing an element of good, you must attach a positive FEELING to that good. Remember, you become stressed by negative feelings and emotion. You need to attach positive feelings to the process of seeing the good.

WELLNESS PRINCIPLE: Your thoughts run your life —
your feelings run your body

Now that you understand that feelings run your body, you begin to understand why pills aren't the answer to handling stress. The only thing stress medications do is to cover up unpleasant symptoms. They do nothing to correct the cause of the symptoms. By regularly following the steps of forgiveness and finding-the-good, you will find you can more easily handle the many different stresses in your life. Symptoms will be eased, energy increased, and both you and life will take on a whole new glow.

We have seen that feelings are formed through your Red and stored in your Yellow. But it's not just your Red and Yellow that are involved. Strong feelings can override the perfection of your Green. Your Green is designed to run your body perfectly. But Red and Yellow messages can be faulty, so your Green responds perfectly to faulty messages. When your body is functioning to survive Red and Yellow perceived threats, your Green perfection will maintain threat-combating physiology. Your Green isn't wrong — perfection can't be wrong. The messages that keep your Green in its defense mode are inappropriate for the circumstances. Every Green response is perfect for the stimuli. So the objective is to neutralize outdated Yellow information. You can do this by using your Red to consciously put positive energy into your Yellow. If your Red and Yellow are going to send information signals to Green, it may as well be information that allows your Green to do its perfect thing without interference.

The forgiveness process is incomplete unless you find the good for yourself in the experience being forgiven. Finding the good is the first step in learning the lesson of every unpleasant experience. Every experience contains some good. Our job is to find it.

FEEL-THE-GOOD BOOSTER

Feeling the good can be a regular part of your day. You don't have to wait until you are ready to go to sleep. You can boost the benefits of forgiving with a mini-find-the-good exercise whenever you aren't concentrating on something else: at work, at home, riding in a bus, waiting to see your insurance agent, or waiting in line at a drive-thru. The process is simple.

As you sit quietly relaxed, recall some of the major situations that currently cause you stress. Select one situation and find something good in that situation. The "something" doesn't have to be big and impressive; just good. Dwell on the good. Be thankful for the benefit you received. Feel the relaxing, peaceful effect when you focus on a positive element in the situation.

After you have focused on the first situation, go on to another and repeat the "feel the good" exercise. Limit yourself to three or fewer incidents for each mini-forgiveness sitting. You will find you return to your work-a-day world refreshed and with a more positive attitude.

Remember, feelings are the key to forgiveness, and forgiveness is the key to upgrading the energy of your Yellow. Memories are the backdrop of all your thoughts and actions. They influence not only your thinking but also your physiology. Red conscious thoughts open the door to Yellow memories. Your Red thoughts come together in a cohesive whole, but the memories associated with those thoughts are stored in several areas of your Yellow. As you think about "Uncle George" in your Red, several "doors" in your Yellow are opened. And behind those doors are the positive or negative "charges" you have put in with previous thoughts and feelings. Each time a door is opened, you have the opportunity to add more positive or negative into the memory behind that "door." If you continually put in negative, only negative is available each time you access that memory. But once you start mixing new positive with the existing negative, the negativity diminishes. Continue to deposit positive and the negative of the memory fades. Mini-feel-the-good boosters serve as the drip, drip, drip method of upgrading negative memories to positive. You begin upgrading Yellow to positive with Red conscious thoughts; you cement the upgrade with positive feelings.

WELLNESS PRINCIPLE: Positive feelings are the cement

of upgraded memories

Perhaps you are among those who can't put a finger on specific disturbing incidents of the past that need forgiving. You might conclude that you don't have a batch of negativity stored behind your Yellow doors. However, if you are a thinking, feeling, adult, living around other people, negative has crept into your Yellow. And never let it be said that we don't try to cover all bases.

Recall those "forgotten" memories that come back only when prompted by a strong associated memory — the Eiffel Tower plate and all of that. A close relative of the "forgotten" memory is the recurring thought we talked about earlier. A recurring thought is one that comes to mind out of context with what you are doing. You're busily engaged in the project of the moment and all of a sudden, for no apparent reason, you think of a neighbor. You don't know this neighbor very well, but you are often irritated with him when he lets his yard become overgrown. This isn't a big deal; but the lack of responsibility he shows for the neighborhood is a constant source of irritation. Although you try to brush off the irritation, thoughts of him repeatedly pop into mind briefly but unexpectedly — out of context for your activity. Recurring out-of-context thoughts are not only baffling and bothersome, they indicate that these memories are affecting, and perhaps controlling, your physiology.

Recurring out-of-context thoughts need attention. The fact that they keep coming back indicates that you haven't "dealt with" the situation or person. You haven't learned the lesson and been thankful for the opportunity to learn. The memories, no matter how insignificant to your conscious mind, continue to influence your physiology. The person behind these recurring out-of-context thoughts is a prime candidate for the subject of the forgiveness process. Even if you believe that there is nothing there to forgive, your body knows better. You don't need a doctor or someone else to tell you that your neighbor, or "Uncle George," is behind your stiff neck. No one else knows what is running around in your Yellow. Only you can identify recurring thoughts that could be the ultimate "cause" of persistent physical symptoms. The conditions that ingrained the subject of recurring thoughts in your Yellow may have happened so long ago that the connection is obscure at best. Who would connect "Uncle George's" treatment of you when you were six with your stiff neck when you are twenty-six or forty-six? Only you can make that connection. And you make it when you become aware that recurring out-of-context thoughts are signals that Yellow memories are overriding Green perfection.

WELLNESS PRINCIPLE: Recurring thoughts are ripe for
feeling the good of forgiveness

Applying the steps of the feel-the-good booster exercise at various times throughout the day can ease the stress in your life. It's rather like taking small sips of water regularly. It keeps you satisfied. When you keep the water or good feelings going in consistently, you reduce the need for great gulps of either. In a short time, you've formed a habit. Before you know it, you have a habit of positive thinking — you think positively most of the time.

THANKS FOR THE MEMORY

An integral part of the forgiveness process is to be thankful for the good we receive with every lesson of life. Thankfulness is the mainstay of the attitude of gratitude that feeds positive feelings to be stored in your Yellow and responded to by your Green.

Let's dissect the feel-the-good emotion to see how it might impact physiology. We've investigated the repercussions of a variety of negative situations, let's see how we might view physiological responses to positive events. Now keep in mind that, as far as I know, there haven't been any scientific, double-blind studies done on the physiology of glee. So we will apply our concepts about how the body works to this "up-side of life" analysis. Let's say that you have just been told that you are being promoted to a job you have coveted for months.

The typical response to good news is elation. "Whoopee," you think. "I made it!" Of course, being the sophisticated adult that you are, you restrain your external exhibition of delight to a modest smile. No dancing around the office; no picture-rattling war whoops. But what's going on inside? Lots of stress — your body changes the way it was functioning. It is in defense homeostasis. Your sympathetic system is dominating. That's why good news energizes you. All systems are on go. The physiological changes allow energy to flow throughout your body. But, not to worry. When you come down from your initial high, your physiology will go back to normal. No residual negative emotions stored in Yellow to keep you defensive for long periods.

In the morning, there you are, dancing on the inside but restrained on the outside. Fortunately, you have at your disposal some means of expressing your emotion that are reasonably socially acceptable. You may snicker or giggle (depending upon your gender), or you may walk around with an uncontrollable Cheshire cat grin. Without you realizing it, your demeanor will probably announce to those who know you that something good has happened. And if you refuse to express the emotions, you will probably find you have difficulty sleeping. The suppressed energy will be expressed in activity of some kind. So it's either express it at the time, or express it by being "so excited" you can't sleep.

WELLNESS PRINCIPLE: Positive or negative, emotions will
be expressed

Positive emotions, like negative emotions, are "Me" centered. They make "Me" feel good. Even if you are pleased by good news for someone else, you experience the pleasant feeling. You can be happy for someone else, and in the process some of the happiness rubs off on you.

What is one of the first responses to good news? In the middle of the exhilaration a feeling of sincere thankfulness erupts. "Thank you!" is offered to either the person who bestowed the good news or to God. Often to both. Without realizing it, in times of delight, as well as in times of sorrow, we acknowledge our connection with a Perfect Intelligence. We may not verbalize this in our conscious Reds, but we know at a more basic level that we, the creatures of this world, are not alone. And we give thanks.

An intense dose of thankfulness can instantly upgrade the negativity in many associated Yellow memory "files." In the promotion scenario, some of the associated memories may involve other people or past events. Have you ever noticed how a boss can suddenly be "not so bad after all" when something good happens. This is the spurt of positive thankfulness that neutralizes — temporarily, at least — some of the earlier "boss negatives" that crept into your Yellow. The positive thankfulness can also neutralize some of the negatives deposited with previous personal "failures" — temporarily, at least. Of course, you can reinstate the negatives with future negative thoughts and feelings about both boss and yourself. When the flush of success has subsided and you "return to normal," you can override the new positive with newer negative drip, drip, drip.

Since thankfulness is "Me" oriented, it is a major self-esteem booster. When you are thankful, you acknowledge that you have received a bonus. And for most of us, our belief system dictates that only the worthy receive bonuses. Hence, the unverbalized realization: I received a bonus; only the worthy receive bonuses; I am worthy. Self-esteem rises.

WELLNESS PRINCIPLE: Thankfulness is the antidote

to low self-esteem

Again, these feelings can be short-lived. And without cultivation, they can be downgraded by negativity. That's why it is so important that you constantly see the good in every event in your life. Seeing the good promotes thankfulness. Thankfulness builds self-esteem. Positive self-esteem allows your body to function at its best.

It's all beginning to come together now. Everything that goes on in your Red and everything that is stored in your Yellow affects how your Green functions. Your Green is intent upon survival. Your Red and Yellow are the conduits of the messages your Green must accommodate to. So your best bet for health, success, and happiness is to make sure that messages from your Red senses put positive into your Yellow memory. Most of the sensory information from your Red is discarded, so most of the messages your Green receives are from your Yellow. When your Yellow memories are predominantly positive, the messages your Green receives are predominately positive. And positive doesn't interfere with either your internal energy flow or your external energy flow.

Forming a regular habit of forgiveness and thankfulness can change your life. A habit of forgiveness and thankfulness is the foundation of a positive attitude. A positive attitude is the foundation of good self-esteem. And good self-esteem is a form of love. Unconditional in which you accept yourself not because of who you are, or what you do, or what you know, or how you look, but in spite of all of those things. And that's what we have been talking about all along. Love. Unconditional love.

> WELLNESS PRINCIPLE: Forgiveness and thankfulness open the door to unconditional love

CLEARING YOUR FIELD

The most positive feeling available to humankind is that of unconditional love. This is the love new parents feel for their child. The child does nothing to earn the love; all it needs is to be. And as the child grows and becomes more independent, even when parents don't like the actions of their child, the unconditional love survives. Unconditional love involves thankfulness. Thankfulness and unconditional love are strong "Me" feelings projected outward. And that's why the "Me" feelings we have been talking about are different from egocentricity. When you practice sincere thankfulness, you project into your field the most precious element you have: the energy of yourself. You were created from perfection and retain that perfection in your Green. Unconditional love is the most perfect commodity you can share. It is a product of your Green. Unconditional love is not a rational feeling. It doesn't come about through logic and reasoning. It isn't part of a barter system. It can't be earned and it can't be bought. Unconditional love comes from your core of perfection. When you feel unconditional love, you project that love into your field. And forgiveness and thankfulness are the seeds of unconditional love.

And that's really where all of our travels are leading us: to a crucial understanding. Although we are "Me-centered" individuals with our own likes and dislikes, and personalities, and beliefs, and thoughts, our purpose is to learn that we are to project, or share, energy as well as consume energy. And we project the most intense energy when we experience and express unconditional love. The steps we have taken to be able to share our own energy are those that reduce the amount of negativity in our thoughts, feelings, and field. We can't eliminate negativity from our lives. But we can certainly learn how to neutralize the negative energy we carry with us in body, mind, and field. And when we learn to do that, we have learned the greatest lesson we can.

Everything you experience in life, every thought, every action, every feeling, every response affects your body and your personal field. Since the health of your body is a reflection of the degree of creative chaos in your field, a physical problem indicates that your field needs attention. Too much organizing negativity has filtered into your field so that not all of the field-energy information is available to your body.

Every life experience is a lesson waiting to be learned. You learn a lesson when you recognize that every experience you have in life benefits you in some way, and you are thankful for the lesson. Sincere thankfulness for the opportunity to learn a life lesson does more than neutralize negative mental "toxicity." Being thankful is the catalyst of your own personal "catalytic converter." And you know the purpose of a catalytic converter — to reduce harmful emission products into harmless products. Forgiving and learning converts negative thought energy that pollutes your field with organizing energy into positive thought energy that slips into your field without disturbing the wholeness of chaos.

In our journey to self-directed health, we have seen how the all-encompassing personal field is the "generator" that provides perfect complete energy to the body. When negative thoughts and feelings impact the field, some of the vital field energy information that is the power source of life is "lost." It isn't lost in space; it is still in your field. But it isn't accessible to you; so it may as well be lost in space. For the body to function at its best, and for you to function at your best, you need access to all of the energy of your fully-equipped energy field. Forgiveness combined with thankfulness and lesson-learning reduces interference in the transmission of complete energy communication.

WELLNESS PRINCIPLE: Forgiveness bridges the communication gap between body and field

We tend to think of the Red conscious mind as the most potent and important level of consciousness. And indeed, it is — for thinking, analyzing, reasoning, and evaluating. However, it's the Yellow that stores the wealth of background information and feelings that are factored into all of our thoughts and conclusions. Without the Yellow, every experience is brand new. Every day would bring a whole new world. No familiar faces or places. You wouldn't be able to recall if you liked pizza, or even what pizza is. And the pizza makers wouldn't be able to remember how to make it. You wouldn't recall what these squiggles on the paper mean. There would be no reference points from which to begin to build your impressions and perceptions. So your Yellow ties your life together. Yet the Yellow is subject to error just as much as is the Red. And when the Yellow contains inappropriate or outdated data, Red perceptions, analyses, and conclusions suffer.

When the Yellow is filled with outdated Personal Programming and impressions of your worth, these outdated data are reflected in your self-esteem. Low self-esteem is negative energy. When your thoughts continually downgrade yourself, your self-esteem suffers. Low self-esteem is devoid of thankfulness. It puts organizing negative energy into your field. The process of sincere forgiving — especially of yourself — upgrades the energy that goes into your personal field.

WELLNESS PRINCIPLE: Low self-esteem is hazardous
to your health and field

Keep in mind that despite our altruistic attempts at being considerate of others, all of us — you and I and everyone else — are essentially "Me" oriented. If we have a negative view of ourselves, we have a negative view of the world. All of our thoughts ae colored by the pervasive negativity. When we are constantly negative, we cannot develop a clear picture of the world around us. So you can see that applying the forgiving-thankful-lesson learning process to yourself for whatever sins of commission or omission you can think of can be one of the most freeing, stress-relieving exercises you can do. Self-forgiveness allows positive to creep in and displace permanent negative.

The process of forgiving, thanking, and learning the lesson is a practical application of the concepts and principles put forth in this book. All of that business about sympathetic and parasympathetic, and the different levels of consciousness, and energy fields, and thoughts, and feelings, and beliefs have headed us toward this point of practicality. Forgiving ourselves and others, being thankful for the lessons we learn, and projecting unconditional love establishes and maintains harmony with Perfect Universal Energy. And for this we can be thankful.

WELLNESS PRINCIPLE: When all else fails, be thankful

Generic Man is the only creature on earth that could be set down in the Garden of Eden and mess up the perfection. We use our conscious Red to try to control everything around us and to improve upon perfection. In the process, we contaminate our internal environment with negativity and inappropriate stimuli, and we inject static into our field. We pollute the air and waters of our planet. We destroy vegetation and wildlife. We alter the balance of nature. And we fill not only our landfills but our own minds with garbage.

However, the Grand Designer didn't give us the ability to think ourselves into a mess without also giving us the ability to repair the damage we do. Recall that intricate physiological and communication systems keep the body's internal environment on an even keel. These are systems that neutralize acids to keep your blood pH at the appropriate level; they direct muscles and tendons to function in concert so you can walk, and; they contain mini chemical laboratories that extract useful nutrients from food. In the same vein, you come equipped with a survival "backup system" of thankful lesson-learning to undo the damage past negative experiences have done, or are doing, to your body.

WELLNESS PRINCIPLE: Forgiving, seeing the good, and
learning the lesson are backup
systems for survival

We have had quite a varied view of the whole-body landscape as we have moved along on our journey to self-directed health. It's time to begin assembling some of the trinkets of information that we've picked up along the way.

Our travels have given us a look at how lifestyle habits and conscious choices might be in conflict with Green wisdom. With this new perspective we can begin to identify some cracks in the foundation of both our personal and corporate health. But our personal temples of life are going to decay rapidly if we just observe foundation fissures without doing something to repair them. And the repairing is up to each of us individually. We know the crisis we've got ourselves into by assigning the responsibility for our health and care to "the experts." We must take responsibility for ourselves and our health. We can strip the gears of the accelerating health care crisis when we learn how to make disease unnecessary. But it's hard to learn how to make disease unnecessary until you learn how you made it necessary in the first place. And that's what we're doing here.

> WELLNESS PRINCIPLE: The Grand Plan Designer has provided us with a means of saving us from ourselves

POINTS OF INTEREST

1.   Forgiveness benefits you.

2.   Forgiveness must be felt to be effective.

3.   Forgiving does not condone, it neutralizes.

4.   The forgiveness process:
           Forgive the other person
           Forgive yourself
           Give the other person permission to forgive
               you.

5.   Forgiving neutralizes negative memories stored in your
       Yellow.

6.   Forgiveness isn't complete until you find some good
       for yourself in the experience that prompts the need for
       forgiving.

7.   Be thankful for the experience that allowed you to
       learn a life lesson.

8.   Forgiving helps reduce organizing negative
       interference in your field.

What God hath created
let no man put asunder.

CHAPTER 15
Practical Health

RED AND YELLOW CONVERGE

Here we are rounding the bend to our destination of self-determined health. Along the way we've run across some concepts and ideas that may have, at first, been foreign to you. We have seen that areas of the six essentials we take for granted — breathing, resting, eating, drinking, exercising, and thinking — involve conscious choices that can send physiological systems into overdrive. We've also seen that the internal responses to those choices are completely out of our conscious control. It doesn't take the proverbial rocket scientist to figure out that if conscious choices are sending our health, success, and happiness down the tubes, we'd better do something to make better choices. And that requires thinking about what you think about. But we didn't start out in life as "accomplished thinkers."

We've seen how our infant perceptions of the world are recorded principally as feelings. These feelings become the first residents in our storehouse of Yellow information. As childhood progresses, we learn by receiving factual and experiential information through the Red and storing it in Yellow. We learn practical things, such as, the sound "HOT" that grown-ups make is usually followed by pain of some sort. And we learn abstract information, such as, at a speed of 60 mph, you travel about 88 feet each second. As we grow, our Reds are very busy. Our Reds handle increasingly complex adult-grade information but our Yellows can get stuck in childhood.

WELLNESS PRINCIPLE: Your "inner child" is a reflection

of early-stored Yellow feelings

We have seen that many of the things we learn from our childhood experiences and perceptions are negative. Children are constantly exposed to negative commands, many of which are barked in anger: "Don't!" "Quit it!" "Keep quiet!" And many children are exposed to physical and emotional abuse. (So much for the "carefree joys of childhood" myth.) Childhood negative feelings are stored in Yellow. As time goes on, more negative feelings attached to similar situations reinforce the original. Your Yellow becomes "stuffed" with negative. And we know what a negative-stuffed Yellow does: it affects physiology and field. Let's recap the process briefly.

We've seen how your Green directs your internal workings, and that you have no control over what it does. Green isn't capricious. It does only what it is designed to do for survival. And it does it perfectly. Green responds to signals it receives from internal feedback mechanisms and from Red perceived sensory stimuli. Perceived sensory information of sight, sound, smell, touch, and taste is evaluated by your Red. The threat potential and/or importance of each separate stimulus is determined immediately. Run-of-the-mill Red information is compared with associated stored Yellow information to give you clues as to how to respond externally — "Please," "Thank you." Behind Red responses — "No thanks, I'm not into string quartets," "Wha'da ya' mean my credit's no good?" — are instant comparisons of hundreds of Yellow-stored past experiences similar in some way to the current situation. Some associations may be very close — the Eiffel Tower plate and Aunt Maud. Other associations may be quite remote — Aunt Maud, Eiffel Tower, steel girders, erector set, Cousin Phillip's birthday. No matter what route the association takes, along with the memory of past events are the memories of the feelings and associated physiology that accompanied them.

WELLNESS PRINCIPLE: Red thought uses Yellow information in logic, reason, analysis, and
evaluation

Most of the information received through the Red is important, but not a threat to your survival. Important information is recognized, possibly acted upon, and stored. Unimportant sensory information — the feel of your clothing on your skin, normal background noises, no-threat sights and smells — is ignored. However, all of the information that settles in your Yellow was important at the time it was received, or it wouldn't have been stored. And Yellow info is accompanied by the feelings that came with it. Most of the sensory information from the outside scampers through your Red before it finds its home in Yellow. Other than in extreme emergencies, your Red doesn't communicate directly with your Green. Red information fans out throughout your Yellow storehouse searching for "thought associates." These associated thoughts harbor feelings from the past. After a fraction of a millisecond, the "feelings" signals arrive at your Green. Your Green responds to the feelings of Yellow information that has already been stored — "ghosts and goblins" of the past.

> WELLNESS PRINCIPLE: Yellow feelings from the past constantly communicate with your Green

And here's the kicker: The information stored in your Yellow was important at the time it was stored, but it may no longer be either important or correct! That means that your Red is using obsolete or incorrect information as a basis for running your life. Your Red is working in an adult world with adult concepts and an adult perspective, but your Yellow is filled with "infantile" associated information. Your Red and Yellow are incongruent. Your Red pulls you toward "grown-up" rationality while your Yellow pulls you back to "kid."

For example, the memory and intense feelings of humiliation and shame stored during your second-grade class play when you said the wrong line at the wrong time were traumatic and important at the time. But that growing-up experience is no longer the focal point of your existence. It doesn't need to be the backdrop for your business presentation to potential investors, or for every other adult encounter you have. However, it can be — if you don't realize that it is the "goblin" behind your overwhelming shyness or your "nervous stomach." The humiliating experience was intense. With your seven- or eight-year old perspective, you responded as though you were in physical peril. And the intensity of those feelings soldered the "picture memory" and "feeling memory" in your Yellow. And there the memories are: poised in the starting blocks ready to leap to the front of the pack of your thoughts at the first hint of another embarrassing situation. When your Yellow-flavored presentation falls flat, you reinforce the original feelings of inadequacy and self-contempt. All of that trauma without actual physical danger. So Green was running your physiology in response to out-dated Yellow information.

But real survival threats take a different route. The old Red-perceived snake-in-the-grass survival threat is quick-and-dirty. It requires an instantaneous response. No time for rummaging through Yellow for "how to respond" comparisons when you're in harm's way. A perceived survival threat zips directly to your Green for immediate action. High intensity threats bypass Yellow and head straight for Green. When you're confronted with danger, there's no time for a committee meeting. And that's good for survival.

> WELLNESS PRINCIPLE: High-intensity   Red-perceived threat stimuli go directly to Green — they don't pass Yellow and they don't collect $200

Your perfect Green isn't the argumentative kind. It responds without thought to either Red or Yellow. There you are, sound asleep, or reading, or changing the furnace filters, or watching TV, and your "stuffed" Yellow pumps out obsolete but power-packed information to your Green. And your Green responds perfectly. Your Yellow interacts constantly with your Green. That's good; it provides continuity to your life. Continuity is one thing; stagnation is another.

Since you put the original information into your Yellow with your Red, you can update your Yellow by using your Red. That's where your conscious choices of thoughts come in. You can choose to think Red thoughts that update outmoded Yellow memories by the drip, drip, drip method. It may seem that Yellow stored information is etched in stone; however, a persistent drip, drip, drip will alter even stone. After all, that's how most of the negativity was stored in your Yellow in the first place — one drip of thought-feeling at a time.

But you're not the same person you were when most of your Yellow was stuffed. With each day's experiences and growth, you become a "different person." You are "different" because you have added new stuffing to your Yellow — new synapses, new connections, new association routes in your brain. And each of these new associations, combined with the old associations, gives your Green new combinations of feelings to respond to.

But suppose your Yellow-stored feelings aren't appropriate for your present life. What happens then?

The Yellow-stored second-grade feelings of humiliation and embarrassment aren't appropriate for your adult status. They were appropriate at the time of the experience; but you really don't need to continue to respond with eight-year-old feelings in the middle of an important business meeting or at a causal social gathering. Yet without you ever thinking directly about that ego-shattering event of long ago, the residual feelings can affect your physiology and your life. The problem isn't the feelings or the memory. The problem is that your conscious Red is working in "adult mode" while your Yellow feelings are zipping along in eight-year-old mode. And since your Red doesn't communicate directly with your Green unless you are in imminent danger, it's your "humiliated eight-year-old" Yellow calling the shots every time you're in a potential "public humiliation" situation. Your Red and Yellow are out of synch. They aren't working harmoniously. We might even say that they are at odds — no wonder you're tired and nervous.

> WELLNESS PRINCIPLE:　Your event memories are your history; your feeling memories are your present and future

My clinical experience has shown that self-perception is the most common area of Red-Yellow disharmony. Memories and their associated feelings are the seeds of self-esteem and self-sabotage. And you don't even realize that you are planting these seeds throughout life. Seeds of physiology-controlling memories are planted in your Yellow by your Red. Red-planted seeds always grow. From the time you become conscious of your surroundings, your Red and Yellow provide a bumper crop of stimuli that your Green must respond to. And you survive. Let's hear it for your Green! Your Green is going to respond to the most threatening feelings in order to keep your systems going as long as possible. Your Red may be humming along happy as a kid in a toy store, but your Yellow may be sending distress messages to your Green.

So the health, happiness, and success objective is to have your Red and Yellow as closely in tune with each other as possible. When your Yellow memories are packed with feelings appropriate to your present conditions, your physiology responds to present conditions. When your Yellow memories are packed with outdated feelings, your present physiology responds to past conditions. And that makes about as much sense as using twenty-year old stock market quotes as a basis for today's investments.

We can see that Red thoughts and Yellow feelings are constant companions that influence not only how we feel but how we respond to the world around us. They are the flavoring in the stock of the mental soup we call the mind. The Red-Yellow influence on your life is constant.

That influence is what is now being heralded as the "mind-body connection." This connection isn't new. It's always been there. The Red and Yellow of your mind are behind most of the responses of your physiology-directing Green. Every thought that runs through your Red affects your Yellow, and your Yellow puts your individual "spin" on those thoughts. It's the "spin" that influences your Green — danger, pleasure, worry, fear, joy. Active Red thoughts are filtered through Yellow memories. And Yellow memories incorporate your feelings, beliefs, attitudes, prejudices, biases, preferences, and interpretations that stimulate the Green. All of this symphony of sensations is a function of that elusive entity, your mind.

THE MIND FIELD

The continuous surge of thoughts, memories, and feelings that flood your Red and Yellow are the most obvious products of your mind. From my perspective, your "mind" is your connection to your personal energy field. It is more than your conscious thoughts, feelings, rationalizations, wants, and urges. Your mind is the "buffer zone" for the energy that drives your body. If you need a road map to locate your mind, look at your brain, your body, and your field.

Your mind produces more than just thoughts and memories. Your mind is more than a thinking machine (that's your Red). Your mind is a primary source of energy communication with your field. Your mind-energy and field-energy blend like the colors of the rainbow. It's hard to tell where one ends and the other starts.

Your mind is the energy that connects you with your Personal Energy Field. It is the buffer zone between you and the Universal Perfect Intelligence. Your mind connects you with the energy of Perfect Intelligence, and it can "shield" you from that energy. In your mind is the sumtotal of all of the energy available to you at any time. Positive energy allows access to the greatest amount of field energy; negative energy restricts that access. Or, to put it another way, positive energy facilitates communication with your field, and negative energy injects static into the communication process. Most of positive or negative communication energy comes from the thoughts you are thinking now and the thoughts you have thought in the past and stored in your Yellow. And since your personal combination of thinking and thoughting is individual and unique, your mind is unique.

WELLNESS PRINCIPLE: Your mind is your unique energy
field, inside and out

Not only is your mind unique, your personal communication field is unique. Throughout your life you have tailored your field with your thoughts. You have taken a tuck here, a dart there, and tightened a seam someplace else. All without realizing what you were doing. And you did this with your Red and Yellow. Not with your Green. Your Green responds without thought. Your Green is an extension of your White field. Your Green, like your White, is perfect. Your Green never changes!

Recall that the original "You" started out as a field that was perfectly complete. Full of creative energy. Full-powered. High-energy. Look at any healthy child to see a healthy field personified. Your personal field was and is chaotic in that systems intertwine with systems that intertwine with other systems that intertwine with yet other systems *ad infinitum*. And your body works at its best when all of the energy of all of those field systems is available. However, your accessibility to your energy supply is not static. It fluctuates according to the quality of the energy of your thoughts. Negative "charges" of thoughts and memories can reduce your access to all of the positive field energy. Contrary to our physical world experiences that opposites attract, when you're out in the energy field it's a whole new ball game: likes attract and opposites repel. So negatively charged thinking attracts more negativity. It closes the gate, so to speak, and keeps some of the positively charged creative field energy from getting through. Your "tank" of creative energy is full, but "negativity plaque" clogs your fuel line.

So it is with restricted communication between body and field. Years of accumulated Yellow negativity restricts access to the full-complement of life-revitalizing energy. There you are, minding your own business, and quietly clogging the lines to your very own life-support mind field.

WELLNESS PRINCIPLE: Eliminating energy "plaque"
is a positive experience

You can begin anytime to combat even years of accumulated "plaque" or negative "charges." Your secret weapon is lesson-learning.

Each time you respond negatively to an encounter, the negativity restricts the availability of some elements of your field energy. However, this restriction isn't irrevocable. Just a little positive can neutralize a lot of negative. And that's what we're after — a field that is high in available energy. The energy is there. The objective is to keep it available to you at all times. It's positive thoughts and feelings in your mind that keep open the channels of communication between body and field.

For every negative circumstance, find and feel as much good in that circumstance as you can, and learn how each circumstance benefitted you. The more positive feeling you put into recognizing the personal benefit, the more negativity you "neutralize." Finding something you can feel good about in every experience keeps you, your physiology, and your life on an even keel. Learning the lesson is the greatest long-term survival strategy you can implement with your Red. We might even say that feeling the good in every experience is the seventh essential of life.

In the previous chapter we talked about forgiving others and ourselves for past offenses. And we said that the forgiving part is only about 40% of the process. Learning the lesson by finding something positive about the experience is the other 60% in the process of removing interference in body and field.

We learn the lesson when we recognize some element of good in every experience we have. Granted, it's pretty easy to see the good in fun, enjoyable, uplifting, or profitable experiences. No trick to that. It's finding an element of good and really *feeling* positive about the less-than-uplifting that's the challenge. Here's just a quick example.

You have interviewed for a job you really want. The interview went well and you were led to believe you were a top contender. But the job went to someone else. A real bummer. Where's the "good" for you?

The good is that: (1) you found that you have the experience and abilities that put you in serious contention for a better job, and (2) the window of opportunity is open for an even better job than the one you didn't get. Those "goods" may initially be small consolation for a big disappointment; however we're looking for molecules, not mountains, of "good." And a positive *feeling* needs to accompany the molecule of "good." Remember, you're not a "victim," and you're not a "martyr."

WELLNESS PRINCIPLE: Find the good — and feel it

As I see it, that's the purpose of everything we do — to find even a molecule of positive about negative situations. This is the growth factor. Life isn't static any more than your body or field are static. Life is a process. And learning how to confront and overcome difficult situations nurtures growth and keeps field communication open. We begin our existence in this world in a field of positive energy. We leave this world when our positive energy is exhausted. Energy may be exhausted in one fell swoop if you're hit by a cement truck doing 60 miles an hour. Or energy may be exhausted little by little by sopping up and storing negativity. It's up to each of us individually to attend to our own field and energy supply. And that's what lesson-learning does for us.

WELLNESS PRINCIPLE: Learning the lesson of every experience clears your mind field

That sounds all very well and good; but how do you start to recognize
good where negative reigns?

You start by recognizing your own unique qualities — and being
thankful for them.

"UNIQUE": WITH A CAPITAL "YOU"

Everyone is unique. Everyone has positive qualities. Yet not everyone
recognizes his or her positive qualities. But the qualities are there. They
are kind to their dog. Or scrupulous about personal cleanliness. Or
considerate of others' feelings. Or a tireless worker. We may tend to
discount our own positive qualities because we figure that they are
standard issue for everyone. So we may acknowledge that we are brave,
loyal, trustworthy, and true, but that doesn't count because most other
people are also. However, that's not the point. Commonality of qualities
is immaterial. None of us has cornered the market on particular positive
qualities. The qualities are universal — available to all. We, as individuals, are unique. We have our own unique combination of qualities. That's
an important distinction. For each of us, the qualities are there; but some
people have trouble acknowledging them. And when we can't see
anything positively "different" about ourselves, we figure that we aren't
worth much.

WELLNESS PRINCIPLE: Positive qualities abound, but our
self-view may be cloudy

You and your life are unique. No one else shares your exact blend of
experiences. No one else shares your precise responses to those experiences. Yet it is your responses that have brought you to where you are
today. In fact, considering your experiences and responses, you couldn't
be any place other than where you are right now. Ponder that for a
moment. You are what you are and where you are because of your
responses to all of the good, not-so-good, terrible, and neutral events in
your life. You are healthy, happy, and satisfied, or you are unhealthy,
miserable, and despondent all because of your particular lifetime of Red
perceptions and Yellow memories that prompted perfect Green responses.

Take your school days, for example. How did you respond to the
academic and social environment of school? Did you respond positively

or negatively? Did you see yourself as "as good as" or "a cut above" your peers? Or did you see yourself as (to use the current politically correct jargon) academically and socially challenged — "not quite as good as everyone else"?

Most of the people who come to me for help believe themselves to be card-carrying charter members of the "not quite as good as everyone else" club. They have developed this belief over time. By the time I see them, their Yellow-entrenched beliefs have done a number on their health. Their conscious Reds have stuffed their non-conscious Yellows with negative feeling-memories about themselves. The memories have solidified into hard and fast beliefs which are continually reinforced with the incessant drip of negative Personal Programming. Attitudes toward themselves range from a solid case of low self-esteem to raging self-hate. And the health of these low self-esteem patients illustrates that they have fulfilled their expectations — they believe and feel they are unworthy, and they prove it. They are even unworthy of good health.

> WELLNESS PRINCIPLE: Stuff your Yellow with negatives and you pepper your life with problems

However, self-esteem isn't an issue of worth or lack of worth. It's an acknowledgement of unique differences. What makes you different from everyone else?

The first thing that springs to mind is physical differences. We have a lot of those. We come in a variety of shapes and sizes. Obvious differences in hair, eye, and skin color, combined with distinctive feature differences that are characteristic of assorted ethnic groups, blend Generic Man into a colorful tapestry of humanity. Each of us comes with a unique blend of genes and DNA. And there are more differences that have nothing to do with appearance. What a dull world this would be if our differences were limited to the physical. Robotsville!

Capping off our multiplicity of sizes and shapes is our variety in mannerisms and personalities. We walk and talk, play and work, gesture, smile, and scowl, think and respond to other people and outside events in our individual unique style. These styles are learned characteristics tempered by physical particulars. Gymnasts, professional wrestlers, computer buffs, accountants, baseball players, engineers, dancers, gourmet cooks, and all of the rest of us march to the beat of unique characteristics of physique and temperament. Personal characteristics develop to conform to current thoughts, past thoughts, and developed beliefs. Therein lies the big difference between you, me, the lady down the street, a tour guide in Sri Lanka, and everyone else. Unique personal characteristics. And these characteristic differences are the products of our unique experiences that we respond to with our unique mind, memory, and interpretations. Personal characteristics are a combination of heredity and experience.

> WELLNESS PRINCIPLE: Heredity shapes your body;
> experiences shape your
> memory and beliefs

The previous chapter talked about how our thinking starts with "Me." So your "Me" centered thoughts are a good place to begin to revamp your thinking to a more positive healthstyle.

Since you are the focal point of your thinking, your attitude toward yourself is the stock of mental soup that flavors all of your other thoughts. If your attitude toward yourself is steeped in bitter herbs, the thoughts that spring from those attitudes will be equally as bitter. Let's look at a fanciful question as an alternative way of thinking about yourself.

If you could be anyone in the world, who would you want to be?

You might come up with an instant answer: Michael Jordan, Madame Curie, Pavarotti, Madonna, Beethoven, Colin Powell — you get the idea. But we're not talking about being only the "public face" or "award winner" part of that person. The question is. "Who would you want to be all of the time, warts and all?" In years gone by (when discretion wasn't a dirty word), we saw only the positive accomplishments of notables, heros, social contributors, and great thinkers. But now we're into full exposure. We're in the era of no-holds-barred-dirt-digging into the private lives of luminaries past and present. Not only the clay feet but the sordid details of the lives of our heroes and heroines are being exposed. So when you decide you want to trade yourself in for someone else, you have to take the angst with the accolades and cash.

Where is all of this leading?

It's leading to the realization that even if you have a rampant case of "I hate me and/or my life," when you think about the things you have had to endure and the mistakes you have made, there probably isn't anyone, repeat anyone, in the world other than yourself whom you would really rather be on a full-time basis. Why?

Because you are living the life that provides the lessons YOU need to learn. "You" don't need to learn Magellan's lessons, or Buddha's lessons, or Jack-the-Ripper's lessons. You, your circumstances, your health, your family — everything about you — are perfect for you to learn your lessons. You and everything about you is perfect for the life course that brought you to this day. You are your own special combination of experiences, memories, thoughts, and responses. No one else could handle the lessons you have had to handle. No one else is operating with your thinking Red or "stuffed" Yellow. No one else has the exact same combination of attributes and "deficiencies" you have. You are Unique. Recognize your uniqueness. Capitalize on it. And most of all, be thankful for it.

> WELLNESS PRINCIPLE: Unique is spelled with a
> capital "You"

RED-YELLOW CONFLICTS

Throughout the preceding pages, we have looked at how thoughts, feelings, and memories — sensory stimuli — affect your body. When you understand how thoughts impact physiology, you can understand what I meant when I said earlier *your disease is your cure*. If you have stayed with me this far, you can see the logic in the mind-body connection. And if you can mess up your life and health with thoughts, you can straighten out your life and health with thoughts. Now it's time to look at some ways to counteract much of the unnecessary, self-inflicted stress that can ruin your days and ultimately lead to physiological exhaustion and disease. No purpose is served if I merely point out that your disease is your cure. Disease is a product of survival responses to stimuli from conscious Red and non-conscious Yellow. If it weren't for the disease response, all of your responses would have stopped — you'd be dead. So we can see that either disease or health is the required output of the particular messages sent to your Green. And those messages come predominantly from Red and Yellow.

Now that we have gone through the "why's" and "wherefore's" of how your thoughts, memories, beliefs, and choices can sabotage your health, it's time to help you develop some mechanisms for making sure your body is on track. And you keep your body on track when you recognize how you benefit from every experience. Each of your experiences is a unique opportunity for you to learn the unique lessons you are offered throughout your unique life.

When you find and feel the good in a bad situation, at least three positive things happen: (1) you project positive energy into your field to cut down on static in your energy communication systems; (2) you "neutralize" negative "toxicity" in your Yellow; and (3) you synchronize Red and Yellow so that they are on the same "wavelength."

We've already reviewed the field energy and neutralizing benefits of feeling the good, and we've touched on the benefits of Red-Yellow synchronization. Let's look more closely at why and how you can synchronize Red and Yellow. First, the "why."

Red-Yellow disharmony is essentially a belief problem. Beliefs are stored in Yellow. But they aren't stored away in the dark recesses of your Yellow and brought out only for special occasions. They are accessed constantly. Everything you think about in your Red is "run by" your "belief department" to see that it fits the accepted criteria. If the Red newcomers don't meet the standards set by your "belief police," you experience what is generally referred to as a "guilty conscience." And as we all know, guilt feelings are very real physical sensations. That's your Red and Yellow "doing battle."

When your Red and Yellow are out of phase, your Green must respond to the beliefs stored in Yellow. Often the out-of-phaseness comes from out-of-date beliefs — kid-sized beliefs in an adult-sized life. Conscious, age-appropriate Red thoughts crash full-tilt into conflicting Yellow beliefs. Remember the young professional woman who was living with her fiance, and young Matt who metaphorically kept shooting himself in his job-foot? Those two are classic examples of Red-Yellow disharmony. And both of these individuals suffered physical and emotional war wounds as a result of their own personal Red-Yellow battles. In life situations, you can override your beliefs with Red-directed actions. You can use your conscious mind to act in any way you please. However, in your physiological life, you aren't the master of your fate. Your Green handles your physiology without your conscious help. As long as there's no tiger nipping at your heels, your Green responds to your belief-packed Yellow. And Yellow beliefs always win.

We can see that physical repercussions to Red-Yellow conflict are quite "normal" when we keep in mind the basic premises of this book: Your body is designed to survive, and you have no conscious control over the physiological survival processes. Conscious Red decisions that conflict with Yellow-stored beliefs constitute a "threat." In Red-Yellow conflict, your Red may not detect a threat, but your Yellow may express one. And your Green responds to Yellow. So when your sixth-sense Yellow signals a stress, your Green responds with defense physiology. You experience body-field interference as Sensory Dominant Stress.

WELLNESS PRINCIPLE: Red thoughts that conflict with

Yellow beliefs cause body-field
interference

One of the secrets to good health is to keep your Red and Yellow in synch so your Green can apply its perfect responses to appropriately-timed stimuli. And when Red, Yellow, and Green chug along in synchronized harmony, the chaos of your White suffers no interference.

But how can you tell if your Red and Yellow are out of synch?

The most obvious clue is that you are up-tight when there's nothing to be up-tight about. Try the shoulder check right now. Are you wearing your shoulders as earrings? Are your shoulder muscles so tight that mosquitos use them as trampolines? If they are, consciously lower your shoulders. Tight shoulder muscles indicate that you are defending against something — and that something is probably settled comfortably in your Yellow. So if you're not being physically threatened, tight shoulder muscles indicate Red-Yellow conflict.

Another example of Red-Yellow desynchronization. As you sit quietly reading these words, is your foot or leg bouncing for no obvious reason? If it is, your Red is signalling "read and relax" but your Yellow is signalling "man battle stations." According to Red, all is right with the world; according to Yellow, danger is around the bend. We have seen that your Green responds directly to your Red only in cases of actual, intense emergencies. As long as no startling emergency sends signals for quick action from Red to Green, your Green responds to Yellow.

WELLNESS PRINCIPLE: Yellow "alert" memories take precedence over Red "resting" thoughts

And a third Red-Yellow conflict indicator is the Recurring Out-of-Context thought (ROT) that we talked about several chapters back. (Funny how all of that "stuff" we talked about earlier is falling into place.) The ROT is "Uncle Charlie" or your former partner or a childhood friend or whatever. Recurring thoughts generally center around a person rather than an incident. And a recurring out-of-context thought is a major clue that your Red attitude toward the person is different from your stored Yellow memories of that person. So pay attention to "Uncle Charlie" or whomever. We're just about to find out what you can do about him/her that will give you body-mind-field relief.

The concept of conflicting messages from your Red and Yellow is a landmark on our journey to self-directed health. This concept sheds a bright light on the question of why we can seem to be doing everything right, yet we end up with a major health problem — high cholesterol or high blood pressure, or heart disease or diabetes, or arthritis or cancer. The bottom line is that the body is responding perfectly. But it is responding to Yellow memories of past traumas and failings rather than to Red thoughts of how we want things to be. We are convinced, in our Red, that we think positively. We think our diet is wonderfully healthful. We are certain that our exercise program is top-notch. We believe that we are controlling the essential variables in ways that *should* result in health, happiness, and success.

What we haven't learned (until now) is that if all of the negative that has accumulated in the Yellow over the past twenty, thirty, forty, or more years of life isn't neutralized, it will be expressed somehow. And that "somehow" is generally as physical disease and discomfort. And the way you neutralize it is the same way you put it there in the first place — with your conscious Red.

Aha! Positive Thinking!

Well, yes and no. Far be it from me to tell you positive thinking isn't good. But helter-skelter positive thinking isn't the answer to neutralizing Yellow-stored negativity. The "positive thinking" must be directed to specific areas of Yellow. And that's what we're going to talk about now.

APPLIED THOUGHTS

The following mental gymnastics are designed to help you re-synchronize your Red and Yellow. You won't work up a sweat or exert your cardiovascular system or pull a muscle when you do these exercises. But you can remove self-inflicted interference, resynchronize your Red and Yellow, and tone your mind-body-field energy systems. These are individual exercises done best in quiet solitude. They include making a couple of movements that may need a little explaining before you start.

You will be instructed to "take a deep breath, and hold it." Keep in mind that some people may be so sick that they should not engage in this part of the exercise except under the supervision of their doctor.

Holding your breath isn't a particularly difficult procedure, but it is very important. You need to *take a deep breath before you hold it.* Don't exhale and hold it; inhale and hold it. Don't just stop breathing in mid-exhale. You don't need to hold your breath for three or four minutes. Hold it until you feel an urgent need to breathe. Depending on how acidic your body is, that may be 10 seconds, it may be 30 seconds, or, it may be a minute. The length of time doesn't matter. It's the process that counts. You see, breathing is an absolute essential; holding your breath creates an internal need for oxygen. Breathing becomes the highest priority for survival. Your Green is actively involved in crisis survival. It taps all resources to find oxygen to satisfy its survival needs. And if there's no new oxygen coming in through the lungs, your Green will conserve as much as possible. What's one of the prime users of oxygen? Tense muscles. So when the oxygen supply begins to ebb, your muscles will relax — it's a survival response.

Another instruction you'll receive that needs a little clarification is, "Move your feet." That doesn't mean get up and dance. But it implies a fairly precise movement. Here's the picture.

You're lying on your back, legs straight, feet together side by side — not crossed. In this position, if you are relaxed, your toes are probably pointing at about the "11 o'clock" and "1 o'clock" positions, more or less. When you come to the "move your feet" instruction, starting where you are at 11 o'clock and 1 o'clock, rotate your feet toward the 9 o'clock and 3 o'clock positions, then move them back to the 12 o'clock position. You probably won't turn them as far as the 9 and 3 positions, and that's fine. Turn you feet outward as far as you can comfortably without working at it. It may be just a matter of a half an inch. The distance isn't crucial; it's the coordination between mind and muscle that is important.

After you have done the side-to-side movement, move your feet up and down. Not your legs, just your feet. Point your toes away from your head, then bring them back so they point straight-up at the ceiling (flex). Point, flex, point flex.

When you've come to the "move your feet" part, do the sideways movements twice and the up and down movements twice. Count them.

You will also be asked to "look up." Your eyes may be closed, but you can still look up. "Looking up" and "moving your feet" are very important parts of the exercises. These are both "do-able" moves, but they aren't common, everyday moves you make without thinking about it. You have to think consciously about what you are doing. Your non-conscious Yellow harbors the memories of how to make the movements. You decide in your Red to move in a particular way, and your Yellow instructs your subconscious Green to carry out the movements. In the process, you coordinate Red, Yellow and Green. Pretty nifty, eh?

I'll list the steps of the basic process first; then we'll look at variations on the basic process that address particular circumstances. The fundamental process is standard. You choose the subjects you think about to suit your particular circumstances. It's a "think and do" procedure. The "thinking" part changes, the "doing" part is constant. Here's the format.

❧ ❧ ❧ ❧ ❧ ❧ ❧ ❧ ❧ ❧ ❧ ❧ ❧

9-Step Process

1. On your back, or "laid back" in an easy chair. Quiet. Relaxed.
2. Close your eyes.
3. Think about the subject you are going to concentrate on — another person, a situation past or present, or yourself.
4. Think about how you *feel* about that subject.
5. Take a deep breath and hold it.
6. With your eyes still closed, "look" up toward your eyebrows and maintain that eye position.
7. Concentrate on how you *feel* about the subject you're thinking about as you ...
8. Rotate your feet (just your feet, not your legs) back and forth to the sides twice, then up-and-down twice (count the movements).
9. Breathe and relax.

❧ ❧ ❧ ❧ ❧ ❧ ❧ ❧ ❧ ❧ ❧ ❧ ❧

This nine-step process is a basic format that can be used to address many areas of Red-Yellow interference. Your job is to identify a specific area of disharmony. Perhaps it is the subject of your recurring out-of-context thoughts. Or it may be a current problem that has been bothering you. Or it could be an experience from the past that you thought you had resolved years ago. Or it could be your self-image that's askew. Start with the area that is most important to you. If you can't identify anything in particular, think about the first person who pops into your mind. That person may well be yourself!

One of the biggest interference-producers is low self-esteem. You can use the basic 9-step process to focus on removing interference created by your Red "picture" of yourself that may not be congruent with your Yellow "picture" of yourself. Remember, people are the focus of virtually all interference, and *you* are a people. My clinical experience shows that the focus of interference for most patients ultimately comes down to themselves. We are "Me" oriented. You can address your "Me" interference by using the basic 9-step process.

WELLNESS PRINCIPLE: Keep your Red and Yellow in synch to help your body stay "in the pink"

The next exercise helps you to coordinate your conscious Red attitude toward yourself with your non-conscious memory Yellow attitude toward yourself. Often the two are at odds. You may mentally chastise yourself in your Red over your faults and foibles, but your Yellow isn't all that unhappy about you. Or, it may be the other way around. You pat yourself on your back with your Red, but your Yellow reminds you that you're really pretty much of a loser. Red thoughts grate against Yellow memories and interfering "sparks" fly. Here's an exercise that can help you synchronize your Red and Yellow self-images.

〜 〜 〜 〜 〜 〜 〜 〜 〜 〜 〜 〜 〜

Synchronize Red and Yellow Self-Image

You are going to "place yourself" on a scale — not a weight scale: a "worthiness" scale. A "how I see myself" scale. The scale ranges from 0 = completely worthless, to 10 = perfect. If you want to visualize yourself standing on a giant ruler, that's fine.

As you lie comfortably, think about yourself, and think about how you think about yourself. In your mind's eye, place yourself at the appropriate number on the imaginary "worthiness scale." You can determine if you have hit the most relevant spot on the scale by closing your eyes and looking up toward your eyebrows. If your eyelids "flutter," you're in the right place. Take a deep breath, hold it, and move your feet back and forth twice, and up and down twice.

If you're not at the right number, your eyelids won't "flutter" when you close your eyes and look up. Mentally move yourself either up or down on the scale. If the eyelids still don't "flutter," move your scale position the other way. Keep moving your self-assessment point away from your original point until you can feel the involuntary flutter of your eyelids. The distance you move from point to point isn't important. You can move by whole units, half units, or tenths. The point is to move. Your body will let you know when you're on target.

As you go through the nine steps, concentrate on yourself. With your eyes still closed and looking upward, think about where you are on the "worthiness scale." Take a deep breath. Move your feet in-and-out twice, then up-and-down twice. Breathe and relax.

Now, think about something positive about yourself and go through the breath-holding, eyes-up, foot-movements again. Think about something you do well. It may be your job or profession, or managing your time, or being considerate of others, or gardening, or organizing. Think about and *feel the positive satisfaction and pleasure you get from your accomplishments*. Close eyes, hold breath, move feet, breathe and relax. This helps you put Red positive feelings into a store of Yellow negative memories about yourself.

ᎧᎧ ᎧᎧ ᎧᎧ ᎧᎧ ᎧᎧ ᎧᎧ ᎧᎧ ᎧᎧ ᎧᎧ ᎧᎧ ᎧᎧ ᎧᎧ ᎧᎧ

The objective of the self-image exercise is to coordinate specific areas of Red and Yellow with positive energy. But this isn't a one-shot, fix-everything exercise. You didn't build your attitude toward yourself all at once and you can't renovate it all at once. Self-esteem is a whole-mind affair. Well-entrenched impressions of yourself are scattered around many associated areas of your Yellow. To get the greatest interference-clearing value for your effort, run through this exercise daily. It helps to keep the "sludge" out of your Yellow.

Although the focal point of interference for most patients is their self-esteem, other areas of interference may need to be addressed. As a general rule, these other areas fall into two categories that were mentioned earlier:

1. The subject of out-of-context recurring thoughts, and
2. Highly emotional situations of past or present.

To clear interference in either of these two broad areas, be as specific as you can about the feelings you have toward the people involved. Identify a person involved and focus on the feelings you have toward that person. Then go through the 9-step process for each individual concerned.

The purpose of these "self-help" exercises is to give you a vehicle for consciously interacting with your Red, Yellow, Green, and White. This is not meant to be the be-all and end-all of health care. Some people need a doctor's assistance. In a clinic setting, the doctor trained in these procedures not only guides patients through the steps of the processes but attends to more serious health problems. If you are sick, a qualified health care specialist is still your best bet for assistance. You shouldn't depend on self-administered synchronization exercises for your total health care any more than you depend on a bottle of aspirin for your total health care. These exercises are self-health boosters. They can help you smooth out kinks in your thinking but they aren't meant to solve major interference or disease problems.

WELLNESS PRINCIPLE: Self-help exercise is maintenance,
not a major overhaul

All of this imagining and mental maneuvering may sound like so much airy fairy nonsense. However, it works. My experience shows that the results of the 9-Step process are "clinically significant." Physiological changes are observed, and, most important, patients feel better!

Keep in mind that your Yellow and Green don't do reality checks. It doesn't matter whether the signals from your Red come from perceptions of the outside world or from your imagination. It's the feelings attached to the signals that impress Yellow and Green. So when you "imagine" (or "image"), your Yellow and Green respond as readily as when you "see" or "hear." So with these exercises you control the thoughts that your Yellow receives. Remember, your Yellow constantly communicates with your Green, and your Yellow knows only what your Red tells it.

> WELLNESS PRINCIPLE: Only Red knows the difference
> between fact and fiction

One more self-help exercise. This one doesn't require any special equipment or set-aside time. It fits easily into your daily activities of going from place to place to do whatever it is you do. It's an exercise to help you establish a habit of thinking about what you're thinking about.

Each time you see a traffic light, think of your own Red, Yellow, and Green. Pay particular attention to the yellow light. Every time you see a yellow light come on, consider it a reminder to (1) get ready to stop the car, and (2) ask yourself, "What kinds of thoughts am I thinking: positive or negative?"

If you are putting a negative spin on most of your thoughts, you'll be reminded that you are interfering with your life and your Green. Your Green responds just like those traffic lights. It responds to energy signals. It doesn't question, it doesn't argue, it doesn't evaluate — it doesn't think! It responds.

So think about what you're thinking about each time you see a yellow light. Your body will thank you with fewer feelings of stress and symptoms.

THE "I" IN THE MIDDLE OF "UNIVERSE"

We have seen throughout these pages that each of us begins as a unique field, develops into a unique person, and experiences a unique life. In the process, each of us builds a unique Red and Yellow. The focus for each of us is on the survival of "self." We, as individuals, think as individuals, respond as individuals, and act as individuals. However, as much as we would like to think that the universe revolves around "Me," in reality, each "Me" is a *part of the universe*. None of us is apart *from* the universe. And although our basic drive in life is to survive as an individual, we cannot survive alone. We weren't designed to survive alone. Generic Man is a corporate animal.

What does this bit of philosophy have to do with health, happiness, and success?

Everything!

We have been examining the effects thoughts, feelings, memories, beliefs, and learning lessons have on "Me." Yet, I'm not advocating a return to the selfish, what's-in-it-for-me, self-centered, "Me generation." You learn your personal lessons in life when you find an element of good in every lesson and recognize a benefit to you personally. Yet in order for a benefit to you to be truly positive, that benefit must not hurt anyone else. As an extreme example, if you rob a bank, you can see the immediate benefit to you of instant ready cash. However, that's hardly a universal positive. You have injured others either physically or financially. And you have injected negative into your mind, body, and field. You know that robbing a bank is "wrong," or you wouldn't go to great lengths to avoid being caught. Intentionally doing something that you know is wrong puts interference into your body and field. And when you put interference into your field, other fields are affected. You are attached by an energy umbilical cord to the energy of the universe. Your energy affects universal energy, and universal energy affects you. It's a wonderfully symbiotic relationship. We might say that each of us is like an independent cell in the vast body of the universe. Each cell has its own job to perform — responses to stimuli — as a part of the whole. So it mustn't respond in ways that injure other parts of the whole. Everything the individual cell (and the individual person) does must benefit the whole. We fight for our own survival, but our survival ultimately depends on the well being of the whole. So it is with our life experiences.

Any action we take, and any benefit we receive, must not intentionally or knowingly hurt anyone else. Although we are "Me" oriented, we are "We" connected. When you focus on finding the good in any experience, make sure it is a universal good that not only benefits you but harms no one else. When you find a universal "good," you find truth. And that's what this book is all about. Looking for universal truths on which to hang our individual hats.

WELLNESS PRINCIPLE: "Truth" is anything that resonates
with Perfect Universal Energy

You can see that if "truth" resonates with Perfect Universal Energy then the opposite of "truth," a "lie," does not resonate with Perfect Universal Energy. Truth in living is the universal growth factor. Learning the lesson of every experience is finding the truth in that experience. Or to put it another way, it is finding the positive energy that resonates with Universal Energy. You can tell when your energy resonates with Universal Energy. Your senses are sharpened, your world is brighter, you are more energetic, and you can see the good in the world around you.

You are more than a visible body. You are an energy being. As such, you are a part of the energy of the universe. Your Yellow memories combined with your Red thoughts and choices can affect your connection to your field. It's all of that "mental energy." If you are looking for health in body, mind, and life, you are in search of truth. And truth lies in synchronizing your mental energy with the energy of your field.

Your body, mind, and field are the dynamic trio that make up the unique "You." Each element of this trio is energy. Each is energy at a particular frequency. Everything you think, believe, feel, say, and do alters the frequency of the energy that is "You." Consequently, you are ever-changing. You and your energy are dynamic. It stands to reason, then, that your best interests are served when you use your dynamic energy in ways that allow your body to function at its best.

The energy of thoughts, feelings, memories, and beliefs are behind many of the ills that plague the world. We have devoted a great deal of this book to focusing on how this happens. Yet thoughts alone won't assure you a healthy, pain-free life. Thoughts are just one of the six essential areas of life. You can think lovely, wonderful thoughts and find the good in every situation and still sabotage your body by making inappropriate choices in the other areas.

WELLNESS PRINCIPLE: No amount of right thinking can
overcome habitual wrong choices

The good news is that you are in control of your life. You may have thought that you were a victim of the whims and wants of others, but you're not. The only thing you might be a victim of is inappropriate responses to events in your life.

Some of the concepts discussed in this book may have been new to you, however, most of the concepts in this book have been around in one form or another for generations. I've just assembled them in a slightly different pattern from those we're accustomed to in our Newtonian culture. However, put together, the concepts I've presented add up to the Golden Rule-plus: Do unto others as you would have them do unto you, and do unto yourself as you would have others do unto you. It all boils down to making appropriate choices in your life. Choices of what you eat, drink, and breathe, how you exercise and rest, and what you think. As long as your choices benefit you and don't harm anyone else, your health and your life will flourish. And that's pretty much the bottom line of the major religions that have survived the centuries.

You live in a dynamic body in a dynamic world. Both change constantly. You may not be able to do a whole lot about the state of the world, but you are the only person who can do something about your health, happiness, and satisfaction in this world.

You are the prime chooser of how you live your life and how you respond to the events in your life. When you understand how your thoughts and actions affect your health, you are in a better position to see that health is not a matter of luck. You are exactly where you should be for your past conscious mental responses and subconscious physiological responses. So, no matter what your state of health, it is perfect. It was perfect for survival in the past, and it is perfect for survival *right now!*

As a unique "You," you have your own strengths and attributes. You are a survivor. No matter how rough the road you have travelled to this point, you have survived. And along the way you have had plenty of opportunities to learn that life is full of challenges. Those challenges are lessons in the making. Remember, no one else can learn your lessons for you. Your lessons are nutrients of life that allow you to keep growing. Although some of your lessons appear to be skirting the edge of your tolerance, be assured that each lesson is one you need to learn for your own dynamic growth. You were designed to survive. And you were designed to grow. Life is a process. A process of growth. Every time you see the good in a challenging situation, you allow the energy of your personal field to enrich your body and mind.

> WELLNESS PRINCIPLE: Energy links the mind-body con-
> nection

POINTS OF INTEREST

1.   Green responds to negative perceptions stored in Yellow.

2.   Yellow information can be updated by Red thoughts.

3.   Negative self-perceptions — low self-esteem — are obsolete information applied to current situations.

4.   We learn lessons in life by finding at least a molecule of good in every situation.

5.   You are a unique blend of experiences, thoughts, memories, and responses.

6.   Red-Yellow conflict can cause energy interference between Green and White.

7.   Only you can learn your lessons.

8.   Truth is anything that resonates with creative energy.

Watch for good times to retreat into yourself.
Frequently meditate on how good God is to you.
                                            - Thomas à Kempis

POSTLUDE

AT JOURNEY'S END, A NEW BEGINNING

The sights along our journey have given us a new way to look at health and our interconnection with the Universe around us. With this new perspective you can see that we, as a nation, have been looking at health the wrong way. We've been hornswoggled by the siren song, "I'm from the government; I'm here to help you." As a result, our medical costs have gone ballistic while our general level of health is headed down the tubes. Fourteen percent of our gross domestic product goes toward what we euphemistically call "health care."[124] Here we are, the most highly developed, sophisticated, technologically advanced country in this world, yet, in 1992 we registered nineteenth among developed nations in infant mortality.[125] But we're not standing still. Oh, no! According to a report aired on CBS TV, 1994 figures put us at twenty-first. How's that for progress?

How did we get into this deplorable situation?

We did it by looking for solutions to diseases rather than recognizing that the diseases are the solution.

Instead of looking at the source of physical problems, we have focused on "fixing" parts that have gone awry. With our vast store of Newtonian knowledge about the way things work, we tend to look at the precision-made body as a set of component, often cantankerous, malevolent parts just waiting to attack. Some of these attacking parts are seen as expendable. Appendixes, gall bladders, and adenoids are excised as superfluous trouble-makers when they act up. Other attacking, or just plain offensive, parts are seen as replaceable. Faulty hearts, lungs, livers, and kidneys are surgically removed, discarded, and replaced with less damaged models. And to subdue parts and/or functions that can't be eliminated, drugs are used to mask or manipulate their activities. Substances are consumed or injected to regulate blood pressure, relax tense muscles, override pain warnings, and generally hide symptoms. But, this isn't all bad — as long as you recognize that drugs are strictly symptom controllers, and you don't expect such intervention to cure you or make you healthy. Remember, your disease *is* your cure.

Surgery and drugs can indeed be life-saving or symptom-controlling. There's nothing wrong with surgery to patch up damage and forestall imminent catastrophes. And there's nothing wrong with drugs to ease symptoms. Drugs help arthritics live more pain-free lives, diabetics live longer with fewer debilitating symptoms, and hypertensive patients enjoy more years of productivity than they might without the drugs. Certainly the occasional aspirin or one of its pain-relieving cousins can be a quick-fix to subdue a day-ruining, work-inhibiting pounding headache. And antibiotics zap pesky "germs" that the patient's body is too disorganized to resist. That's good. Especially if you are the one who is on the receiving end of greater comfort and an easier life. But none of these strategies address the fundamental *cause* of the problem that prompted them.

In this book I have made a big thing of the concept that your physical body is a reflection of your field. The first-cause of pain, disease, or a severe case of "The Punies" is over-organization of field information. Your field energy becomes shackled, and only bits and pieces of lower-frequency energy get through. Under conditions of energy-restriction, affected organs and systems of the body work overtime to handle the stress. These affected parts become exhausted, and exhaustion leads to symptoms and disease. It's a personalized energy-crisis and a whole-body problem. Fixing parts is a short-term solution to a short-term survival problem. Addressing the cause of the energy-shortage is a long-term solution. When your energy quotient is on target, "fixing" is unnecessary.

WELLNESS PRINCIPLE: "Fixing" parts can make some perfect survival responses less bothersome

Your parts never do anything wrong. They can't do anything wrong. They can do only the processes they were designed to do — and that's never wrong. Parts respond perfectly in ways that will keep the body alive for as many instants as possible. The problem isn't in the responses or the responding parts. The problem is in the internal messages that prompt the responses — messages, or stimuli, that affect the whole body. The responses are perfect; it's the messages that are inappropriate.

Parts merely carry out functions according to the messages they receive. These messages come from the conscious mind and internal feedback systems. They are self-instructing messages along the lines of, "Oh-oh, that looks/sounds like an attack — defend," or "Jerk, you don't deserve this good luck — sabotage the situation," or "Don't let him/her/them see that you're upset — keep this feeling bottled up."

No doubt about it; you live at the physical level and your body functions at the physical level. When you have a headache or broken arm, or are angry or frustrated, the physical is involved. Yet we have seen that many physical and physiological responses are prompted by memories stored in your Yellow non-conscious. These memories are learned responses. And they are powerful. But they are often outdated — obsolete. Nonetheless, they can keep your body responding perfectly even though the message stimulus is inappropriate. Outdated memory messages that dictate particular subconscious physiological responses not only require the body to perform correct functions at inappropriate times, but they put up roadblocks to communication with your personal field. Communication between the information source and the information receiver is muddled. We have seen that your body is organized according to information from your personal field. This field is in its best form when it is chaotic — fully-equipped with creative energy.

A chaotic, creative, energy field contains all of the energy "know-how" information available in the Universe. This information is most accessible and usable when your personal field is also chaotic. As your personalized information zone becomes more organized, the fewer pieces of data from "On-High" are able to wriggle their way over, under, or around rigid barriers of organization. We call this interference. Interference between field and body is like interference between radio transmitter and radio receiver.

> WELLNESS PRINCIPLE: Interference is anything that re-
> stricts information flow between
> field and body

That's hardly a "scientific" explanation of interference in your field. But it summarizes how interference projected into your perfect field limits the amount of essential field-information available to you. Interference doesn't alter the perfection of your field. Interference reduces accessibility to your full complement of perfect energy information.

> WELLNESS PRINCIPLE: Your body organizes itself best
> through the full-scope of informa-
> tion from your chaotic field

As scientific technology advances, the energy fields in and around the body can be measured by sophisticated equipment, such as EEGs and SQUIDs. In the community of science, measurable fields around the body are seen as by-products of living. In this book, I take a different view: energy fields are more than interesting by-products of life; they are essential life-developers. My search and re-search for truth convinces me that the field is the defining source of life, not the result of it.

> WELLNESS PRINCIPLE: The field is the design template of
> function, not the leavings

On our trip to the integrating energy field, we looked at the process of development. We found that this marvelous field is invisible to the naked eye yet measurable by sensitive equipment. We saw that from the single unified egg and sperm to the 75 trillion-celled complete person, a field of perfect energy envelops the physical being. Researchers have found that photographs of a seed taken by ultra-sensitive equipment reveal the field of the seed to be in the shape of the mature plant — not the shape of the seed. I believe that we can extrapolate from tree-seeds to people-seeds. They're both energy-intense and energy-developed.

We know that not every union of egg and sperm results in a lasting new life. Either egg or sperm may be less than perfect. Nevertheless, if the two unite, perfect energy directs development of the whole. The perfect field assures the best possible response from the union. If the response is inadequate, the development process is ended. We call this process spontaneous abortion. If the response is barely adequate, the development process may be less than ideal; we call the result "birth defects." However, the response is perfect for the conditions.

Egg and sperm come equipped with their own individual energy fields. Before their union each is synchronized with the mother and father respectively. At union/conception these fields unite to form the unique pulsating field of a new individual. It is this unique field that makes each of us unique. Each person's unique integrating field is a "buffer zone" between that person and the greater Universal Intelligence that many of us call God.

Identical twins have identical fields until they have developed to the point of receiving separate stimuli from emotions or consciousness. At that point, to an outside observer the physical appearances of the twins may remain virtually identical, however, the separate personal fields take on characteristics of their own. The packagings develop in tandem; the contents evolve independently.

WELLNESS PRINCIPLE: Form follows field

Although I refer to the physical body and the extended field body, as I see it, the two are one. At the quantum level, both are energy in action — quarks, leptons, and the more familiar electrons. The more minute the particles under the scrutiny of quantum or subatomic investigations, the harder it is to tell the difference between force and matter. As Nobel Prize-winning physicist Leon Lederman says, "One of the most intriguing developments today is that the very distinction between force and matter is blurring. It's all particles. A new simplicity."[126]

Electrons have been measured as both particles and waves. The energy in our physical particle-bodies is the same as the energy in our extended wave-body field; but it's in a different form. Although the concept that the body and field are the same energy in different forms may appear to be a large, non-Newtonian pill to swallow, we have no trouble accepting the concept that steam and ice are both water in different forms. When we view ourselves as a particular form of energy — energy beings — we can see that instead of being primarily a physical entity coupled with moderate doses of thoughts, emotions and spirituality, we are primarily lumps of particle-energy (ice) drawing on a more powerful wave-energy (steam) source than ourselves. We can see that we are more than just physical beings looking for uplifting emotional and spiritual experiences. In reality, we are spiritual energy looking for grounding or satisfaction within our physical bodies. Or, as Cardinal Newman is credited with saying: We try to please ourselves without displeasing God too much.

WELLNESS PRINCIPLE: We are spiritual beings undergo-
                      ing a physical experience

If we are energy beings with a personal buffer-zone field that extends beyond the visible flesh-and-blood body, where do "I" begin and end, and where do "You" begin and end?

At our current stage in the corporate intellectual development of Generic Man, the precise physical scope of the personal buffer zone hasn't been firmly established. But it's there and it's physical. My clinical experience shows that an individual's feelings register to a distance of approximately two inches outside his or her visible body. So we can say that the buffer zone extends *at least* two inches beyond the physical body. I suspect, however, that the personal field that integrates energy information is greater in size than that. And I am convinced that the activity of your personal field affects, in some way, the fields of those around you and, ultimately, the Universal Field of Intelligence.

Everything we do is a developmental process. We develop by learning the lessons of life. This philosophy is summed up in the words of Bernard M. Baruch: "The art of living lies less in eliminating our troubles than in growing with them."

> WELLNESS PRINCIPLE: Nothing happens to us; everything happens for us to learn our own lessons

Life is a developmental process. From the union of egg and sperm, we develop into a physical, complete being according to the template of our field. The body, we can see. We know the field is there — it's us. When we realize that the body is the vehicle that allows us to learn through life, we understand that life is a process of cultivating and growing with our field.

So it all boils down to learning a succession of small lessons in order to fully comprehend THE BIG LESSON.

The ultimate lesson — as I see it — is to learn that you are a part of, not apart from, the Universe. You and I, Uncle Charlie and Great-Grandmother Estelle, Katherine Hepburn and Boris Yeltsin, Charles Manson and his prey, Genghis Khan, and everyone else affect the energy of the Universe. Individually, we are minuscule energy conductors within the Universe. Recall the interlaced Venn diagrams we discussed earlier. Each of us is in charge of his or her own unique blend of "energy circles."

We are all bits of energy that affect other bits of energy that affect bigger bits of energy, that affect even bigger bits, and so on. We can see a similar situation in the bits and pieces of the body. Each part of a cell is an integral part of that cell, and that cell is an integral part of an organ, and that organ is part of a system which, in turn is a part of and contributor to the well-being of the whole. Oxygen-carrying red blood cell, invader-fighting white blood cell, heart cell, bone cell, kidney cell, you name it, all have their jobs to do — under circumstances of the moment. Each contributes to the workings and survival of the whole body. The difference between body and field is size. Your "whole body" is you, the individual. The "whole body" of energy is the Whole Body of Universal

Intelligence.

Each of us functions in his or her own personal field which radiates a direct connection to Universal Intelligence. And since we live in a communal society, our radiant personal fields phase in and out of contact with the radiant personal fields of others. These phasings are pleasant when two or more fields resonate harmoniously. Resonating, positive energy radiates between converging fields — fields around electrons, atoms, molecules, cells, tissues, organs, systems. Inside and out, we are aglow with interwoven, radiating energy fields. This aura of energy is behind the "radiant glow" of a new mother or bride. It is this radiant energy that we see stylized in artists' renderings of their impressions of Christ, the Buddha, the Virgin Mary, Cherubim, Seraphim and other heavenly beings. We call this positive radiating resonant energy "Love" — specifically "Unconditional Love."

> WELLNESS PRINCIPLE: Unconditional Love radiates posi-
> tive energy

The challenges that confront us in life are directed toward allowing us to learn how to contribute "Unconditional Love" to the Grand Plan. We're not talking eroticism, lust, obsession, or hormonal surges. We're talking about the love that is directed toward others despite their imperfections. This love carries no expectation or need for pay back. It's unconditional. Non-judgmental. Just sincere appreciation and genuine affection. No strings attached. It's the love most easily described as the love of parent for child. Mom and Dad don't stop loving little Kate just because the child has a dirty diaper. And they don't turn off their "Love" for a surly, rebellious teen-ager — although their "like" may falter a bit. Unconditional Love has nothing to do with approving of or agreeing with actions and attitudes of others. Unconditional Love is free of judgment, free of "if-only's," free of interference — free-flowing.

Unconditional Love is the ultimate positive feeling. And feelings are energy generators. Positive feelings harmonize with your personal field. Your personal field is perfect and positive, so positive feelings enhance the positivity and take nothing away from it. Negative feelings, on the other hand, suppress or lower energy from your personal field. Strong feelings affect both body and field. And strong positive feelings — love, acceptance, joy, appreciation — are the ideal "field fuel."

Feelings of Unconditional Love are easy to come by when all is going well. But how do you muster up "Unconditional Love" in the midst of an agonizing lesson?

Finding Unconditional Love in the loss of a cherished family member or life-supporting job isn't easy. But it is not only possible, it is necessary for your mental and physical health. That's where the "learning" comes in.

We learn by recognizing and appreciating that everything that happens in our life is an opportunity to find an element of good in that experience. Some lessons are easier to recognize than others. Finding the good — the Love Quotient — in the birth of a wanted, healthy child is a snap. Finding the good — the Love Quotient — in the subsequent death of that child is hard.

We can find the good in this example only when we understand that every child, cherished as he or she is by his or her parents, is also an individual with his/her life-lessons to learn. We, with our conscious intellect, cannot know what these lessons are. However, from the parents' point of view, the "good" in an experience as painful as losing a child might be the recognition of the increased joy and challenges the child brought to his or her family. Seeing the good — with feelings of Unconditional Love in every experience of life — enhances the flow of energy between the physical body and the personal field. Each instance of field enhancement improves the harmony and resonance among body, mind, and field and the source of all life, the Ultimate Power of Universal Intelligence — God. And that is our ultimate goal — to resonate harmoniously with the Ultimate Power.

> WELLNESS PRINCIPLE: Finding the positive side of every
> situation and learning the lesson
> resonates with harmonious energy

When you realize your role in the Big Picture, you can recognize that whatever your features, faults, or failings, you are a vital contributor to the Big Picture. And everyone else, whether you like them or not, is a vital contributor to the Big Picture. We contribute positively to the Big Picture by promoting harmony between our teeny-tiny personal field and the all-encompassing, in-charge, universal field of Universal Intelligence. And we promote harmony through the positive thoughts, feelings and emotional energy we pump into our personal field. When we realize that we are a unique blend of perfect energy, low-self esteem and self-denigration become virtually impossible. How can you hate yourself — or anyone else, for that matter — when you realize that you are following a unique path of unique lessons. I don't know what lessons you are here to learn, and you don't know what lessons I am here to learn. So how can we fault one another for the course each takes in the learning process.

Whatever our lessons are, we do the very best we can with our personalized lesson-plan.

And when you understand that life is a succession of lessons, you realize that there's no way you can be a victim. Life's lessons don't have victims; they have students. No one else can learn your lessons for you and no one else is to "blame" for your responses to your lessons. Others may be unwitting participants in your lessons, but the lessons are yours. And until you learn the things you are supposed to learn, you'll repeat the course.

WELLNESS PRINCIPLE: There are no drop-outs
from the lessons of life

So there you have it, faithful reader. Good news. You are NOT a victim. Your conscious choices of what you eat, drink and breathe, how you rest and exercise, and especially what and how you think and feel determine the health of your field, the health of your body, and your happiness and success. And your thinking determines your conscious choices. That's one of the big attractions we find at the end of our journey to self-directed health — our very own Rosetta Stone that reveals that our choices are behind whatever level of health, happiness, and success we have achieved. In this book we have focused primarily on thought choices. If you have been wrestling with a physical problem that has been treatment-resistant, the *cause* of your problem could be either thoughts or diet. Now that you have a "new view" of thoughts, feelings, beliefs, and energy, you might find it helpful to investigate the diet side of your life by reading *Your Health, Your Choice*. Between the two books, you'll be in a position to see whether your thoughts or your diet is most in need of revamping. And don't be surprised if it is a little (or a lot) of both. Diet is important and thoughts are important. Your diet affects your internal environment; your thoughts affect your internal environment, your field, and your life.

WELLNESS PRINCIPLE: What you think is what you get

The major lesson of life is to learn to live in harmony with Universal Intelligence. The practical application of this lesson is to learn to live in harmony with the other students who attend the school of hard knocks with you. By living harmoniously with both Universal Intelligence and fellow travelers, you won't interfere with the chaotic, creative nature of your fully-charged personal field of energy. In an ideal, negative-free world, you would project energy of only positive thoughts and feelings into your field. But let's face it, who lives in an ideal, negative-free world? Since most of us don't, it's up to each of us to play the hand we've been dealt in this game of life in the most positive way possible. If you are the rare individual who generates positive thoughts exclusively, you have already learned the secret to success in life. If you don't live in that rarified atmosphere of continuous positive thinking, you can still eliminate the lion's share of negativity from your thoughts and life. Just follow the four-step thought-directing formula described earlier: Recognize. Cancel. Forgive. See the good.

More good news. You have the greatest influence on your mind, body, field, and life. You are in charge of your health, happiness, and success. No one else can give any of these to you. And no one else can take any of them away. It's all in the way you respond. If you're not satisfied with the way your life and/or health have been going up to now, it makes sense to change the way you respond to life's wrinkles and blips. You can do it. You're not a victim. You are in charge.

> WELLNESS PRINCIPLE: Health, happiness, and success are
> positively dynamic

In a nutshell, that's the message of this book — and what's a book without a message.

ENDNOTES

1. Barber, John. (Sept/Oct 1988). Equinox. "Worried Sick: Scientists discover how stress and emotion affect the course of disease," pp. 91+.
2. Black, Dean. (1994). *Regulated to Death: How Too Much Healthcare Bureaucracy Is Making Our Nation Sick*. Phoenix, Arizona. p. 48.
3. Ibid, p. 17.
4. Ibid, p 30.
5. Ibid, p. 47.

6. Becker, R. O. *Cross Currents: The Perils of Electropollution, The Promise of Electromedicine*. Los Angeles: Jeremy P. Tarcher, Inc. 1990. p. 69.

7. Guyton, Arthur C. *Physiology of the Human Body*, 6th ed. New York: Saunders College Publishing. 1984. p. 214.
8. Ibid., p. 214.
9. Marino, Andrew A., Ed. *Modern Bioelectricity*. New York: Marcel Dekker, Inc., 1988. p. 2.
10. Ibid, p. 6.
11. Becker, *Cross Currents*, op. cit., p. 70.
12. Guyton, Arthur C. *Textbook of Medical Physiology*, 7th ed. Philadelphia: W.B. Saunders Company, 1986. p. 997.
13. Guyton, *Physiology of the Human Body*, op. cit., p. 630.
14. Ibid.
15. Ibid.
16. Gerber, Richard. *Vibrational Medicine: New Choices for Healing Ourselves*. Santa Fe, NM: Bear & Company, 1988. p. 63.

17. Becker, Robert. O., and Gary Selden. *The Body Electric: Electromagnetism and the Foundation of Life*. New York: William Morrow, 1985. p. 45.

18. Guyton, *Textbook of Medical Physiology*, op. cit., p. 37.
19. Becker, *Cross Currents*, op. cit. , p. 57.
20. Becker, *Body Electric*, op. cit., p. 182.
21. Becker, *Cross Currents*, op. cit., p. 57.
22. Gerber, p. 51.
23. Ibid., p. 52.
24. Chopra, Deepak. *Quantum Healing: Exploring the Frontiers of Mind/Body Medicine*. New York: Bantam Books, 1989. p. 45.
25. Ibid., p. 213.
26. Greenwood, Michael, and Peter Nunn. *Paradox and Healing: Medicine, Mythology & Transformation*. Victoria, B.C.: Meridian House, 1992. p. 212.
27. Guyton, *Textbook of Medical Physiology*, op. cit., p. 7.
28. Chopra, *Quantum Healing*, op. cit., pp. 41-42.
29. Goetz, Phillip W., Ed. in Chief. *The New Encyclopaedia Britannica*, Vol. 24. Chicago: Encyclopaedia Britannica, Inc., 1989, pp. 798-814.
30. Thomas, Clayton L., Ed. *Taber's Cyclopedic Medical Dictionary*, 15th Edition. Philadelphia: F.A. Davis Company, 1985, p. 1716.
31. Barber, John. op. cit., pp. 91+.
32. Guyton, *Physiology of the Human Body*, p. 200.
33. Guyton, *Textbook of Medical Physiology*, p. 686.
34. Ibid.
35. Thomas (Ed.), p. 160.
36. Guyton, *Physiology of the Human Body*, p. 218.
37. Guyton, *Textbook of Medical Physiology*, pp. 694-695.
38. Guyton, *Physiology of the Human Body*, p. 218.
39. Guyton, *Textbook of Medical Physiology*, p. 277.
40. Ibid., p. 548.
41. Ibid.
42. Ibid.
43. Guyton, *Textbook of Medical Physiology*, p. 656.
44. Ibid., p. 548.
45. Csikszentmihalyi, Mihaly. *Flow: The Psychology of Optimal Experience*. New York: Harper & Row Publishers, 1990, p. 26.

46. Ibid.
47. Ibid., pp. 28-29.
48. Guyton, *Textbook of Medical Physiology*, p. 648.
49. Ibid.
50. Ibid.
51. Ibid., p. 608.
52. Lederman, Leon. *The God Particle: If the Universe is the Answer, What's the Question?*. Boston: Houghton Mifflin, 1993, p. 63.
53. Ibid., p. 103.
54. Ibid.
55. Penrose, Roger. *The Emperor's New Mind: Concerning Computers, Minds, and The Laws of Physics*. New York: Oxford University Press, 1989, p. 24.
56. Ibid.
57. Ibid.
58. Ibid., pp. 24-25.
59. Gerber, p. 58.
60. Ford, Kenneth W. "The Large and the Small." *The World Treasury of Physics, Astronomy, and Mathematics*, (Timothy Ferris, Ed.). Boston: Little, Brown and Company, 1991, p. 27.
61. *Encyclopaedia Britannica*, Vol. 9, p. 503, Vol. 23, p. 702.
62. Becker, *Body Electric*, p. 61.
63. Becker, *Cross Currents*, pp. 21-22.
64. Davies, Paul. *God and the New Physics* New York: Simon & Schuster, Inc., 1983, p. 61.
65. Gerber, p. 416.
66. Ibid., p. 33.
67. Ford, Ibid., p. 28.
68. Ibid., p. 26.
69. Eccles, J., Sperry, R., Prigogine, I., Josephson, B. *The Reach of the Mind: Nobel Prize Conversations*. Dallas: Saybrook Publishing Company, 1985, p. 60.
70. LeDoux, J.E., Romanski, L., Xagoraris, A. Indelibility of subcortical emotional memories. Journal of Cognitive Neuroscience, 1(3), 238.
71. Chopra, *Quantum Healing*, p. 73.
72. Becker, *Cross Currents*, p. 70.
73. Chopra, *Quantum Healing*, p. 48.

74. Guyton, *Textbook of Medical Physiology*, p. 37.

75. Leonard, George. *The Silent Pulse: A Search for the Perfect Rhythm That Exists in Each of Us*. New York: E.P. Dutton, 1986, p. xii.

76. Magoun, H.I., Sr. *Osteopathy in the Cranial Field*, Third ed., Kirskville, Missouri: Journal Printing Company, 1976, pp. 23-42.

77. Gerber, p. 28.

78. Ibid., p. 85.

79. Asimov, Isaac. *Understanding Physics: Vol. II, Light, Magnetism & Electricity*. New York: Barnes & Noble Books, 1993, p. 52.

80. Davies, *God and the New Physics*. p. 168.

81. Ibid., p. 137.

82. Ibid., p. 107.

83. Guyton, *Textbook of Medical Physiology*, pp. 36, 37.

84. Chopra, *Quantum Healing*, p. 73.

85. Ibid., p. 67.

86. LeDoux, et al., p. 238.

87. Goleman, Daniel. "Emotions win out: Brain pattern keeps logic from defeating fear." Anchorage Daily News, Sept 3, 1989, pp. D1+.

88. Gregory, R. I., Ed. *The Oxford Companion to the Mind*. New York: Oxford University Press, 1987, p. 220.

89. Guyton, *Textbook of Medical Physiology*, p. 676.

90. Edelman, Gerald M. *Bright Air, Brilliant Fire: On the Matter of the Mind*. Basic Books, 1992, p. 118.

91. LeDoux, Joseph. "Emotion, Memory and the Brain," Scientific American, June 1994, p. 57.

92. Ibid., p. 56.

93. Ferris, Timothy. *The Mind's Sky: Human Intelligence in a Cosmic Context*. New York: Bantam Books, 1992, p. 122.

94. Pelletier, Kenneth R. *Mind as Healer, Mind as Slayer: A Holistic Approach to Preventing Stress Disorders*. New York: Dell Publishing Co., Inc., 1977, p. 69.

95. Redfield, James. *The Celestine Prophecy*. Hoover, AL: Satori Publishing, 1993.

96. Brennan, Barbara Ann. *Hands of Light: A Guide to Healing Through the Human Energy Field.* New York: Bantam Books, 1987, p. 22.

97. Helmstetter, Shad. *What to Say When You Talk to Your Self.* New York: Pocket Books, a division of Simon & Schuster Inc., 1982, p. 20.

98. Guyton, *Textbook of Medical Physiology*, p. 546.

99. Ibid., p. 547.

100. Ibis., p. 657.

101. M. Ted Morter, Jr. *Your Health, Your Choice: Your Complete Personal Guide to Wellness Nutrition & Disease Prevention.* Rogers, AR, 1990.

102. Guyton, *Textbook of Medical Physiology*, p. 673.

103. Ibid, p. 674.

104. Goetz, *The New Encyclopaedia Britannica*, Vol. 27, p. 301.

105. Guyton, *Textbook of Medical Physiology*, p. 277.

106. Ibid., p. 608.

107. Ibid., p. 5.

108. Chopra, Deepak. *Perfect Health: The Complete Mind/Body Guide.* New York: Harmony Books, 1990, p. 263.

109. Pelletier, pp. 307-308.

110. _____. "Body Notes," *Health*, Jan/Feb 1994, p. 32.

111. Poppy, John. (Oct '94). "Walk This Way." *Men's Health*, p. 118.

112. Guyton, *Textbook of Medical Physiology*, p. 816.

113. Ibid., 778.

114. Guyton, *Physiology of the Human Body*, p. 5.

115. Guyton, *Textbook of Medical Physiology*, p. 386.

116. Ibid., p. 2.

117. Morter, p. 55.

118. Guyton, *Textbook of Medical Physiology*, p. 442.

119. Ibid.

120. Ibid., p. 449.

121. Morter, M.T., Jr. *Correlative Urinalysis: The Body Knows Best.* Rogers, AR: B.E.S.T. Research, Inc., p. 33.

122. Guyton, *Textbook of Medical Physiology*, p. 443.

123. Anand, C.B. and Linkswiler, H.M., "Effect of Protein Intake on Calcium Balance of Young Men Given 500 mg Calcium Daily." J. of Nutrition. 104:695-700, 1974.

124. Babazono, A. and Hillman, A.L., "A Comparison of International Health Outcomes and Health Care Spending," *International Journal of Technology Assessment in Health Care*, 10 (1994): 378. Cited in *Regulated to Death: How Too Much Healthcare Bureaucracy Is Making Our Nation Sick* , unpublished manuscript by Dean Black, 1994, p. 1.

125. Lin, K., et al. "International infant mortality rankings: A look behind the numbers," *Health Care Financing Review* 13 (1992): 105-18. Cited in Black, unpublished manuscript, p. 1.

126. Lederman, Leon, op. cit., p. 51.

INDEX

protein 49, 57, 210, 234, 258, 260, 276, 277, 282-285, 287-294, 297
psychic isolation 156, 157, 173
pulse 15, 54, 118-121
quantum 4, 27, 34, 49, 56, 103-106, 109, 112, 114-117, 128-131, 134, 138, 139, 179, 349
regeneration 31, 32
reproduction 28, 117, 132
rest 2, 13, 15, 16, 43, 47, 51, 71, 73, 78, 86, 107, 117, 128, 136, 151, 152, 155, 157, 168, 177, 185, 194, 195, 201, 207, 208, 221, 223-225, 228-233, 239, 244, 245, 248, 260, 265, 267, 280, 282, 291, 293, 296, 330, 343, 353
reticular activating system 87
ridicule 77, 170
salt 123, 286, 291
self-esteem 5, 97, 101, 142, 158, 165-171, 173, 202, 211-213, 217, 220, 314, 315, 317, 325, 330, 337, 339, 344
Sensory Dominant Stress 8, 9, 11, 12, 14, 17, 69, 75, 139, 151, 303, 333
sixth sense 75, 82, 303
sleep 26, 43, 50, 59, 65, 87, 160, 161, 187, 225, 230-233, 242, 265, 306, 311, 314
smoking 144, 198, 199, 201, 228, 229, 243
stimuli 2, 8-10, 12, 23, 36, 37, 40, 44, 47, 50, 51, 57, 60-62, 65, 66, 68, 69, 71, 76, 77, 80, 86, 87, 89, 97,

99, 115, 116, 125, 127, 138, 139, 153, 159, 171, 176, 189, 190, 195, 196, 199, 204, 222, 223, 225, 259, 302, 303, 305, 310, 318, 322, 324, 325, 332, 334, 341, 347, 348
stimulus 8, 14, 40, 44, 46, 47, 50, 51, 57, 61, 78, 85, 99, 127, 135, 138, 144, 156, 160, 161, 196, 199, 219, 223, 302, 322, 347
stress response 8, 47
subatomic 25, 26, 35, 103, 115, 129, 130, 132, 148, 349
subconscious mind 4, 11, 51, 54, 83, 178
superconscious 83, 84, 98, 99, 101
survival homeostasis 72
survival physiology 139, 144, 242
sympathetic nervous system 67-69, 140
symptom 10, 22, 119, 141, 142, 158, 346
symptoms 2, 7-11, 14, 21-23, 28, 36, 37, 40, 50, 60, 74, 76, 108, 109, 117, 120, 124, 125, 137, 141, 151, 157, 162, 169, 181, 199, 213, 222, 232, 236, 242, 259, 297, 310, 312, 340, 346
thalamus 59, 86, 88, 153
thankfulness 124, 313-317
timing 40, 51, 69, 74-77, 127, 221, 224-226, 242, 245, 249, 253, 256, 266, 273, 276, 293
toxicity 139, 221, 224-226, 228, 229, 245, 259, 276, 299,